✦ THE HERITAGE GUIDE ✦

SICILY

A complete guide to the island, its towns,

monuments, and incomparable landscapes

Touring Club of Italy

Touring Club of Italy

President and Chairman: *Giancarlo Lunati*

Chief Executive Officer: *Armando Peres*

Managing Director: *Marco Ausenda*

Editorial Director: *Michele D'Innella*

Coordination: *Anna Ferrari-Bravo*

Senior Editor: *Gemma Mattei*

General Consultant: *Gianni Bagioli*

Jacket Layout: *Federica Neeff*

Map Design: *Cartographic Division - Touring Club of Italy*

Authors: *Ilario Principe* (Sicily: the environmental picture); *Letteria Tripodo* (The characteristics of settlement; chapters 4, 8, 9, 10); *Elena Del Savio* (chapters 1, 2); *Francesco Tranchida* (chapter 3); *Maria Pia Di Gaetano* (chapter 6); *Maurizio Mannanici* (chapters 5, 7).

Translation and adaptation: *Antony Shugaar*

Copy Editor: *Derek Allen*

Drawings: *Antonello* and *Chiara Vincenti*

Layout and editing: *Studio Tragni*

Production: *Giovanni Schiona, Vittorio Sironi*

Picture credits: *Action Press*: M. Pedone 171; *Archivi Alinari*: 21; *Archivio Ketto Cattaneo*: 18; *Barbagallo*: 40, 98, 108, 117, 118, 122, 143, 144, 179, 180; *M. Casiraghi*: 11; *Controluce*: 68, 70, 86; *Controluce / C. Fusco*: 91; *E. Dati*: 125, 136, 172, 189; *A. Garozzo*: 20, 27, 30, 39, 45, 54, 79, 81, 85, 101; *Image Bank*: G. Colliva 106, 165, F. Fontana 169, Mahaux 196, G.A. Rossi 25, 53, 102; *W. Leonardi*: 15, 16, 74, 82, 87, 90, 132; *G. Leone*: 51, 63; *M. Lo Verde*: 138; *Marka*: L. Fioroni 160, F. Giaccone 121, 127, 15?; L. Marioni 193, *M. Mazzola* 181; *P.S. Ongaro*: 11, 37, 42; *Laura Ronchi*: P.S. Ongaro 12, 48, 56, 59, 140, 200, E. Zinna 130; *Santini*: 76.

Cover: The temple of the Dioscuri in Agrigento, by *G. Colliva (Image Bank)*

Picture p. 3: *Temple of Castor, Agrigento* (Laura Ronchi / P. Negri).

Pictures pp. 4-5: *Vases at the Museo Eoliano, Lipari* (Barbagallo); *Façade of the Cathedral, Syracuse* (M. Lo Verde); *Local folk at S. Biagio Platani, Agrigento* (W. Leonardi).

Typesetting and colour separations: *Emmegi Multimedia- Milano*

Printed by: *G. Canale & C. - Borgaro Torinese (Torino)*

© 1997 Touring Editore - Milano
Code L2G
ISBN 88-365-1521-5
Printed in April 2000

oreword

he detailed tour of Sicily proposed by this guidebook, part of "The Heritage uide" series, takes us through one of Italy's most resourceful and captivating gions, a region that offers an extraordinary wealth of history and art, l set amid a countryside of breathtaking intensity and variety. The largest land in the Mediterranean, Sicily has been a vital focus of all the ancient vilizations that navigated this ancient sea.

he outline of the island's geography and long history is followed by a guide its cities and sights, divided into 10 chapters, with 29 different excursions at cover the entire island, starting from the capital, Palermo, the subject of e first chapter. From here we travel down the west coast and round to grigento, then on toward agusa at the southernmost tip the island, before returning to the Tyrrhenian coast isiting the outlying islands so), leaving until last our ploration of the island's scinating interior. All these neraries and excursions are lustrated with street plans id road maps and plans of chaeological sites, together ith a host of illustrations and awings. On the way we scover the legacies of the oenician, Greek, and oman occupation of the land, which were followed in ore recent historical times by succession of Muslim, orman, Swabian, Angevin, d Aragonese dominion. ich culture left its mark on e territory and on the towns id cities, though perhaps the ost memorable aspect of cily's architecture is the lively aroque style that pervades the entire island.

Temple of the Dioscuri (Agrigento)

he guide is completed by a section of travel tips and useful addresses, with sts of hotels and restaurants, places to shop, cafés and pastry shops, and not ast the main art galleries, museums, and archaeological sites.

Contents

Information for Travellers and Index of Places and Monuments

Excursion Key Map
and Index of Maps and Plans

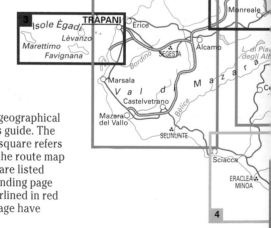

The key map shows the geographical
subdivisions used in this guide. The
number in the coloured square refers
to the chapter in which the route map
occurs. The route maps are listed
above with the corresponding page
number. The cities underlined in red
and listed on the front page have
a city map.

MAR MEDITERRANEO

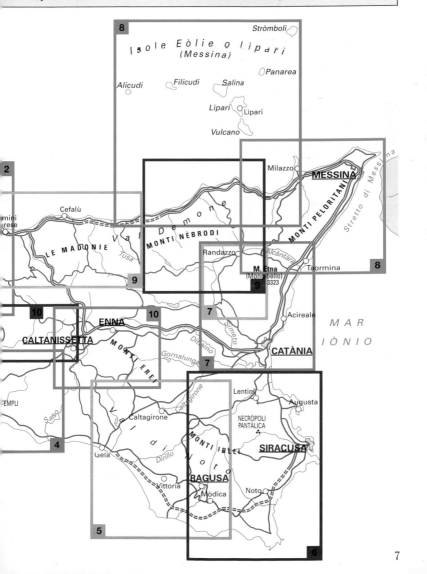

How to Use this Guidebook

■ We have attempted to use the original Italian names of all places, monuments, buildings, and other references where possible. This is for a number of reasons: the traveller is thus made more comfortable with the names as he or she is likely to encounter them in Italy, on signs and printed matter. Note also that maps in this book for the most part carry the Italian version of all names. Thus, we refer to Piazza Pretoria and Parco dell'Etna rather than to Pretoria Square and Etna Park. On first mention, we have tried to indicate both the Italian and the English equivalent; we have renewed this dual citation when it is the first mention in a specific section of text. In Italian names, one of the most common abbreviations found is "S." for "saint" (and "Ss." for "saints"). Note that "S." may actually be an abbreviation for four different forms of the word "saint" – "San", "Sant'", "Santo", and "Santa". Many other terms, while generally explained, should be familiar: "chiesa" is a church, "cappella" is a chapel, "via" is a street, "ponte" is a bridge, "museo" is a museum, "biblioteca" is a library, "torre" is a tower, "campanile" is a bell tower, "giardino" is a garden, "parco" is a park, "pinacoteca" is an art gallery, "teatro" is a theatre, "piazza" is a square, "ospedale" is a hospital, "porta" is either a door either a city gate.

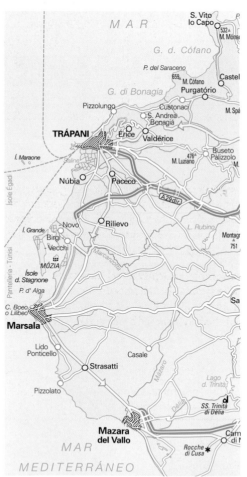

Maps and Plans

The itineraries and excursions described in this guide are accompanied by *route maps,* in which the suggested route is traced in yellow, with an arrow denoting the direction followed by the description in the text. All the main towns and cities have an accompanying *city map;* here the suggested itinerary is marked in blue. A key to the symbols used can be found on page 10. The principal monuments and museums together with the hotels, restaurants, and other public facilities are marked directly on the maps, and are followed by a reference to their location on the map or street plan (e. g., I, A3, meaning map I, square A3); hotels and restaurants are marked with letters in bold. The notation "off map" indicates that the monument or location mentioned lies outside the areas shown on the maps. Floor plans of monuments are marked with letters or numbers for iden-

ification, and corre-
pondingly linked to the
descriptions in the text.

The Places to Visit

In all descriptions of monuments or landmarks dif-
ferences in typography
names shown in **bold** or
in *italics*) larger or smaller
type size, and one or two
asterisks (*) indicate the
importance of each mon-
ument, museum, or other
site. Written descriptions
are illustrated with drawings and photos that help
the reader to visualize
works of art or architec-
ture which he or she
should not miss.

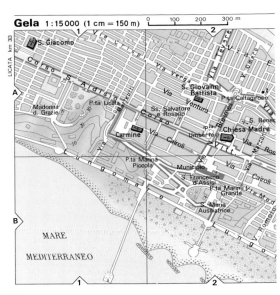

Information for travellers

A compendium of useful addresses, hotels and restaurants which suggests a selection of the finest hospitality facilities. Specific criteria are described on page 206. We
provide information which is up-to-date as of the writing of this book. The reader should
be aware that some subsequent changes may have occurred in hours or schedules.

Notice regarding telephone numbers

As of the 18th December 1998, each location's telephone code must also be dialled
for local calls and are listed next to the symbol ☎ in the section Information for Travellers, page 206. For those calling from abroad, the local code (including the 0) must
be dialled after the international code for Italy, followed by the subscriber's number.

The so-called Valley of the Temples, with the town of Agrigento in the background

Conventional Signs Used in the Maps

City maps

Lines of communications

Highways

Highways and throughfares

Main roads

Other roads

Pedestrian ramps

Secondary roads

Trails

Roads under construction

Railroad lines and stations

PORTO DI MARE ⓜ Subway lines stations

x—x—x—x—x Cableways

•—•—•—•—• Chairlifts

+++++++++ Cable cars

Monuments and buildings

of exceptional interest

quite interesting

interesting

Other indications

Public offices

Churches

Hospitals

i Tourist information offices

P Principal parking areas

Gardens and parks

Contour map showing elevation and grade

Arcades

Excursion maps

Lines of communications

Excursion, with direction followed

Detour from the route

A1 Highway, with route number

Main roads

Other roads

Shipping lines

Towns and cities

o Places to see along the excursion

Urban area

o Other places

Symbols

⌐ Churches

H Castels

::: ∴ Ruins

⌒ Caves

* Waterfalls, natural curiosities

⌂ Mountain huts

≍ Mountain passes

. Mountain peaks

347 Elevations

✈ Airports

Borders of countries

Sicily: the environmental picture

xtending over 25,708 square kilometers, Sicily is the largest and the most populous island in the Mediterranean Sea, and it is the southernmost and the largest region of Italy; it comprises 8.5 percent of the total surface area of the country. As of 31 December 1990, the population of Sicily was 5,196,822 individuals, which is to say, 9 percent of the national population. In terms of latitude, Sicily lies along the same strip that crosses the Mediterranean coastal area of Western Africa, while Trapani lies almost on the same meridian as Rome, and Messina lies on the meridian that runs through the lake of Lesina at the juncture of the Gargano peninsula with the mainland. This strategic location has long made Sicily a stepping stone linking East and West, North and South across the Mediterranean Sea: in particular, Sicily lies at a distance from the Tunisian coast at Cape Bon of only 140 km., while

Sicilian puppets, one of the symbols of the island

the distance between Messina and Siracusa (Syracuse) is 180 km., and the distance between Messina and Palermo is 230 km.

The distinctive shape of the island – an isosceles triangle – resulted in its being called early on Trinacria, or island of three promontories; this is the name the island was given in antiquity. The modern name of Sicily comes from the the the tribes of the Siculi or the Sicani, two of the earliest populations of the island (the third ancient tribe residing here is that of the Elimi), and the name of Sicily appears as early as the Homeric sagas. Divided until 1927 into seven provinces, only one of which lay inland, Sicily was redistricted in that year into nine provinces (the two new provinces were Ragusa, which took the place of the formerly designated Caltagirone, and Enna), a division that is still in effect. The division into seven provinces had been done at the decree of Ferdinand I as late as 1817; from the time of the Arab occupation on, the island had been split into three sections, known as the Valli: Val di Mazara to the west, Val di Noto to the southeast, and Val Démone to the northeast; these three areas converged at the Monte Altesina (1,193 m.) between Enna and Nicosia, not far from the actual geographic center of the island.

The islands and the coast

The insular nature of Sicily is mitigated by the closeness of the mainland of Calabria, which lies at a distance of only 3 km. across the Stretto di Messina (Strait of Messina), and by an array of islands and islets lying at various distances off the long sides of the island's perimeter. The group of the Eolie (Aeolian Islands), which lies in the province of Messina, in administrative terms, is the most numerous island group, and includes 7 major islands: the three largest are Vulcano, Lipari, and Salina, aligned along the meridian, and clustered close together, and the two pairs of islands, Alicudi and Filicudi to the west and Panarea and Stromboli to the north, as well as a certain number of rocks and shoals of smaller size. Of these, the loveliest are Strombolicchio and Basiluzzo. Much farther off is the other island along the northern coast: this is Ùstica, which has a surface area of 8.6 square kilometers and which forms part of the province of Palermo, from which it lies at a distance of 57 km. To the west of Sicily lies the small island group of the Egadi, near the coast of Trapani, to which they belong in administrative terms; this group features the three larger islands of Favignana, Levanzo, and Marettimo and the smaller landmasses of Maraone and Formica, while the island of Stagnone and Mozia can be considered, in morphological terms, as continuations of the salt marshes of the larger island, from which they are separated only by a narrow channel. Also part of the province of Trapani is the relatively distant island of Pantelleria, which lies at roughly a hundred km. from Cape Granitola, midway between Mazara del Vallo and Selinunte, and just 70 km. from Cape Mustafà in Tunisia. The small island group of the Pelagie, part of the province of Agrigento, is scattered even further out in the central Mediterranean Sea: Lampedusa, the largest island in this group, is no less than 205 km. from the Sicilian coastline (as opposed to a distance of just 113 km. from Tunisia and 150 km. from Malta); Linosa is set roughly forty km. north of Lampedusa, and to the west is the uninhabited shoal of Lampione, which has a lighthouse and nothing more. Malta, as well, with Gozo and Comino and the smaller surrounding islets, once belonged to the crown of Sicily, from the cession undertaken by Charles V in 1530 on behalf of the Knights of the Holy Sepulchre (Cavalieri del Santo Sepolcro), up until the treaty of Paris (1814), which placed Malta under English rule.

The coastal perimeter of Sicily extends for 1,039 km., but that distance increases to 1,500 km., if we include all of the smaller islands that surround it: beginning with the three capes of Peloro over Messina, Lilibeo at Marsala, and Passero at the southwestern extremity, the Tyrrhenian coastline extends 440 km., the coastlines along the Mediterranean Sea toward Africa extend 312 km., and the Ionian coast stretches for 287 km. These coasts are not perfectly linear, though there are no major marked variations in their structure. The northern coast, lying perfectly along the parallel, running counterclockwise from Messina, presents first the narrow peninsula of Milazzo extended toward Vulcano, followed by the minor outgrowths of Cape Calavà and Cape Orlando; the coast then runs straight, except for the curve of the gulf of Termini Imerese, nearly all the way to the valley of Palermo, guarded by Cape Zafferano to the east and by Cape Gallo to the northwest. The gulf of Castellammare is far more pronounced and deeper than all of the other gulfs in Sicily, and it is bounded to the west by the high and steep promontory of Cape San Vito. The coast remains tall and dramatic all the way to Trapani where, with the salt flats characterizing the land-

A farm in the countryside around Trapani, where the highest quality wines are produced

cape, we see the beginning of the low-lying table-land that runs along the more properly Mediterranean coastland: between Marsala and Cape Passero there are virtually no noteworthy geographic features, and the few short promontories or the slight sandy bluffs do little to interrupt the sense of sameness that is so typical of this part of Sicily. Between Messina and Cape Passero the coast once again runs straight and rather high as far as Catania, and then opens out on a line with the only real plain in Sicily, at the mouth of the river Simeto. The marked promontory of Augusta gives its name to the gulf of Augusta, with another promontory looming to the south, terminating in Ortigia; the gulf is marked at its center by the peninsula of Magnisi, just as, to the south of Ortigia, Cape Murro di Porco first, and the other frequent features dotting the coastline interrupt the line, creating micro-environments of considerable charm.

There are very few areas along the Sicilian coastline that are not served by roads, though for the most part the roads tend to run at a certain distance from the sea, leaving vast expanses of coastline quite untrammeled, especially along the steeper and wilder coastal areas, and those furthest from the major cities; these now constitute wilderness areas of considerable interest. Straight though it may be, the Sicilian coastline does open out in a certain number of harbors – the old wheat ports – which the geographic conditions of the sites in which they are located have at times made truly exceptional, even in the remarkable panorama of the Mediterranean Sea; this is true, for instance, at Messina, where industry and development stretch back to Roman times. The lack of harbors along the southern coast, facing Africa, has resulted in a relative economic stagnation, making this an area that is socially and economically backward; villages such as Palma di Montechiaro or Sicullana have for decades been the poorest and least-developed places in all of Europe. Only recently, with the improvement of the roads, the promotion of high-quality agriculture, and the creation of some industries, with – however – all of the social and environmental ills that come with industry, has this enormous territory begun to emerge from its centuries of isolation.

The morphological nature of the territory: landforms and volcanoes

While its form is clear and its coasts are linear, it remains quite difficult to describe in simple terms the overall morphology of Sicily. First of all, 61 percent of the territory is classified as hilly (as against the national average of 42 percent), while 25 percent of the territory is covered by mountains (in Italy as a whole, the figure is 35 percent), and only 14 percent is occupied by the few plains available (as opposed to the 23 percent of Italy). The only genuine alluvial plain is the Piana di Catania, or perhaps to a lesser degree, the coastal fringe of low sand dunes arching southeast of Gela; the rest of the plains are a few open

areas set in the limestone of the main promontories, as is the case with the Conca d'Oro of Palermo and the neighboring rolling plains of Carini and Alcamo, or the areas of debris near relatively high reliefs, such as is the case at Milazzo or in the area around Trapani, or the high and slightly sloping plains which, in the area facing Africa, crumble into a limestone breccia, the tufa stone of the area between Trapani and Castelvetrano and the Iblei, or else spread out into the broad sand dunes of the area around Agrigento. The coastal alluvian plains are quite narrow, limited as they are by the complex and often steep mountains overlooking the sea, and ever since antiquity this has been the site of the richest agriculture, especially the citrus *groves*; this has also been the area best served by communications and means of transportation.

In orographic terms, there are four major mountain groups in Sicily. The most noteworthy of these groups is represented by the alignment of the northern chain, which continues – in its basic structure – the chain of the Calabrian Apennines; this is not a homogeneous chain however, and in it we can distinguish at least three sections: the Peloritani, entirely similar to the Calabrian chain which never rises above an elevation of 1,300 m.; the Nebrodi, or better yet, to use the local term, the Caronie, which rise to an altitude of 1,800 m. and which are generally marked by bare summits; and lastly the Madonie, which rise to an altitude of nearly 2,000 m., and are characterized by handsome oak forests and, higher up, by beech groves. The mountains of western Sicily, on the other hand, at times appear as irregularly grouped massifs, in some cases isolated, and if so, quite large because relatively unconnected with the surrounding features, and in certain cases, constituting full-fledged islands, as is the case in the Egadi. There are no clearly distinguishable alignments or ranges, save in the case of the link with the Madonie, which in some sense connect with the morphology of the Palermo area (through the Rocca Busambra, 1,615 m.). The so-called "sulphur-bearing highland ("altopiano solfifero"), which occupies the central and the southern part of the island, sloping slightly down toward the sea, can almost be considered an area of debris of two major geographic features endowed with a more sharply defined identity: this is in fact a heterogeneous complex of ledges, broad hilly saddles, and vast valleys; it is possible to detect an organizing principle, even in the geological composition of the soil, which presents a chalky and sulphur-bearing structure, broken up by numerous and varied horizons of a diverse nature, but invariably characterized by hills that are sere and yellowish, save for the springtime, when the wheat tinges them with an intense green. Toward Enna (931 m., the highest regional capital in all of Italy), the "sulphur-bearing" highland ("altopiano solfifero") congeals into another system of limestone ledges and saddles, suited to serve as watersheds between the two southern slopes of the island; these are the Monti Erei, linked in turn to the system of long tablelands, the Iblei, that are so distinctively characteristic of the area around Siracusa and the entire southern expanse of Sicily. The landscape here appears flattened, and even the highest elevation – the Monte Lauro, 986 m., near Buccheri – only just rises from the surrounding territory, which seems to constitute one vast stretch of land embracing the sea. These white limestone tablelands tending toward the golden yellow that is so typical of the buildings of Sicilian Baroque common in fact in the Val di Noto, are crisscrossed by watercourses running in long, narrow cuts, often with vertical walls, *quarries* that in the past have housed remarkable prehistoric and protohistoric civilizations.

But what most of all distinguishes in an unmistakable manner the island of Sicily are its volcanoes, and in particular, Mount Etna. Visible from incredible distances, this imposing and perennially smoking cone is not only a feature of the landscape and the morphology; with its great and remarkable silhouette and its distinctive personality, it suggests an idea of Sicily that does not fit into any of the environmental categories of the Mediterranean region. Mount Etna is the largest active volcano in Europe, and its elevation varies, as is the case of all volcanoes; nowadays it is roughly 3,323 m. Despite the impression that the volcano may give when observed from a distance, this is not a uniform cone, nor are the craters at the summit the active ones; indeed, the entire structure is still provisional (this volcano is only 500,000 years old, and can therefore be considered a relatively young volcano) and reflects a complex geological history of eruptions, which is translated into the numerous folds and irregularities along the slopes of Etna and the hundreds of cones and conelets which are the relics of the 135 eruptions documented in historical times. The other two active volcanoes of Sicily, Stromboli (924 m.) and Vulcano (500 m.), are roughly comparable with Etna in size, but they are rooted at a depth of 2,000 m. below sea level; as a result only their summits are visible. Particularly noteworthy is the summit of Stromboli, with its cone emerging directly from the water, and incessantly active.

Lakes and rivers

Sicily may be rich in fire, but it is considered poor in water, and not because there is any real lack of rainfall (roughly 600 mm. of precipitation a year, on average), but rather because that rainfall is poorly distributed and is soon lost in soil that is generally not permeable; the effects are at times disastrous, destroying crops and villages. To forestall these unfortunate occurrences, manmade reservoirs and lakes have been built; the only natural lake is the Lago di Pergusa, unless we count the "bivieri," or ponds behind the dunes, which nowadays can be found only along the littoral strip of the southern coast. The orographic alignment to the north, overlooking the Tyrrhenian coast, allows only numerous and short rivers, like those found in the Calabrian area (there is roughly one every 5-6 km. of coast-

e) from exceedingly limited watersheds; all the same, the waters of these streams man-
e to nourish flourishing citrus groves and other fine crops. The river beds extend and
e basins of water become more extensive for the watercourses that empty into the
editerranean Sea, but the actual flow of the streams tends to become much smaller due
the lower amount of rainfall in this area; that flow also becomes intermittent due to the
permeable nature of the ground, which reduces flow in the summer practically to noth-
g. The Salso or the Imera Meridionale, with its 144 km. of length and its 2,000 square kilo-
eters of basin, is the most important of the rivers of Sicily, and the Platani, which emp-
s into the sea near Eraclea Minoa, with 110 km. of length and 1,785 square kilometers
basin area is the third largest; the other streams along this area of the Sicilian coast
he Belice, the Gela, the Acate, or Dirillo, and so on – present rather extensive basins
t small flows of water. This is not the case for the eastern slope, where we find the
rgest river system on the island, formed by the Simeto-Dittaino-Gornalunga, with a main
ream running some 113 km. and a feeder basin extending over nearly 4,300 square kilo-
eters, including that rich source of water that is Mount Etna, covered with abundant
ow for much of the year. To the north of Etna, on the other hand, is the Alcantara, gath-
ing the waters of the mountains, while the Monti Peloritani empty numerous torrents
to the Ionian Sea.

limatic conditions and vegetation

Sicily is not endowed with much water, it does have a remarkable abundance of sunlight:
ere is an average of 133 beautiful sunny days in Siracusa, 130 in Taormina, 125 in Cata-
a, 110 in Messina, 98 in Palermo. Catania holds the European record for sunshine, with

average of 2,518 hours a
ear, while Palermo has an
verage of 2,200 hours: all
ese statistics tell us, how-
ver, is how much light
ere is in the sky, and beause of the location of the
land, that means an un-
aralleled amount of light,
ore than anywhere else
Italy or continental Eu-
ope. The mildness of the
limate along the coasts,
ith an annual average tem-
erature ranging between
7 and 19 degrees Celsius,
owever, drops, and con-
iderably, toward the
ountains and plateaus of
he interior, where the
Mediterranean influence
ades, and there are much
harper variations in tem-
erature, with more fre-
quent precipitation – even
nowfall – and chilly win-
ers. In the summer, how-
ver, and especially in August, it is not rare for there
o be very high tempera-
ures, and it was in fact in

The islands of Pelagie constitute an uncontaminated natural environment characterized by a rich marine and land fauna

August in Sicily that in 1885 the highest temperature ever recorded in Italy was reached
- 49.6 degrees Celsius. Typical of Sicily is the hot sirocco wind, generally humid on the eastern coast and dry on the western coast, which generally blows for three days running from
he south, often bringing with it dust and sand from African.

t is difficult to say whether the Sicilian climate ever allowed anything in the interior of the
sland that was different from the arid and sere landscape, that is today so widespread and
which was so closely bound up with the latifundium, or large landholding, and with grain

15

farming. The evergreen Mediterranean scrub, or "macchia" (French, "maquis"), which ce tainly must have covered much of the coastline of Sicily, extending into the hinterland well, has virtually vanished, save for a few areas that have not developed rapidly, remaini on the outskirts of the major routes of communications; and when there are forests, eve forests comprised largely of high-branched trees, high on the mountain ridges, they mu have greatly suffered in relation to the historical events to which the island has been th ater and witness; in any case these forests have generally been fought back to a few fra mentary patches, found most often along the northern range and around the splendid slop of Mount Etna, which is to say in the areas that are furthest from crowding and overus or at any rate, most difficult to reach and to deforest, and in those areas where deforestatio has taken place on a large scale, as for example on the slopes of Mount Etna, often the va ished forests are replaced with magnificent chestnut groves. It comes as no surprise at a

Mediterranean faces and colours permeate the whole island

then, that the plants that are now found in Sicily do not come at all from the island itsel but were imported in the more-or-less recent past: grapevines and olive trees as well a almond, pistachio, pomegranate, and other fruit trees came in antiquity from the Near Eas the hazelnut tree came from Campania; the carob, the palm tree, the mulberry, cotton, sug ar cane, lemon, and bitter oranges were all introduced by the Moors, while the sweet or ange, still called the "arancio portogallo," was in fact brought by the Portuguese in the 16t c. from China, while from the islands of the Sunda Strait came the tangerine, which was in troduced no more than two centuries ago, while the prickly pear and the agave arrived i the 17th c. from Central America.

Agriculture and other economic activities

What remains is wheat, and ever since the time of the ancient Romans, when Sicily was con sidered the breadbasket of the empire, Sicily has literally always built its economy and it society on a foundation of wheat. Now things are a little different, because alongside th traditional latifundium planted in grains – in no way undercut by the agricultural reform of the 1950s, indeed probably a little less profitable, since grains do not require the little patches of land that the reform attempted to foist off on the Sicilian working class – ther has developed a substantial and variegated sector of specialized intensive crops, in the wak of the considerable array of public works designed to improve irrigation; these crops are grown both in the fields and in greenhouses, especially located along the coastal areas and in the better-protected and more-fertile interior valleys. Extensive zones were then con verted to the cultivation of specialty shrub and bush crops, as well as olive and almond trees, but especially grapevines, which in particular have largely and widely substituted – in the area of the Bèlice, in the wake of the emergency assistance that came in the af termath of the earthquake, and not always bringing the best of results – the old grain crops with their three-year rotations.

he ambivalence found in the agriculture, which remains the locomotive of the Sicilian conomy and employs twice the Italian average, is found as well in the industrial sector. ere – even though many of the most notable Italian crafts traditions have managed to ave themselves because they are such a deep-rooted part of the local cutlure – suffice to think of the fields of ceramics, the industrial undertakings in the 19th c. linked to the roduction of wine, the conservation of fish, shipyards, and that is not even to mention ne mining of sulphur, which, in what we might call its "heroic" phase, had a very short un, no more than two decades – all these new enterprises were soon mired in crisis beause they were unsuccessful in meeting the demands of the market, nor the *capital-inensive* investments in industrialization, so rich in money and poor in employees, manage o get past the short-sighted objectives of a number of well-funded multinationals, both om Italy and from the outside world. The discovery of oil in Gela and the Ragusa area, r Ragusano, at the end of the 1950s, authorized in some way or other the construction f major refineries and elephantine chemical plants; off the waters of Gela and especial in the roadstead of Augusta, or Rada di Augusta, there are seabeds particularly suited r super-tankers; instead of docking to load up with crude oil, they bring the petroleum eeded to run the plants, because the size of the oilfields was far less than had been predicted, and oil exploration had to be extended out to the continental shelf off the areas eing developed. Instead of integrated industrial development, which had been the ob-ctive of the state funding, there was a terrible and irreversible disequilibrium created n the territory, which led to the massive destruction of irreplacable resources, and, by social mechanism of the encouragement – but not the satisfaction – of expectations, and roken promises, the kind of broken promises that have loomed so large so often in the istory of Sicily and its contacts with the outside world. All this eventually resulted in damge to the environment and civil and moral breakdowns, undercutting the remarkable intitutional advantage given Sicily on 15 May 1946, when the region was given a special tatute and an autonomous (semi-independent) status, even before the constitution of the alian Republic entered into force (1948).

he character of the island and its inhabitants

his breakdown appears to most people nowadays to be a distinctive characteristic of Sici-, also because it has not remained trapped in its territory, but rather has emerged, ex-loring the outside world with a vigor and an audacity that had not been expected of the icilian people. We should not indulge in facile stereotypes, however, and the develop-ent of Sicilian history and culture can teach us much in this connection. A profound lo-al tradition, in fact, leads us to a powerful and distinctive presence in all Sicilian towns nd villages of customs, traditions, and habits that manage to express not only a personality f great scope and a quality of life that is translated into literary and artistic forms of na-ional and international renown, but in particular a discrete and profound social fabric, asually dialectic and open to the stimuli and influences of civil society, wherever they nay come from. We are not talking merely of the folkways and the colorful Sicilian tra-itions that, in some sense, complete the image of this island of sunshine that has been ssigned to Sicily. It is true that the Sicilian cart has been banished from the streets by oise and violence, and that the puppet theater is present only as a relic, and perhaps a purious relic, only because of the good efforts of a few generous fans; but processions, eligious festivals, family celebrations, mystery plays, and so on, survive in considerable umbers to tell of a history that even today lives on in the humblest layers of society. It s from this history that we must begin if we wish to have anything other than a false and heerful image of this surprising island.

The characteristics of settlement

Sicily nowadays is considered to be a polycentric region, a place of several cities, becaus in Sicily there has developed an equilibrium among the roles – and of course the ranks of three major cities: Palermo, in the western corner; and Catania and Messina, on the eas ern shore. Perhaps it would be more accurate to say of Sicily that it is a place with two cer ters. For if Palermo is the regional capital and the capital of the island for more than a mi lennium now, Catania is, after Naples, the most thriving center of industrial manufactu ing in the Italian south, or Mezzogiorno d'Italia; Messina, although it is a vital "land" gat between Italy and Sicily, plays no other real role, aside from that service. For more tha a century now, Catania has contended with its rival Palermo, trying to replace it as the lea ing city in the island's economy. Moreover, if we consider the infrastructure of the island highway system, we may note that, while one highway, on the east coast, runs from Mess na to Catania and another highway, through the interior, provides a direct link betwee Catania and Palermo, in comparison, on the Tyrrhenian coast, between Messina an Palermo, the proposed highway has remained unfinished.

What pushes us to compare Messina with Catania is the population of the cities themselves Messina, in 1981, had roughly 276,000 inhabitants, while Catania had roughly 100,000 mor

We should briefly mention the urban structur of the two cities. In the case of Messina ther is a strip of "countryside" between the urba center and the surrounding townships, whil for Catania it is possible to speak of a metr politan area: the townships adjoining the cit center now constitute outlying quarters c the city itself; and at times, they are not eve the most outlying areas; consider for exampl the case of Aci Castello, which is an integra part of the urban fabric. The city structure then, extends without a break from Piazz Stesicoro, the heart of Catania, as far as the la va flows of Mount Etna, and the areas of th townships in the so-called "cintura," or "belt. As a result, the greater metropolitan area c Catania has a population not of 400,000; rathe it is closer to a million. Each day, it is est mated, more than 500,000 people mov through the city's streets.

Archimedes was born in Siracusa in the 3rd c. B.C.

But the prosperity of Catania and its powerful role on the island are of recent origins. I the 18th c., it was still Messina and Siracusa that determined the fate of the easter coast, and with Palermo, they composed the system of cities that ran Sicily.

Historical Sicily

It is difficult to set forth a sufficiently clear chart of Sicilian historical developmen through the birth and development of its systems of settlements. For too long, the islan has been treated as a territorial and administrative entity all of its own, and too often th role played in political history by Sicily has been incorrectly analyzed, when it was rec ognized at all. A crucial issue in any evaluation, is the question of historical and cultur al unity. One historian suggested at the turn of the 20th c. that Sicily had received fron Greek rule a character that vitally affected all subsequent development, and not only c its own history, but of the history of all Italy, and even that of Europe. In more recent years there has been a revival of interest among scholars in the philo-Islamic aspects of Sici ian culture. Everything, or nearly everything, in Sicily, becomes a derivation of Arabic cu ture: from etymologies and inflections in the language, to social behavior, sweets, and or namental plants.

Whether it was from the Greeks or the Moors that the prime influence on the formation c Sicilian culture came, the problem remains the same: in order to understand Sicilian his tory, it is necessary to divide it up into periods marked by various occupations, right u

the unification of Italy. The history of Sicily has always had a lot of give-and-take with
e history of northern Africa, even if the earliest settlements, dating back to the upper Pa-
olithic, were found especially along the northern coasts; thus far there are very few traces
African culture, especially between Siracusa and Marina di Ragusa.

eek and Roman domination

ne earliest inhabitants were Sicani, Elimi, and Siculi, of unknown origin, but certainly not
original. The first signs of organized life on the island date back to the 8th/7th millennium
C., while in the 5th millennium there was a development and proliferation of the Aeolian
wns linked to trade in obsidian. Interestingly, there are also finds – again from the Aeo-
n islands – that indicate that as early as the 16th c. B.C. there was intense trade with the
egean Cretan-Mycenaean cultures.

is common belief that the Phoenician presence on the island was only due to trading re-
uirements, and that it was limited, especially after the arrival of the Greeks, to the west-
n regions. Here, aside from the Phoenicians, the Greek colonists found Sicani and Elimi
d, to the east, Siculi, well organized into a dense network of cities, built, for the most part,
highlands overlooking extensive territories. On the east coast, the first colonies began
flourish: Naxos in 735 B.C., Syracusai in 734, Leontinoi and Katane in 729, Megara
daea in 728, Zancle and Selinunte in 628, Mylai and Gela in 689, Akragas in 581, Lipara in
6. Some of these towns were new foundations, while others simply settled on the site of
existing indigenous village, but the innovation, which clearly points to Hellenic influence,
as the partial or total reorganization of the urban space, in accordance with orthogonal
hemes of distribution of the various zones.

nese characteristics of Greek urban planning were consolidated and became evident, in
e 7th c. B.C., when the colonies took on the status of Poleis. In Megara a regular network
streets defined blocks that surrounded a trapezoidal agora. In Casmene, a military out-
ost of Siracusa (Syracuse), the excavations have brought to light a dense succession of
arallel streets, and, also dating back to the 7th c. B.C., the alignments of buildings and tem-
es in Naxos. The Phoenicians took up residence in the western corner of the island, as
d the Carthaginians, and laid the foundations for the formation of a solid system of cities,
pable of withstanding the Greek advance. The cities founded and reinforced in the 7th
B.C. under Punic and Phoenician influence are Mozia, Palermo, and Solunto.

ne 6th c. witnessed an almost total Hellenization of the indigenous towns, in part due to
e foundation of tyrannies in all of the "poleis" in the island. Hippocrates in Gela, in Akra-
as and Himera, one of the fiercest opponents of the Carthaginians; and in Syracuse, Gelon.
nder their rule, the early Sicilian cities grew considerably, from the 5th c. on, in accordance
ith the plans developed by the architect and urbanist Hippodamus of Miletus: an or-
ogonal network of main roads (plateiai) and secondary roads, which cut out standard-
zed city blocks, leaving ample space in the central areas for public functions.

the 5th c. B.C., following the attempted revolt of the Siculi, there was a general consolidation
Greek control and supremacy, over the cities in the interior as well, but by the end of the
me century, the Carthaginians had destroyed the system formed by Selinunte, Imera, Gela,
d Kamarina. Syracuse held out, and under the tyranny of Dionysius, between the end of
e 5th and the beginning of the 4th c. B.C., reached the peak of its power. Aside from the en-
uing urban expansion, Syracuse extended its spheres of influence and staked the preservation
its power on its control over the Strait of Messina through the creation of a triangle of the
ty guarding this exceedingly important stretch of sea. Messina on the cape, or Capo
eloro, Taormina on the Ionian Sea, Tindari on the Tyrrhenian – these were all possessions
Dionysius I and it is interesting to note the way in which this tyrant had a thorough and
omplete knowledge of the geography, not only of the island, but indeed of all southern Italy
d the surrounding waters. A number of scholars, moreover, underscore the importance
Dionysius (see Holm) in the history of early-Italian civilization, as the creator of such a pow-
ful state, in Sicily, that it successfully opposed the advance of the Carthaginians, thus al-
wing the preservation of Hellenism in Sicily and in Europe.

he reinforcement of the coastal strongholds was accompanied by a renewed interest in
e towns of the interior, now that the Carthaginians were out of the running, in the wake
the defeat of 386 B.C. The Greeks regained control of Henna, along with Akragas, Selin-
nte, and Gela. In the second half of the 4th c. B.C., these cities once again became free
oleis," and Timoleon, the Greek general who restored democracy in Sicily, undertook an
tense project of urban renewal.

ew in terms of conception of space and style, these scenic settings, often distinguished by the use of a stoa (portico) around the agora, as at Morgantina, were developed duri the Hellenistic age, especially during the reign of Hieron II of Syracuse, which is to say the beginning of the 3rd c. B.C. During this same period there was a development of re dential quarters with richly decorated (with mosaics and murals) aristocratic homes. The was also a consolidation, between the end of the fourth and the beginning of the 2nd c. B. of the form of the theater, which was directly imported from the motherland; the theate of Syracuse, Eraclea Minoa, Segesta, Solunto, and Morgantina, all survive in their origi form; while the theaters of Tindari, Taormina, and Catania, were transformed through t adaptation of the orchestra to an arena for gladiatorial fights.

With the end of the second Punic war and the conquest of Syracuse in 212 B.C. by Marc lus, Sicily passed into Roman hands, and was divided into two provinces and its cities we classified into four categories: libere (or free, Segesta and Palermo), foederatae (those w

had been allied of Rome), decumanae (the a versaries of Rome), censoriae (the die-hard the territory of these last named cities we confiscated to give them to Roman citizer In the Republican phase, there were limit Roman cultural contributions to the dev opment of this Sicilian town.

In the early empire there was an agricultu rebirth, a result of a renewed interest in t countryside. "Vici" and "pagi" were forme small villages with a purely agrarian eco omy.The Piana di Gela, as it is settled in t present day, preserves practically un tered this organizational structure of t "borghi." With the Romans, the prima routes of communications, which had ready been traced out for many millennia the succession of peoples that had liv here, along with the territorial infrastru tures, such as aqueducts, irrigation ar other canals, ports, and fortifications. No of the cities, however, took its basic patte of settlement from the Romans, in part consideration of the effects brought abo the new exchange economy, to which t various towns, linked effectively by t

A Virgin Mary mosaic on the façade of Palermo Cathedral

road networks, soon adapted: the consular road, or Consolare Pompea, along the coa between Messina and Palermo; the Consolare Valeria, between Messina and Siracusa (Sy cuse); the present-day state road 120 which passes through Troina, Randazzo, Cesarò, ar Petralie, and which leads to Palermo through the interior; the present-day state road, Statale Meridionale Sicula with the ports of Licata and Termae Selinuntinae (Sciacca). Th we see the possibility of a full-fledged territorial plan and the complete urbanization the territory.

In the late empire, the development of the latifundium, an administrative structure that w of enormous importance to the economic history of the island, went hand in glove with t construction at the center of each latifundium of sumptuous villae: suffice it to mention t example of the villa of Piazza Armerina. With an overall policy of intensive exploitation the land, the island became a major site for the production of wheat and other foodstu to feed the empire, to the point that it won itself the nickname of "breadbasket of Rom In the 3rd c. A.D., Diocletian, in his effort to reorganize the provinces of the empire, attribute new importance to the role of Sicily, making it a "regio suburbicaria", a direct depende cy of Rome, in other words. Through a system of attribution of privileges and the gene ous distribution of funds, there formed the immense landholdings, or latifundia, which we to become the foundation for the administration of the region for centuries to come.

Early Christian Sicily

The literature concerning early-Christian Sicily is not vast. While Milan, Ravenna, and Rom were being rebuilt with the first basilicas in the 4th c., and Rome and central Italy especial were preparing to accept the power of the church, Sicily was welcoming exiles from t

st: Monophysitic heretics, persecuted in the iconoclastic campaign, and monks. And it
it this point that the real break comes between the history of this island and that of the
ropean continent. Even though, in fact, during the five centuries of Roman government,
ily never played a role of great importance in the affairs of the empire, its interests were
ver overlooked. The distance from the Alps made it safe from the invasions that dev-
ated the central and northern regions of Italy, but it could not protect it against the greed
Byzantine administrators who took possession of it, following the Eastern Schism. The
ne emissaries of the Eastern Emperor attempted to make Sicily a base for the reconquest
the western part of the empire, with its capital in Rome. There was an enormous rein-
cement of the Greek element in the population, to the point that in this island, Greek was
oken almost exclusively.
important role was played by the Eastern monks who, with their monasteries, located

the outskirts of towns and vil-
es, formed active communities,
couraging the spread of the Greek
e in Sicily, and reinforcing the de-
ndency of the Sicilian clergy upon
e patriarch of Constantinople. So
he larger cities were being rou-
ely plundered by corrupt Byzan-
e administrators, leading to the
pular power of major towns and
ies, there formed, almost as an
set, a dense network in the rural
eas of small inter-related villages,
mmunicating one with another
ng the roads that had served for
llennia for the migration of sheep,
e "trazzere," as they were later
med, with a term that is probably
Moorish origin. Dating back to
is crucial point in history was the
bdivision of Sicily into three sub-
gions, which were named, under
e Moors, Val Demone, Val di Noto,
d Val di Mazara. The first extends
om the northern course of the riv-
Imera to that of the river Simeto;

*Our Lady of the Annunciation by Antonello da
Messina at the Palazzo Abatellis in Palermo*

e second lies between the Simeto and the southern Imera; the third is located on the re-
aining western area, with Palermo as the chief town.

rab domination

he Moors, who arrived in Sicily in the first half of the 9th c., introduced a new system for
e management of the territory, underaking a full-fledged agrarian reform. They proceeded
break up the latifundium, assigning small lots of land to the direct care of the peasants,
d encouraging the free exchange of the goods thus produced. They developed and per-
cted the best system of water supply that the island had ever had, based on the safe-
arding of the wooded areas on the interior, so as to ensure the existence of a moist lo-
l microclimate, and on the preservation of large marshy areas alongside the main
vers. The Moors were skilled engineers, and they reinforced the bridges and aqueducts
ilt by the Romans, but also built new ones: it is still possible to see those Moorish struc-
res, like the lovely bridge near Càccamo. The agrarian landscape of medieval Sicily, then,
ust have been dotted with hamlets and fortresses, on every ridge, guarding every wa-
rway, everywhere, save in the Val Demone, where the sizable Greek Christian population
ndered the penetration of Islam.
he passage of Arabic culture to Sicily, however, is also documented by the survival in many
the island's cities, to the present day, of urban layouts with an irregular grid, so typical
Moorish culture. One study of the Islamic town plan pointed out how unnecessary or-
ogonal thoroughfares and blocks were in an urban context made up of minarets and hous-
, in which, therefore, the radial propagation of the voice of the muezzin tended to sug-
st a model of cities made of concentric circles. The articulation of space into lanes and

courtyards is particularly evident in the historical centers of nearly all the western citi
which were not plagued by earthquakes. Dating from the Moorish period are the locatic
of the settlements and the urban fabric, as it were, of them, while there are no longer trac
of houses of worship, such as mosques, etc. Sicily became an important base for the
pansion of Islam toward the peninsula.
Palermo was chosen, in A.D. 831, as the capital of the Emirate; the city grew and was c
ebrated as one of the loveliest cities in the known world.

Norman Sicily

Norman Sicily in the 11th c., in the descriptions offered by Edrisi, the Arabic geograph
at the court of Roger, appears as a synthesis of two worlds – the typical world of the sou
eastern Mediterranean Sea, of Muslim influence, and another world that had been co
structed in the high Middle Ages in western Europe. The deep mark that the Normans I
in the Sicilian landscape comprised the efficient apparatus of military cities dotting the lo
"service roads" which run along the coasts and to the interior of the island. It would a
pear that the countless foundations and refoundations of cities in this period were all p
scribed by a territorial plan; we find them in various strategic locations. The "plan" m
have called for the reinforcement of the port towns along the coasts, and, on the interi
the definitive routes of the "penetration" routes, with the formation of a system of citi
equidistant one from the other, guarding the immense valleys.
The Normans brought Sicily back under the jurisdiction of the Church of Rome; they i
stored the feudal system, assigning the control of the latifundia, or large landholdings, r
only to lay barons, but also directly to monasteries and convents. The Norman policy
settlement, moreover, was distinguished by the custom of spending on the constructi
or restoration of a church, which often constituted the nucleus for a new quarter or a no
city, which were often encouraged to grow by the establishment of a colony of Lombard
In the large cities, such as Palermo, which became the capital of the kingdom, the expa
sion was often accompanied by massive jobs of urban reconstruction, with the co
struction of churches and official palazzi, and not without a reinforcement of the defensi
structures of the place.

From Frederick II to the end of Spanish domination

Frederick II continued the project of reinforcing defenses, especially for the cities
Catania, Enna, and Siracusa. In the meanwhile, the enormous privileges bestowed upon t
barons led to the formation of a landed aristocracy that exercised unbounded power, fil
in the province and later in the city. In the fourteenth and fifteenth centuries, two famili
shared all power in western Sicily: the Chiaromonte and the Ventimiglia families. Favor
by the Prammatica di Re Martino, which was decreed in Catania in 1406 and then extende
to the other cities (a law that ensured the right of the private citizen who wished to bui
a home to obtain the expropriation, to his own advantage, of the lands bordering that pro
erty, in order to increase the beauty of the city), those families filled the towns of the F
lice and the hinterland of the Agrigento area with Chiaromonte architecture, or "a
chitetture chiaromontane," as the towns of the Madonìe and the Monti dei Nebrodi we
filled with the towers of the Ventimiglia family. Often, these buildings were erected to i
dound to the power of the lord, but it is not rare to encounter examples of great comp
sitional elegance, as is the case with the "Palazzo Steripinto" of Sciacca.
In 1415 the Spanish government sent the first viceroy to Sicily. There began a long peri
of subjugation, ending only in 1712. But the island was an important possession, at the hea
of the Mediterranean Sea, for Charles V, who spared no effort to defend it from Turkish i
vasion, with massive fortified works around the most important coastal cities. The 16th
was also a time of the refeudalization of the countryside and of the program of extensi
farming, launched by the crown. In the vast areas of the interior, new farming towns d
veloped, with regular checker-board plans, which were to attract the populations of t
larger cities, such as Enna and Caltanissetta.
In the era of the Counter Reformation, the 17th c., the cities were already solidly laid o
along the directions suggested by the main monastery structures and complexes. Pe
spective demanded the use of straight thoroughfares, scenically ending in a monument
building or a city gate, as in Carlentini, a city-fortress with broad streets lined with elega
buildings, striding in succession toward one of the monumental gates of the city. The "
azza" took on great importance in Sicilian Baroque urbanistic planning, as a logical sol
tion to the other fundamental element, the "croce di strade," or cross of roads. An eloque

mple can be seen in the Quattro Canti di Città in Palermo. For the layouts of new cities, re was a tendency to use the feudal models of the form of the cross and the eagle, sym- s, respectively, of the Roman Catholic Church and the Holy Roman Empire. An excep- to this rule is Ragusa, with its remarkable fish-shaped plan.

m the 18th c. to the 20th c.

713, the treaty of Utrecht decreed the end of Spanish domination, and Sicily passed to house of Savoy. While in the Val di Noto work was begun on the reconstruction of the es, destroyed by the earthquake of 1693, in 17th-c. Baroque style but also in accordance h a modern urbanistic design, in other cities the close late-Baroque was opened up, and re began to be parks and public promenades.

h the admission of Naples to the kingdom in 1735, Palermo lost its ancient standing as capital of a kingdom. In 1812 Ferdinand IV conceded the Constitution and feudal priv- es were abolished. Finally, with the unification of Italy, the south, which was still gov- ed by medieval laws, came up against the capitalist economy of industrialized nations. e great enterprise of extracting sulphur from the mines of central Sicily began. The ex- t of the mineral led to the growth of some of the port cities in contact with the mining ns, such as Catania. In the same centuries, great public works were undertaken, fun- nental structures for the bourgeois city. The chaotic form with which the first indus- l experiments went forward caused inevitable damage to the cities. The solution was nd with a first set of general regulatory plans, between the end of the 19th c. and the n of the 20th c., but the First World War made the efforts of the planners quite useless. as to be necessary to wait for the 1960s until there was a concrete response to the prob- of the reordering of the architecture of the cities of Sicily.

e Mafia

e imposition and the exercise of power by a rigidly – even "militarily" – organized group, h the purpose of controlling the economic activities of a place and the surrounding ter- ories: these could certainly be considered as the essential components of the phe- nenon of the Mafia. The Mafia, in origin a tool of economic and political power, was trans- med over time, itself, into an economic and political power. The Mafia originated in the liest decades of the 19th c., when feudal power was abolished, in 1812. From this date , the barons began to hire their own personal troops of soldiers, the "compagnie d'ar- " with which they were able to preserve the privileges that they had enjoyed until that ment. These "armed companies," composed of unscrupulous lowlifes and criminals, de- ded the property of the barons, using the weapons of abuse, intimidation, and violence. e members of these companies enjoyed more than just economic rewards; they also ob- ned the political protection of the baron from the authorities, who might pursue them their crimes. The Mafia, therefore, became a sort of counterpower, or perhaps we should , a power that was parallel to that of the State. The absence of any serious repression m the state, and the fierce vendettas against those who were unwilling to submit to the controlled power of the Mafia, allowed the growth and reinforcement of the much lament- culture of "omertà," which has so much to do with the definition of "mafiosità" offered many serious historians. The Mafia, at the end of the nineteenth and the beginning of e twentieth centuries, underwent considerable changes. Its interests expanded, from the untryside it came to take over the cities; it established close ties with politicians, and abbled in politics directly, supporting its own members for elected office (Commissione nchiesta Franchetti-Sonnino 1876, from M. Pantaleone, *Mafia e Droga*); and finally, it be- me international, establishing ever closer ties with the American Mafia. Under Fascism, e Mafia, apparently, was for a certain period on the ropes, but during the Allied Occu- tion and during the years directly following WWII, it found new vitality, playing a major e in the issue of Sicilian separatism.

e phenomenon of the Mafia in all its forms certainly constitutes the least appealing as- ct of Sicily, at the present time. In recent years especially, the Mafia, with its frontal at- k on institutions and its massacres, has become regular front-page news. Despite this, e most encouraging aspect appears to be – aside from a greater commitment of the state more widespread awareness on the part of the Sicilian people that the Mafia must be acked and fought day by day, freeing an island from all that the culture of "omertà" has posed for too many long years.

Italy: Useful Addresses

Citizens of Australia, Canada, New Zealand, and the United States can enter Italy with a v₁ passport, and stay for a period of not more than 90 days; citizens of Great Britain and land, as members of the European Union, can travel either with valid passport or with va identification card.

Foreign Embassies in Italy

Australia:
Corso Trieste 25, Rome, tel. (06) 852721

Canada:
Via G.B. de Rossi 27, Rome, tel. (06) 445981

New Zealand:
Via Zara 28, Rome, tel. (06) 4402928

United States of America:
Via Vittorio Veneto 119/A, Palazzo Margherita, Rome, tel. (06) 46741

Great Britain:
Via XX Settembre 80/A, Rome, tel. (06) 4825441

Ireland:
Piazza Campitelli 3, Rome, tel. (06) 6979121

Foreign Consulates in Italy

Australia:
Via Borgogna 2, Milan, tel. (02) 777041

Canada:
Via Vittor Pisani 19, Milan, tel. (02) 67581

New Zealand:
Via G. D'Arezzo 6, Milan, tel. (02) 48012544

United States of America:
– Lungarno A.Vespucci 38, Florence, tel. (055) 2398276
– Via Principe Amedeo 2/10, Milan, tel. (02) 290351
– Piazza Repubblica 2, Naples, tel. (081) 5838111
– Via Re Federico 18/bis, Palermo (consular agency), tel. (091) 6110020

Great Britain:
– Via S. Paolo 7, Milan, tel. (02) 723001
– Via Crispi 132, Naples, tel. (081) 663511

Ireland:
Piazza San Pietro in Gessate 2, Milan, tel. (02) 55187569

Italian Embassies and Consulates Around the World

Australia:
12 Grey Street - Deakin, Canberra, tel. (06) 273-3333
Consulates at: Adelaide, Brisbane, Melbourne, Perth, Sydney.

Canada:
275 Slater Street, 21st floor, Ottawa (On-

tario), tel. (613) 2322401/2/3
Consulates at: Montreal, Toronto, Vanc ver.

New Zealand:
34 Grant Road, Wellington, tel. (4) 4735. - 4729302

United States of America:
1601 Fuller Street, N.W., Washington D tel. (202) 328-5500/1/2/3/4/5/6/7/8
Consulates at: Boston, Chicago, Philac phia, Houston, Los Angeles, Miami, N York, New Orleans, San Francisco.

Great Britain:
14, Three Kings Yard, London W.1, ₁ (0171) 3122200
Consulates at: London, Manchester, Ec burgh.

Ireland:
63/65, Northumberland Road, Dublin 4, ₁ (01) 6601744

ENIT

In order to have general information and do mentation concerning the best known place Italy, you can contact the offices of the E. Nazionale Italiano per il Turismo (ENIT), run the Italian government; they are open Mon- from 9 to 5.

Canada:
Office National Italien du Tourisme/Itali Government, Travel Office, Montreal, Q bec H3B 3M9, 1 Place Ville Marie, Su 1914, tel. (514) 866-7667/866-7669, fax 3 1429

United States of America:
– Italian Government Travel Office, N York, N.Y. 10111, 630 Fifth Avenue, Su 1565, tel. (212) 2454822-2455095, ᵢ 5869249
– Italian Government Travel Office, Chica 1, Illinois 60611-401, North Michigan ⟨ enue, Suite 3030, tel. (312) 644-0996, ₁ 644-3019
– Italian Government Travel Office, Los ⟨ geles, CA 90025, 12400, Wilshire Blvd., Su 550, tel. (310) 820-0098/820-1898, fax 820-63

Great Britain:
Italian State Tourist Board, London W 6AY, 1 Princes Street, tel. (0171) 408-12₁ fax 493-6695

Palermo and the Conca d'Oro

traditional image of Palermo (elev. 14 m., pop. 698,556; maps on pages 26-27 and 30-31), amidst the greenery of vast citrus groves at the foot of the distinctive promontory of nte Pellegrino, celebrated by view painters and etchers of the 18th and 19th c., has col-d with the conditions of the 20th c., and with the changes brought about by the con-erable growth of the city, which has historically played the role of "capital," and even more ious, the speculative growth that ever since the end of WWII has played a fundamental e in the development of the modern city and the equilibrium of the entire territorial sys-1. This, indeed, may be described as the last act in a series of urban developments that, r the last five centuries, have profoundly modified the natural characteristics of the site ere, in ancient times, the first settlement grew: a low-lying and extensive promontory, wa-d on either side by rushing streams, the Papireto to the north and the Kemonia to the th, extended out into the sea in the heart of a broad bay protected from the winds.

e historical center of Palermo with Cala, the city's original port, in the foreground

e phases of the settlement's growth clearly show three areas that can be distinguished terms of their basic structure within the context of the present-day city: the once-walled y, within whose perimeters, established as early as the Islamic age, the history of the tlement developed from its origins all the way up to the 18th c.; the 19th-c. city, anchored the two theaters, the Massimo and the Politeama, and jutting into the harbor; the more cent city, lying along the axis of the Viale della Libertà and jutting northward toward the ain known as the Piana dei Colli. The Pheonicians landed here in the 7th c. B.C. and, es-plishing themselves in the inland, more elevated section of the promontory, established rading post with the early Sicilian and Greek peoples then occupying this territory. The pidity with which the settlement expanded, alongside the unquestioned considerations safety and stability, demonstrate the maturing of a city structure that by the 4th c. B.C. volved the fortification of the entire surface of the promontory, breaking it up into the o walled areas of the Paleàpoli (Paleapolis), the earliest core, walled as early as the 6th B.C., a sort of citadel, and the Neàpoli (Neapolis), the new city overlooking the harbor. ie ease with which it was possible to anchor, and the remarkable structure of the har-r itself (originally some 500 meters further inland than the present-day Cala) served to entify the settlement with the name of Panormos, meaning "all harbor," taken from a Greek rm that, in a city that was never ruled by the Greeks, shows not only the intensity of the s with the adjoining and neighboring Greek colonies, but also the aspiration to assim-te the character of a more mature and refined culture.

lied with Carthage following the war of Himera (480 B.C.), Palermo progressively took a more important role in the political setting of the Mediterranean, becoming the chief inic base in Sicily. Under the Romans, who conquered it in 254 B.C., the city saw its pres-

25

tige decline, while the political and economic interests of Sicily shifted to the east-west
is that tied Siracusa (Syracuse), the capital of the province, to Lylibeo, headquarters of
propraetor: the harbor preserved its strategic importance, and the value that accrue
it from the fact that it lay at the heart of the sea routes of the Mediterranean, while Pa
mo itself became a municipium, with a senate comprising 100 citizens, as well as the he
quarters of quaestor. Occupied by the Vandals and later by Odoacer, in A.D. 491 Paler
was conquered by Theodoric and in A.D. 535 was brought by the general Belisarius un
Byzantine rule. The Arabs conquered the city in A.D. 831, during the earliest phases of th
occupation of the island. When, in A.D. 948, Sicily became an autonomous emirate, Pa
mo served as its capital, and, taking part in the vast economic and cultural empire Isl
it generated a complex urban organism that was clearly bound up with the social and
litical structure of Islam. The city expanded outside of its walled perimeter, along the ba
of the two watercourses and along the progressively developing delta of the rivers Kemo
and Papireto. The ancient settlement became the privileged center of life in the city a
the core of the city government, while new and larger quarters developed around the p
itself, a part that was further protected and fortified by a castle, near which a citadel v
built in 937, in time the headquarters of the emir and the Muslim ruling class.

In the middle of the 11th c., while Islamic strength in the central Mediterranean was
clining, Palermo revealed the complex features of a cosmopolitan metropolis, who
boundaries were to remain substantially unchanged right up to the modern era, and who
development was to condition the shape and future layout of the city. With the subsequ
Norman conquest (1072) and the ensuing alliance between monarchy and clergy, soli
fied by the coronation of Ruggero II (Roger II) as King of Sicily (1130), the city became a
ant building yard, intended to consolidate, through material construction, the author
of the crown and the episcopal cathedral, and it was through the contributions of Arab
Byzantine, and Latin master craftsman that there developed that remarkable architectu
synthesis that now survives in the glory of the Cappella Palatina (Palatine Chapel) and t
Duomo (Cathedral) of Monreale.

In 1266, the city and its surrounding region passed from Swabian rule to that of the Anj
but shortly afterward, the dramatic events that followed the revolt of the Vespro (Sicili
Vespers, 1282) led to the succession of Aragonese dominion, replacing that of the hou
of Anjou: the triumph in this period of the great feudal families offered Palemo a chan
– now that it had been supplanted as capital by Naples – to enjoy a limited autonomy a
to undertake ambitious programs of construction and a general reorganziation of the
ban layout, through the power of the ruling aristocracy.

The imposing palace-fortresses of the Sclafani and the Chiaramonte families stand as t
chief fulcrums of the new city layout, constituting the prototypes of a remarkable arc
tectural form that characterizes the civil and religious building of the 14th c.

The position of Palermo on the Mediterranean checkerboard, during the years of the gre
est hostility between the Turkish and Spanish empires, led to a radical restructuring of t
city that profoundly modified its layout and overall appearance and image. Palermo's r
as a stronghold, as well as the capital of a viceroyal province under Spain, led to a rer
vation of public spaces and a different layout of the political and military headquarters. Wh
ensued was the most substantial and spectacular urban reconstruction of Palermo do
during the 16th c., which, in close conjunction with the renewed fortifications, led to a p
found renovation of the city's central area, creating an internal longitudinal axis of co
munications (a main artery that also served as a ceremonial and official avenue) along whi
lay the squares of the chief institutions of the city and the most prestigious buildings
the nobility and the religious institutions.

From the Baroque experience to recent urban structures

The construction, in the early years of the 17th c., of the Via Maqueda, perpendicular to t
Càssaro, and the creation, at the center of the intersection, of the Piazza Vigliena, actua
gutted a broad swath of the city and triggered, with the establishment of a second chief arte
a total revolution in the existing structure of the city: the urban image that was thus cre
ed is symbolically summed up in terms of the politics of the period, and the Catholic Count
Reformation, by the concave settings of the four Cantoni Centrali, or central corners. Th
marked the beginning of the Palermitan Baroque movement, a period during which the ci
was profoundly transformed through a process of renovation that exalted the splendor
power over the two centuries of ecclesiastic and feudal rule. The many and often contr
dictory reforms that – under the pressure of the growing crisis of the old regime – chara

zed the rule of the house of Bourbon (Sicily, following the short rule of the houses of Savoy
Austria, passed under Bourbon rule in 1734), triggered a series of urbanistic and cul-
l projects that aimed at a more intelligent and responsible growth of the city.
development of the economic and political bonds that linked Palermo to the rest of
ope at large in the first half of the 19th c. clarified the broad outlines of a program of
struction and urban renovation that aimed at a complete implementation of the bour-
is model. In the setting of the "belle époque," marked by a lively growth of industrial

nufacturing and a general increase in pros-
ity that culminated in the Esposizione
ionale (National Exposition) of 1891, Paler-
established the two major theaters, the
tro Massimo and the Teatro Politeama, as
anchors and strongpoints of its new im-
; this image, during a remarkable period of
ativity, dominated by the figure of Ernesto
ile, took the city to the high point of Italian
erty (the Italian version of Art Nouveau). The
struction of the Strada della Libertà, an ex-
plary model of 19th-c. urban culture, gave a
initive push to the northward expansion,
ating a profitable and spectacular repre-
tative axis along which to establish new
idential settlements, while at the same time
gering the de facto abandoment of the his-
ical center. The center, worn out by a slow
progressive desertion in favor of the new res-
ntial neighborhoods, and badly damaged by
bombing it suffered during WWII, is only just
ginning the difficult process of renovation in
ler to lead the city to a new economic and so-
l level.

*The magnificent fountain which
dominates Piazza Pretoria*

1 The earliest fortified settlement

e earliest inhabited section of Palermo
cupied the most easily defended part of
arrow promontory, extending between
o rivers, set in a deep inlet. Here, the
oenicians, arriving in the 7th c. B.C., es-
lished a trading station by fortifying a
uare area that coincides, roughly, with
e area that now lies between the Palazzo
i Normanni and the Cattedrale (or Cathe-
al; roughly corresponding to the present-
y Piazza della Vittoria). The settlement
ew rapidly, and the entire summit of the
omontory was enclosed, in the 4th c.
C., by a new set of walls that, while pre-
rving the earlier settlement, uphill
aleàpoli, or Paleapolis), extended the
w settlement (Neàpoli, or Neapolis) down
ward the port basin, which then ran deep
d inland as far as what is now Via Roma.
e sudden expansion that came in the
ake of the Islamic invasion and the foun-
tion, around the length of the old walls,
new and populous quarters, confirmed
is area known as the "Càssaro" as the
art of the city of Palermo, and such it re-
ained in the medieval city as well, when

the foundation of the Reggia Normanna
(Norman Palace) and the Cattedrale (Cathedral) established the "Galca" (the ancient
Paleàpoli, or Paleapolis) as the the political
and religious center.
From the complex of the Piazza della Vit-
toria-Piazza del Parlamento, which extends
before the Palazzo dei Normanni, the itinerary extends along the narrow roads that
cut through the compact structural mass of
the Càssaro, reaching the Piazzetta S. Giovanni Decollato, with the Palazzo Sclàfani;
continuing along the Via dei Biscottari it
runs into the Piazza Bologni, surrounded by
handsome Baroque palazzi. After climbing
up to the left along the Corso Vittorio
Emanuele, central artery of the area and major "marble way" through the medieval city,
straightened and widened in the 16th c.,
past the Biblioteca Regionale (library), one
emerges into the Piazza della Cattedrale, set
between the Cattedrale and the Palazzo Arcivescovile (archbishop's palace).

Piazza della Vittoria (II, E-F3). This square
lies at the center of the area occupied by the

earliest fortified settlement, the ancient Paleàpoli, or Paleapolis, known in the centuries following the Islamic invasion as the Galca (from the Arabic "al-Halqah," or enclosure wall). Originally bounded by the high ground of the Palazzo Reale, it took on its present-day urbanistic layout around the middle of the 16th c.

The chief site of public events and official parades, and the location, in 1820, of the victorious insurrection of the people of Palermo against the local Bourbon garrison (commemorated in the present-day name), this square is almost entirely occupied by the palm gardens of *Villa Bonanno* (with ruins of Roman homes).

Palazzo dei Normanni* or Palazzo Reale (II, F3). Now the headquarters of the Assemblea Regionale Siciliana, or Sicilian parliament, this building is one of the most important monuments in the city of Palermo in terms of its historical and artistic importance. It was built by the Arabs in the 9th c., on the site of what was probably a Punic and Roman fortress; the façade, which dates from the 17th c., shows features (the Torre Pisana, or Pisan tower) dating back to the Norman expansion, which transformed the original fortress into a sumptuous palace and the political and administrative headquarters of the state. Beginning in the middle of the 13th c., with the decline of Swabian dynasty and the decline of Sicilian political life, the building so lost its former standing that by the middle of the 16th c. it lay in abandonment and serious neglect, with the exception of the Cappella Palatin. In 1555, the Spanish viceroys decided to use it once again as their residence, and they carried out radical renovations. In 1921, study and work began on the project of uncovering traces of the original buildings, which were thought to have been entirely destroyed, with the exception of the Torre Pisana, the Cappella Palatina, and the hall known as the Sala di Ruggero in the Gioaria. The surprising result, to the contrary, was the rediscovery of nearly all of the rooms recorded by history, as well as others whose existence was previously unknown. In the *Torre Pisana* was discovered the chamber of treasures, or Stanza dei Tesori, with a double entry door, surrounded by battlements covered by majestic vaults, illuminated by narrow windows with double splaying: the four large urns that are sealed into the floor could contain hundreds of millions of golden coins.

On the second story is the entrance to the

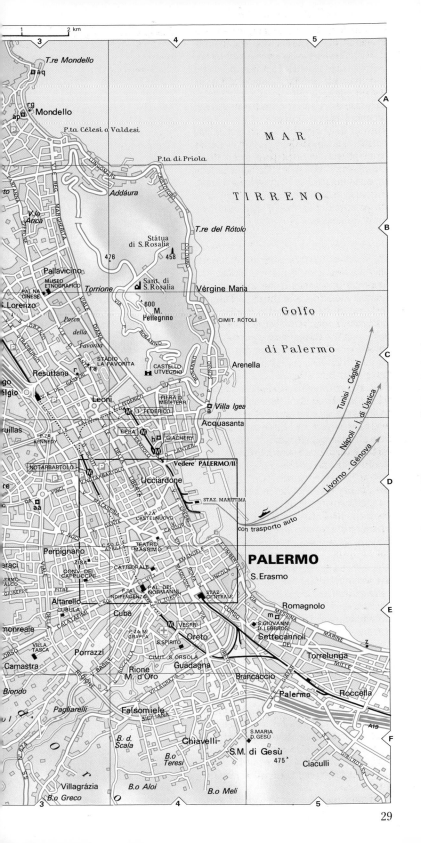

T.re Mondello
aq
rg Mondello
ap
P.ta Célesi o Valdesi

MAR

P.ta di Priola

TIRRENO

Addáura

V.le
Anca
MARGHERITA

T.re del Rótolo

Státua
di S.Rosalia
476   458

Golfo

Pallavicino
MUSEO
ETNOGRAFICO
PAL.NA
CINESE
Torrione
Sant. di
S.Rosalia

Vérgine Maria

S.Lorenzo
Parco
della
Favorita
600
M.
Pellegrino

di Palermo

CIMIT. ROTOLI

Resuttana
STADIO
LA FAVORITA
CASTELLO
UTVEGGIO

Arenella

Tunisi - Cágliari

Leoni
FIERA D.
MEDITERR.
M J. FEDERICO

Villa Igea

Napoli - I. di Ústica

FIERA M
GIACHERY
M

Acquasanta

NOTARBARTOLO M
NOTARBARTOLO
LIBERTÀ

Ucciardone

Vedere PALERMO/II

Livorno - Génova

STAZ. MARITTIMA

P.ZA
CASTELNUOVO

con trasporto auto

Perpignano
CONV. DEI
CAPPUCCINI
ZISA

TEATRO
MASSIMO

PALERMO

S.Erasmo

CATTEDRALE

Romagnolo
MESSINA
S.GIOVANNI
D. LEBBROSI

Altarello
CUBULA
Cuba
PAL. DEI
NORMANNI
P.ZA
INDIPENDENZA
STAZ.
CENTRALE

Settecannoli

monreale
VESPRI
S.SPIRITO
Oreto
Torrelunga

VILLA
TASCA
Porrazzi
Rione
M. d'Oro
CIMIT. S.ORSOLA
Guadagna
Brancáccio

Camastra
Palermo
Roccella

Biondo
Pagliarelli
Falsomiele
VILLAGRÁTIA
A19

B. d.
Scala
Chiavelli-
S.MARIA
D. GESÙ
S.M. di Gesù
475
Ciaculli

Villagrátia
B.o
Teresi
B.o Aloi
B.o Meli

B.o Greco

1   2 km

Cappella Palatina**, a splendid monument from Norman times, founded by Ruggero II in 1130. The interior constitutes one of the highest known instances of the integration of architecture and the figurative arts: basilican in form, it features a nave and two aisles divided by exceedingly subtle oval arches; in the raised sanctuary, with three apses, the central square is bounded by mosaic transennas and surmounted by a hemispheric dome set on corner niches. The floor is in mosaic; the walls have a marble wainscoting. The central nave has a magnificent wooden caisson ceiling (circa 1143) and "muqarnas," painted with Kufic figures and inscriptions; the small side aisles have pitch roofs, with painted beams: the whole constitutes the largest cycle of Islamic paintings to survive to the present day. At the beginning of the nave is the vast *royal throne*, encrusted with mosaics; near the sanctuary, on the right, is a rich mosaic *ambo*, supported by striated columns, and a splendid *Paschal candelabrum* (4.5 meters tall), carved with acanthus leaves, figures, and animals: all these date from the 12th c., and they combine Romanesque, Arabic, and Byzantine elements. The wooden choir is modern.

Mosaics** cover the upper sections of the walls of the side aisles and the sanctuary, and glitter with a golden background. The oldest ones are those in the sanctuary, which date back to 1143: in the dome, *Christ Pantokrator gives a benediction*, amidst angels, archangels, prophets, saints, and evangelists; on the arches of the presbytery, the *Annunciation* and the *Presentation in the Temple*; in the vault of the apse, note the *Christ giving a benediction*. Dating from a slightly later period (circa 1154-66) are the mosaics with Latin inscriptions in the central nave, depicting *Stories from the Old Testament*; still later are the mosaics of the little side aisles.

On the upper floor are the **royal apartments**, normally closed to visitors. Of special interest is the *Salone d'Ercole* or *Sala del Parlamento*, built in 1560-70 and decorated in 1799 with frescoes by Giuseppe Velasquez: currently, it is used for sessions of the Assemblea Regionale Siciliana, or Sicilian parliament. Forming part of the royal apartments is the *Sala dei Viceré*, a hall featuring portraits of the viceroys and lieutenants of Sicily, a *dining room* that was once an open atrium, with high oval arcades supported by corner columns and, adjoining this room, the hall, or *Sala di Re Ruggero*, magnificent with its mosaics depicting hunting scenes (circa 1170) that

cover the upper sections of the walls, eaves of the arches, and the vaults, pressing – in the refined decorations w animals and plants – the pictorial influe of the Persian Middle East.

On the upper story is the observatory, *Osservatorio Astronomico* (closed to public), set in the upper section of the To Pisana, founded in 1786, at the behest of Bourbon government, by Giuseppe Pia: who was its first director.

Porta Nuova (II, E-F3). This massive g done in the Mannerist style features a sin broad fornix, or aperture, is surmounted a small loggia, and topped by a cusped jolica roof, and was built in 1583 along straight avenue of the Càssaro in the pl of an existing 15th-c. gate, to commen rate the entrance of Charles V into the c upon his return in 1535, from his victory Tunis: badly damaged in the lower sect of the outer front, where there are four te mons, it was rebuilt in 1669.

S. Giovanni degli Eremiti** (II, F3). One the best-known monuments from the N man period of Palermo's history, it was built at the behest of Ruggero II (Roger II 1136, on the site of an earlier Gregor monastery. The construction, consider the distinctive and essentially Arab arc tecture, should be attributed to Islam craftsmen.

The *interior* has a single nave divided i two bays, and surmounted by a dome. T presbytery, with apses and surmounted a small cupola, is flanked by two squa rooms, also with apses: rising over the l hand apse stands the bell tower; from t

S. Giovanni degli Eremiti

ht-hand apse, with a dome, one passes in- the structure of an existing building, ected between the 10th and 11th c. (per- ps a mosque), comprising a rectangular l, originally featuring two aisles divided five pillars (on the left wall, note the re- ains of *Virgin Mary with Christ Child and ints*, a fresco dating from the 12th c.), a orish portico with five arches, since de- oyed, and a square open courtyard, once e cemetery for courtiers. In the hand- ne garden, note the remains of a Moorish tern and a small cloister which belonged the original Benedictine convent, from e late Norman era.

ngside is the church of *S. Giorgio in Ke- nia*, adjoining the former convent of the dri di Monte Oliveto (Fathers of Mount ve), which overlooks the Via dei Benedet- i with an 18th-c. façade; further on, in Pi- za Montalto, are the remains of the gate, *Porta di Mazara*, dating from the first lf of the 14th c.

lazzo Sclàfani (II, E-F3). Imposing and ssive, with a square plan and a large ntral atrium, this building, now housing mandi Militari, or offices of military offi- rs, was built by Matteo Sclàfani in 1330, d was erected according to tradition in st one year; the dynamic interweaving of ches with intarsias in black tufa stone closes in the first order a series of elegant in-light mullioned windows, while below at, in the compact curtain wall, original- without apertures (the windows were ilt at the end of the 19th c.), there is a very e portal with a pediment surmounted by aedicule and an eagle. With the decline the family of the Sclàfani the palazzo, ich had become Spanish property, was ansformed in 1435 into a hospital. By the ddle of the 15th c., the atrium was deco- ted with a cycle of frescoes, featuring a iumph of Death, detached following WWII, d now in the Galleria Regionale della Si- ia (art gallery of the region of Sicily).

lazzo Speciale (II, E4). Built by the prae- r of the city in 1468 and largely rebuilt dur- g the 17th and 18th c. by the Valguarnera mily, and later by the Raffadali family, no had become the owners of the building, preserves in its façade the mullioned win- ows and the mouldings of the original, Cat- onian-style façade. Set on this façade, in e second half of the 17th c., was built the rge portal that leads into the inner atrium.

azza Bologni (II, E4). This vast rectangu- r plaza opening out onto the Càssaro,

built in 1566 by the Bologna family, which had built its palazzo here, is given a unified appearance in its powerful Baroque façade by the later construction of the surrounding palazzi: *Palazzo Ugo* (to the south), built in the early years of the 18th c., with a loggia over the entrace and marble statues from the school of the Gagini; *Palazzo Villafran- ca* (to the west), built in the 17th c. in the place of the demolished home of the Bologna family, with a broad façade rebuilt around the middle of the 18th c., with two symmetrical portals and with large deco- rative heraldic crests in stucco; *Palazzo Belmonte-Riso* (to the north, on the Corso Vittorio Emanuele), built to plans by Ve- nanzio Marvuglia in 1784, with the heraldic crest of Ignazio Marabitti.

Collegio Massimo dei Gesuiti (II, E4). This institute of higher education was an expres- sion of the cultural domination enjoyed by the Jesuit order, virtually monopolistic from the middle of the 16th c. until 1767, was transformed in 1778 into a public library, and now serves as the site of the library of the region of Sicily, or *Biblioteca Regionale Si- ciliana*; one enters through the portal of the former church of S. Maria della Grotta (1615). The palazzo, badly damaged during WWII, has been subjected to radical restoration. A broad staircase, built at the expense of the interior of the church, leads up to the li- brary, or Biblioteca, with a collection of some 400,000 volumes, including collec- tions of hand-written texts, collections of correspondence, illuminated codices, and incunabula.

Cattedrale**, or Cathedral (II, E3). This major architectural monument, encloses, in the stratification of styles produced by the manifold renovations undertaken, a great portion of the history of the city. Built in 1184 by the archbishop Gualtiero Offamilio on the site of an existing basilica, trans- formed by the Arabs into a mosque and then restored by the Normans to a place of Christian worship, it stands on the square of the same name (Piazza della Cattedrale), which was built in the 15th c., and sur- rounded by balustrades adorned with stat- ues during the following century. In the 14th, 15th, and 16th c., it underwent con- tinual additions and alterations which all the same did nothing to alter fundamentally the ancient structures; between 1781 and 1801 it was subjected to a radical transfor- mation which resulted in the changing of the basilican plan to a Latin-cross plan, with the addition of side-aisles and the wings of the

Palermo/II

1:15 000 (1 cm = 150 m)

MONDELLO km 11 - AEROPORTO km 31

A29 km 15

MONREALE km 8

SCIACCA km 92

32

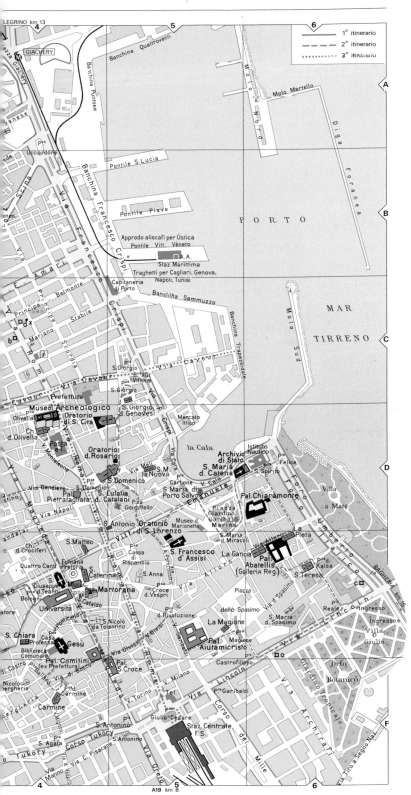

transept, and the addition of the cupola.
The **main façade**, overlooking the Via Matteo Bonello, preserves the appearance it was given between the 14th and 15th c., with two tall and slender towers with mullioned windows and slender columns, barely indicated blind arches, and multiple oval arches with slender columns set in the corner ribbings. The central portal, dating from the first half of the 15th c., is surmounted by a twin-light mullioned window; it also features on the keystones of the interior the heraldic crests of the house of Aragon and of the Senate of Palermo; in the aedicule is a 15th-c. *Madonna*. The 18th-c. wooden doors have been replaced by modern bronze doors, with Episodes from the Old and the New Testaments and from local history (Filippo Sgarlata, 1961). Two tall oval arches link, across the Via Bonello, the façade to the *bell tower* that faces it; it is medieval in its massive lower volume. Set in the *left-hand façade* of the church – the most extensively reworked side – a portico in the Gagini style dating from the middle of the 16th c. was included in the late-18th-c. reconstruction, and depicts on its elevation the portal from 1659. At the beginning of the *right-hand façade*, overlooking the square, set between little towers is a broad portico, a magnificent example of Catalonian-style flamboyant Gothic, built in 1429-30 by Antonio Gambara, with three tall oval arches (in the first column on the left, probably already part of the church when it was converted into a mosque, is a carving of a passage from the Koran). The pediment, adorned with Gothic motifs, open out into a rich and broad portal (1426) with handsome wooden doors (1432). The *absidal façade*, enclosed by little corner towers similar to those of the façade, curves around three apses, carved with a motif of intertwined arches, and covered with an in-

tarsia decoration. This is the section of building that most faithfully preserves original 12th-c. forms.

The **interior**, completely transformed tween 1781 and 1801, has a Latin-cross p and has a nave and two side-aisles, divi by pillars, each of which includes four s der granite columns, originally part of previous basilican church. The interi rich in works of art, among which we w point out sculptural elements of a disn tled Gigini tribune, now set in the presb and the transept, and statues by France Laurana and Antonello Gagini. At the fo the right side-aisle are the famous *Tombe periali e Reali* (royal and imperial tom majestic in their simplicity: the sarcopha (Roman, with hunting scenes) of Costa d'Aragona, or Constance of Aragon, wi Federico II (Frederick II, d. 1222); the to of Enrico VI (Henry VI, d. 1197); the tom Federico II (Frederick II, d. 1250; the ur so contains the remains of Pietro II d'Ar na, or Peter II of Aragon, d. 1342); the cophagus of Guglielmo, or William, the D of Athens (d. 1338), son of Federico II d' gona, or Frederick II of Aragon; the tom Ruggero II (Roger II, d. 1154); the tomb of empress Costanza, or Constance, his dau ter (d. 1198). In the presbytery are a carved wooden *choir*, of the Catalor Gothic school (1466), an *episcopal throne* assembled in part with mosaic fragme from the 12th c., and a *Paschal candelab.* from the same period, with mosaics. Ab the altar of the left transept, note the wo en *Crucifix* from the early 14th c., an exc tional piece of work in the "dolorous-G ic" of the Rhine style, taken from the sir demolished church of S. Nicolò la Ka The *crypt* is divided by granite columns to two transverse aisles with cross va (12th c.). The front aisle is partly occup

The complex mass of Palermo Cathedral, surmounted by a late 18th century dome

the base of the church's apse. To the
ht of the presbytery, the chapel of S.
alia conserves the remains of the city's
ron saint in an ornate silver urn.

azzo Arcivescovile, or archbishop's
ace (II, E3). Founded by the archbishop
one di Bologna, this building features, in
façade overlooking the Piazza della Cat-
rale, rebuilt in the 18th c., the remains of
original 15th-c. construction: an elegant
alonian Gothic triple-light mullioned win-
v, in the corner on the left, and the geo-
ric basket-arch portal, with the insignia

of the Beccadelli-Bologna family. From the
second courtyard on the left, one can enter
the **Museo Diocesano** (currently closed for
renovation), or museum of the diocese, created in 1927 and expanded in 1952; this museum features marblework from the Cathedral, paintings and statues from churches
that had been suppressed or destroyed
(among them are triptychs and panels of the
Sicilian and Tuscan schools of of the 12th to
15th c.), and lovely sculptures, friezes, and
capitals, dating from the Sicilian Renaissance and Baroque, originally from the
Cathedral.

The medieval quarters and the Four Corners

s itinerary runs into the compact and
htly chaotic fabric of the walled city,
nded to the south by the train station,
tazione Centrale, and to the north by the
atro Massimo. Juxtaposed upon this
se-knit urbanistic system was laid, dur-
the 16th and 17th c., the construction of
crossroads (Croce di Strade) of the
rso Vittorio Emanuele and the Via Maque-
built to optimize communications with-
he city, but also with the idea of giving
ermo a new and monumental image and
ew administrative structure (the city
ken into four parts), culminating in the
nstruction of the Quattro Canti (literally,
ur Corners).
m the Via S. Agostino, with the 13th-c.
urch of S. Agostino, one crosses the Via
queda and, following the Via Bandiera,
e reaches the Piazza di S. Domenico and
church of S. Domenico. From here, the
te continues along the Via dei Bambinai
e name refers to the presence of crafts-
n who shaped wax figures), with the Or-
rio del Rosario di S. Domenico, and Via
uarcialupo, with the church and the Or-
ry of S. Cita, and one finally reaches the
e-Renaissance church of S. Giorgio dei
novesi. Along a labyrinth of little streets
ose names recall the presence of various
afts activities (Via Argenteria Vecchia,
silversmiths; Via dei Chiavettari, for
ksmiths; Via dei Materassai, for mat-
ss-makers; Via dei Maccheronai, for pas-
nakers), and which are made more live-
by the nearby market known as the Vuc-
ìa, the oldest market in Palermo, one
ches the Corso Vittorio Emanuele: after
ossing this major artery, you continue
ng the Via Paternostro (formerly the Via
Pisani), one of the most important thor-
ghfares of the medieval city, along which
u will see the 13th-c. church of S.

Francesco d'Assisi and the Oratory of S.
Lorenzo. As you head down the Corso toward the sea, you will reach the Renaissance churches of S. Maria di Porto Salvo
and S. Maria della Catena, which adjoin the
harbor area overlooking the Cala, where
in centuries gone by merchants from Genoa,
Pisa, Amalfi, and Naples kept their fondaci,
or storehouses. Not far away is the 14th-c.
Steri, the palazzo of the powerful Chiaramonte family. In the Via Alloro, a major residential street of late-medieval Palermo,
now in ruins, stand – one adjoining the other – the church of the Gancia, from the 15th
c., and, from the same period, the Palazzo
Abatellis, which now houses the Galleria Regionale della Sicilia, or regional gallery of
Sicily, a rich collection of art history, from
Sicily and elsewhere. Take the Via Torre-
muzza to reach the church of S. Teresa della Kalsa, in the heart of a quarter that bears
the same name, as well as a fortified citadel
built by the Moors in A.D. 937 for the emir
and his viziers, and then you will continue
along until you reach the southern boundary of the medieval city, marked by the
broad Via Lincoln, built in the 18th c. along
the perimeter of the walls. From here you
can enter the botanical gardens, or Orto
Botanico and the adjoining gardens of Villa Giulia, which – taken together – form the
largest green space in the city. Along the Via
Garibaldi, where the Renaissance Palazzo
Ajutamicristo stands, one heads back into
the medieval city, and after passing one after another the straight avenues of Via Roma and Via Maqueda, one heads along the
Via del Bosco, flanked by lordly homes
from the 16th to the 18th c., finally reaching
the church of the Carmine. After passing
through the church of the Gesù, one reaches the Piazza Bellini - set near the Baroque
crossroads, or Croce di Strade - the city

center of medieval Palermo, with the monumental churches of the Martorana and S. Cataldo, and the adjoining Piazza Pretoria. Piazza Vigliena – better known as the Quattro Canti – is the point of departure for the tour of Baroque Palermo, with the four arms of the cross (Corso Vittorio Emanuele and the Via Maqueda), with their array of 17th- and 18th-c. façades, constituting the most noteworthy creation of that period.

S. Agostino (II, D4). The façade, constructed in the early years of the 14th c. with the generous support of the Sclafani and Chiaramonte families (who also placed their heraldic crests here, along the sides), has a stern Gothic portal with a niched pediment and an exquisite rose window. The side portal dates from the 15th c. and has been attributed to Domenico Gagini (the lunette dates from the 16th c.); in the vestibule there is a late-Roman sarcophagus and a 16th-c. holy-water font. The *interior*, completely redone in 1671, has a single nave and walls punctuated with pillars, as well as a rich decorative array of stuccoes by Giacomo Serpotta, completed between 1711 and 1729; among other things there is a panel by Simone di Wobreck (mid 16th c.) and a 14th-c. panel and Crucifix. Adjoining the church is a 16th-c. *cloister.*

S. Domenico (II, D4-5). This church is one of the most noteworthy Baroque monuments in all of Palermo, and its broad and light elevation, adorned with stucco statues and flanked by two tall belltowers, overlooks the Piazza di S. Domenico, which was built in 1724 following the demolition of old buildings that were hemming in the church. It was erected in 1640, to plans drawn up by Andrea Cirincione, on the structure of an existing church, founded along with the convent in 1300, and rebuilt to a larger scale in 1458; the façade was added in 1726, following the construction of the new square. In the vast *interior*, built to a Latin-cross plan, with a nave and two side-aisles divided by stout columns, with the tombs and cenotaphs of noted Sicilians, making this the Pantheon of the city of Palermo (among others, one-time Italian prime minister Francesco Crispi is buried here). Note the handsome marblework by Antonello Gagini and the Gagini school.

Oratorio del Rosario di S. Domenico* (II, D5). In order to tour this oratory, contact the custodian, at no. 16 in the Via dei Bambinai. The interior* is a masterpiece of elegance, with the exquisite stuccoes by Giacomo Ser-

potta, who created a spectacular array o
legorical statues (depicted on the colum
the second figure on the right, represen
Strength, is the lizard, or in Sicilian dial
the "slrpuzza," emblcm of the artist), p
and reliefs; above the altar is a little cup
from the cornice of which look down lac
knights, and boys. On the walls, note the .
teries, painted by Pietro Novelli, Giacome
Verde, Matthias Stomer, and Luca Giorda
in the vault, note the *Coronation of the V*
Mary, by Pietro Novelli. On the altar, note
Madonna del Rosario*, or Virgin of
Rosary, with St. Dominick and the pat
saints of Palermo, a magnificent canvas
Antonie van Dyck, commissioned in Pale
at the turn of 1624, and completed by hi
Genoa in 1628.

S. Cita or **S. Zita** (II, D4-5). Although
church is known by these two variants on
same saint's name, it is actually dedicate
S. Mamiliano, or St. Mamilian, and was fou
ed in 1369, rebuilt in 1586-1603, and c
pleted with its façade in 1781; it was ba
damaged by bombing in WWII, and has si
been restored. The interior, built to a La
cross plan, contains works of sculpture fr
the original church, including a numbe
masterpieces by Antonello Gagini.

Oratorio di S. Cita (II, D4). This oratory is
mous for the stuccoes that adorn the in
rior (if you find it closed, enquire at
nearby church). From the small door,
high on a set of steps, you cross throug
late-16th-c. loggia with a double order, a
you enter the rectangular interior, c
pletely covered with magnificent stucco
by Giacomo Serpotta. Carried out in vari
phases between 1688 and 1718, these st
coes depict allegorical statues, spectacu
flights of putti, and little representatio
of the Mysteries of the Rosary. On the
trance wall, note the *Battle of Lepanto*, w
two putti, on either side of a tropaeum
arms. Along the walls, there are benches
the brothers of the order, with mother
pearl intarsias.

S. Giorgio dei Genovesi (II, C5). This chu
was built by the colony of Genoans in Pa
mo in 1576-81; the façade, simple and un
suming, has two orders, and is given a
partite division by pilaster strips, with
crowning element formed of large deco
ed cornices. The *interior* (usually closed;
church, which has been deconsecrated
periodically the site of temporary exh
tions), an elegant layout with a Latin-cro
plan, has a nave and two side-aisles, with

s formed of bundles of marble columns,
h a high cupola at the intersection of the
ns of the cross. Handsome sepulchral
ques, largely from the 16th and 17th c.
ie dates from 1756), cover much of the
oring.

rancesco d'Assisi (II, E5). This church,
ignificant marker of the presence of this
ndicant order in this neighborhood of
rchants, beyond the Corso Vittorio
anuele, was built for the third time, be-
een 1255 and 1277, but in time it was
ojected to a variety of modifications: in
: 14th and 15th c., the side chapels were
ded, while in 1533 the wooden roofing
s replaced with a cross vault, and in
39 the presbytery was elongated. Deco-
ed and frescoed in the 17th c., it was
ther embellished in 1723 by Giacomo
rpotta with exceedingly fine stuccoes. It
s however damaged in the earthquake of
23, and restored in the Neoclassical style.
imaged by bombing in 1943, a radical
storation was undertaken, restoring to
he original appearance of the 13th c.
e façade, restored toward the end of the
th c., has a remarkably fine flamboyant
thic portal, built in 1302, with a small log-
in the pediment, frescoed at the turn of
: 20th c., surmounted by a lavish rose win-
w, rebuilt to the model of the rose window
the church of S. Agostino. The side portals
te from the end of the 16th c. Along the
ht side and outside of the apses, it is pos-
ole to make out several elements belong-
g to the earliest structure. The **interior** fea-
res a nave and two side-aisles set on cylin-
ical pillars, with broad Gothic arches. In
e central nave, note the allegorical statues
Giacomo Serpotta (1723); in the side
sles, there are Gothic and Renaissance
apels. Among the artworks to be seen
re, let us mention major sculptures by An-
nello, Antonio, and Giacomo Gagini, Pietro
: Bonitate, and Francesco Laurana (the
st two are probably responsible for the
ortal of the 4th chapel on the left), in the
esbytery, and a handsome carved wood-
choir from the 16th c. The church pos-
sses a considerable treasure, with reli-
ous canvases and furnishings dating back
om the 15th to the 19th c.

ratorio di S. Lorenzo* (II, E5). This ora-
ry, built after 1569 by the Compagnia di S.
ancesco, a Franciscan religious organi-
tion, contains a magnificent stucco dec-
ation on the interior, a masterpiece from
e later period of Giacomo Serpotta (1698-
'10). Ten symbolic statues, including fig-

ures of *Charity and Almsgiving*, eight smaller stories, full of lively details (*Scenes from
the Life of Saint Lawrence and Saint Francis*),
a large panel with a *Martyrdom of Saint
Lawrence* in the far wall, and everywhere a
spectacular array of flying festive putti, and
higher up, a number of male figures all compose a brilliant and magnificent whole, full

*The oratory of S. Cita with stucco work
by Giacomo Serpotta*

of grace and elegance. Around the walls,
note the handsome seats, intarsiaed in
mother-of-pearl, supported by carved wood-
en brackets (18th c.). The altar once featured a Nativity of Jesus, a large canvas by
Caravaggio (1609), but the painting was
stolen in 1969.

S. Maria di Porto Salvo (II, D5). This church
was built in 1526, perhaps to plans by Antonello Gagini, and it served as the backdrop to the straightaway formed by the
Càssaro Nuovo (now Corso Vittorio
Emanuele), but the establishment in 1581 of
the last section of this thoroughfare (known
as the Càssaro Morto) resulted in the
church's being mutilated in the apsidal
area, which was given a façade in the same
style, punctuated by pilaster strips and
with a portal by Giacomo Gagini.
The *interior*, which features handsome architecture, possesses a nave and two side-
aisles set on raised pointed arches and covered with a cross-vault (note the magnificent star-studded vault arching over the
old presbytery); the side chapels are separated by stout Renaissance pillars, which replaced the old ones in 1581 in order to support the rooms that had been built over

the vaults. The interior contains noteworthy late-Gothic sculpture and paintings, including a wooden 15th-c. *Crucifix* and a triptych with the *Virgin Mary, Christ Child, and Saints*, from the 16th c.

Palazzo Chiaramonte* (II, D6). This palazzo is also known as *Steri* – from the Latin term "Hosterium," meaning fortified palace – and it is a clear indication of the prestige of the most powerful feudal family of Sicily in the 14th c. The building has a square plan and a central atrium, and it was begun by Manfredi Chiaramonte in 1307, and was completed with its decorations in 1380. The exterior, although it has been extensively altered, still shows along the front and the sides the forbidding lines of the original, three-story construction, with the first floor appearing massive and closed, and the other two open, with broad double-light and triple-light mullioned windows, elegantly decorated with intarsias done in lava stone. In front of the palazzo in 1396, the last member of the Chiaramonte family, Andrea, was beheaded for his rebellion against king Martino I of Aragon. In the middle of the 15th c., the Steri became the headquarters of the viceroys of Sicily, and in 1601 it became the headquarters of the Tribunale del S. Offizio (the church courts; in the *Carceri Filippine*, a long area split up by pointed arches set on columns, which can be reached from an inner courtyard, there are drawings, paintings, and writings of the nameless victims of the Inquisition); it was later occupied by various tribunals, from 1799 to 1960, the year in which the offices were transferred to the new hall of justice, or Palazzo di Giustizia. Once it became the site of the new Rettorato Universitario, or university administration, it was subjected to extensive restoration, but is not open to the public. The large hall on the second story has a wooden ceiling painted with decorative motifs that hearken back to the Muslim tradition and with Bible stories and stories of knighthood, by Simone da Corleone, Cecco di Naro, and Darenu da Palermo (1377-80). In the loggia, set on pointed-arch columns, which runs around the inner courtyard, note the two handsome twin-light mullioned windows (one of which has been damaged), with unusual ashlars.

S. Maria della Catena* (II, D6). This church is named for a chain, or "catena," that was used to close off the city's old port, and was built in the early years of the 16th c. It is a splendid example of the Catalonian Gothic style, mixed with Renaissance elemen and some have attributed it, though with documentation, to Matteo Carnalivari stands high atop a stairway, and befor stands a portico with three basket arch Beneath the portico are three portals, w bas-reliefs, by Vincenzo Gagini, leading to the interior. On the left side, with sin mullioned windows and pillars, is a Gag portal. The *interior* has a nave and two si aisles, divided by slender Renaissan columns; the nave has ribbed vaults, a side barrel vaults; it has a raised presbyt and three apses. In the chapels, note the liefs and statues of the Gagini school.

Porta Felice (II, D6). This majestic structu a city gate, stands at the mouth of the C so Vittorio Emanuele. It was named after t wife of the viceroy Marcantonio Color who ordered it built (1582) in order to co memorate the completion of the last secti of the Corso, which he had undertaken was set as a counterpart to the Porta N va, which stands at the opposite end of t straightaway.

Museo Internazionale delle Marionette D6). This international museum of ma onettes and puppets, housed in the Ass ciazione per la Conservazione de Tradizioni Popolari, in Via Butera 1. It po sesses more than two thousand items, cluding hand-puppets, puppets, ma onettes, shadow puppets, backdrops, a stages: there are puppets from Palerm Trapani, and Naples; marionettes and pu pets from various countries; Indian, Gre Turkish, Malaysian, Balinese, Thai, a Cambodian shadow puppets; stick puppe from Java and Mali.

S. Maria degli Angeli, known as **La Ganc** (II, E6). Built at the turn of the 16th c. on t site of an earlier church dedicated to Sai Jerome, this church was a hospice for Fra ciscan monks: the façade, in undresse square ashlars, is opened by a Gothic po tal with a delicate bas-relief on the arch. The *interior*, profoundly transformed in t second half of the 17th c., has a single nav with a lacunar ceiling, lined by chape Over the main entryway is an organ dati back to 1620, probably the oldest organ Palermo, built by Raffaele La Valle. Amor the furnishings of the church, we wou point out: the *Virgin Mary and Saint Cathe ine and Saint Agatha* (Madonna of Monse rat) by Antonello da Palermo (1528); b tween the 5th and the 6th chapel on th right, a pulpit composed of fragmentary e ents of the Gagini school; in the chapels the right and left of the presbytery, stuc- es by Giacomo Serpotta; *Wedding of the gin Mary* and *Nativity*, by Vincenzo da via (16th c.); *Pietà*, a relief dating from the h c. There are also reliefs by Antonello gini and statues of the Gagini school.

azzo Abatellis* (II, E6). This sumptuous sidence was begun in 1490 by Matteo rnelivari, and was completed five years er, for the Maestro Portolano del Regno d the praetor of Palermo, Francesco atellis. It is a compact structure with un- essed stone ashlars, set on a square plan d styled in the forms of the Catalonian e-Gothic, with various Renaissance de- ls. The *façade* is embellished on the main or by elegant three-light mullioned win- ws, and it rises on either side in two tow- s, with a rich Gothic decoration; the broad rtal contains a bundled motif of staffs d batons braided with cabling, and is rmounted by three heraldic crests. It was ry badly damaged during WWII, and was en restored and adapted by Carlo Scarpa 1954, as the site of the **Galleria Regionale lla Sicilia*** (art gallery of the region of ily), a museum installation of the highest ality, featuring works of sculpture and inting, especially dating from the 14th 16th c. In the atrium and in the courtyard, th their portico and loggia, there are ws of sculptures, dating from the era pri- to Romanesque all the way up to the th c. Following this, in the halls on the ound floor, there are wooden sculptures m the 12th to the 16th c. and stone stat- ry from the 14th and 15th c., including the nowned **bust of Eleonora of Aragon***, a

e famous st of eonora Aragona

masterpiece by Francesco Laurana (ca. 1471). Among the paintings, note the **Triumph of Death***, a spectacular fresco from the Palazzo Sclàfani, done around 1450, with a depiction of Death on horseback, shooting with his arrows a group of festive young people. In the rooms on the second floor, there are numerous paintings on wooden panel from the 14th and 15th c., of various Italian schools; among these is the small and very famous panel of the **Annunziata*** (Our Lady of the Annunciation) by Antonello da Messina. Also present are various works by Flemish artists; among them we would note in particular the renowned **Malvagna triptych*** by Jan Gossaert (1510). The last sections are dedicated to painting from the 16th, 17th, and 18th c.

S. Teresa (II, E6). This church is one of the most noteworthy works of Palermo Baroque, and was built by Giacomo Amato between 1686 and 1706. The immense façade dominates the Piazza della Kalsa; in the luminous interior, there are decorative stuccoes by Giuseppe and Procopio Serpotta. Not far off are the ruins of the **church of S. Maria dello Spasimo**: built in 1506 and later converted into a hospice for the penniless it now houses exhibitions and shows. Here Raffaello painted a canvas depicting Jesus Falling Beneath the Cross, known as the Spasimo di Sicilia (Spasm of Sicily), now in the Museo Prado in Madrid.

Villa Giulia or Villa Flora* (II, E-F6). This magnificent Italian-style garden was designed in 1778 by Nicolò Palma, and was enlarged and decorated in 1866; it takes its name from Donna Giulia, wife of the Spanish viceroy Guevara. The first public green space in the city, it is based on a geometric design with concentric rays on a square plan; in the central square, there are four Neoclassical exedrae with niches, and, in the fountain in the center, a dodecahedron upheld by a putto. In the broad walkways, note the busts of illustrious Palermitans.

Orto Botanico (II, E-F6), or botanical garden. Set next to Villa Giulia, and designed to integrate that large park, this botanical garden was established in 1785. The square building in the middle, with Neoclassical pronaoi on the two opposite façades, is known as the *Ginnasio*, and contains the herbarium. The most interesting feature is the garden, encompassing roughly 10 hectares, or 25 acres, with a great and abundant array of

A specimen of ficus in the botanic garden

specimens from every climate and type of vegetation to be found on earth.

Church of the Magione (II, E5). Founded in 1191 by Matteo d'Ajello on behalf of the Cistercian monks, this church was given by the Holy Roman Emperor Henry VI in 1197 to the order of the Teutonici, who held it until their expulsion, in 1492, by command of Pope Innocent VIII. One enters the church through a Baroque portal that opens, on the left, onto the street of the same name (Via della Magione). The *interior*, with three aisles divided by marble columns and pointed arches, features a vast transept and three apses; there is an open-beam ceiling (rebuilt). In the flooring (rebuilt), note the large funereal slabs of Teutonic knights. At the far end of the right side-aisle, note the marble triptych dating from the 16th c.; in the left apse, note the small Renaissance portal. On the left of the church, there are interesting remains of a 12th-c. *cloister*, with small pointed double-lintel arches, set on small twin columns with exceedingly elegant capitals, built prior to the cloister of Monreale, by the same craftsmen.

Palazzo Ajutamicristo (II, E5). Built by Matteo Carnelivari in 1490-95 at the behest of Guglielmo Ajutamicristo, it became the property, a century later, of the Moncada di Paternò, who planted a magnificent garden there. The architecture of the building, in bare stone ashlars, reveals a Renaissance influence in the forms of late Catalonian Gothic. Entering through the portal at n. 23 in Via Garibaldi, you will cross a first courtyard, and then, on the left, you will enter a courtyard with a magnificent portico, with basket arches set on columns and a pointed-arch loggia, adorned with tondos and rhomboids set in the pendentives of the arches. Beneath the portico, note the round- and pointed-arch portals, and traces of twin-light mullioned windows.

Church of the Carmine (II, F4). Rebuilt from 1626 on to plans by Vincenzo La Barbera and Mariano Smiriglio, this church displays an unusual cupola, completed in 16.. with an exceedingly ornate tambour (te.. mons set between columns) with the interior sheathed in polychrome majolica. The.. are statues by the Gagini, stuccoes.. Giuseppe and Giacomo Serpotta, and pa.. ings by Tommaso de Vigilia (15th c.). Behi.. the main altar is a small late-Gothic altar w.. a cross vault, with frescoes between t.. ribbings. From the left aisle, you can en.. the *cloister*, with three sides featuring 14.. c. arches set on Renaissance columns.

Church of the Gesù * (II, E4). This is the f.. church built by the Jesuits in Sicily, whe.. they arrived in 1549, and where they qui.. ly gained in influence. This church was l.. gun in 1564, and was considerably enlarg.. with the addition of the side chapels (15.. 1633) and a new cupola in the middle of t.. 17th c. The *interior*, built to a Latin-cro.. plan with three aisles, has deep interco.. municating chapels, transept, and aps.. presbytery as well as a cupola, and cons.. tutes a magnificent example of Sicili.. Baroque art; every corner is sheathed.. polychrome intarsia, marble adornmen.. and stucco reliefs, with a great profusion.. sculpture and paintings, all works done.. a small army of artists over the course.. two centuries; we should mention, amo.. the more respected supervisors of th.. spectacular 'mantle of decorations,' the J.. suits Lorenzo Cipri and Angelo Italia. All th.. survives of the original pictorial decor.. tion are the frescoes in the first bay of t.. vault of the nave, signed by Filippo Ra.. dazzo (1743), and those in the vault of t.. presbytery (the others are replacement.. done by Federico Spoltore in 1954-56). In t.. presbytery and in the apse are preserve.. the exceedingly lavish original decoratio.. in which the sculptures by Gioacchino V.. taliano stand out. The chapel to the left.. the main chapel, the Cappella di S. Anna,.. entirely sheathed in marble decorations.. To the right of the church stands the wester.. front of the **Casa Professa**, with a portal da.. ing from 1685 and a cloister from the 17th c.. through which you can reach the *Bibliotec.. Comunale*, or city library, founded in 17.. and moved here in 1775, eight years after th.. expulsion of the Jesuits from the kingdom..

Martorana ** (II, E4). This Norman churc.. was built in 1143 by Giorgio d'Antioch.. (George of Antioch), admiral of King Rog.. II, and is also known as *S. Maria dell'Amm..*

lio; it overlooks Piazza Bellini with a roque façade that resulted from reconuction in the 16th c. Entrusted to the eek clergy in 1221, in 1433 it was given by ng Alphonse of Aragon to the nearby nedictine monastery, founded by Eloisa rtorana in 1194; it took her name. Over : centuries, it suffered both destruction d additions, and modern restorations ve in part freed it from those additions. Of : original structure, it is possible to see m the square the campanile and, bend the façade, the rough-hewn body of e church, topped by a small hemisphercupola, set on a polygonal tambour, nated on the exterior by inset architece. Since 1937, the church has been the cathedral of the diocese of Piana degli Alnesi, and services are conducted in acrdance with the Greco-Byzantine rites. ke a stairway up to the base of the **camnile****, square in plan, dating from the h c., open at the base with a pointed-arch :ade with corner columns, further up re are three orders of large twin-light lllioned windows, beneath which one en's the **interior*** of the church. The interior s originally made up of a square struce, divided into a Greek cross by four lumns supporting a cupola, with three

e church of S. Cataldo and the Martorana

ises; it was connected to the campanile by ortico, which was replaced in the 17th c. ' a series of bays. The church proper, ich once had marble sheathing along e lower sections of the walls, is decorat on the higher areas of the walls almost tirely in **mosaics****, which constitute, gether with the mosaics of the Cappella latina, the oldest series of mosaics in all Sicily. The iconographic scheme and the stribution of the mosaics correspond to e most orthodox of Byzantine canons; e style, as well, despite the numerous fferent artists who worked here, hearns back to purest tradition of the middle

Byzantine period. They depict *Christ Pantokrator*, surrounded by *archangels, Prophets, Evangelists; Apostles*; the *Nativity of Jesus* and the *Death of the Virgin Mary; Annunciation* and the *Presentation in the Temple*. There are mosaic transennas before the apses; the flooring, restored, is original. In the first portal on the right, dating from the 9th c., and set here in 1599, note the interesting carved wooden doors, an excellent piece of Moorish craftsmanship (12th c.).

S. Cataldo* (II, E4). This is another church from the Norman period, built around 1160 by the admiral, or Ammiraglio Majone di Bari; it however better preserves – in part due to the radical restorations done in the 19th c. – the clean and square forms of the original architecture, with blind arches along the building's face, in living rock; the cornice with parapets and the three little hemispherical domes raised above the tambour; in the tripartite façade, there are single light mullioned windows, closed by transennas. The **interior**, with its remarkable bare walls, which never were coated with mosaics, is a rectangle (10 x 7 m.), divided into three aisles by six columns, taken from ancient buildings, with varied capitals, which support Moorish-style arches, and with three apsidioles. The nave is surmounted by three little cupolas, set on corner niches. The mosaic is original: so too is the altar, upon which is carved a cross, a lamb, and the symbols of the Evangelists. The church is the headquarters of the order of the knights of the holy sepulcher, or Ordine dei Cavalieri del S. Sepolcro.

Piazza Pretoria (II, E4). This monumental square, leveled and built up in the 16th c., dominated by the domes of the two diametrically opposed churches of S. Caterina and S. Giuseppe dei Teatini, is entirely hemmed in by buildings of considerable architectural merit, and is almost entirely occupied by the immense fountain known as the **Fontana Pretoria***, the creation of a Florentine sculptor named Francesco Camilliani (1554-55); the fountain is adorned with statues of deities, allegories, heads of animals, and herms. On the southern side of the square, straddling Piazza Bellini, stands the *Palazzo Senatorio*, or *Palazzo del Municipio*, also known as the *Palazzo delle Aquile* after the marble eagle that stands above the portal. Built in 1463, with a square plan, and made of stone ashlars, it originally turned its main façade principale toward the Piano di S. Cataldo; enlarged and renovated in the 16th and 17th c., it was restored in 1823. In the façade are set numerous commemorative plaques and, on the top, in a niche, there is a statue of Saint Rosalia (1661).

Quattro Canti (II, E4). Via Maqueda, which was built by the viceroy Maqueda in 1600 by brutally ripping through the ancient structure of the city, crosses the Càssaro at a right angle (at the time, it was known as Via Toledo, now it is Corso Vittorio Emanuele), and creates, in the center of the large crossroads that identifies the Baroque section of Palermo, the spectacular *Piazza Vigliena*, also known as the Ottangolo (Octangle), Teatro del Sole (Theater of the Sun), and, more commonly, the Quattro Canti (Four Corners). In the symbolic apparatus, so to speak, of this new ceremonial square, which

ileged position in the new urban cent that was created by this crossroads. I gun in 1612, construction was completed 1645, and decoration was undertaken fre the middle of the 17th c. and throughout t 18th c. The church is topped by a soari cupola, with a tambour decorated wi twinned columns, with the interior of t cupola covered with majolicas. The *inter* is spectacular, and is built to a Latin-cro plan, with three aisles divided by 14 mor lithic marble columns, with a central cup la set on eight colossal twinned column which are also monolithic, and small cup las along the lesser side-aisles. There is la ish decorations on the vault over the nav with stucco ornamentation by Paolo Cor and frescoes by Filippo Tancredi, by a

One of the stalls at the local "Vucciria" market, an explosion of colours and tradition

reproduces – in the decorations of the corners – the four-part division of the city itself, there was concealed the reformist intent of a project of great urban renewal. The four façades of the corners, adorned with balconies, cornices, windows, and niches set in three orders, were designed in 1608 by Giulio Lasso and completed in the architectural aspects in 1620. In the first order, there are four fountains with statues of the Seasons; in the niches of the second order, there are statues of the Spanish kings Charles V and Philip II, III, and IV; in the niches of the third order, there are statues of saints Christine, Ninfa, Olive, and Agatha, patron saints of the city; in the crowning element, note imperial and royal crests.

S. Giuseppe dei Teatini (II, E4). This church is set on the southern corner of Piazza Vigliena, and develops its side elevation on the Piazza Pretoria, and occupies a priv-

large damaged during the war, but loving restored since. The vault of the cupola frescoed by Guglielmo Borremans, and t pendentives are done by Giuseppe V lasquez. The plastic decoration of the vau of the transept is by Giuseppe Serpott while the frescoes are attributed to Gugli mo Borremans. Beneath the church, as if were a crypt, is the *church of the Madon della Provvidenza* (there is an entrance the left of the main entrance).

Corso Vittorio Emanuele (II, E4). In t western section, running toward the Ca tedrale (cathedral), there is a line Baroque palazzi that have been heavily re ovated. In the eastern section, facing t 16th-c. elevation of the monastery of Caterina, stands the **church of S. Matte** built between 1633 and 1647, with a pov erful Baroque façade, three orders, in gre marble, adorned with statues. The interi splendidly decorated with marble work, th statues in stucco by Giacomo Serpot- and frescoes by Vito D'Anna in the cupo- The main altar is rich in gilt bronzes d precious stones, agate, and lapis lazuli.

a Maqueda (II, D-E4, F5). From the Quat- Canti you will first walk through the rthern section of this street. You will im- diately see the *Palazzo Merendino* (no. 7), built by Venanzio Marvuglia in 1785-88, und a stern colonnaded atrium. On the her side of the street, following the im- essive late-18th-c. façade of *Palazzo Ru- ñ*, stands the former *Casa dei Crociferi* ith fragments of a cloister on the interior) d the **church of S. Ninfa dei Crociferi**, ting from the first half of the 17th c., in the man late-Renaissance style; on the inte- or is a dramatic stucco group of the *Cru- ixion*, by Giuseppe Serpotta. Further ong, the 17th-c. *Palazzo Branciforti* (no. 3), clustered around a porticoed court- rd, features, on the interior, handsome corated and frescoed halls; then comes e *church of the Madonna del Soccorso*, ilt in 1603, with a Gagini portal. ong the southern section of this street, just er Piazza Pretoria, stands – directly across m the Piazza Bellini – the *former convent the Teatini*, dating from the turn of the th c. (dating from the same period is a

handsome cloister), radically renovated at the turn of the 19th c. to house the University of Palermo. Just past the intersection with the *Via dei Calderai*, a working-class market street selling metal crafts products, stands the 17th-c. **church of S. Nicolò da Tolentino**: it contains a number of structures dating from the Renaissance (baptismal font and two tabernacles) and canvases by Pietro Novelli (17th c.). Further along is the *church of S. Orsola*, with a Mannerist façade from the first half of the 17th c.: on the interior, there are stuccoes by Giacomo Serpotta and paintings by Pietro Novelli. Adjoining it is the sumptuous *Palazzo Comitini*, built around the middle of the 18th c., with handsome frescoed halls. On the opposite side of the street stands the *Palazzo S. Croce-S. Elia*, one of the loveliest pieces of Baroque architecture in Palermo, likewise dating from the middle of the 18th c., with large pedimented windows, wrought-iron balconies, and sumptuous frescoed halls, with majolica floors. Further along extends the three-portal façade of the *Palazzo Filangeri di Cutò*, built in the first half of the 18th c. Beyond the *Porta Vicari*, a gate that stood in the southern walls of the city, marking the end of the Via Maqueda, is the *church of S. Antonino*: it contains the last Crucifix done by Fra' Umile da Petralìa, left unfinished upon the death of the artist, who is buried here.

3 The modern section of the city

is itinerary, running from the central ain station, or Stazione Centrale (Piazza ulio Cesare) to Piazza Vittorio Veneto ong Via Roma, Via Cavour, Via Ruggero ttimo, and Viale della Libertà, follows the oroughfares that marked the growth of e modern city and pioneered the expan- on that, from the middle of the 19th c. on, as to shift the center of Palermo out of the alled city. Already as early as the middle the 16th c., on the occasion of the con- ruction of the new seaport, there was a roposal for the enlargement of the urban rimeter through the development of a st area next to the northern city walls; but was not until 1778 that the plan for the ddition" proposed by the Pretore Re- lmici, drawn up in accordance with the oss-intersection grid that had already en tested in the old town, established e bridgehead of later urban development ith the extension to the north of the Via aqueda. The construction of the Viale lla Libertà, undertaken by the new city overnment that arose following the revo-

lutionary disturbances of 1848, further confirming this direction for the growth of the city, offered an occasion for a radical redesign of the city's structure, and for a new, middle-class approach to city space: the new road, whose course forms, along with the Via Ruggero Settimo, Via Maqueda, and Via Oreto a straightaway extending for over 6 km., took on the role of thoroughfare for the future residential expansion, though in a context that was still primarily suburban. The construction, beginning in the 1860s, of the Teatro Massimo and the Teatro Politeama with their respective squares, set as hinges between the new and the old city, served to accelerate the processes of urbanization that tended to class this part of Palermo as the new, or modern city. The transfer of the population to the new quarters was encouraged by the urban "renewal" of the second half of the 19th c. (Via Roma, which cuts brutally through the medieval structure of Palermo, dates from 1865), which, with the construction of other new thoroughfares in the historic center of town, in fact turned it into an area for the passage of traffic.

From the central train station, or Stazione Centrale, built in the distinctive "Umbertino" style between 1879 and 1886, this route runs along the straight Via Roma, a 'modern' commercial thoroughfare that was completed in 1922; lined with Neoclassical and Art-Nouveau ("Liberty") buildings, the Via Roma runs parallel with the Via Maqueda. Following the intersection with the Corso Vittorio Emanuele, the Via Roma runs along the massive building of the former Convento dei Padri Filippini, which now houses the important Museo Regionale Archeologico, and then intersects with the Via Cavour, the northern boundary of the walled city, which ends on the right at the seaport (Porto) and to the left runs into the Piazza Verdi. The elegant Via Ruggero Settimo, heart of modern Palermo, which runs from here to the piazza of the same name, links the two largest theaters in Palermo – the Teatro Massimo, in Piazza Verdi, and the Teatro Politeama, in Piazza Ruggero Settimo – and then continues along in the Viale della Libertà, symbol of the modern city. This road ends in the circular Piazza Vittorio Veneto, near the entrance to the Parco della Favorita.

Museo Regionale Archeologico ** (II, D4). This regional archeological museum is one of the most important of its kind in all of Italy, considering the vastness and the quality of the collections, and especially for the complex of Siceliot sculpture from Selinunte; it was founded at the turn of the 19th c. as the Museo dell'Università (university museum), and moved to its present site in 1866. The collections – divided into sections in accordance with typological criteria and according to its site of provenance – occupy numerous halls distributed over the three stories of the building. On the *ground floor* are halls of underwater archeology (containing, among other things, the most complete collection of ancient anchors on earth), the halls of Oriental-style sculpture (Phoenician, Greek, Egyptian) and classical sculpture (including epigraphs, architectural fragments, and sarcophagi): note in particular the twin steles from Selinunte depicting couples of deities, plastic creations by local artists, with clear Punic and Hellenistic influence; also note the architectural fragments from the temples of Selinunte, in stone and painted terracotta; the lion's-head rain gutters from the temple of the Victory of Imera (5th c. B.C.). The most important items in this section are the larger **sculptures**** from the temples of Seli-

nunte, a remarkable series of great importance, not only for their beauty, but al for the light they cast on Siceliot sculptu at large: there are *three splendid metop from Temple C*, *four superb metopes fr Temple E*, and, in the center of the hall, a 5 c. B.C. bronze statue known as the **Ephe of Selinunte***. The Etruscan collection, fr Chiusi, includes funereal cippi with reli decorations, numerous funerary urns, i stone, terracotta, and alabaster, with a d piction of the deceased on the cover, s cophagi, cinerary urns, and vases in ter cotta and bucchero.

On the *second floor*, there are other colle tions of varied material from numerous d ferent sites; from Marsala, Selinunte, Moz Segesta, Tèrmini Imerese, Imera, Randazz and Sòlunto: oil lamps, votive terracott funerary aedicules. The collections bronzes are divided into small pieces (st uettes of Greek, Etruscan, and Roman h roes; mirrors; votive objects) and larg items: among the latter is the *ram* from racusa (or Syracuse, 3rd c. B.C.), a work remarkable realistic power, and the gro depicting *Hercules as he kills a stag*, fr Pompeii (Roman era). Two halls are de cated to Greek and Roman sculpture, a there are many small halls devoted to go smithery and numismatics.

On the *third floor* are the prehistoric c lections, collections of Greek cerami (from the proto-Corinthian and the Corint an to Attic), Roman mosaics and frescoe and Italiot ceramics.

Porto (II, B-C5) or port. This was a fund mental piece of infrastructure for 19th Palermo, and the chief point of departure, the 20th c., for Sicilian emigration to Nor and South America; the port of Palerm the largest in Sicily, represents with its nav shipyards (Cantieri Navali) an essenti nexus in the economic structure of the cit It is protected by moles and an offsho breakwater, rebuilt after the disastrous s storm of 1973. The northern mole dat back to 1567, when, once it became evide that the old natural basin of the Cala was n longer adequate for military security in th Mediterranean Sea, it became necessary move the port further north, with a proje that was widely considered grandiose an exceedingly expensive. After the unificati of Italy, the growing commercial requir ments of the city led to larger and improve defenses: an area of shallow seabed wa dredged, and naval shipyards and a sma drydock were installed. Partially destroye by bombing in WWII, it was rebuilt and in

...oved, including the trapezoidal mole, ...ere it is possible to see a number of ruins ...he old "sea castle," or Castello a Mare.

...atro Massimo (II, D3-4). Situated in Piaz...Giuseppe Verdi, which was rebuilt, at ...e end of the 19th c., in the wake of massive ...molition, to suit the theater, this is the ...in opera house in Palermo and one of the ...gest theaters in Europe (7,730 square ...ters of surface area). The masterpiece of ...ovanni Battista Filippo Basile, it was begun ...1875 and completed by his son Ernesto in ...97. The building presents a broad eleva...n, extending outward in the center with ...Corinthian hexastyle ...onaos set on a high stair...se, with a cupola set on a ...gh tambour. On the *inte-*...*r* is a splendid hall with ...e rows of boxes and a ...llery, seating a total of ...000.

...atro Politeama (II, C3). ...is theater was built by ...useppe Damiani Almey-...between 1867 and 1874, ...classical forms of Pom...iian inspiration; it domi-...tes the Piazza Ruggero ...ttimo. The front has a jut-...ig structure that is remi-...scent of a triumphal arch, and is adorned ...th a vast high-relief, crowned by a quadri...(chariot) and spirits on horseback.

...ie halls on the top floor contain a modern ...t gallery, the **Civica Galleria d'Arte Mo-**...**erna Empedocle Restivo**, a major collec...on that was installed in this setting in ...10. The works exhibited here present a ...ie panorama of modern and contempo...ry Italian art, especially in the Sicilian ...tting, and constitute a continuation of ...e array of art exhibited in the regional art ...llery, or Galleria Regionale di Palazzo ...batellis (in which there are artworks from ...e Middle Ages throughout the 18th c.). In

terms of sculpture, there are works by Domenico Trentacoste, Stefano De Lisi, Benedetto Civiletti, and Ettore Ximenes; and for painting, among the important names, let us mention Antonio Mancini, Giovanni Boldini, Carlo Carrà, Renato Guttuso, Felice Casorati, Gino Severini, Mario Sironi, Massimo Campigli, Remo Brindisi, Corrado Cagli, Domenico Purificato, and Fausto Pirandello.

Fondazione Mormino (II, A2). This foundation is the cultural institution of the Banco di Sicilia, and it houses the interesting collections owned by the great Sicilian

The Teatro Politeama

bank, in the 19th-c. Villa Zito, in the Viale della Libertà 52. Aside from the major collection of Greek ceramics, most of which come from archeological digs financed by the Banco di Sicilia, there is also a numismatic collection on display, documenting the history of Sicilian coinage from the times of the house of Aragon to the reign of the house of Bourbon, a collection of majolica, and a stamp collection, including the remarkable stamps of the kingdom of Sicily (Regno di Sicilia) engraved by Tommaso Aloisio Juvara and stamps from the kingdom of Naples (Regno di Napoli). Also of interest is the collection of prints and engravings with Sicilian subjects.

.4 The Conca d'Oro and Ùstica

...ne broad area of territory that is known as ...e Conca d'Oro, comprising the land im...ediately surrounding Palermo, extends ...om the slopes of Monte Gallo to the west ...l the way to the promontory of Monte ...atalfano to the east, and is bounded inland ...y the massifs of Monte Castellaccio, Monte ...uccio, Monte Caputo, Monte Grifone, and ...onte Porcara; all of these peaks, save for

the last, stand between 800 and 1,000 meters high. Given the characteristics of the morphology and the settlements, it is possible to divide the Conca d'Oro into three areas. The area to the northwest consists essentially of the Piana dei Colli, an area of considerable urban development in the 19th c. following the construction of the Viale della Libertà: this territory was inhabited by peasant villages, and in the 17th and 18th c., it was covered with spectacular residences built by the nobility of Palermo, attracted by the fine climate, and anxious to vacation amidst the lush greenery of parks and gardens. The construction, in 1799, of the large royal park of the Favorita, which became a public park following the unification of Italy, laid the foundation for a final set-aside of this area of the Conca d'Oro as an area for leisure time and enjoyment, reinforced by the reclamation of the marsh of Mondello and the construction, at the turn of the century, of a garden-town that was to serve as a beach resort for the well-to-do. The great attraction of this area pushed the expansion of Palermo ever northward, and in the last few decades the city has invaded the entire plain with an extensive and compact residential area.

The central area of the Conca d'Oro is a territory that has been inhabited ever since antiquity, an area with which the city has woven, over the course of its history, an intense and fragmentary relationship. In the 9th c., the Moors transformed this plain, so rich and abounding in water, into a vast and flourishing garden dotted with farms and agrarian compounds, building spectacular residences. This was primarily a vacation spot, and the Normans unified it in the 12th c. into a single royal landholding, establishing a system of parks including the Parco Vecchio, in the southeastern area of the Conca d'Oro, centered around the Castello della Favara, and the larger Parco del Genoardo, which contains the castles of the Zisa, the Scibene, the Cuba, the Cuba Soprana and, at the extreme south, the Castello del Parco. On the mountain slopes, the Benedictines, who were present here as early as the 6th c., at San Martino delle Scale, founded the monasteries of Monreale, Castellaccio, and Baida; in the 15th c., the Minori Osservanti established themselves on the slopes of the Monte Grifone. Over the course of the 16th c. the territory once again became a site of leisure and entertainment for the city aristocracy, which transformed many agricultural buildings into seasonal vacation homes and built, in the centuries that followed, many sumptuous villas. The construction, at the end of the 16th c., of the great thoroughfare, the "Stradone di Mezzomonreale" (now Corso Calatafimi) at first pushed urban expansion outside of the city walls in a southwesterly direction; it then moved definitively, in the 19th c., in the direction marked out by the Viale della Libertà. The eastern strip of the Conca d'Oro is a fertile valley, crossed by the river Eleutero

and closed off to the east by the Mo.. Catalfano, on the slopes of which, ov looking the sea, there developed in Rom and Punic times the settlement of Sòlun The broad plain, heavily farmed, w crossed by the old consular road, or V Consolare, which linked the capital of S ly with the cities along the northern coa in 1658 the prince, or Principe di Bute built his new residence on a little hill he quickly triggering a mass return of the o er well-to-do families of the aristocracy Palermo, who, in the course of fifty yea built in the surrounding area the most sp tacular Baroque villas of the Conca d'O. Around the middle of the 18th c., the building of Villa Butera and the constructi of two straight thoroughfares led to t foundation of the town of Bagherìa, who development, feverish and uncontrolle soon reached the surrounding residence destroying the great parks and even da aging the homes themselves. In the peri following the second World War, a ma sive residential tourism has covered t coastline, resulting in a dense network seasonal homes, blighting large areas considerable beauty and environmental i portance.

The northwestern strip of the Conca d'Oro

Parco della Favorita*

This is a vast public park at the foot of t. Monte Pellegrino; its array of woodlan and forests is a fundamental treasure greenery wedged between the city and t. beach resort of Mondello; the usual e trance to the Parco della Favorita (I, C3-4) through the gate, or Porta Leoni, whic opens onto the Piazza Leoni. Established Ferdinand III of Bourbon in 1799, whe ejected from Naples by the armies Napoleon, the king took refuge, for himse and his court, in Palermo, the park cove a surface of some 400 hectares, and w originally created as a hunting and fishir preserve, and as a botanical garden fc agricultural experimentation, of which t. king was particularly fond. Today, the. are a number of notable sports faciliti here. Running lengthwise, the park crossed by two long boulevards, known the Viale di Diana and the Viale di Ercol the latter boulevard terminates at the fou tain, or *Fontana di Ercole*, a round basin the center of which stands a massive Dor column, surmounted by a statue, a copy the Farnese Hercules (Ercole Farnese), no in the Museo Nazionale in Naples.

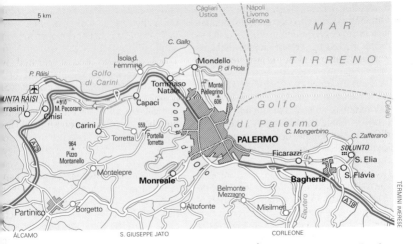

lazzina Cinese

ilt in 1799 by Venanzio Marvuglia at the hest of Ferdinand III of Bourbon, the lazzina Cinese (I, B-C3), or Chinese pavil , is a picturesque interpretation in the oclassical style of various Chinese motifs. s not presently open to visitors.

is was the favorite residence of the king d of his consort Maria Carolina, during eir forced stay in Sicily, and it was also me to Admiral Nelson and Lady Hamilton. is building is a singular product of the d-of-the-century taste for "chinoiseries," teresting also because it present bizarre xtapositions of disparate stylistic ele ents, such as the Gothic-arch porticoes on e ground floor, the vestibule, and the lumned classical-style terraces, and the rrets with open spiral staircases, built Giuseppe Patricolo.

useo Etnografico Siciliano Pitrè*

ounded by the Palermitan ethnologist useppe Pitrè in 1909, and later enlarged d reorganized in this space (1934-35) by useppe Cocchiara, the ethnographic mu um, or Museo Etnografico Siciliano Pitrè , B-C3), one of the most interesting muse ns of its sort in all Europe, occupies the alls adjoining the Palazzina Cinese. The ob cts that make up the rich collection and hich document the lifestyles, customs, d folkways of the Sicilian people, are assified according to the various activities which they belong, and are displayed in e rooms originally occupied by the ser ants, arranged around a cross-shaped ourtyard. There are a great variety of tra itional activities shown here: hunting, fish g, spinning and weaving (linen and em roidery done by women of the Rione Kalsa, ostumes and garb of Sicilian peasants,

carpets from Èrice, costumes worn by the Sicilian-Albanian women), shepherding and farming, ceramics produced by Sicilian craftsmen, games and toys and musical in struments. Also on display are carriages and sedan chairs, Sicilian carts, creches, vo tive offerings, and a working puppet theater.

Monte Pellegrino

The ancient Heirkte, called by the Moors "Gebel Grin," and described by Goethe as "the loveliest promontory on earth," is now the Monte Pellegrino (I, B-C3-4), a distinctive limestone mountain standing 606 meters tall, closing off to the north the gulf, or Gol fo di Palermo. Craggy on every side, it is covered with patchy vegetation, and here and there reforested with pines, especially on the southwestern slope.

On its slopes, there are grottoes of geolog ical and prehistoric interest.

Santuario di S. Rosalia

This sanctuary (I, B4) dates back to 1625 and comprises a grotto that has been trans formed into a chapel of the convent, with a 17th-c. façade, built into the rock; in an aedicule to the left is a marble 18th-c. stat ue of St. Rosalia. The saint, who is tradi tionally said to have been the daughter of the duke, or Duca Sinibaldo, lord of Quisquina, and nephew of William II, born in 1130, lived here in penitence for many years, until she died in 1166. Her bones were un covered on 15 July 1624 after a miraculous apparition; they were transported to Paler mo, where it was thought that they had caused a halt in the outbreak of the plague; it was for this reputed miracle that the saint was proclaimed patron saint of the city. On 4 September, there is a popular pilgrimage to the grotto, with a procession.

Mondello

Extending along the curve of the little bay that lies between the Monte Gallo and the Monte Pellegrino, Mondello (elev. 11 m.) is the "lido," or beachfront of Palermo (which lies some 10 km. away) as well as one of the best-known beach resorts in Sicily. The oldest core of the resort is comprised by a fishing village that lies at the northern extremity of the inlet, around an old tonnara, that was still in operation at the turn of the 20th c.; all that remains of it, absorbed into the fabric of the village, is a cylindrical 15th-c. tower (another cylindrical watch tower, also dating from the 15th c., stands isolated on the rocky spit that stretches around to encircle the bay). The surrounding countryside, which was marshy and unhealthy until the 19th c., was reclaimed between 1892 and 1910 and leased to the Belgian company "Le Tramways de Palerme," which developed a garden-city here. In the climate of the Belle Époque, the first homes were built, incorporating stylistic concepts and architectural features of the late-Floral style (the *Kursaal-by-the-Sea*), as early as the First World War; but it was between the two wars that the little town developed and grew, taking on a strongly elitist flavor. This elitist sense has been vanishing since the Second World War under the crush of mass bathing and vacationing and the pressure of the new buildings that have sprung up in the surrounding greenery.

Set above the nearby beach of the Addàura, in the spur of the Monte Pellegrino which runs down to the Punta di Priola, half-hidden amid the greenery are the *grottoes of Addàura* (meaning, laurel), caves of considerable speleological and above all paleontological interest; note the human and animal figures carved into the walls, dating back to the upper Paleolithic.

From Mondello, continue along the state road ward the airport of Punta Ràisi, and you reach the intersection (176 km.) for **Carini** (e 170 m., pop. 21,076). This little town, built on slopes on the site of a Moorish settlement fr the 10th c., took its name from Hyccara, wh must once have existed in the vicinity, and wh was destroyed in 415 B.C. by the Athenian stat man Nicias. The *castle*, which was adjoined b fortified village, probably dates back to Norm times, but was rebuilt in its present form in 16th c. The castle, along with the fief of Car probably belonged to the Chiaramonte, Mon da, and La Grua Talemanca families. The *chu of Matrice* (Assunta) has a late-18th-c. façade. interior is decorated with Neoclassical stucco and frescoes (1795), and features an *Adoratio the Shepherds*, by Alessandro Allori (1578).

If you head back down to the state road, and c ve another 12 km., past the jutting form of Pu Ràisi, you will reach **Terrasini** (elev. 33 m., p 10,544), a fishing and farming town, where y will find an interesting civic museum, or *Mus Civico*, broken into three sections: natural histo archeology, and ethno-anthropology. The e no-anthropological section includes the musei of Sicilian carts, or *Museo del Carretto Sicilian*

The central area of the Conca d'Oro

Zisa**

This is one of the best examples of the F timid architecture of the Norman period. was begun under William I and was co pleted under William II around the yea 1165-67. The Zisa (II, D-E1) (from the Arab "aziz," splendid) is a high and compa building with a rectangular plan; the he metic cubic shape of the structure, broke on the short sides by two slender squa towers, is interrupted by three orders slight blind arches, which originally e closed little twin-light mullioned window and ended at the top in a cornice with a Arabic epigraph, removed in the 16th

The Mondello beach, one of the most famous seaside resorts in Sicily

nd replaced by battlements. It became
rivate property, and over time the owners
nade numerous transformations and adap-
tions; after a period of neglect, it was pur-
hased by the Sicilian region, or Regione Si-
liana, which undertook its restoration.
his was the seasonal residence of the Nor-
nan kings, once surrounded by an immense
ark and overlooking a body of water in
vhich it is mirrored, the building has an ex-
eedingly complex interior, composed of
ublic rooms and private suites; the latter
end to extend over numerous floors.

uba*

nother splendid piece of Fatimid archi-
ecture in the Norman park of the Genoar-
o (now part of a barracks), built by William
in 1180, the Cuba (II, F1) is, like the Zisa,
tall building with a rectangular plan, com-
act and squared off in its volume, with
at avant-corps at the center of each front.
lind arcades extend the height of the ma
onry surface, and enclose stacked blind
indows and elongated niches; at the top, a
and with an Arabic epigraph bears the
ame of the king and the date of foundation.
the 14th c. Giovanni Boccaccio made this
e setting for a novella in the "Decamerone"
Day V, 6). It was purchased by private cit-
ens; in the 16th c. it became a leper colony,
nd under the reign of the Bourbons, it was
corporated in a cavalry barracks. This
ermetic architectural structure originally
ood at the center of a manmade pond,
urrounded by a garden, and was a pleasure
avilion. Inside, after a vestibule, there was
large square hall, rising the height of the
uilding, with a central atrium.

onvento dei Cappuccini

uilt in 1621, the Convento dei Cappuccini
, E-F1) stands on the site of an earlier
uilding complex. The church, which was
novated and enlarged in 1934, still pre-
rves on the interior wooden altars dating
ack to the 18th or 19th c., as well as other
ne furniture and artworks, including a
ooden *Crucifix* from the late Middle Ages.
ote the funerary monuments, on the enance wall, erected by Ignazio Marabitti be-
ween 1753 and 1764. The monastery is
own especially for its *catacombs*, men-
oned by Ippolito Pindemonte in his work,
e "Sepolcri." This is a vast subterranean
metery where, beginning in the 17th c.
d continuing until 1881, in long corri-
ors, wealthy Palermitans were buried.
ere are roughly 8,000 bodies, a few of
em mummified but most of them in a
eletal state; many are standing, others are
seated, others still are contain in caskets or
crystal urns. Women, "professionals," and
ecclesiastics are all in separate corridors.

Monreale*

This busy little city lies 8 km. from Palermo,
and is set on a spur looking out over both
the valley of the river Oreto and the Conca
d'Oro; Monreale (elev. 310 m., pop. 26,256)
is the leading tourist attraction in the area
around Palermo; it is renowned for the
beauty of the views and, first and foremost,
for its superb cathedral, or Duomo. It developed beginning in the 13th c., clustering
around the Benedictine abbey that was
made the see of an archbishop (1183); it was
one of the largest and wealthiest such arch-
bishoprics in Sicily. Subsequent growth
was consolidated in the 16th c. with the
settlement here of numerous religious orders, followed by the construction, during
the 17th and 18th c., of many churches,
convents, and educational institutes; all of
them give the little town a distinct Baroque
identity and appearance.

Duomo** (B3), or cathedral. This architectural masterpiece from the Norman period, in which expressions of Muslim,
Byzantine, and Romanesque culture combine to create one of the highest creations
of the Italian Middle Ages, stands in the Piazza Vittorio Emanuele, the center of the village. It was founded by William II in 1174 and
was rapidly completed, along with the
abbey, the Palazzo Reale, and the Palazzo
Arcivescovile, with which it formed a single
organic complex. The *façade*, in Piazza
Guglielmo II Normanno, set between two
enormous square towers, is preceded by an
18th-c. portico, with three arches, and set
on columns in the Doric style, crowned by
balustrades; beneath it is a magnificent
centered pointed-arch portal, adorned with
carvings and mosaic strips; the bronze
doors*, a creation by Bonanno Pisano
(1186), are divided into 42 panels, with Bib-
lical scenes in relief, accompanied by ex-
planatory legends in the vernacular (as opposed to Latin). The entrance is through a
simple portal with bronze doors, dating
from 1179, opening under the portico on the
left side.
The **interior*** is immense (102 x 40 m.),
and has three aisles, divided by columns,
most of which are ancient, with pulvini and
ancient and lovely capitals with clipei
(shields) of deities set amidst cornucopias,
supporting pointed-arches of the Moorish
variety; the cross vault is of the Byzantine
type, with a square plan (bounded by four

broad pointed arches and enclosed in the front by 19th-c. mosaic transennas), without a cupola and with three apses, decorated on the exterior by intertwined arches set on small columns. The mosaic flooring, with porphyry and granite disks, features marble bands interwoven in broken lines, and is the original pavement; it was completed in the 16th c. A component of particular interest is constituted by the **mosaics**** with gold background, which cover (over a surface of 6,340 square meters) the walls of the aisles, the sanctuary, the apses, and above the high socle of marble slabs. These mosaics were done between the end of the 12th c. and the middle of the 13th c.; they were partly done by local craftsmen, who studied under Byzantine mosaicist, and partly by Venetian master mosaicists. They depict the stories of the Old and New Testaments, with legends written in Latin and Greek. In the central apse, high in the vault, there is a colossal half-figure of *Christ Giving Benediction*, with the Greek legend "Pantokrator" (all-powerful); beneath it, is the *Virgin Mary with Christ Child Enthroned*, and the legend "Panacrontas" (all-chaste), flanked by angels and apostles; below are saints.

To the right of the façade of the cathedral, o Duomo, is the entrance to the **cloister**** o the very old Benedictine monastery, or Convento dei Benedettini; it too was founded during the reign of William II (last quarter o the 12th c.). It is a square measuring 47 x 4 m. The pointed arches of the portico, with double arch lintel and a distinctive large torus in the intrados (this is a particularly Is lamic feature), are supported by 228 twinned columns, with a rich variety of ornamentation, many of them with mosaic intarsias and others carved with arabesques. In the southern corner there is a square enclosure*, with three arches on each side and little fountain in the center; the jet of wate spurts up from a small column in the shap of a stylized palm tree. High above the side of the cloister opposite to the church rise the strong wall of the old *Benedictin monastery*, punctuated by blind, pointe arches; the interior, now open to the sky, i divided into three aisles by pillars; in the fac ing wall, twin and single-light windows.

Collegiata (A3). This church presents 17t c. architecture, which was altered in th two ensuing centuries; in its apse is a *Cr cifix* done on majolica tiles from the 17th c

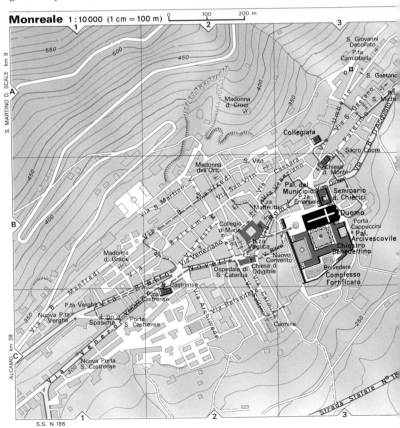

Monreale 1:10 000 (1 cm = 100 m)

side, in the three aisles with columns
corated in stucco by Giacomo Serpotta
723), there are noteworthy canvases
om the 17th and 18th c.

astellaccio. At a distance of 5.3 km, from
onreale, this im-
osing construc-
on features sev-
al donjon towers,
uilt in the 12th c.
t the summit of the
onte Caputo as a
rtress and a sanitori-
m for the Benedictine
onks of Monreale.
bandoned at the end
the 16th c., it went
o ruin. Restored in
398, it became the
roperty of the Club
pino Siciliano, which adapt-
d it for use as a mountain hut, es
blishing the Stazione Alpina
stellaccio and undertaking the
forestation of the summit.

n Martino delle Scale*

a distance of 9.5 km. from Monreale, San
artino delle Scale (elev. 589 m.) is a pop-
ar hillside resort, set amongst extensive
ne forests, dotted with vacation accom-
odations. On the large plaza that over-
oks the valley stands the *Benedictine
bey*: founded, according to tradition, by St.
regory the Great, in the 6th c., and de-
royed by the Moors in 820, it was rebuilt
1346 and, enlarged in several stages be-
een the 16th and 17th c., it was complet-
d in 1770 by G. Venanzio Marvuglia. The
ormous construction, articulated around
rious courtyards and porticoed cloisters
th arched loggias, it was at one time a ma-
r center of culture, and is now in part oc-
pied by the Benedictines, who officiate at
e church services, and in part by the dis-
bles, who run a large charitable institution.
e 16th-c. church has an interior with a sin-
e vast white nave, with side aisles set be-
een large pillars, a deep transept and a
pola. One should note the monumental
th-c. carved wooden choir, and numerous
intings by the Palermitan painter
useppe Salerno, known as the Zoppo di
ngi. In the part of the monastery inhabit-
 by monks, you will find the cloister of St.
nedict (Chiostro di S. Benedetto), with
lumns and arches, dating back to 1612.

ughly 15 kilometers to the north of the town is
e monastery, or **Convento di Baida**, set on a se-

cluded promontory. It was founded in 1388 by
Manfredi Chiaramonte for the Cistercians. The
church preserves its original double-pitch façade,
preceded by a portico with three pointed arches,
with a twin-light mullioned window atop it, enclosed within an arch; beneath the portico, note
the marble Renaissance portal, by Antonio Vanel-
li (1507). The interior
has a single nave, with
a whitewashed 18th-c.
architectural face; the
presbytery section
dates back to the 14th-c.

*The Duomo of Monreale:
detail of cloister column*

S. Maria di Gesù*

The church of S. Maria
di Gesù (I, F5) stands in
the Borgata Guadagna,
on the southeastern out-
skirts of Palermo, on
the lower slopes of the
Monte Grifone. You will
enter a small terraced garden, now a cemetery. Up high on
the right is the church (1426), preceded by a little square with a 17th-
c. fountain, with an octagonal basin
adorned by four lions and surmounted
by a basin, from which exquisite putti
extend. In the façade, note the marble portal with figures of the Apostles (1495); on the
left side is a pointed-arch portal, topped by
an aedicule with the Virgin Mary in relief,
dating from the 16th c. On the left, note
the elegant Catalonian Gothic portal (15th
c.) of the chapel, or Cappella La Grua-Tale-
manca. The *interior* has a single aisle, with
a raised presbytery, opened by a Gothic
arch; it contains 16th-c. sarcophagi, including that of Antonio Alliata, by Antonello Gagini (1512). In the apse are 15th-c. frescoes. To the right of the church, there are
relics of the 15th-c. *cenobium*, or religious
community, with a *cloister* featuring stout
columns with the original capitals; note the
funerary monuments and fragments of
sculpture.

Not far away, toward the center of town, near the
hospital, or Policlinico, is the cemetery, or
Cimitero di S. Orsola (I, E4), or *Cimitero di S.
Spirito*, founded by the Viceroy Caracciolo in
1782, with an orthogonal layout and with monuments and chapels of a fine 19th-/20th-c. architecture. Within the enclosure, at the far end
on the left, is the Norman church of **S. Spirito***
or the Chiesa del Vespro. Founded by the archbishop Gualtiero Offamilio in 1178, it has a solid
masonry structure, bounded along the right side
and in the transept by pointed arches, which intertwine in the apsidal area, vividly adorned
with volcanic-stone inlay, with ashlar windows,
closed by transennas. The *interior* (if it is closed,
contact the custodian of the cemetery) is austere
and remarkable, with three aisles divided by

pillars made of square-hewn blocks of stone, with a higher and broader presbytery, and three apses. The open-beam ceiling shows remains of the original decorations in the nave. Behind the main altar, *Crucifix* on shaped panel, from the 15th c.; on the sides of the presbytery, sarcophagi from the 16th c.

S. Giovanni dei Lebbrosi

In Corso dei Mille (eastern outskirts of Palermo), the church of S. Giovanni dei Lebbrosi (I, E4) is one of the earliest churches of the Norman period, founded by Roger I in 1071 and completed in the following century, when a leper hospital was added (1150). The church, which is thought to have been the work of Moorish craftsmen, stands at the center of a palm garden, and before its façade stands a little portico, topped by a campanile, built in 1934 as a part of the very drastic restoration project. The *interior*, which is basilican, and has three aisles supported by pillars, as well as a hemispheric cupola set on niched pendentives, above the raised transept, and three apses. Above the altar is a *Crucifix* on a shaped panel, dating from the 15th c. To the right of the church, there are the scanty ruins of a Moorish building, the castle, or Castello di Iehia (in Italian Giovanni, in English John), to which the church was once joined.

The eastern strip of the Conca d'Oro

Bagherìa

A populous trading town set on gentle slopes amidst green expanses of citrus groves, medlar trees, and olive groves, overlooking the sea and the Monte Catalfano, Bagherìa (elev. 78 m., pop. 47,085), at a distance of 15 km. from Palermo, concentrates in its territory a number of the loveliest Baroque villas in the Palermitan countryside. The town grew up around the structure of the Villa Butera, built by the Principe Giuseppe Branciforte, who retired to the countryside in the 17th c., and began the cultivation of the surrounding lands. Other villas rose nearby and in the surrounding area, and a century later, in 1769, Salvatore Branciforti rebuilt the old residence and created a thoroughfare, on a straight line running due north, toward the Mare di Aspra (Corso Butera), intersecting at a right angle with another thoroughfare terminating at the Chiesa Madre (Corso Umberto); these established the layout of the later development of the town. Along the two thoroughfares, the spread of cement and development has been ineluctable, filling in over the past century the greenery of the surviving parks and growing up around the villas, virtually strangling them.

Villa Cattolica was completed in 1736; it rigid volumes – enlivened by two exedrae, of which one contains a great staircase – stan at the center of a cruciform courtyard surrounded by the low structures of the secondary buildings. This is the town's modern art gallery, of *Galleria Comunale d'Arte Moderna e Contemporanea*, established in 197 around a considerable collection donated by Renato Guttuso, and subsequently enriched by artworks donated by various artists. Aside from the numerous paintings by Guttuso, and the various watercolors by the painter's father, Gioacchino, there are art works by Mirko Basaldella, Robert Carro Mario Schifano, Domenico Quattrociocch Ernesto Treccani, and Carlo Levi. It is currently closed for renovation.

Villa Butera, built in 1658 by Giuseppe Branciforte, has a newer façade, added by Salvatore Branciforti in 1769. To the left of the 18th-c. façade, which is crossed on the second story by a balcony, and bearing th heraldic crest of the family in the attic above the clock, you will enter a courtyard here is the elevation of the construction dating back to 1658, with a double-ramp staircase, covered with climbing plants, which leads up to the entrance of the second floor, surrounded by festoons and draperies made of stucco, held up by two putti wh flank the marble bust of the founder.

Villa Palagonia, built in 1715 by Tommaso Maria Napoli (and later continued by Agatino Daidone) at the behest of Ferdinando Francesco Gravina, prince of Palagonia an Pretore of Palermo, is the most renowned the villas of Bagherìa; described by Giovanni Houel (1776) and lauded by Giovanni Meli, it made a strong impression on Goethe It has vivid architecture, which become

Villa Valguarnera in Bagherìa

strip of coastline near Baghería with Capo Zafferana in the background

ectacular and theatrical in the façade of e little central mansion, with the lively ossed-tongs staircase and the ribbing in llow tufa stone against white plaster. On e second floor there is an elliptical stibule, frescoed with the *Labors of Hercles*; the adjoining hall has walls encrusted th marble-work and has a pavillion ceiling vered with mirrors. The four-sided ensure, in the midst of which stands the lit-mansion ("palazzina"), presents a great riety of persepctives and is crowned by a lebrated and choreographic procession of otesque depictions, mostly monstrous, msily sculpted beginning in 1747, as a oduct of the whimsy of the grandson of e founder; both shared the same name – rdinando Gravina Alliata. Sadly, even this eation of 18th-c. forerunners of the suralists has been spoiled by modern con-uction, which emerges beyond the fence d clusters in on every hand. Even the ry long boulevard punctuated by exe-ae, which began on a line with the Corso tera (where the entrance portal still ands, isolated, between two monstrous ures) has been absorbed in the chaotic ex-nsion of the city and transformed into a y street (Via Palagonia).

la Valguarnera* is not open to the pub-Built in 1721 to plans by Tommaso Maria poli, this is the most sumptuous of all the las, and it enjoys the best location, in e midst of a park girt by terraces and lustrades. Before it lies a broad, double-edra plaza; it has a façade that is concave the center, to accommodate the crossed-igs staircase that leads up to the sec-d story; the rear façade, facing the sea, is rectilinear, and the attics of both façades feature statues by Ignazio Marabitti.

Sòlunto*

Situated on the southeastern slopes of the Monte Catalfano, at a distance of about 3 km. from Baghería, the ruins of Sòlunto (elev. 235 m.) constitute a major urbanistic document of Punic civilization in Sicily. Soloeis or Solus was, with Mozia and Palermo, one of the three chief Punic cities in western Sicily. The town was founded toward the middle of the 4th c. B.C., and it remained under Carthaginian rule until, around 250 B.C., it was conquered by the Romans. At the end of the 2nd c. A.D., it was abandoned, perhaps voluntarily, by its inhabitants. In the ruins (it was destroyed by the Saracens) there is a prevalence of Hellenistic and Roman forms. The excavation of "Soluntum" began in 1826; it was begun again in various periods; major sectors of the settlement have yet to be unearthed. The relics from the digs are largely in the archeological museum, or Museo Archeologico of Palermo.

The city, which appears in its Hippodamean urban layout, had a regular plan: the main street, running roughly north and south, and its parallels, are crossed at right angles by the transverse streets, which run east to west, in some cases with steps, forming "Insulae," or blocks, of houses, and by narrow passageways ("ambitus"), for the drainage of rainwater downhill. The cobblestone paving is pretty well preserved; the terracotta paving of the main street is typical. In the "insulae," ruins o houses with square plans, various in siz (from 400 to 550 square meters), with pla ter walls, often painted (fragments can be seen in the Museo di Palermo), with flooring in "opus signinum" and in mosaic, with thresholds and steps and in some cases shops. It is interesting to note the quantity

One of the many finds unearthed in Ùstica

(one per house) and variety of cisterns, some of them with complex systems for gathering water, ensuring an adequate water supply in a city without natural springs. At the entrance to the ruins is an *antiquarium*, in which there are capitals, statues, architectural elements and fragments, casts of coins from the mint of Sòlunto and all sorts of material from the most recent excavations; cartographic documentation of the ancient city explains various aspects of it. On the slope of the hill, to the west of the *agora*, stands the Roman-Hellenistic *theater* (you climb up to the left after the exedrae), of which you can clearly see the few remaining fragments of the steps of the cavea and the scaena. Alongside it is a small semicircular building with steps, probably an "odeon" (for dances) or a "bouleutèrion" (for public assemblies), very well preserved.

The island of Ùstica

Linked to the port of Palermo by a regular service of ferryboats and hydrofoils, and located 52 km. to the north of cape, or Capo 'lo, Ùstica is the emerging tip of a great extinct underwater volcano; its geo-l structure is similar to the Aeolian is-nd it has a surface area of 8.6 sq. km. idge of hills, which culminates in or Punta Maggiore (also known as

the Punta di Guardia di Mezzo), elev. 244 m crosses the island transversely, separati the district, or Contrada di Tramontana, the north, from the smaller districts, Contrada di Mezzogiorno and Contrada Spalmadore, to the south. The island, wi a mild, though decidedly maritime climat has fertile plains, intensely cultivated wi vineyards, wheat, figs, prickly pears, a legumes, where there also grow hemp w low and the occasional olive tree. The coas are exceedingly jagged and generally stee this is a famed beach resort and a great traction for divers of all sorts; there a diving events each year. The island is a m rine nature reserve, and in 1987 on t western side of the island, the first regic al marine park (Parco Marino Regional was established. Archeological finds atte to the successive presence on the island prehistoric populations (2nd millenniu B.C.), Phoenicians, and Romans. From t 8th c. to the 11th c., Ùstica was ruled by t Saracens; here, the Normans built t church of S. Maria and the convent, Convento dei Benedettini, which the Sa cens destroyed when they took over the land again in the 14th c., exterminati and scattering the population. Various forts to occupy and populate the islar made thereafter by the Spanish gover ment, were unsuccessful. It was not ur 1763, the year following the last Sarac raid, that the island was fortified and c onized by the Bourbon government, wi roughly a hundred families from the lands of the Eolie and a garrison of 250 s diers. Natives of the Eolie, or Aeolian lands, the population of Ùstica still p serves the customs, garb, and dialects those islands.

From the *Cala S. Maria*, which is equipp with landing piers, a road made up of thr ramps runs up to the town of **Ùstica** (ele 49 m., pop. 1,188), set on a tufa ledge betwe two inlets, and in the shadow of Capo F conara, on the summit of which stands Bourbon fortress. The town was founded 1763 in accordance with an orderly plan straight streets and rectangular blocks. the south of the little town, in the *Torre d. Maria*, there is a *Museo di Archeologia S tomarina*, or museum of underwater arc ology, with material from the wrecks of cient ships and fragments from the s merged city of Osteodes. A decent road ru all the way around the island, while m tracks and walking paths allow hikers take interesting strolls.

The territory to the south of Palermo

...e territory under consideration is bounded on the west by the valleys of the rivers Ia-
...and Bèlice, to the south by the massif of the so-called Monti Sicani, with the notable sum-
...ts of Monte Cammarata (elev. 1,578 m.) and the Monte delle Rose (elev. 1,436 m.), and
...the east by the rivers San Leonardo and Plàtani. The route (a total of 164 km.) originates
...Palermo and – after passing Altofonte, the residence and hunting preserve of king Roger
...e Norman (in the Palazzo Reale, king Peter II of Aragon was born), immediately before
...ich, on the right, there is a turnoff for San Giuseppe Jato and San Cipirello – the route
...rives after 23 km. in Piana degli Albanesi, the most important of the four colonies of Al-
...nians in Sicily (the other three are Palazzo Adriano, Contessa Entellina, and Mezzojuso).
...u then head south, amidst rolling hill country, covered with fields, and after skirting the
...eat woods, or Bosco della Ficuzza, extending out at the foot of the Rocca Busambra, you
...ll get onto the state road 118, which links Palermo and Agrigento; head toward Agrigento,
...d some 34 km. later you will reach Corleone, a major farming town. After a turnoff that
...kes you through Bisacquino, Chiusa Sclàfani, Giuliana, and Palazzo Adriano, you will con-
...ue toward Prizzi. The route as far as Lercara Friddi, a town that was founded in the 17th
...includes two more detours: to Santo Stefano Quisquina and to Castronuovo di Sicilia.
...u will then head back to Palermo with a stretch of 61 km. along the state road 121, which
...rts, successively Mezzojuso, Cefalà Diana (with the old Moorish thermal baths), and Mis-
...eri; by this point, you are on the eastern outskirts of Palermo.

Piana degli Albanesi, to Corleone, and to Lercara Friddi

n Giuseppe Jato
...is town (elev. 467 m., pop. 9,460) was
...nded on a feudal landholding acquired in
...79 by Giuseppe Beccadelli di Bologna e
...avina on a site once occupied by a ham-
... and a little Jesuit church; the Jesuits
...d once controlled this fief. Like the near-
San Cipirello, the town has an orthogo-
...l grid. Without any real break in the urban
...ric, next comes the town of San Cipirello
...ev. 394 m., pop. 5,048), an agricultural
...nter that developed after a terrible land-
...de from the Monte Iato destroyed, in
...38, two-thirds of the town of San
...useppe. In 1864, San Cipirello became a
...wnship, becoming independent from the
...wn that had engendered it. Located there
...a little *museum*, in the Via Roma no. 320,
...turing materials found in excavations of
...e ancient Iato (see below). Besides the
...o large caryatids and the two telamons
...m the theater, there is architectural ma-
...ial and ceramics, from the temple of
...hrodite. Opposite, stands a small eth-
...anthropological museum housing tradi-
...nal implements.

...the southern slope of Monte Iato, to the east
...San Giuseppe Jato, excavations that have
...en going on for a number of decades now are
...covering the remains of the ancient city of
...as or Ietae: it is possible to see the structures
...he *theater*; in the flatter area, the *agora* stood,
...X 40 m. in size, the central point of the city,
with three sides closed off by porticoes; to the
west of this, the *"bouleutèrion"*, a small council
hall; roughly 200 m. to the west are the ruins of
a small *sanctuary* dedicated to Aphrodite, and a
Hellenistic peristyle house.

Piana degli Albanesi
The population of Piana degli Albanesi (elev.
720, pop. 6,129) speaks an Albanian dialect
and professes the Catholic religion, with
Greek rites. This town was founded at the

Piana degli Albanesi: S. Demetrio

Orthodox rites ceremony at the church of S. Giorgio in Piana degli Albanesi

end of the 15th c., when groups of refugees, fleeing central-southern Albania following the Turkish invasion, obtained permission from King John II of Spain to settle in areas of western Sicily, virtually uninhabited, and to preserve their religion. The customs and folkways that have been handed down over the centuries are revealed during ceremonies, baptisms, weddings (note the spectacular wedding gown worn by the bride), festivals, and during religious rites.

The town, given the difficult morphology of the terrain (a slope that runs down toward the broad hollow which contains the source of the right branch of the river Bèlice), has an irregular plan, crossed by the straight thoroughfare of Corso Giorgio Kastriota (an Albanian national hero). The *church of S. Giorgio*, transformed in 1759, is the oldest church in town. The interior has a single nave: the presbytery is closed off by an iconostasis, adorned with recent icons by the Greek painter, Stefano Ermacolas; in a niche on the left wall, St. George, a wooden equestrian statue by Nicolò Bagnasco. The *church of S. Demetrio*, which is the cathedral, or Chiesa Madre, is a Greek rite church, begun in 1590; it has been partially modified by recent restorations. The interior, built to a Greek-cross, with three aisles, is decorated with frescoes by Pietro Novelli (17th c.). Albanian costumes, traditional objects, and ethnographic material is on exhibit in the anthropoligical museum, or *Museo Antropologico*, established at no. 213 in Corso Kastriota.

Bosco della Ficuzza

You can visit this forest, and at 500 m. from the entrance there is a well equipped are an unusual sight for western Sicily: an e ceptional green expanse, well maintaine (4,000 hectares of deciduous forest, larg ly comprising oak trees) and covering t northern slope of the Rocca Busambra. 1910 the adjoining forest of Godrano w added to the Ficuzza. A road runs from t town of *Ficuzza*, to the left of the square which the Casino stands, and into t woods; from here you can set off on hike The *Casino di Caccia*, or hunting lodge, bu in 1803 by the architect G. Venanzio Ma vuglia at the behest of the king Ferdinand in a stunning setting, stands out against background of greyish limestone walls.

Corleone

This inland farming town has a vast ar well-watered territory; Corleone (elev. 5 m., pop. 11,261) is set in a valley surroun ed to the east and the south by limesto and sandstone mountains, which erosio has modelled into bastions and tower: pa ticularly distinctive is the so-called "Caste lo Soprano" (elev. 661 m.), to the ea topped by a *"Torre Saracena"*, or wate tower, and the "Castello Sottano", an enc mous boulder that stands, alone, on t right bank of the river that runs through t town to the south.

Corleone probably existed in Byzanti times, and it was of considerable econo ic and military importance during the Mo ish occupation (the inland road linki Palermo and Sciacca passed through her It was conquered around 1080 by the No mans, and in 1095 it was ceded by Cou Roger to the diocese of Palermo, and 1176 it was assigned to the abbot of Mo reale. At the turn of the 15th c. (1418) a m jor landslide damaged the upper part the city, near the castle, or Castello Sopr no, destroying the church of S. Giulian and badly damaging the quarter, Quartiere di S. Giuliano; similar landslid (in some cases aggravated by violent floo ing), due to the clayey nature of the grou upon which the structure stands and t presence of underground and surface wate have repeatedly caused serious damage the interior of the city and especially the eastern and southern outskirts, close to the river bed. The general impoveris ment of the economy and of the island's r sources during the 17th c. (largely due the enormous taxes and the donations i posed by the Crown) had particularly se ous consequences in Corleone, forced n once but twice to pay heavy ransoms le the town be sold by the king; there was w process of social and economic decay, hich seriously conditioned the history of is town right up to recent times.

e **Chiesa Madre**, dedicated to St. Martin , Martino), was built in 1382, probably the site of an existing church, enlarged the first half of the 15th c., and complet- with its cupola in 1663; it acquired its pre- nt-day appearance primarily in the 18th when it was further enlarged and deco- ted with frescoes in the cupola. The im- ense interior, with three aisles, contains merous artworks, including a number at were rescued from other churches – sed to worship – in the city; among them e handsome wooden sculptures from the xteenth and 17th c. The 18th-c. *church of e Addolorata*, built to a central plan,

around 1753, is decorated on the interior with stuccoes and frescoes from the same period. The **church of S. Rosalia**, built in the 17th c., contains numerous artworks of various origin, including a canvas of the Nativity, attributed to Vito D'Anna; *St. John the Evangelist on the Island of Patmos*, by Giuseppe Velasquez; *St. Benedict* by Pietro Novelli; wooden 15th-c. *Crucifix*, known as the Crocifisso della Catena.

Bisacquino

Situated in a panoramic position overlooking the southwest slope of the Monte Triona (elev. 1,215 m.), Bisacquino (elev. 744 m., pop. 5,484) takes its origin from the Moorish hamlet of "Busackuin" (named for the great abundance of water to be found in this site).

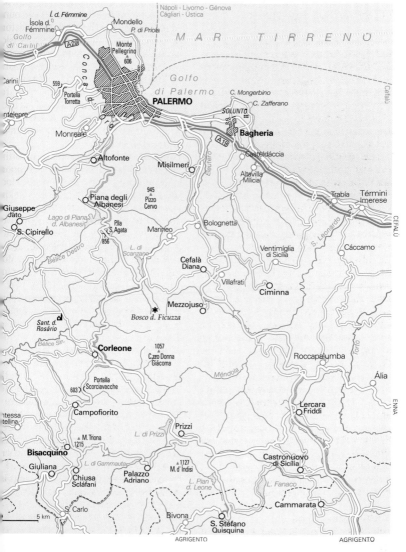

The **Chiesa Madre** (dedicated to St. John the Baptist) was built in 1713 by the Cardinal Francesco Giudice on the same site as the 16th-c. Chiesa Matrice; all that remains of the previous structure was the bell tower. On the interior, three aisles, and exquisite stuccoes from the 18th c. The civic museum, or *Museo Civico*, recently established in the former monastery, or ex-Convento dei Cappuccini, focuses primarily on ethnography and anthropology, but it also has an archeological collection of local finds. There are reconstructions in various rooms, of all the most important episodes of peasant life prior to industrialization, from agrarian and pastoral activities (the entire cycle of wheat, the olive-oil mill, the stall) to social activities (the home, weaving, and embroidery), and the various trades and callings. The archeological section contains Greco-Punic artifacts dating back to the 6th/5th c. B.C., from the Monte Triona.

Roughly seven kilometers to the west of Bisacquino is all that survives of the immense abbey, or **Abbazia di S. Maria del Bosco di Calatamauro**. There is documentation of the existence of a hermitage on this site as early as the 13th c.: in the 14th c., the hermits subscribed to the Benedictine rule, and in 1401 the abbey was established; at the end of the 15th c. the abbey was ceded to the order of the Olivetani, who remained there until 1784. This impressive complex was built between 1583 and 1646; around the two large *cloisters* stand the immense structures of the abbey, which open out with a scenic view of a vast expanse of western Sicily. Adjoining the monastery is the monumental *church*, irreparably damaged by the earthquake of 1968 and by later collapses: all that stands of it today is the façade and the campanile.

Chiusa Sclàfani

A town of medieval origins, lying on a slope and closed off to the southeast by the Serra dell'Omo Morto, Chiusa Sclàfani (elev. 658 m., pop. 3,677) was founded in 1320 by the Conte Matteo Sclafani, probably on the site of an existing hamlet. Beginning in the 16th c., with the arrival of numerous religious orders (Dominicans, Carmelites, Conventuals of St. Francis, Augustinians, Olivetans, etc.), the urban layout began to evolve, and is still largely recognizable today; in the middle of the 17th c. a very bad landslide swept away much of the central area of the town, creating a fracture in the urban structure that can still be seen today.
The *Chiesa Madre* (S. Nicolò di Bari), a church that was founded in the 14th c. and rebuilt between 1772 and 1813, has a large interior with a cupola. The Via Greco, which runs through the oldest and most charming section of the town, is characterized by numerous lanes and courtyards with inte[resting] pavement, still well preserved, lead[s] to the enormous Piazza Castello; her[e] flanked by a cusped campanile, stands t[he] *church of S. Sebastiano*, with a single nav[e,] the interior is particularly rich in decor[a-]tion, featuring frescoes and stuccoes of t[he] school of Serpotta.

Giuliana

Set on an isolated basalt crag, high above t[he] valley of the river Malotempo, Giuliana (ele[v.] 710 m., pop. 2,478) already existed durin[g] the Moorish occupation. During the 14th c., at the behest of Frederick II of Aragon, th[e] town was fortified with a long enclosu[re] wall and an imposing castle, probably rebu[ilt] on the site of an existing fortress. During t[he] long feudal period, the center of town w[as] enclosed within the old walled perimet[er] (which was demolished in the 19th c[.]) strongly marked by a complex mediev[al] layout, and characterized by a massive pre[s-]ence of religious buildings, dating back [to] the 16th and 17th c., by the numero[us] monastic orders that settled here.
At the top of the town stands the castle, [or] *Castello*, constituted by two structur[es] that contain the ceremonial and livi[ng] quarters, and by a massive tower with [a] pentagonal base. Inside the perimeter [of] the enclosure wall stands the complex [of] the **monastery of the SS. Trinità**, built t[o-]ward the middle of the 17th c. by the Oliv[e-]tan monks of S. Maria del Bosco; t[he] *church*, rebuilt on the site of an existi[ng] church (dedicated to St. Catherine), ha[s a] single nave, with frescoes dating back [to] the 17th c. Set on a vast clearing to t[he] north of the castle is the cathedral, [or] **Chiesa Madre**; originally built in the 14th c., it constituted a notable example of 14th c. architecture in Sicily, but, after subse[e-]quent renovations, it was demolished [in] 1919, and replaced, on the same site, b[e-]tween 1935 and 1938, with the prese[nt-]day building in a Neo-Gothic style. On t[he] southern side, a late-Gothic portal was [in-]stalled, originally from the church of [S.] Antonio; numerous panels in carved sto[ne] from the old cathedral were set along t[he] retaining wall to the north. On the inter[ior] is a marble baptismal font from 1593.

Palazzo Adriano

Situated on a slight incline, on the slopes [of] the Cozzo Braduscia, in the high valley of t[he] river Sòsio, the present-day Palazzo Adria[no] (elev. 696 m., pop. 2,767) was built in the se[c-]ond half of the 15th c. by a colony of Gre[ek] banian refugees. The urban plan is characterized by a radial/concentric layout, which has its point of confluence in the central square, or *Piazza Umberto I* (formerly Piazza Grande), upon which both of the principal churches front. The Greek-rite church on the right as you reach the square), is dedicated to the Virgin (*S. Maria Assunta*; Our Lady of the Assumption), and was built at the end of the 15th c., and enlarged in the 18th c.; facing it is the Chiesa Matrica, or Cathedral, of the Latin rite, dedicated to Our Lady of the Lamp, or *S. Maria del Lume*, and built in the 18th. Also overlooking the square are the *Palazzo Dara* (town hall) and *Palazzo Mancuso*; at the center, an octagonal fountain dating back to 1607. Particularly noteworthy is the northern section of the town, which constitutes the earliest core; in a concentric array, the blocks wind over the little hill, around the ruins of the old *castle* and of the first church dedicated to St. Nicholas (15th c.).

izzi

ing on the southern slope of the mountain the same name, Prizzi (elev. 966 m., pop. 154) has a vast scenic view of the valleys the rivers Sòsio and Vicaria. The origins the town are linked to the old settlement Hyppana, situated on the mountain, or ontagna dei Cavalli, where abundant cheological material has been found, from rious periods of history (from Punic to man times). The present settlement began to develop, beginning in the 12th c.; according to the description of the Arabic ographer Idrisi, Prizzi is a small fortified orgo," or village, abounding in water and surrounded by vast areas covered with lds of wheat. The earliest inhabited town, ich clustered around the castle, occupies e higher part of the mount, and is marked-characterized by a medieval layout, with ense grid of roads and lanes, in some caso steep that they have steps. The **Chiesa** **adre**, which stands on an elevated location, was built in the 16th c. on the site of earlier church of S. Giorgio; the interior, ch three aisles, contains a statue of *St. chael Archangel*, by Antonello Gagini. om the Largo Matrice, if you continue in esterly direction, you will reach the ruof the *castle*, built at the turn of the h c. and rebuilt by the Chiaramonte fam-

ily; today, the few remaining fragments are in part incorporated in a number of homes.

Santo Stefano Quisquina

Situated on a gentle slope of the Serra Quisquina, Santo Stefano Quisquina (elev. 730 m., pop. 5,628), surrounded by fertile farmlands, was inhabited during the Moorish period. During the reign of Frederick II of Aragon (1296-1337) the fief of Santo Stefano was held by Giovanni Caltagirone; in

Piazza Umberto I, central square of Palazzo Adriano

this period, probably, there already existed the earliest core of the present-day town. From that original nucleus, which probably was consolidated around the present-day Chiesa Matrice, the town continued to develop from the 16th c., in an expansion that can still be recognized in the regular layout of the long rectangular city blocks.

In the *Piazza Castello*, raised and characterized by a stone fountain dating from the 18th c., stands the 18th-c. *Palazzo Baronale*. The *Chiesa Madre*, founded in the 16th c. by Federico Chiaramonte, is dedicated to S. Nicolò di Bari (St. Nicholas of Bari).

Castronuovo di Sicilia

This small town which originated in the Middle Ages stands on the left bank of the river Plàtani; Castronuovo di Sicilia (elev. 660 m., pop. 3,604) is situated upon a slight slope, dropping down to the southeast, in the shadow of the Monte Kassar. Numerous traces of constructions on the vast highland that extends on the summit of the mountain, testify to the existence of an ancient settlement of proto-historical origins, later Hellenized. Following the destruction of this fortified town (probably during Roman times), the inhabitants gathered on the steep crag of S. Vitale (to the west of the present-day town), where it is still possible to see ruins of buildings from the Byzantine period and from later periods. Between the 9th and the 11th c., on the eastern high plain, downhill from the fortified crag, near abundant springs, there developed two small villages ("borghi"), originally located outside of the town precincts; in the 13th c. the Borgo Rabat, closer to the crag, was enclosed within the perimeter walls (no longer in existence) which protected the original nucleus of the present-day town. The settlement of the Padri Carmelitani and the Padri Conventuali di S. Francesco to the east of the city walls (middle of the 14th c.) and the construction of the new church of the Madre della SS. Trinità (1404) marked the progressive abandonment of the settlement set on the highland of S. Vitale and the rapid development of the town downstream, which soon grew beyond the boundaries of the town walls.

The **Chiesa Madre** preserves, of the original construction (1404) the side portal and a number of pointed-arch windows; the interior, with a single nave and side chapels, renovated many times, contains numerous works of artistic interest, partly from other churches that no longer exist (including a Gagini statue of the *Madonna della Catena*; a canvas from the school of Rubens depicting the *Flagellation of Christ*; a painted 14th-c. *Cross*; a marble statue of *St. Peter Enthroned*, by Domenico Gagini). From Piazza Duomo, if you head west, through the complex urban layout, articulated into lanes and courtyards, you will reach the *church of S. Caterina* (16th c.): the interior, adorned with precious marble altars and stucco work by Antonio Messina, contains a number of canvases from the 18th c. A little further along is the fountain, or *Fontana del Rabato*, rebuilt in 1531.

Lercara Friddi

Lying along the slopes of the peak, or Pizzo Lanzone (elev. 917 m.) on the interior of the broad hilly area that separates the basin of the river Torto from that of the river Plàtani, Lercara Friddi (elev. 660 m., pop. 7,602) was founded in the fief of Friddi by the Spanish aristocrat D. Baldassarre Gomez de

Amescua with a "licentia populandi," or cense to colonize, in 1605. The new foundation stood not far from an existing "fóndaco" (Arabic term, for a stopping place a trading market), located along the royal way, or Regia Trazzera that linked Palermo and Agrigento. Of fundamental importance in the economic history of this town, at the turn of the 19th c., was the mining of sulphur from the rich and numerous mines that dotted the territory; Lercara then gradually became the most important town in the northern sulphur-bearing basin of the island, which extended over a surface area of roughly 4 square kilometers, including the groups of the Colle Croce, the Colle Madonna and the Colle Serio. All the same, by the eve of the Second World War, the development of this industry was hindered by the lack of good roads, by the outdated mining equipment, by high costs, and by strong competition from other sulphur-producing countries; the crisis culminated in the closure of the mines. The urban layout of Lercara is characterized by an orthogonal road grid which has its fulcrum in the main square, the Piazza Duomo, on the east side of which stands the cathedral, or Chiesa Madre.

Mezzojuso

Set on the slopes of the wooded hill, Colle la Brigna, whose walls serve as a backdrop to the town, dominated by the campaniles of the two cathedrals, or Chiese Madri, Mezzojuso (elev. 534 m., pop. 3,2..) takes its name from "Manzil Jusuf," meaning "village of Joseph," a Moorish hamlet that stood here before. In the 15th c., it became an Albanian town, after refugees fled here from the onslaught of the invading Turks; the main square there are two Chiese Madre atop one staircase is the *church of the Annunziata*, founded by the Normans and of Latin rite; lower down is the *church of S. Nicolò*, built in the 16th c., and of the Greek rite; both have undergone Baroque renovations. On the interior of the second church are six late-Byzantine panels, from

Lercara Friddi: a solfatara

iconostasis that has since been disman-
ed; on the main altar, dating back to the
th c., in polychrome marble, there is an
ory *Crucifix*, on a 17th-c. ebony cross. At
e northwestern extremity of the town is
e **church of S. Maria delle Grazie**, with a
onastery. Built in 1501, it was officiated
om 1650 on by Basilian monks of the Greek
e. It was modified around the middle of
e 18th c.: on the interior, there is an
onostasis with Byzantine panels dating
ack to the 15th c.; on the walls, note the
escoed medallions, with the Doctors of the
eek church. The monastery has housed,
nce 1968, a workshop/laboratory for the
storation of old books.

falà Diana

e foundation of the town of Cefalà Di-
a (elev. 563 m., pop. 1,031) dates back to
e second half of the 18th c. ("licentia pop-
andi," dating from 1684). The name, of
certain origin, may derive from the head-
ape of the spur upon which stands the
stle. The fortress was part of a system of
rtresses strategically arranged along the
ute that leads to Palermo. The town
ands on a slope behind the castle, and has
ayout based on an orthogonal grid, re-
lving around the central square. The
uses that date back to the foundation
nerally are built to a plan with a single
om divided up into two or three sectors,
ommon typology in towns of this period.
e *castle*, which may be of Moorish origin,
in ruins.

ninna

uated in a hollow to the south of the Piz-
S. Anania, Ciminna (elev. 530 m., pop.
51) may correspond to the Moorish ham-
of "Has," which the Arab geographer
isi described as rich in crops. Punic and
man finds uncovered in the surrounding
untryside confirms the existence of ear-
r forms of settlement. In the Norman era,
e "borgo" must have clustered around a
stle, of which not a trace survives. You
ll enter the town along the straight thor-
ghfare of Corso Umberto I and, before en-
ing the Piazza Umberto I, you will come
the *church of S. Domenico*, which contains
o works by Antonello Gagini: a statue of
e Virgin Mary (1532) and a ciborium
521). In Piazza Umberto I stands the
rch of the *Purgatorio*, which contains a
h-c. polyptych depicting the Virgin Mary
d Saints. The *church of S. Francesco* pre-
rves, in various locations, parts of a dis-
ntled marble polyptych of the Gagini

school, and a papier-mâché Crucifix (1521).
The **Chiesa Madre** (S. Maria Maddalena),
which was founded in the 16th c. on a highland, atop another, earlier structure, has undergone considerable renovations, from
the 17th c. on, and preserves, of the earlier
structures, a Gothic rose window and a
massive campanile (1519). In the Baroque
interior, which has three aisles, divided by
pillars, there are stucco decorations, and a
16th-c. wooden ceiling; the carved wooden
choir dates back to 1619. In the chapel of the
right aisle, closed by a stone arch that was
placed here in 1531, is a copy of the *Spasm
of Sicily* by Raphael, by Simeon of Wobreck.
The *church of S. Giovanni Battista* is the
largest in the town, after the Chiesa Matrice; it was built, to plans by Paolo Amato
(17th c.), on an ancient oratory of the Con-
fraternita del SS. Crocifisso, a brotherhood
that venerated the 16th-c. *Crucifix* now behind a grate, just past the main altar.

Misilmeri

Misilmeri (elev. 129 m., pop. 20,072), a farming town, grew up on the site of a Moorish
hamlet, the "Manzil al Amir" (Hamlet of the
Emir), around the ruins of a Norman-Moor-
ish castle, which dominated a long stretch
of the valley of the river Eleutero, an obligatory passage between Palermo and the
hinterland. In the 16th c. Misilmeri was refounded and repopulated: a previous settlement from the Norman period, which
clustered around the castle, founded by
the Moors (Qasr al Amir), can be recognized in the higher section of Misilmeri,
where the houses are clustered in a circle
around the ruins of the castle. The town was
shifted downhill, and in 1553 the main
church, or Chiesa Madre was built. It was
upon the site of that church, and along the
royal way, or Trazzera Tegia, later a state
road, the route that serves as the main
street for the entire town (Corso Vittorio
Emanuele), that the new settlement with a
geometric structure was laid out. The ruins
of the *castle* dominate the large settlement:
ruins of walls and polygonal towers belong to the reconstruction done by the
Chiaramonte family (14th c.) and a further
expansion done in 1487 by Matteo Carnelivari. The **Chiesa Madre** (church of S. Giovanni Battista) possesses an altarpiece depicting *Our Lady of the Immaculate Conception*, by Vito D'Anna (1768), who also did
a Via Crucis on slate (1767), and various
18th-c. wooden *statues*, including one of
Our Lady of the Immaculate Conception, by
Pietro Marabitti (1734).

3 Western Sicily

At the western extremity of the island, there has been considerable influence – in ter[m]
of historic formation and in the development of human occupation – from contact with o[th]
er civilizations. Relationships with the material and political cultures that flourished in t[he]
western Mediterranean Sea – and more specifically with the cultures of Africa and the Ib[er]
ian peninsula – counterbalanced by the peripheral effect of other civilizations, mo[re]
common in the eastern areas – such as Greek civilization, or that of the Italian penins[ula]
– exerted enormous influence in this area.

With the abandonment or destruction of the settlements of classical antiquity, what [re]
mained was the excellent network of Roman roads, serving as the skeleton of a new la[y]
out and organization of the territory in the High Middle Ages. In particular, the Arabs, b[e]
tween the 9th and the 11th c., undertook a process of reorganizing the structures of s[et]
tlement, production, and administration, establishing an influence that was to affect t[he]
history of the island right up to modern times, especially in this part of Sicily, where Islam[ic]
penetration was much deeper and where the damage done by feudalism was more serio[us]
with the Norman conquest and the spread of the "latifundium," or large landed estate, t[he]
relationship between city and countryside altered irrevocably, causing an irreversible c[ri]
sis in the last few centuries of the Middle Ages.

A geographic revolution in the settlement of the island was undertaken, beginning in t[he]
middle of the 16th c., by the baronial class, with the repopulation of immense uncultiv[at]
ed feuds, though there was also an element of political and economic consideration involv[ed]
This immense drive to construct and build led to a radical change in the structures of t[he]
territory and in the general system of communications; hence the Sicilian settleme[nt]
grouped into large compact centers, which serve as counterpoint to the virtually em[pty]
countryside, which at the most are dotted with the infrequent presence of farms.

Following the unification of Italy, there was a progressive and increasingly acute isolati[on]
of the western territories of Sicily, which had become peripheral to the areas undergo[ing]
development; this peripheral status – if we make exceptions for the few towns with co[n]
siderable capacity for production, such as Marsala and Mazara del Vallo – translated [in]
to a general impoverishment of social and economic components.

3.1 Trapani, Èrice, and the salinas

This was a major seaport and an important industrial center until relatively recent
times. The closure of the historic seaport of
Lilibeo in the Stagnone, the splendid la-
goon that extends to the north of Marsala,
in the late 16th c., shifted the maritime traffic of the western Mediterranean Sea to the
port of Trapani, which prospered greatly in
the 18th and 19th c. thanks to the industries
of salting fish and the shipyards, which
took the place of the coral working that
once flourished here; the city of Trapani established major salinas (salt pits or saltworks) along the coast of the Mediterranean
Sea, in Africa and in Asia, right up until the
earliest decades of the 20th c., and crews
and officers from this area long manned
the great tuna-fishing boats.

Trapani (elev. 3 m., pop. 69,497; plan on
page 64) is nowadays a city of the service
industries.

As an emporium and a strategic seaport
under the Phoenicians, the harbor of Trapani grew in importance when it becam[e]
naval base and the keystone of the Pu[nic]
system of defences in Sicily. Beginning w[ith]
the Roman conquest of the city, howev[er]
despite the increase of population thanks [to]
the transfer of the Ericines, there bega[n a]
slow decline, which extended into t[he]
Byzantine Age.

The Moorish invasion of the island su[c]
ceeded in giving Trapani, from the 9th c. [on]
a new period of prosperity; and it was p[re]
cisely with the arrival of the Arabs that t[he]
city was rebuilt, taking on numerous fe[a]
tures typical of Islamic town planning. T[his]
period of prosperity continued even f[ol]
lowing the Norman conquest, with the [de]
velopment of maritime trade, accompani[ed]
by the skilled local manufacture of coral a[nd]
gold jewelry.

The consequential growth in populati[on]
led James II of Aragon (1286) to enlarge t[he]
town, organizing new residential areas w[ith]
the reclamation of peripheral land s[o]

unding the old city walls. During the same riod, construction began on the new system of defences, which included areas of expansion, with a new fortress erected to the ortheast (Castello di Terra).

he saturation of the areas remaining free me about, as is common in the history of is area, between the 14th and 15th c., th the establishment in the city grid of the rge convent buildings. In e 16th c., a plan of modnization fostered by arles V led to the conruction in the city walls of werful bastions, isolatg the city from the mainnd by means of a navigae channel, which linked e inlet of the port with e inlet of the walls, known the Tramontana; this annel has since been led in, and is now the Via XX Gennaio.

ith the demolition of the ty walls in 1862 there ben a new phase of expanon of the city, justified the need to find resintial areas inland; it coesced along the main oroughfare of Via G.B. rdella, which nowadays tends to the slopes of onte Èrice. The reconruction that followed the mbing of 1940-43, acmpanied by the demands of the new city, led a definitive shift of the nter city outside of the storic center, with a rearkable revolution of the rritorial layout of modern-day Trani.The tour begins from the 'peripheral' nctuary of the Annunziata, which, with e adjoining Museo Pepoli, constitutes e of the most interesting aspects of a tour the city. Beyond the 19th-c. Piazza Vitrio Emanuele, one of the narrow lanes at runs off from the Via Garibaldi takes e on a stroll through the medieval quarrs, where ancient churches stand alongde the Jewish ghetto, while Corso Vitto Emanuele leads, among 17th-c. palazzi, the "punta della falce," or point of the ckle. It is pleasant, in the summer enings, to mingle with the people of Trani, in Piazza Garibaldi and Piazza Lutelli, sitting in one of the many ice cream ops, enjoying the cool sea breezes.

Not far from the city, one obligatory stop is nearby Èrice, which looks out over the surrounding territory from its mountain perch (there is a daily bus service, from the train station of Trapani, an advisable replacement for the use of cars), and, along the road to Marsala, the salinas and the remarkable museum of salt, or Museo del Sale.

South of Trapani, the landscape is characterized by salinas

Santuario dell'Annunziata* (A6). This sanctuary is the leading monument of the city, and was built between 1315 and 1332, but in 1760 it was radically redone on the interior, with the older division into three aisles transformed, by Giovanni Biagio Amico, into a single nave. The original façade remains, with an immense rose window and the Norman Gothic portal from the early 15th c.; the massive Baroque campanile that stands beside it, a symbol of the continual reconstruction of the complex, dates from 1650.

Inside, note the chapel of fishermen, or *Cappella dei Pescatori* (on the right) and the chapel of sailors, or *Cappella dei Marinai* (on the left), both of which date back to the 16th c., and built in tufa stone: the for-

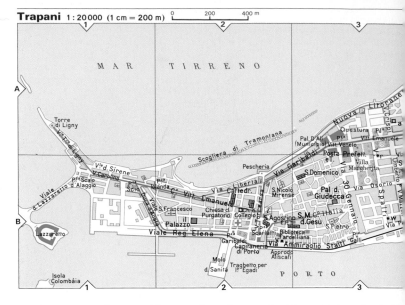

Trapani 1 : 20000 (1 cm = 200 m)

mer has a square plan topped by a cupola (the decorative seashell motifs refer to those to whom this chapel is dedicated), the latter stands out for the remarkable monochrome punctuation of the architecture, given by the distinctive yellow color of the tufa stone, typical of so many buildings in this part of Sicily. On the other hand, the chapel of the Virgin Mary, or *Cuppella della Madonna* (the sanctuary proper, which can be reached from behind the main altar) dates back to 1530, and stands out for the polychrome marble decorations of the walls and floors: the large marble arch, adorned with exquisite reliefs (*prophets and sibyls with God the Father*), is by Antonino and Giacomo Gagini (1531-37), while the *Virgin Mary with Christ Child**, known as the "Madonna di Trapani," on the altar, is by Nino Pisano.

Museo Regionale Pepoli* (A6). This regional museum is housed in the former *monastery of the Carmelite Fathers of Trapani* (Padri Carmelitani di Trapani), an imposing building from the 17th c., though it was originally founded in the 14th c. along with the Santuario dell'Annunziata; the museum has undergone numerous changes over the years, and it offers a thorough-going history of the art and culture of Trapani and its territory, from antiquity nearly to the present day.

Among the sculpture, we should mention the *St. James the Elder** by Antonello Gagini (1522) and a holy-water font dating from 1486. The art gallery includes paintings dating from the 14th to the 18th c., and among

them we should note: *Madonna* by the Ma[ster] ter of the Polyptych of Trapani, *Pietà** [by] Roberto di Oderisio, triptych by Anton[ello] Massaro, *St. Francis with Stigmata** by Titi[an]. The archeological section is made up [of] finds from Èrice, Selinunte, and Lilibeo. What distinguishes the museum, making [it] particularly interesting, are however [the] masterpieces of the *local applied arts*: fi[ne] sculptures in wood, canvas and glu[e,] ivory, seashells, semiprecious stones, c[re]ations in coral, silver, and ceramics, wi[th] fine pieces set in different halls on t[he] second story. Above all, what is notew[or]thy here is the unrivalled skill of Trapan[i] artists in the working of coral. The o[b]jects of this particular profession, famo[us] as early as the 16th c., were born from t[he] imagination and the skill of a Francisc[an] monk, Fra' Matteo Bavera, who execut[ed] several of the pieces displayed here: [a] large gilt bronze *lamp*, with coral a[nd] enamel (1633), a coral *Crucifix*, set on [a] cross made of ebony, tortoise-shell, a[nd] mother-of-pearl.

Piazza Vittorio Emanuele (A3). This squa[re] marks the western extremity of the *Via G*[. Fardella], a thoroughfare built during t[he] 19th-c. expansion, and it features an *equ*[es]*trian statue of Vittorio Emanuele* (1882) alo[ng] with the fountain of the triton, or *Fonta*[na] *del Tritone* (1951), adjoining the *Vi*[lla] *Margherita*, the city's public park, dati[ng] from the 19th c. Overlooking the adjoini[ng] Piazza Vittorio Veneto is the *Palazzo d'*[? (1904), which is the city hall, and the A[rt] Nouveau ("Liberty," as the Italian has]

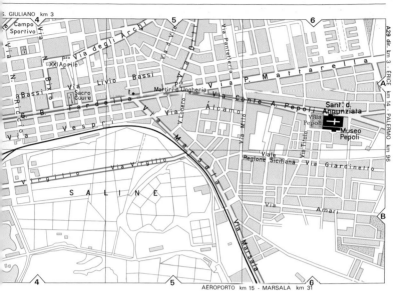

izzo delle Poste e Telegrafi (post office telegraph office, 1924).

Garibaldi (B2-3). The former Rua Nova remarkable setting, lined by Baroque zzi and churches that overlook it; one uld particularly note the magnificent de of *S. Maria dell'Itria*, built in 1621 later enlarged (inside, it is possible to ire 17th-c. sculpture and paintings) , at the end of the road, the church of *ia SS. del Soccorso*, founded in the 15th id partly rebuilt in 1874, featuring hand- e Baroque choir lofts.

omenico (B3). Rebuilt between the 17th the 18th c., the church preserves – of original 14th-c. construction – the rose low in the façade and traces of the orig- structure in the apse, where the *sar- hagus of Manfredi* (1318), son of Freder- ll of Aragon, is preserved. The so-called el, or *Cappella Pepoli*, behind the apse, erves considerable fragments of the inal frescoes, dating from the 14th c. *cifixion*) and the 15th c. (*St. Catherine* other saints; dating from the same pe- is the *Virgin Mary with Christ Child* to the t of the entrance); the exquisite Baroque el with polychrome marble decora- s, which Giovanni Biagio Amico built g the left wall, features on its altar a rare den *Crucifix** in the Iberian style, known olorous-Gothic (13th/14th c.).

church of S. Nicolò Mirense (B2), which can eached from S. Domenico by taking the Via eca, is the second-oldest church in the city

(it was built in A.D. 536) and it boasts the title of basilica; in 1749 the plan of the church was mod- ified to plans by Giovanni Biagio Amico, into a Latin cross with three aisles (the marble *triptych* on the main altar is of the Gagini school; the *bap- tismal font* is a gift from Charles V).

Palazzo Senatorio (B2). This Senate Palace, built by Gioacchino Cavaretta, between 1699 and 1701, on the site of the former Loggia dei Giurati, is one of the finest ex- amples of Baroque civil architecture, with its framework with two orders of free-stand- ing columns, set against a façade adorned with statues, linked on high by a console- balcony which overlooks the Corso Vittorio Emanuele. Adjoining the palazzo is the clock tower, or *Torre dell'Orologio*, one of the five towers depicted in the city's heraldic crest.

Corso Vittorio Emanuele (B2). Formerly the Rua Grande, this broad and long thor- oughfare dates back to the development of the city in the 13th c., and it constitutes – with the beauty and size of the public and private buildings that line it – the draw- ing room of the city.

Church of the Collegio (B2). Begun in the 17th c., and dedicated to the Immaculate Conception, this church is the work of Na- tale Masuccio; it presents a sumptuous Mannerist-Baroque façade, rich in marble decorations, which joins to its sleekness a certain magnificent splendor, thanks to the elegant columns and the two statues of women, standing in the place of caryatids. The *interior* features three aisles, with the vault and walls of the central aisle, or nave, decorated with stucco panels (*Bibles scenes*) in half-relief, highlighted in gold; in the apse stands an *icon* of the church's namesake (the *Immacolata*), carved in half-relief in white marble, a masterpiece by Ignazio Marabitti.

Cattedrale (B2), or cathedral. Dedicated to St. Lawrence (S. Lorenzo), this cathedral was built in 1635 on the site of an existing church, built in the 14th c., while the elegant Baroque façade, with portico, dates back to 1740 and was built to plans by Giovanni Biagio Amico; inside, there are three aisles set on columns, with decorations in the early Baroque style; also note the 17th-c. *Crucifixion*, attributed to the Trapanese painter Giacomo Lo Verde.

Directly across from the façade of the Cattedrale, or cathedral, take the Via Generale Domenico Giglio, to reach the **church of the Purgatorio** (B2), built in 1683, with an elegant and lively façade with two orders (Giovanni Biagio Amico, 1712) decorated with *statues of the Apostles*.

The *Mysteries*, or better, the *groups of the Passion*, housed in the church are tied to a procession which is one of the most important sacred events held in Trapani. It traces its origins back to the determination of the Church, at the turn of the 16th c., to impose order and composure on the less easily controlled living groups who portrayed the passion and death of Jesus; the 20 wooden groups, completed in the 17th-c. and made of wood, cloth, and glue, in fact, depict, with nearly life-size characters, this moment in the life of Christ.

Torre di Ligny (A1). This tower was erected in 1671 in honor of the arrival in Trapani of the viceroy Claudio Lamoraldo, prince of Ligny, at the northwestern extremity of the sickle-shaped breakwater of the port; it now houses the museum of prehistory, or *Museo della Preistoria*.

Isole Colombaia (B1). These islands, set opposite the fishing port, and surrounded by shallow waters (you can see the seabed from the sidewalks along the Viale Regina Elena), were the site of the construction in the 14th c. of an octagonal tower, which in the following century was put to use as a fortress; in the 17th c. it was converted into a judiciary prison; it no longer serves that function, and it now awaits restoration.

S. Agostino (B2). This church is actually dedicated to St. John the Baptist, and not to St. Augustine; it was built in the 15th c. near the hospice of the Knights Templar

Trapani: the palazzo della Giudecca

(Cavalieri Templari; this is also known as church of the Templars, or Chiesa dei T~~plari~~, and was entrusted, during the r~~eign~~ of Frederick III to the Augustines, who ~~es~~tablished a monastery there; it was ~~later~~ used by the city senate as a site for offi~~cial,~~ religious, and civil ceremonies. It was ~~seri~~ously damaged by bombing in 1942; o~~f the~~ original structure, what survives is the ~~sin~~gle, foreshortened hall, and in the faç~~ade~~ the magnificent rose window, with littl~~e in~~tertwined arches and alternated fretw~~ork,~~ with a Gothic archivolt portal.

The square that contains the church ~~fea~~tures a fountain of Saturn, or **Fontana ~~di Sa~~turno**, built in 1342 by the Chiaramon~~te~~ family, lords of the city, in commem~~ora~~tion of the aqueduct which they also ha~~d or~~dered built.

The **Biblioteca Fardelliana** (B2-3), a library ~~that~~ occupies the 18th-c. former church of S. Giac~~omo~~ Maggiore (it is reached by following Via S. A~~gosti~~no and Via dei Biscottai), was founded in 18~~30 by~~ G.B. Fardella di Torrearsa; it contains app~~roxi~~mately 118,000 volumes, a number of valuab~~le in~~cunabula and 851 manuscripts; of particula~~r in~~terest are the 15 illuminated codices dating ~~from~~ the 14th and 15th c. and an exceedingly fine ~~col~~lection of engravings (*historical views of the* ~~Tra~~*pani area*) from the 17th and 18th c.

S. Maria del Gesù (B2-3). Dating back to ~~the~~ first half of the 16th c. (built at the behe~~st of~~ Charles V, along with the convent that ~~was~~ destroyed during the Second World ~~War,~~ with a plan similar to that of the Duom~~o of~~ Monreale), this church has a façade ~~with~~ Gothic/Renaissance features and a h~~and~~some portal with decorations in the

nian style. In the *interior*, with a nave
d two aisles, which were originally di-
led by pointed arches, ribbed vaulting of
e left apse and the presbytery has been
covered, with small late-Gothic columns;
e chapel, or Cappella Staiti (to the right of
e presbytery) contains, beneath an ex-
isite marble *buldachin* by Antonello Gagi-
(1521), the *Madonna degli Angeli**, a
zed terracotta statue by Andrea della
bbia.

lazzo della Giudecca (B3). This building
one of the most important relics of the
vish heritage in Sicily, and was built at the
hest of the aristocratic family of the
mbra (hence the other name by which it
till known) inside the area of the ghetto.
e building has been renovated exten-
ely over the course of the centuries: all
t survives, dating from the turn of the
h c., testifies to the "stile plateresco," an
hitectural style that spread in an exu-
rant and fanciful manner in Spain be-
en the end of the 15th c. and the last few
rs of the 16th c., and which spread wide-
hroughout Sicily. Damaged by the brutal
nts of history (the entire left side was de-
lished in the 19th c.), the building still
sts a tower, rusticated, a large portal,
l in the wing that was spared demoli-
n, apertures with lavish cornices and
umns.

Èrice*

This little town (elev. 751 m., pop. 29,420;
plan below), set high on an isolated mountain at the western edge of Sicily (on particularly clear days, it is possible to see the
summit of the majestic cone of Mount Etna
at the other end of the island; Monte San Giuliano was long the only point of visual reference for sailors on the other side of the
nearby islands of Ègadi), is a magnificent medieval village that has survived intact to the
present day: Èrice is in fact a remarkable synthesis of mythology and history, art and
culture, landscape and environment, fanta-
sy and reality. Its origins are exceedingly ancient: it is said to have been founded by
the mythical Èrice, son of Venere and Bute,
who became king of the Elimi, an ancient
tribe that settled here, extending as far as
the nearby Segesta; surviving from that period, a massive legacy, emblematic, with
legends inscribed in letters that have not yet
been deciphered (Phoenician?), giant walls,
described by archeologists as Elimo-Punic.
Èrice is a historical town and a center of
artistic heritage of considerable interest.
With its cobblestone streets and its remarkable urban layout, it met the require-
ments of a population that lived on a limited amount of land: the considerable steep
climbs explain the twisting nature of the
lanes and streets, which also had to be
sheltered from the strong winds, and that of

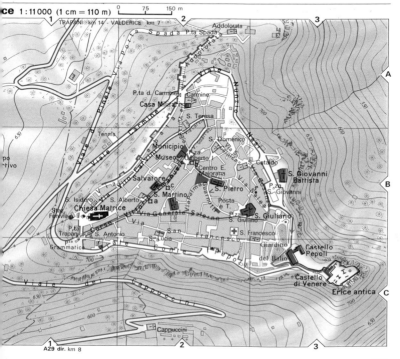

ce 1:11 000 (1 cm = 110 m)

The Castello Pepoli in Èrice

the narrow "vanelle," passageways so narrow that only a single person can get through at a time. Aside from the streets, the most typical and best-known aspect consists of the little courtyards.

Besides being the headquarters of a scientific institute, the Centro di Cultura Scientifica "Ettore Majorana," Èrice hosts – through the course of the year – major cultural events, such as the 'days of the arts,' or "Le Giornate delle Arti" (temporarily suspended), and an international week of medieval and Renaissance music (Settimana Internazionale di Musica Medievale e Rinascimentale). In particular, you should note the Mystery Procession (Processione dei Misteri), on Good Friday.

If you enter through the gate, or *Porta Trapani* (B-C1), one of the three entrances in the enormous *enclosure walls* (the lower part of which dates back to the eighth/seventh c. B.C., with Roman reconstruction; the upper section dates back to the Norman period), you will find yourself on the *Corso Vittorio Emanuele*, once the 'royal way,' or Via Regia, along which stood between the 13th and 14th c. the main civil and religious buildings. Among the handsome Baroque elevations along the "corso," we should mention those of the *Palazzo La Porta* and the *Palazzo Platamone* (B1-2), behind which extends the square that contains the **Chiesa Matrice*** (B1). This church is dedicated to Our Lady of the Assumption, and was erected in 1314 and then renovated (especially the interior) in 1865. The façade, facing the town walls, is preceded by a 15th-c. pronaos, beneath which stands a hand-

some Gothic portal. Facing it is an isolat campanile, with Gothic twin-light mullion windows in the Chiaramonte style, possi built at the behest of Frederick of Aragon a watch tower (1312).

The direction of the "corso" divides into t Via Albertina degli Abbati, which skirts t *church of S. Martino* (B2), rebuilt in t 17th/18th c., and then reaches the p *chrurch of S. Giuliano* (B2-3), rebuilt in t 18th c., but founded by the Normans. A dating from this era is the church of *Cataldo* (B2-3), beneath which, on the br of a great cliff, the church of *S. Giovanni I tista* (B3) was built in the 12th c., rebuil the 15th c. and again in the 17th c. (t side portal dates from the 13th c.).

If you climb up toward the southwest tip the triangular walls, you will reach the 19 c. garden, or *Giardino del Balio*, beyo which extended the platea of the anci acropolis. Here stands the castle, or *Cas lo Pepoli* (C3), formerly the site of the "b lo" (governor's palace) and converted i a villa in the 19th c. (not open to the publ On the isolated crag of the acropolis the 12th and 13th c. was erected, with use of ancient materials as well, the called castle of Venus, or **Castello di Ven** (C3), crowned with parapets; inside, sch ars have identified the site of the temple the Venus of Èrice (Venere Ericina).

From the fork in the road, the Corso Vit rio Emanuele continues uphill; on the l dating from the late-13th or the early-14th is the *Palazzo Chiaromonte* (B2), which longed at one point to an order of Bened tine nuns. At the end of the "corso" stan the centrally located *Piazza Umberto I* (E a 19th-c. version of the venerable town "l gia." Located in the municipal comple: the civic museum, or **Museo Civico Co ci**, which houses, among other thin archeological finds from the necropolis Èrice, including a *head of Aphrodite* dat from the 4th c. B.C.

The tour can end with a trip down to the I torical center of the town, i.e., the medie crossroads where the *S. Pietro* (B2) stan it was built in the late 14th c. and was reb in 1745 to plans by Giovanni Biagio Am Nowadays, the former monastery hou one set of offices of the Centro Culturale tore Majorana."

The salinas

Among the most notable of the Sicilian s works, these salinas have been a major ture in the urban landscape, until relat ly recent times, of Trapani and the ent coastal area as far as Marsala. Described e Arab geographe Al-Idrisi during the gn of Roger the Norman, these saltworks joyed great prosperity under the house of agon, and from the 18th c. until just a few cades ago: toward the end of the 19th c., e salinas of Trapani numbered roughly ty, and their product was exported to rway, where it was used in the process- of cod. Nowadays, this traditional in- stry is in crisis, and few of the plants re- in active.

e distinctive landscape of the salinas to south of the city can be observed by dri- g along the coast road to Marsala and en turning off every so often down to- rd the coast, where one might find it in- teresting to inspect more closely the occa- sional plant that is still in operation (piles of salt are covered with terracotta tiles to protect them from the rain); there are "aero- motori" (windmills), with their towers; in the older ones, which once had sails just like old-fashioned Dutch windmills, recent restorations have installed metal blades, like the more modern windmills that dot the American west.

A stop in the *Contrada Nubia* (elev. 7 m.), where you will arrive after a short detour from the coast road to Marsala, will allow you to reach the interesting salt museum, or *Museo del Sale*, installed in an old salt-grind- ing mill, restored by its owners.

2 The islands of Ègadi and Pantellerìa

apani is a point of departure for boat rvice to the islands of Ègadi, served by fre- ent connections by ship and by hydrofoil. e service, which is more frequent in sum- er, with several trips a day, is run by the mpany Siremar (in Palermo: 091/582688; Trapani: 0923/540515) and by the com- ny Alilauro (passengers only, no cars; apani: 0923/24073). The hydrofoil termi- l is in Trapani, in the Via Ammiraglio liti. With the exception of Favignana, ich is the largest island and which has a od system of roads, we recommend ainst bringing cars.

order to reach Pantellerìa, the best point departure is once again Trapani, and u can simply call the same shipping com- nies that serve the islands of Ègadi. This and is also equipped with an airport, h daily flights from and to Rome, with in- mediate stops at Palermo and Trapani.

e islands of Ègadi

the sea to the west of Trapani and rsala lie the islands of Ègadi (pop. 4,335), insular fragments of the tip of a long-ago tri- angular Sicily. Composed of limestone and sandstone, the little island of Lèvanzo, the rocky and secluded Maréttimo, and espe- cially the largest island, Favignana, have been enjoying great popularity in recent years, a popularity that only seems to grow; the recent establishment of a nature pre- serve status – or Arcipelago a Riserva Mari- no-Paesaggistica – is an attempt to put a halt to reckless development in the interests of preserving the natural environment.

Inhabited back in prehistoric times (there are important graffiti in the cave, or Grotta del Genovese on Lèvanzo) and once the site of a Phoenician-Punic settlement, these islands became Roman in 241 B.C.; there is further historical mention of them in the middle of the 16th c., when the Spanish crown sold them to the family of the Pallavi- cino-Rusconi of Genoa.

Favignana. Capital of the islands of Ègadi, this is the largest island in the group (19 square kilometers), as well as being the

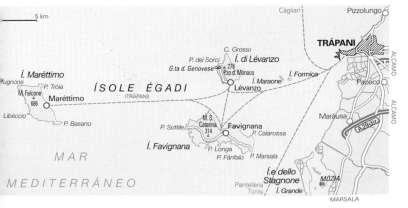

southernmost; it rises to an elevation of 314 m.

It has been an island-fortress and an island/tuna-fishing station, as well as an island-prison (the Spanish, the Austrians, and the house of Bourbon all used it for ordinary criminals and for political prisoners). The archaeological digs are of particular interest (strictly guided visits, tel. 0923-921411) with the famous *Bagni delle donne romane* (Roman Women's Baths).

The quarries of fine-grained quaternary seashell tufa stone, excellent as a building material, have long served as a major resource here: from grottos as immense and as intricate as great cities were taken the "cantuna," or tufa blocks, with which entire towns were built in Sicily, in Tunisia, in Libya. But the main resource here has always been the sea. This sere, arid, and fascinating island, exposed to winds and salt air, forms a barrier in the progress of schools of tuna as they make their way around Sicily; along with the islet of Formica and the shoal of Maraone, it serves as a huge turning buoy for the migrations of the tuna fish, which at the end of the spring come close to the coasts to breed, and which are caught in the "tonnare."

The stations were divided into "tonnare di corso," situated on the northern and western littorals, with the aim of catching the fish during their migrations toward their breeding areas, and "tonnare di ritorno," located on the southeastern coast, along the routes followed by the tuna following their breeding season.

The stations in the sea ("impianti a mare") were basically nothing more than a system of nets and floating buoys, which halted the fish and directed it toward a series of rectangular chambers, and finally the so-called "chamber of death," with fine and very strong netting. Here the tunas

that had been caught were killed off in a ce mony – the "mattanza" – that is cruel but pack with cultural and anthropological significanc The stations on the land ("impianti a terra") so constituted a complex of great historic a economic importance; they served as supp plants to the fishing boats, storing nets, boa and harpoons, but above all they contained fish-processing and fish-packing plants. The were very large complexes arranged aroun large esplanade near the sea ("marfaraggio") Of the roughly 50 "tonnare," or tuna-fishing s tions that once existed in Sicily, only the one Favignana (which has always been the large still operates with any degree of continuity, p cessing each year from 1,000 to 1,500 met tons.

Lèvanzo. It is worth coming here just for t *Grotta del Genovese** alone, famous for prehistoric graffiti; this cave penetrates t mountain on the western coast (you c reach it by following a mule track, but i also very charming to take a boat). T enormous dark grotto – 8.5 m. in width, m. in depth, and 4 m. tall – bears on its wall 'messages' left some five to ten the sand years ago, when Lèvanzo and Fa g nana were still joined to Sicily and were habited by firstly Mesolithic and, later, olithic tribes: it is possible to make out a *ries of animals*, graffiti with exceedin light lines and remarkable naturalistic p fection, and four *human figures* shown i ritual dance.

Maréttimo. The westernmost of the Èga this island is a world unto itself, and nothing in common with the two other lands. Here there is no group fishing, with ceremony of the "mattanza": here the fi erman works alone and faces the boundl sea, on tiny boats marked with an odd flo ish on the bowsprit, strangely reminiscen

The "mattanza" of the tunas, a tradition which continues to this very day in Favignar

The suggestive village of Maréttimo, on the eastern coast of the island

Viking craft. No hotels have been allowed in Maréttimo, but the inhabitants provide accommodations in their own homes.

Pantellerìa

After Malta, this is the largest of the islands surrounding Sicily, with a surface area of 83 square kilometers and a population of 7,484 inhabitants. Set in the middle of the Canale di Sicilia, it is a prime attraction to those who love the sea, with all its wild beauty, with coastlines abounding in inlets and points, coves and grottos set amongst sheer rocks. For those who love fishing or underwater photography, this is the place. Communications with Sicily, which is further away than the African coast, are good: there are daily flights and boat services, which do much to reduce the island's isolation, and to encourage tourism.

Pantellerìa clearly bears signs of its birth from the sea (the most recent eruption was in October 1891): the Montagna Grande, which rises to an elevation of 836 m., is a relic of a volcanic cone, and the "cuddie," 24 highlands that stand around that cone, are also ancient craters. A number of examples of secondary volcanism are also present: the "favare," huge geysers of watery steam (circa 100 degrees Celsius), expelled thunderously from crevices in the boulders; the dry baths, or "stufe," natural grottos with steam vents that are used as a treatment for rheumatism; the "caldarelle," hot springs that bubble forth at temperatures ranging up to 70 degrees Celsius; the "mofette," with fumes of carbon dioxide; the "buvire," wells of brackish water.

For those who are seeking something more than the admittedly considerable charms of the sea, Pantellerìa offers relics, features, and curiosities that cannot elsewhere be found all on the same island. The "sesi," first of all; and then the "dammusi," cubic houses of Moorish origin, or the gardens.

The story of the "sesi" is an enigmatic chapter in the history of Pantellerìa: a mysterious people from the Neolithic age, a people that perhaps arrived here from the coasts of Libya, and took refuge along the harsh and hostile coast that looks out toward Africa, in the area of Mursia. This people, a tribe of hunters, fishermen, and gatherers, had no writing; and yet it succeeded in leaving traces of its existence in a cyclopean enclosure wall, erected for the village's defense, and in the funerary monuments – called "sesi" to be specific – which are great cairns (tumuli) of rough stone in regular blocks, of considerable size, with a hemispherical shape, inside which were one or two cellae. There were more than 500 of these remarkable prehistoric monuments, in some sense similar to the "nuraghi" of Sardinia; nowadays, there survive only a few dozen (in particularly good condition is the *Sese del Re* or Sese Gigante, the largest of them all), in that over the course of the centuries the stone that composed the "sesi" were used in the construction of the distinctive houses of Pantellerìa, the "dammusi."

It was the Moors, who ruled the island for 400 years (the name Pantellerìa derives

from "Bent el-Rhia," daughter of the wind), that transformed its appearance by cultivating every square inch of soil (they were responsible for the introduction of the cultivation of the "zibibbo," a sort of muscatel grape, which still grows here alongside plantations of capers and lentils); the Moors live on in the place names, in the dialect, and in the distinctive houses and garder The "dammusi" have thick walls and a cu la roof, which both serves to collect rain w ter and to keep the interior cool in the su mer and warm in the winter. They we originally used as summer homes, and the vineyards as tool sheds, and are nc reused as tourist accommodations.

3.3 The southwest coast and the Valle del Bèlice

There are many faces to the territory around Trapani – and those faces are geographic, as well as economic and cultural. The coastal area that bounds the Canale di Sicilia alternates gulfs with promontories, opening out over the sea with spectacular scenic views (splendid view from Selinunte); there are expanses of vineyards in the area just slightly inland (the area around Trapani is the home of the finest Sicilian wines).

The central area of the basin of the river Bèlice is known as the Valle del Bèlice, especially because of the violent earthquake in 1968. The exasperating slowness of the reconstruction made the provisional settlements, built in the emergency following reconstruction, practically permanent. The passing visitor can hardly help but notice, alongside the eloquent ruins of the towns, the shacktowns, now largely abandoned, and the ghost villages that are perhaps even sadder than the ruins themselves.

This is also the area where you are most likely to find "bagli" (the name comes from the Arabic word "bahal," or courtyard), built as early as the 17th c. (though some trace them back to the Middle Ages) for the organization of life in the "latifundium," or large landholdings. These were buildings, often several stories tall, enclosed by a defensive wall made of stone, with a few small windows and a large central courtyard (the "baglio" proper) paved with slabs of stone and cobbles arranged in elegant geometric patterns; they were built in such a way as to contain the residence of the owner (usually on the second floor), the stables and other housings of the animals, the wine cellars, storehouses, storage areas for farming tools, and – quite often – a chapel as well. It was necessary to create, at the center of every feudal holding, large and efficient farm structures, which when needed could also serve as fortified strutures (in some of them, which are closer in appearance to castles than to the country homes, there are turrets, enclosure walls, and loophole windows), and this coincided with the common practice of extensive farmlan (especially grains) and livestock breedi and grazing.

The Tyrrhenian coast, finally, appears hea ily marred by developments (often illeg in the vacation homes market along t splendid coast.

This route, which runs in a great circle e tending a total of 174.8 km., heads south first, along the state road 115, Sud-Oc dentale Sicula, from which it is possible see, beyond the Ègadi, the islands of t Stagnone (the ruins of Phoenician Moz are worth a detour). In a distance of 31.4 k you will reach Marsala, the largest Sicili wine-producing town and the home of t celebrated Marsala wine. After the fishi port of Mazara del Vallo, the route runs land to Castelvetrano, set at km. 73 along t route. From this town, another 12.2 km. driving takes you to Selinunte, one of t most important ancient-Greek archeologic sites in the entire Mediterranean Sea.

After you leave the coast, you will dri along the sadly famous valley, or Valle d Bèlice, along the state road 119/Gibellir reaching the new site of the town of Gib lina, designed and rebuilt from scratch f lowing the earthquake of 1968, and, aft taking the state road 188A, you will arrive Salemi. From here, you can continue to C latafimi, renowned for the decisive battle the expedition headed by Giuseppe Garib di, and, having passed (at km. 114.6) Seg sta (another archeological site, which particularly important and interesting d to the ancient origins of the settlement a the size of the temple), you will reach camo, a large farming town and the main dustrial center in the district.

It is just a few kilometers from Àlcamo to t gulf, or Golfo di Castellammare, followi westward along the coast road of the inl On your right, you will pass the turnoffs the Riserva Naturale Regionale dello Zi garo and the area around the Monte Còfa (from the little bay of San Vito lo Capo y can admire the other slope of the nature serve) and then you will return to Trapa

ozia*

 the south of Trapani, the sea forms a la-
on, the Laguna Stagnone, closed to the
st by an island, the Isola Grande, and to
e east by the Sicilian coast; from this
dy of water emerge – aside from the ver-
nt crests of the island mentioned previ-
s – the islets of Santa Maria and San Pan-
eo. These were the precise features typ-
lly sought out by the ancient Phoeni-
ans for a settlement: a small island near
e coast, surrounded by shallow water,
ensure adequate defense against enemy
tack and a safe anchorage for ships, on
ores swept by the prevailing winds. And
was here, in fact, on the island of San
ntaleo, that the Cartaginians founded, at
e end of the 8th c. B.C., the city of Mozia;
s possible to take a boat to the ruins, from
ittle pier on the Sicilian coast.

Given its ideal location, both close to Africa
and an obligatory point of passage along the
main trade routes to Spain, Sardinia, and
central Italy, the island soon housed one of
the most prosperous Punic (i.e., Carthaginian) colonies in the Mediterranean Sea. The
presence of the Greeks in Sicily – with whom
the Phoenicians sometimes traded and
sometimes engaged in hostilities, led to a series of wars, with first one then the other
prevailing; in the end, Mozia was destroyed
at the behest of Dionysis II of Syracuse, in
397 B.C.; the survivors moved over to the Sicilian coast, founding the city of Lilibeo,
present-day Marsala.
Mozia was fortified by a massive perimeter
of *enclosure walls*, punctuated by watch
towers and penetrated by *gates* at the four
points of the compass (two are still in good
condition). When the fortifications were

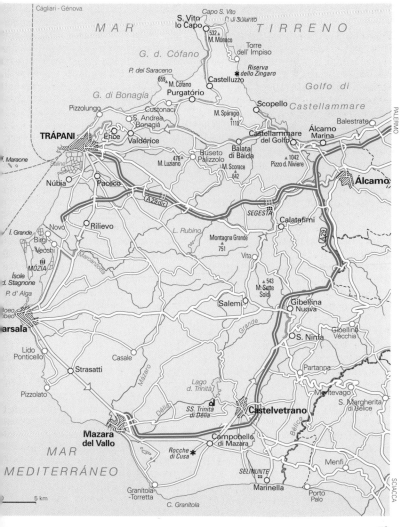

built, around the middle of the 6th c. B.C., the archaic necropolis that had been used to bury the dead since the very foundation of the city fell out of use because it was cut off by the wall; from that point onward the people of Mozia buried their dead on the mainland, bearing them over a causeway across the face of the sea. Of that causeway, which started from the north gate, and joined the island at the coastal settlement now known as Birgi (the causeway was 1.7 km. long and wide enough to allow the passage of two carts side-by-side), there still survive various traces beneath sea level, while on the island there are still ruins of a limited *port facility*.

Among the sacred areas that have been discovered, the *tophet* is unquestionably the most interesting one: it consists of an open-air sanctuary, inside of which is a burial ground in which were placed the remains of the human sacrifices made to the god Baal Hammon, in vases. The Phoenician religion, in fact, demanded that every first-born male should be sacrificed to the gods; every human deposit, so to speak, was marked by a stele, carved with symbolic or anthropomorphic depictions, in a number of techniques (from graffito to engraving, and from high relief to full in the round relief) or else painted (this latter sort of stele showed Egyptian and indigenous cultural influences, as well as Phoenician ones).

In an excellent state of conservation is the ancient "*cothon*," a careening basin used in the maintenance and repair of ships, which, after the larger one in Carthage, is the only one that has been found in the western Mediterranean Sea; the structure had both commercial (the economy of Mozia was based on trade and, probably on the production of ceramics) and military functions (the city was clearly the base of a major naval fleet).

The **Museum** was founded by Joseph Whitaker, one of the first foreign lovers the island, and its first archeologist; Whitaker moved to Sicily for purposes of business, and undertook the campaigns of excavation of the ancient settlement. The museum was established in a wing of his villa and the recent reconstruction of that building has done little to undercut its 19th-c. lure. It contains the roughly 10,000 items that Whitaker found during his exploration and that were uncovered during more recent digs, including a magnificent *statue an auriga**, or charioteers, depicting young man dressed in a long tunic; made marble from Asia Minor (this is almost certainly a Greek original from the 5th c. B.C. probably taken as plunder of war), an eloquent piece of evidence of the continuity ties between western Sicily and the eastern Mediterranean Sea.

Marsala

The survivors of Mozia, which was destroyed by Dionysius II of Syracuse in 3 B.C., took refuge on the nearby promontory of Lilibeo (now Capo Boeo) and, in conjunction with the Elimi and Sicane early cilian tribes that lived here, founded a new settlement, which in fact they named Lilibeo. With the passage of time it became the most important Punic base in Sicily, the point that it was finally their last enclave on the island. The surviving inhabitants wanted it to be – Mozia had been – wealthy and practically impregnable: expanding over an area of roughly 100 hectares, the city was washed on two sides by the waters of the sea and girt strongly, to the landward side, with walls that stood as much as 7 m. in breadth, and by a broad moat (a network of underground passages made it possible to make sudden sorties against besiegers). Sadly, all that survives of the massive defensive works are descriptions by Polybius and Diodorus, because nothing or practically nothing, mains of the original settlement.

The city remained impregnable until 241 B. when the Romans, following their victorious battle of the Ègadi against the Carthaginians, conquered Mozia and made it the chief naval base in the central Mediterranean Sea, well as a stronghold along the routes to Africa.

After a period of decline which was followed by

A clay mask unearthed in the sacred tophet area in Mozia

nquest by the Moors (830), the city be-
me once again the chief port on the
rican routes and the bridgehead for Mus-
immigration to the island; use of the
y's port, which was named "Marsa Alì" or
arsa Allah" (hence, Marsala), encour-
ed renewed growth, with a renovation of
e existing layout in accordance with Is-
nic patterns of settlement.

tween the 12th and the 14th c., the city
urned to the Latin sphere of influence,
nsolidating its medieval layout and re-
ganizing its urban fabric, with the con-
uction of numerous churches, monas-
ies, and convents for the mendicant or-
rs. The city sided with the house of
agon and against the Angevins, and the
agonese – once they seized power – fa-
red Marsala, making it even more im-
rtant as a trading town. Aside from its im-
rtance as a port town, Marsala based its
osperity upon the production of a fertile
terland, which produced in particular
eat and sugar. The flourishing economy
o encouraged a general urban renova-

tion, linked to the city's growing military
might: the city became one of the leading
strongholds in Sicily, and was enclosed
within a perfectly square and symmetrical
enclosure with bastions, inside of which a
cross-roads grid linked the four gates to
the large central square, the Piazza della
Loggia. The city thus created an exemplary
Renaissance model, which was in turn giv-
en a Baroque appearance with the construction and in some cases reconstruction, between the 17th and 18th c., of the
main civil and religious buildings.

Charles V made an extremely ill-advised
decision, in 1575, to block up the port in an
attempt to defend the city from pirate raids:
from that point on, Marsala declined in importance as a great trading center. The little town reappeared in the center stage of
history once again at the time of Garibaldi's
great expedition, which began from a landing at this port.

Marsala (elev. 12 m., pop. 80,177; plan
shown above) is nowadays a thriving farming and manufacturing town, with a monu-

75

mental center of considerable quality, enclosed within a 16th-c. walled square, where many relics survive. On the whole, the historic center is nicely preserved, maintaining a complex of fine homes, avoiding the sort of decay that blights other towns, with concerted efforts to preserve and safeguard the town's important patrimony.

Part of Marsala's fame is tied to the fine liquorous wine by the same name, which comes from a species of grape known as the Vitigno Grillo which, along with the Vitigno Catarratto, dominates the "alberello"-style grapevines that abound in the warm and colorful landscape; we should note, that the success of Marsala wine was the product of the initiative of a number of British entrepreneurs who came here at the end of the 18th c.

It was one of the frequent sirocco tempests that hit the western shores of Sicily that pushed John Woodhouse, in 1773, to seek haven in the port of Marsala. He tasted the local wine and was completely won over; he then shipped a considerable amount to England, adding a little brandy to preserve it during the voyage. His fellow Englishmen were so enthusiastic about the new wine that it immediately began to compete with the prestigious Spanish liquors that were already on the market; like those fortified wines, Marsala could be taken to sea for years without going bad, and it soon became standard fare in the warships of the Royal British Navy.

The Florio wine cellars with barrels of Marsala wine

Via XI Maggio (B2). This road runs along the ancient "càssaro," which may have been laid out as early as Carthaginian times, but which has straightened and realigned during the Baroque period. Among the many sacred and residential buildings (16th/18th c.) which line it, we should make note, just past the Piazza della Repubblica, of the 16th-c. monastery, or *Monastero di S. Pietro*, with a handsome tower with a majolica cusp.

From the Piazza Matteotti, the southeastern terminus of the Via XI Maggio, by following the distinctive little lanes of Marsala, you can reach *S. Matteo* (B2-3), the first Chiesa Matrice of the town, founded in the 11th c. and later rebuilt.

Palazzo Senatorio (B2), or senate building. Overlooking the *Piazza della Repubblica*, heart of the city, this building was erected beginning in 1576, and completed with

façade, with broad arcades and a squa͏͏ tower, or Torre dell'Orologio, in the 18th͏

Duomo (B2), or cathedral. The first stone the Chiesa Madre, dedicated to St. Thom͏ of Canterbury, was laid in 1628 on an ear͏ er (1176) Norman foundation, even thou͏ the imposing façade, adorned with statu͏ and flanked by two small bell towers, w͏ not completed until 1956; the interior, w͏ three broad aisles, punctuated by t͏ columns, is adorned with works of art by t͏ Gagini and their school.

Behind the apsidal area of the Duomo is t͏ tapestry museum, or *Museo degli Arazzi*, ͏ cupying a few specially adapted room͏ and containing eight magnificent Flemish *pestries**, property of the church in th͏ they are a gift of the Archbishop of Messi͏

who in turn had received them from Phi͏ II of Spain.

Museo Archeologico* (B1), or archeolo͏ cal museum. Located in the Baglio Anselr͏ it contains prehistoric materials from t͏ area of Marsala and Mazara del Vallo, c͏ jects from Punic Mozia, finds from the ri͏ necropolises of Lilibeo, as well as artifac͏ from the early-Christian and the mediev͏ city. The jewel of the museum is a **Pun͏ ship*** (the sole example in the world o͏ "liburna," an agile warship roughly 35 m.͏ length), discovered and salvaged by t͏ submarine archeologist Honor Frost in 19͏ it is thought that the ship formed part of t͏ Carthaginian fleet which, in 241 B.C. fac͏ the Roman fleet in the battle of the Èga͏ The wreck is of particular importance b͏ cause it has shown scholars the ship-bui͏ ing technique that was used in Cartha͏ apparently involving prefabricated un͏

...rsala: the Duomo and the town hall

...sembled in the shipyard; no one can yet ...plain, on the other hand, why the nails, ...ough they have remained underwater for ...any centuries, should not have rusted.

...ot far from the Baglio Anselmi stands – ...one – the church of *S. Giovanni Battista*, ...th a Baroque portal; through the interior, ...ou can enter the so-called cave of the Sibyl ...Lilibeo (*Antro della Sibilla Lilibea*); this ...byl, according to legend, lived here and is ...uried here. Visits on request (tel. 0923-...4097).

...sula Romana* (A1), or Roman block. In ...is area, accessible from the Viale Vittorio ...eneto, remains of a quarter of the ancient ...oman city have been unearthed; the most ...ubstantial section of this area comprised ...large *villa* from the 3rd c. A.D., with vari-...us rooms. Adjoining it are the remains of ...*bath building*, with a polychrome mosaic ...oor. In the archeological area, storehous-...., cisterns, and numerous tombs from an ...rly-Christian necropolis have also been ...nearthed.

...azara del Vallo

...et at the mouth of the river Màzaro, and ...verlooking the Canale di Sicilia, this town ...the descendant of a Phoenician trading ...olony (about which we have accounts from ...hucydides; further documentation is pro-...ded by the discovery of coins and tools), ...d a later trading colony that came from ...elinunte. They continued to flourish un-...er Roman rule, when the population be-...ame quite heterogeneous; that last quality ...a constant in the history of this city, open ...o a wide range of exchanges and cohabita-...ons, with the greatest mutual respect.

...ne of the happiest periods in the history of ...is town came under Moorish rule: the ...loors began their invasion of Sicily with a ...nding at Mazara, which they made the ...apital of one of the three administrative dis-...icts ("valli") into which they divided the is-...nd.

...ith the advent of the Normans, the city was ...ade an episcopal see, and the fortified

castle, or Castello – of which only the ruins of the portal still survive, following the de-molition done after the unification of Italy to build the platform of a promenade near the sea – constitutes the defensive bulwarks of the walls that form a square around the en-tire city; in each side of that square there is a gate (Porta Palermo, Porta Mokarta, Por-ta Salaria, and Porta Cartagine; in 1696 an-other gate was added, the Porta Salvatore). It was also during Norman domination that the cathedral, or Cattedrale, the church of S. Nicolò Regale, and the little church of S. Maria della Giummare (or Madonna dell'Al-to) were all built.

The importance of the clergy in this city can be seen in the continuous construction of ecclesiastical buildings tied to the various religious orders, who pushed in the 17th and 18th c. for a new equilibrium of the urban-istic components with the Baroque recon-struction on the main squares, first among them the Piazza Maggiore (now Piazza del-la Repubblica), leaving perfectly visible, however, the road grid of the Muslim layout of the town.

Mazara del Vallo (elev. 8 m., pop. 47,750) is nowadays not only a major farming town; it is also one of the largest and best-equipped fishing ports in Italy; work related to that sector of the economy has caused the resi-dential section of town to 'explode,' but the old center, happily, was spared; here, the labyrinth of lanes and little streets – which often take their names from ancient guilds or from the trades – blind alleys, little arch-es, and courtyards is reminiscent of the general layout of the cities on the other side of the narrow channel. The geograph-ic location of this town, so close to Africa, makes it an ideal bridgehead to that conti-nent, as well as one of the liveliest and most bustling cities in all of Sicily.

Overlooking the Baroque *Piazza della Re-pubblica* (C2), is the *Seminario dei Chierici*, a porticoed structure with a broad loggia above (1710), housing the Diocesan Museum and an interesting Library with 17th-c. texts, and the bishop's palace, or *Palazzo Vesco-vile*, built in 1596 but restructured at the be-ginning of the 18th c. Blocking off the east-ern side of the square is the side of the cathedral, or **Cattedrale***, founded in 1093 and rebuilt in 1690-94; over the portal, note the relief depicting *Count Roger* (Conte Rug-gero) *on horseback, trampling a Muslim* (1534). The presbytery contains a *Transfig-uration** by Antonino Gagini (1537) amidst stuccoes by the Ferraro family.

Between the Cattedrale and the Lungomare Mazzini extends the park, or *Giardino Pub-*

blico Jolanda (C-D2), on the site of the long-since destroyed Norman castle; of the castle all that survives is an *arch* overlooking the bustling *Piazza Mokarta*, backbone of the city's growth in the 19th and 20th c., at the southern edge of the ancient city.

From Piazza della Repubblica, the Via XX Settembre leads to *Piazza del Plebiscito* (C1-2), where it is possible to observe the Baroque façade of the *church of S. Ignazio*, dating from the early 18th c. The adjoining *Collegio dei Gesuiti* contains the **Museo Civico**, or civic museum, with Roman archeological finds, fine medieval sculptures (*elephants bearing pillars* in the Muslim style of the 12th c., *little pillar-bearing lions*), sculptures and drawings by Pietro Consagra.

If you follow the canal-port along the Molo Caito you will reach the **little church of S. Nicolò Regale** (B1), a Norman building dating back to 1124, with a square plan and three apses. Not far off is the important *canal-port* (A-B1), constituted by the estuary of the river Màzaro.

You can then enter the *Via Bagno* (B2), which was the main street of the Muslim city and the thoroughfare of the medieval trading quarter, serving as a link between countryside and port. Then you may take the *Via dei Goti* (B2), in the heart of the working-class residential district, that is still strongly marked by Moorish urban features; go to the **church of S. Michele** (B-C2), adjoining the Benedictine convent. Founded in the 11th c. and rebuilt in 1637, it has a lavish interior, decorated with marble-work and stuccoes, and with twenty allegorical statues by the school of Serpotta (1697).

The Via S. Michele leads to the **church of S. Veneranda** (C2), with a spectacular Baroque façade dating from 1714, set on a Norman plan. If you pass the *Casa Scuderi* (in Via Pino), with the remains of a cylindrical 15th-c. tower and a little portal in the "plateresco" style, you will reach the *Via Garibaldi* (C2), the main business street of the historic center, along which you can return to the Piazza della Repubblica.

Castelvetrano

This large farming town – specializing in olives and grapes – (elev. 187 m., pop. 30,272) took its origin from the ancient early Siciliar populace of "Legum" (in the area of Piazza Garibaldi a major necropolis from prior to the Greek period was uncovered in the 19th c.) and, later, from the colonies of veterans from Selinunte brought here to guard foodstuffs (hence the Latin name of "Castrum veteranorum"). The earliest in-

formation that we have concerning settl ment in this area, following the Greek pe od, dates back only to the 12th c., when v have documentation concerning a lar farmhouse built during the period of Moc ish colonization. The grid of the historic center, with its complex and intricate urb structure, is indicative of the successi superimposition of two different urban mc els: one is radial, and dates back earlier, the medieval formation of the inhabite center; the other has crisscrossing gric with large square lots, cut by an endless a ray of blind alleys and courtyards, a clear dication of the Islamic urban tradition.

Of the monuments here (Castelvetrano ha a considerable outpouring of art, especia ly in the 17th c.), we should mention: on t Piazza Garibaldi, in the heart of the litt town, the **Chiesa Madre**, which was beg in 1520 and completed in 1579; the *Palaz Pignatelli*, built in the 13th c. but conside ably renovated over time; the *church of t Purgatorio*, built in 1642 on the site of an o religious building, and now housing the A ditorium "Lorenzo Perosi"; the delightf fountain, or *Fontana della Ninfa* (Orazio N grone, 1615), which adorns Piazza Umbe to I (facing the left side of the Chiesa Madre Along the straight thoroughfare of V Garibaldi, which runs off to the south fro the central square, you can reach – by fe lowing the Via Francesco la Croce – t civic museum, or **Museo Civico**, which co tains archeological finds from Selinun and paintings and sculpture from churche that are no longer in use (alabaster *statue the Virgin Mary with Christ Child*, by th workshop of Francesco Laurana, 1467).

In the Piazza Regina Margherita, which reached, from Via Garibaldi, by the Via Fr Pantaleo, stands the *church of S. Domenic* built beginning in 1470 but later renovate (inside, the presbytery and the choir are b decked with lavish decorations in frescoe and stuccoed terracotta). Across from th church stands the *church of S. Giovan Battista*, founded in 1589 and renovate heavily in 1797-1802 (in a niche in the pre bytery, note the marble *statue of John th Baptist*, signed by Antonello Gagini and da ed 1522).

It is worth taking a short detour (3.5 km.) to th west to see the **church of the SS. Trinità Delia**, a fine and beautiful piece of Norma Moorish architecture, set in the pleasant gree ery of a handsome park: dating back to th 12th c., the church presents a square mas crowned by a little red cupola in the Mooris style; around the windows, as the sole decor tive motif, run smooth cornices.

linunte*

e name of this town comes from the
me of the river that flows to the west of
e ancient city, the "Selinon" (now the riv-
Modione); this name in its turn comes
m the Greek name for wild parsley ("seli-
n"), which grows abundantly on the site
this settlement, and which was a symbol
the city, as is shown by the ancient coins
Selinunte. Thucydides and Diodorus Sicu-
tell us that Selinunte was founded, under
e leadership of Pammilos, by the colonists
m Megara Hyblea (it is still uncertain
ether that was in 628 or 650 B.C.), be-
ming the westernmost Greek colony in
ily. Originally an ally of Carthage and, fol-
ving the battle of Himera, with Syracuse,
s town enjoyed sudden and vigorous
wth that soon put it on a collision course

Harris and Samuel Angell, who discovered
the metopes that once decorated the temples, now housed in the archeological museum, or Museo Archeologico of Palermo,
along with other notable finds.
The archeological complex of Selinunte (plan
on pag. 80) is divided into four zones: the
acropolis, the ancient city, the eastern temples, and the Sanctuary of Malophoros. Instead of beginning the tour from the southern edge of the acropolis – where the temples
stand – we recommend climbing directly up
to the immense fortifications that separate
the acropolis from the site of the ancient city,
and then to climb down to the Sanctuary of
Malophoros and, lastly, to visit the majestic
remains of the religious buildings.

The ancient city (A1-2). Located on the hill

ne of the magnificent Selinunte temples, evidence of the city's great past history

th Segesta over disputes concerning ter-
ory and rivalries; it was defeated brutal-
and destroyed by Segesta, allied for this
casion with Carthage, in 409 B.C., in one
the most terrible massacres of the an-
ent world, a destruction which was com-
eted, at the end of the first Punic war, by
e Romans, who tore down the few hous-
that remained standing. In the Christian-
zantine and Moorish era, small groups of
ople continued to live in the acropolis,
t in the Middle Ages, even the name of
linunte was lost, buried under the ruins
a terrible earthquake, which wiped out
e last few remaining structures.
was only the middle of the 16th c. when
e Dominican monk Fazello correctly iden-
ied the area of the old city; excavations
d not begin however until 1823, at the
ging of two English archeologists, William

of Manuzza, to the north of the acropolis,
only recently has this section been the object of campaigns of digging, campaigns
that have unearthed a road and the ruins of
various homes; after the destruction in 409
B.C., much of the settlement must have
been used as a necropolis by the survivors
of Selinunte who still lived on the acropolis.

Acropoli* (B1-2), or acropolis. This acropolis stands on an irregularly shaped ledge
sloping slightly down toward the sea, and
overlooking a long stretch of sea in one of
the most alluring areas of all of the Mediterranean coast of Sicily . The enclosure walls
that surround it, and which we still see today, admittedly renovated repeatedly, was
built between the end of the sixth and the
beginning of the 5th c. B.C., making use of
materials from previous defensive works,

systematically razed to the ground. Well preserved, on the other hand, are a *gate* that has been sealed up, on the eastern side of the enclosure wall, and the *northern gate* at the end of the long road that cuts lengthwise across the center of the acropolis. The plateau is in fact crossed by two thoroughfares that intersect at right-angles, dividing the enclosed area within the walls into four quarters. This area contains, aside from many public and religious buildings, five temples, overlooking the river Gorgo di Cottone and the port – now filled in – which lay at the river's mouth; because of the limited excavations that have been done there and the extent of the devastation, the ruins have still not yet been completely explored and analyzed (each temple is still indicated by letters of the alphabet, since we still do not know exactly to which deity each was dedicated).

The *temple D*, built at the end of the 6th c. B.C. and possibly dedicated to Poseidon or to Aphrodite, had six columns on the short sides and thirteen columns on the longer sides, with the entrance facing east, as in all the other temples.

Not far away is the *temple C*, the oldest temple (middle of the 6th c. B.C.) of all those on the acropolis and, most probably dedicated to Apollo; in 1925-26 14 columns on the northern front were rebuilt and re-erected (it had respectively 6 and 17 per side); this temple is now practically a symbol of Selinunte; a number of metopes from the trabeation and the colossal gorgon's mask from the pediment are now in the regional museum, or Museo Regionale di Palermo.

Next, heading south, you will find the lit temple B, dating from the Hellenistic peri and possibly dedicated to Empedocles, t famous scientist and philosopher of Ag gento, who is thought to have overse the project of draining the water from S nunte.

The *temples A* and *O* – which are very cl together and so exceedingly similar in th hexastyle peripteros plan that it is thoug that they were dedicated to Castor and P lux – are more recent; they were in fa built between 490 and 480 B.C.

If you head down, from the westernmost tremity of the chief transverse street in acropolis, to the river Modione, you can tou on the right bank of that river – the less-th spectacular, but exceedingly important ruins the ancient **sanctuary of the Malophoros** B1), dedicated to Demeter – goddess of ferti and harvests, and here described as a bearer apples or pomegranates – and comprising small altar, a large altar for sacrifices, the temp well known in antiquity, this place of worship s vived the decline of the city itself, used first the Carthaginians and later hosting Christ and Byzantine communities. The importance this complex, which still poses many diffic problems, lies in the remarkable nature of the tive offerings that have been found here (lit steles crowned with pairs of human heads, c beside the other) and the fact that a part of population that coexisted here was not Gree

The eastern temples* (A-B3). Probably s rounded by a single enclosure wall, the are the most imposing temples of Se nunte and they give some idea of the wea and importance of this Greek settleme in the 6th c. B.C.

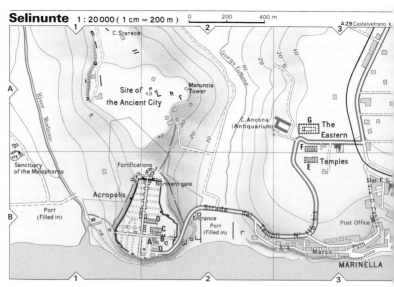

berto Burri's "Labirinto" and the remains of a house devastated by an earthquake

ᴉe *temple G**, commonly thought to be a
ᴉmple of Zeus, is one of the largest temples
classical antiquity (110.36 X 50.1 m.) and
ᴉas never completed (its construction, un-
ᴉrtaken around 550 B.C., was probably
ᴉt complete at the time of the destruc-
ᴉn of the city): we have evidence of this in
e variations in style (archaic in the east-
n front, classical in the western front)
at occurred as it was being built. From the
ᴉormous mass of ruins, there now emerges
ᴉly a single colossal column, restored in
ᴉ32, standing 16 m. tall and measuring 3.5
. in diameter.
ᴉ the right of the road lie the ruins of the
ᴉmple F, the smallest one (61.8 X 24.43 m.)
ᴉd the one that has been most severely
undered; it may have been dedicated to
ᴉhena and was built in the archaic style be-
ᴉeen 560 and 540 B.C. The nearby *temple
***, in a very pure Doric style (5th c. B.C.),
ᴉas dedicated to Hera (Juno); a hexastyle
ᴉeripteros (67.7 X 25.3 m.), it was rebuilt in
ᴉe middle of the 1950s, and now looms
ᴉainst the landscape of Selinunte creating
though the restoration is questionable –
remarkable and striking effect.

ibellina
ᴉhis town is a symbol of the tragedy of the
ᴉèlice, destroyed by an earthquake in the
ᴉght between 14 and 15 January 1968;
ᴉibellina (elev. 227 m., pop. 5,027) was re-
ᴉuilt at a distance of 18 km. from the rubble
ᴉ the ancient town, founded in the Middle
ᴉges. The emblem of the new town is a
ᴉar, a metal colossus built in 1980 by Pietro
ᴉonsagra and set at the entrance to the
ᴉew town.
ᴉhe new town of Gibellina was conceived as
ᴉcity-qua-museum, in which works of con-
ᴉmporary art are displayed along the
ᴉads, along a regular urban grid, serving to

alleviate the desolation of the aftermath of
the earthquake. Some of the leading contemporary artists were asked to contribute,
among them many Sicilians (Consagra,
Fausto Melotti, Giuseppe Uncini, Nino
Franchina): each tried to offer a personal
contribution to the difficult task of the
recreation of a once lovely town. Other artworks by contemporary masters, especially Sicilians, are on exhibit in the *Museo Civico* in the Viale Segesta. Among those artists,
we should mention Renato Guttuso, Fausto
Pirandello, Antonio Sanfilippo, and Mario
Schifano.
In accordance with a project by Alberto
Burri the **ruins of Gibellina**, destroyed by
the earthquake, have been progressively
covered with a giant slab of white cement:
a vast sheet spread over the landscape,
apparently uniform but actually lacerated
by a number of openings, each of which
leads into a labyrinthine network of paths
that correspond to the grid of roads of the
little medieval village.
The ruins of ancient Gibellina now host,
each summer, performances of the
Oresteia: this is a theatrical project of considerable scope, which sinks its roots into
the mythology of Mediterranean culture, a
mythology which is represented through
ancient, modern, and contemporary texts.

Salemi
The Elimi were the first inhabitants of this
site, and the city built on these highlands is
probably the town of Alicia, about which
Diodorus Siculus wrote (where the ruins of
the apse of the Chiesa Matrice now stand,
once stood the acropolis on which was
erected a temple to Venus). This was the
theater of conflict between Selinunte and
Segesta, fighting in alliance with the latter
beginning in the 8th c. B.C., and the town

flourished in particular under Moorish rule; it was the Moors who gave the town a new name: "Salem," place of delights. The reconstruction of the castle, or Castello (13th c.) and the settlement of mendicant orders of monks here (12th-16th c.) encouraged the reorganization of the city's layout, culminating in the construction of the Jesuit college, or Collegio Gesuitico, and many other palazzi.

One's first encounter with Salemi (elev. 446 m., pop. 12,321) takes place, from the Piano di S. Francesco, along the spiral climb up to the top of the hill. The finely calibrated Moorish layout, with remarkably complex blind alleys, which lead into increasingly secluded little courtyards, and steep staircases on the brink of exceedingly steep slopes; the monumental right-angled construction of the Jesuit complex, with its dense accompanying array of churches and patrician residences; the looming presence of the castle, or Castello, still seemingly jutting out to embrace the fragments of the city walls; the majestic ruins of what was once the cathedral, or Duomo, until the earthquake devastated it; and from there the mind's eye ranges down to the silent wreckage of the quarter, or Quartiere del Carmine on the slope behind the apse and the new area in which reconstruction was done, downhill from the old center of town: these are the features that characterize the town, not entirely torn apart by the earthquake, in part thanks to the considerable work that has been put into restoration.

In the higher section of the little town, next to the presbytery of the cathedral, or *Duomo* (rebuilt in 1615-1764 and destroyed by the earthquake), stands the castle, or *Castello*, dominated by the tall mass of the round tower, in which it is possible to make out the Swabian-Norman style (it was rebuilt, atop an existing structure, by Frederick II)

and the traces of long history of destructi and transformation. The college of the J suits, or **Collegio dei Gesuiti**, although it d abolish once and for all the continuity of tl Muslim urban fabric (in order to build it 1600 an entire medieval quarter had to l demolished), gave the urban setting strong addition of monumentality, whi takes on a theatrical flavor in the façade the *church of the Collegio*. The compl contains the civic museum, or *Museo Ci co*, with its artworks rescued from the ru ble of shattered churches, which collapse in the earthquake, and a collection of so venirs and memorabilia of the Risorgime to (1870).

Calatafimi

The name of this town is of Moorish orig (from "Kalat al-Phini"), though the Islam village stood around a Byzantine fortres the Castrum Phimes (castle of Euphymius Populated by Berber peasants attracted l the richness of the surrounding farmland Calatafimi was conquered by the Norma army, and became part of the royal estat the house of Aragon was responsible for tl reconstruction of the castle and the encl sure walls of the town. When it became feudal landholding of the counts, or Conti Mòdica, it grew, encouraged by the arriv of the mendicant orders, flinging up ne quarters inside and around the walled are Further development took place betwee the 15th and 16th c., when the chief tho oughfare (Via XV Maggio), which links tl two monumental focal points of the Chies Madre and the church of S. Michele, was e tended in both directions along its axis: the northeast, toward the sanctuary, c Santuario della Madonna del Giubino, forr ing the Rua Grande (Via Garibaldi); and the southeast (Via Mazzini-Corso Vittor Emanuele) along the axis linking it up witl

Splendid views may be enjoyed from the Greek theatre of Segesta

e territory of Bèlice. The earthquake of
8 here too caused considerable dam-
e, both in the architectural heritage and
the lesser structures; the subsequent
n for the reconstruction and improve-
nt of the historic center has not yet been
ly implemented. The chief monuments of
latafimi (elev. 338 m., pop. 7,636) are:
e *church of S. Michele*, rebuilt in the 16th
the *Chiesa Madre*, founded in the 12th c.
d enlarged in the 16th c.; the so-called
nto Romano, a remarkable name (liter-
y, 'Roman weeping') for this ossuary-
onument built just outside of the town, in
mmemoration of the battle against the
urbon army, resulting in Garibaldi's vic-
ry on 15 May 1860. But this little town is
rth visiting, especially for the Festa di Pri-
vera or Festa del Crocifisso, which takes
ce 3rd May and is one of the most au-
entic Sicilian popular festivals, celebrat-
in commemoration of a number of mirac-
ous events, tied to an ancient Crucifix,
ich occurred in 1657.

gesta*

is was, along with present-day Èrice, one
the chief settlements of the Elimi, a peo-
e of uncertain origins (Thucydides said
at they were the product of a mix of local
pulations with fugitives from Troy and
ocaea; Vergil wrote that Segesta was
nded by the Trojan hero, Aeneas). Of
ehistoric origin, Segesta (or "Eghesta," ac-
rding to the Greeks) extends over the
pes of the Monte Bàrbaro, at an elevation
304 m., in a strategic location, overlook-
g a vast territory. The main chapter of its
story has to do with its conflicts with
linunte over the border, marked by the
per course of the river Màzaro; conflicts
at, beginning in the 6th c. B.C., were ulti-
ately fatal to Selinunte. Destroyed by the
rant of Syracuse, Agathocles, inasmuch as
was an ally of Carthage (end of the 4th c.
C.), Segesta found new wealth and pros-
rity, in part thanks to the trading port of
stellammare, which was particularly im-
rtant during Roman times; then there
sued a slow decline, ending with devas-
tion by Vandals and Saracens.
the ancient town, still being excavated,
me traces remain: the ruins of a number
square towers and of a gate from the old
rtifications.
iraculously intact, on the other hand, is
e **temple****, a hexastyle peripteros (61.15
26.25 m.) in the purest Doric style, which
r the past 2,400 years has stood, solemn
d imposing, on a hill to the west of the
onte Bàrbaro, in a sere and deserted land-

scape that emphasizes the grandeur of the structure. Scholars still debate the function that the temple was meant to serve (the only open-structure temple known in the ancient world) and why it seems to have been left unfinished: one of the hypotheses is that the Elimi built it with a view to making magnificent a sacred area in which indigenous religious rituals were performed, intentionally leaving it open to the elements; others believe that construction was interrupted because of the war that broke out with Selinunte in 416 B.C. (this is now the most widely held hypothesis, even though on the interior of the peristyle there is no trace of the cella in which the rites were celebrated. The **theater***, which dates back to roughly the middle of the 3rd c. B.C., stands right on the top of the mount, at an elevation of 400 m., in a location overlooking the urban setting; it has one notable characteristic: unlike the other buildings of the same sort, it faces north, and this is probably so that it would offer an enchanting view of the hills and the distant sea. Little or nothing remains of the scaena, which must have been adorned with pillars and columns; under the scaena a number of excavations have unearthed the remains of existing constructions, which date back to the 10th/9th c. B.C. In summer, classic dramas are performed in the theater.

Segesta gave its name to the hot springs, or *Terme Segestane*, which can be reached by turning off from the state road 113 in the direction of Àlcamo. The springs, which were already known in Moorish times, pour forth on both banks of the river Caldo, as well as inside a grotto which has formed a sort of natural sauna (the steam reaches a temperature of 38 degrees Celsius); the sulfurous waters sulfuree (45 degrees Celsius) are used for baths, mudpacks, and inhalations.

Àlcamo

The old Arabic name, which is the origin of the modern name, was "Manzil Alqamah," which means 'station of the lotus fruit.' This large farming town lies on one of the main roads linking Palermo with Trapani, in the heart of a broad valley abounding in vineyards, in a territory that – in Moorish times – boasted three large farm complexes corresponding to three fortified strongholds. Under the Normans, Àlcamo became part of a large feudal holding, controlled first by the Peralta family, and later by the Chiaramonte and the Ventimiglia families. The oldest core of the present-day town still has the original 14th-c. urban grid laid out by the latter family: an orderly plan of streets at right-angles and regular blocks with a crossroads; at the extremities of those roads stood the main urban and architectural complexes of the 14th c.: the castle, or Castello to the south, the market square, or Piazza del Mercato to the north, the convent, or Convento dei Francescani to the east, and the Chiesa Madre to the west.

The insertion into the urban fabric of numerous religious orders (15th/17th c.) encouraged the development of the city, which is divided into quarters and which extends, beyond the medieval enclosure walls, in a westerly direction along the extension of the chief thoroughfare (Corso VI Aprile). The center of the Baroque section, then, was the Piano Maggiore (Piazza Ciullo), which lies almost as a hinge linking the old center and the new expansion, consolidated – with the construction of the church of the Collegio – into the function of city center that it still serves.

This city (elev. 258 m., pop. 42,621; plan shown below) underwent a chaotic urban development, that, even though it preserved the basic urban characteristics, in fact marked the slow decline of the historic city, with the creation of the new res-

idential quarters that have spread the s[...] tlement all the way out to the slopes of [...] Monte Bonifato.

The elongated *Piazza Ciullo* (B2), on[...] known as the Piano Maggiore, is the cen[...] of life in this little town, opening onto t[...] western section of the since-demolish[...] 16th-c. walls. Here stands the *church o[...] Oliva*, built in 1723 by Giovanni Biagio A[...] ico on an existing structure dating fr[...] the 16th c.

At the southern edge of this plaza was bu[...] in 1648, the *church of the Collegio* (B2), [...] joining the complex of the Jesuits, wit[...] harmonious façade with friezes, stucco[...] and sculptures. If you continue past t[...] church along the Via Mazzini, you will rea[...] the enormous *Piazza della Repubblica* [...] C2), which has been turned into a gard[...] Closing it off to the north is the castle, [...] **Castello dei Conti di Mòdica**, built in t[...] higher section of the town during the 14[...] c. It has a rhomboid plan and cylindri[...] towers, with parallelepiped towers at t[...] corners; on the northern elevation, the[...] are traces of twin- and triple-light mullion[...] windows, in the Catalonian Gothic sty[...] and a splendid rose window. The cas[...]

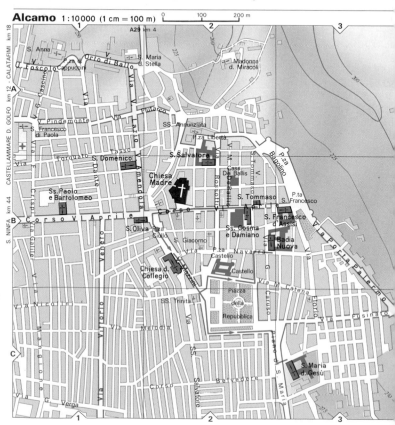

Alcamo 1:10000 (1 cm = 100 m)

14th century castle in Àlcamo

l house an ancient library and the Ethno-
phical and Contemporary Art Museums.

er crossing the square, you can cross the Pi-
S. Maria, to the *church of S. Maria del Gesù*
), possibly founded in the 15th c., enlarged in
7, and rebuilt in 1762.

m the Piazza Castello, within the area of the
lled "borgo," the Via Navarra leads to the
rch of the Badia Nuova (B2-3), designed by
vanni Biagio Amico; it contains allegorical
tues by Giacomo Serpotta.

uching the Piazza Ciullo to the north is
Corso VI Aprile (B1-3), the ancient "stra-
imperiale," or "imperial road," a funda-
ntal axis of the historical center, marked
late-Baroque and Neoclassical architec-
re. If you follow the "corso" to the east,
u will find, on the Piazza IV Novembre, the
iesa Madre (B2), founded in the 14th c.
d rebuilt in 1669; all that survives of the
iginal structure is the campanile, with
illioned windows and a handsome marble
rtal.

the intersection with the Via Rossotti, in
e heart of the village, which was founded
the 14th/16th c., stands the *church of the
Angelo Custode* (B2), rebuilt to plans by
ovanni Biagio Amico. On the Via Mari-
o De Ballis stands the *Casa De Ballis*
2), a handsome Gothic building that pre-
rves its 16th-c. tower, adorned with triple-
ht mullioned windows, as well as a jutting
t of bracketed parapets.

rther along on the "corso," we should
ention: on the left, the *church of S. Tom-
aso* (B2), a noteworthy example of 15th-c.
chitecture, with a lavish Gothic portal; on
e right, the Baroque *church of the Ss. Co-
a e Damiano* (B2), adjoining the
onastery of S. Chiara, built in 1721 to
ans by Giuseppe Mariani.

Castellammare del Golfo

This town was founded as a trading center
for the two Elimi towns Segesta and Èrice;
during the high Middle Ages, under Moorish
rule, it became an impregnable stronghold,
with a fortress perched on a promontory
jutting over the sea. It was the Moors who
gave the center its new role – dubbing it "Al-
Madarig" (meaning, the steps), possibly after a particularly steep street – as a major
trading station at the confluence of routes
leading inland, establishing cargo loading facilities and a tuna-fishing station ("tonnara"). This little town, which became prosperous under the rule of the house of
Aragon (1281-1410) chiefly through trade in
wheat, experienced further growth with
the development, behind the castle, or
Castello, of an ancillary village, or "borgo":
founded in 1560, it was enclosed by walls
and a ditch and organized along a thoroughfare that ran lengthwise. The urban
expansion that took place between 1600
and 1800 was also considerable, and at first
followed a model of a crossroads, and later
with a system of streets and blocks that
extended up to the slopes of the mountain.
The town (elev. 26 m., pop. 13,515), set in
the lovely gulf, or Golfo di Castellammare
and at the foot of a high and harsh mountain
banked with luxuriant vegetation, slopes
gently down to the sea, as far as the little
peninsula where, between two magnificent
sandy beaches, the castle, or *Castello*,
stands, renovated in Norman and Swabian
times and then rebuilt entirely under the
house of Aragon. Among the religious build-

The entrance to the Scurati caves

The splendid bay of Scopello with its old tuna-fishing station and rock stacks

ings here, we should mention the 18th-c. *Chiesa Madre* and the *little church of the Rosario*, widely known as the church of the "Madonna di l'Agnuni," with a handsome 16th-c. portal. From 19-21st August the very popular festival of Maria SS. del Soccorso, with the evocative sea procession.

Preserve, or Riserva dello Zingaro*

From Scopello to San Vito lo Capo there are a number of kilometers of coastline that still conceal uncontaminated nooks and crannies: coves, stack formations, coastal towers, and, above all, one of the last remaining areas of Mediterranean vegetation; here, thanks to a massive effort on the part of ecological organizations and public opinion, there was established, in 1981, over an area covering some 1,600 hectares, a regional natural preserve, or *Riserva Naturale Regionale*, a paradise for those who love nature and crags looming over the sea. The vegetation is that found in hot arid climes: lentisk bushes, carob plants, patches of euphorbia, broom, olive trees, dwarf palms, which, despite their names, can grow to be as tall as two meters. In terms of the fauna, the existence of appropriate ecological niches has encouraged the presence of numerous animals, some forty species of birds (peregrine falcons, kestrels, and buzzards); and then rabbits, porcupines, and foxes. Of great biological value are the seabeds off the shores of the protected areas, which present interesting phytobentonic habitats.

At the edge of the preserve is **Scopello** (elev. 106 m.), a small peasant village, which was built around an 18th-c. "baglio," on the site of an older Moorish hamlet, and

renowned for its tuna-fishing station, whi is documented as far back as the turn of t 13th c., and active until recent times. T development of the town as a beach reso has made Scopello a fashionable destinati for vacationers, who crowd it during t summer, and for the people of Palerm during the weekends.

Monte Còfano

This dolomitic promontory looms far abo the sea, and was for a long period a func mental point along the route followed Phoenician ships from the islands of Èga to Palermo. Human settlements around th promontory and the bay certainly da back, however, to the Paleolithic, as shown by a number of shards, amphora and crockery found both on the seabe and in the cave dwellings of Grotta Ma giapane, at the foot of the mount, and at Sc rati. The area of the Còfano was populate in Phoenician, early-Christian, and Norma Moorish times, as is shown by the tow that overlooks the slope of Castelluzzo. The landscape is truly African, with the o casional fig tree, carob, and lentisk tre the only patches of greenery save for th distinctive dwarf palm trees; breaking u the enormous allure of the environme are the great cuts in the earth, made to e tract the marble of Custonaci, especially c the slope facing Valderice.

The nearby town of **San Vito lo Capo** (ele 6 m., pop. 3,567), a lovely tourist attra tion and beach resort, was, even in Roma times, an important maritime port; ev dence is offered by the basins used for fis farming, ruins of which can be seen near th "tonnara" of S. Vito.

Agrigento, the Agrigentino, and the islands of Pelagie

charm of the landscape of southern Sicily consists of its colors, which are made more liant and sharply drawn by the intense light of the sun, which shapes these lands, differentiating them from the northern regions. The hills, which are an almost uniform en in the springtime, turn an array of colors, in summer and fall, that run from the gold-yellow of ripe wheat to the dark brown of freshly turned soil, contrasting sharply with blue of the sky.

ng the sea, the hilly cliffs, eroded by the wind, form a coastline with very few natural ts, and therefore poorly suited to the construction of ports. This was the main reason y the ancient Greeks waited so long before colonizing the area (the center of which was igento), and were only driven to do so by the need to better monitor and control the bitions of Carthage. And it was precisely, and paradoxically, the failure of the city to de-op toward the coast, due to the lack of a structure so fundamental to communications a port that allowed the preservation, in Agrigento, of Sicily's richest archeological trea-e. Serving as a counterpoint to the only two major coastal towns Sciacca, at the west-most extremity of this area, and Licata, at the opposite extreme, are the many rural set-ments in the hinterland, founded between the 15th and 17th c., high atop hills and mounts d in the center of vast feudal landholdings, overseeing the cultivation of the interior, in tain cases, working the sulphur mines.

ile wheat was once the leading agricultural duct, it is now an excellent table grape, own as the "Italia," which is allowed to ripen wly until late winter, protected by heavy plas-sheets. Following the crisis brought about by closure of the sulphur mines ("zolfatare") d by the drop in demand for wheat, the farm-economy is slowly recovering, in part be-se of the establishment of cooperative associa-ns. One common characteristic found throughout territory, with the possible exception of Eraclea Mi-a, is a wide array of reflections of Arab culture. We d these reflections in the very names of the towns, en those of recent foundation; in the structure of the es and the courtyards in the older quarters, de-ned to shelter from the heat of the sun and the blast of the sirocco; in the techniques irrigating the fields, and even in the character of the popolation. And once again, we clear-see, in this entirely Sicilian area, a frontier between the Arab world and Europe.

Greek vase on display at the Museo Archeologico Regionale

1 Agrigento**

you look at Agrigento from the hill of the mples (Collina dei Templi), the modern ildings that serve as a backdrop to the aces between the columns almost seem if there has been a massive develop-ent in recent times, perhaps as a logical ntinuation of the ancient magnificence of e city. Instead, there is a sharp hiatus tween the present-day city and the city of e past: the present-day city is distracted d listless, caught in a world that it would kind to call provincial, cut out of the ain Sicilian routes, and turned in on itself; e ancient city, preserved for our admira-n as if by a miracle, still imparts its vo-

cation to open toward the outer world. But the hiatus, the gap, is in space and in time, but it is primarily in culture, the same gap described unhappily by Pirandello and de-nounced in anger by Sciascia.

The territory of Agrigento has been inhab-ited ever since prehistoric times, as is shown by the discoveries from an Aene olithic site at Serraferlicchio, while the ear-liest signs of a Greek presence date back to the 7th c. B.C. (necropolis of Montelusa, on the coast, to the west of San Leone), al-though it was not until 581 B.C. that the peo-ple of Gela, together with a group of Greeks from the homeland, founded "Akragas" –

this was one of the last Greek colonies in Sicily – locating it midway between Gela and Selinunte, controlling the coast that overlooked Africa, thus providing protection for the rest of Sicily against Carthaginian invasion. Between 570 and 555 B.C. Phalaris, the first tyrant of the city built the first enclosure walls (much of which can still be seen), establishing the shape and size of the original urban core; the first years of settlement were marked by conflict with Carthage. Once the Carthaginians had been eliminated – albeit temporarily – in 480 B.C., in the battle of "Himera," one hundred years after its foundation "Akragas" was able to expand its dominion as far as the Tyrrhenian Sea; the territorial boundaries to the east and west were marked respectively by the course of the rivers Salso and Plàtani; in this period, documents record that the city had a population of roughly 200,000, including many illustrious thinkers, artists, and scientists (suffice it to mention Empedocles), with the construction at almost the same time of the splendid temples on the southern hill, as well as the completion of the acropolis on the Rupe Atenea and on the northwestern heights.

In 406 B.C., "Akragas" fell to yet another attack by the Carthaginians, who conquered it and held it until 310 B.C.; in that year, the Corinthian statesman and general Timoleon, in his plan to liberate Sicily, moved on the town from Syracuse, retook it, and restored a regime of Greek democracy; the ruins of the so-called Hellenistic and Roman quarter are clear evidence of the economic and social rebirth that the city experienced after this.

The Romans, who settled here permanently in 210 B.C., renamed it "Agrigentum," and renewed the entire sector of farming and trade, laying the foundations for the major trading port that this town was later to become, during the Byzantine era. Toward the end of the 7th c., the inhabitants left their homes in the valley and moved up to the top of the acropolis, in a mass migratory process that scholars are still unable to explain fully. This settlement constituted the core around which was built the Moorish city, which as early as the 9th c. had been proclaimed capital of the Berbers in Sicily, with the name of "Gergenti": aside from the name, which was slightly altered to Girgenti, the city preserved into the 20th c. numerous place names that originated during the Moorish occupation (Via Bac Bac, Porta Bibbiria, Quartiere del Rabato), as well as the twisting lanes and the charming courtyards.

The 11th c., with the arrival of the Normans – who did not hinder, and indeed en-couraged trade with North Africa – wa time that witnessed the reaffirmatior the role of Girgenti in the interior of Si and in the control of the stretch of sea tween Sicily and Africa. The ensuing grov of the "borgo," or village, was halted the depopulation caused by the foun tion of numerous farming towns in the I terland; a project that was begun in 15th c. and perpetuated until the 18th when the bishop Lorenzo Gioieni stre ously promoted a substantial social rec ery, that was to lead to a shift of the m thoroughfare of the city from the Via D mo to the Via Atenea. In the first half of 19th c., with the construction of the new enue, or Viale della Vittoria, work beg on the expansion that pushed outward fr the Porta di Ponte, an ancient obstacle stopping point on the Via Atenea, wh was then demolished and replaced wit sort of propylaeum. During that century, initial phase of stagnation in new constr tion was followed by a period of chac development, of wildcat construction th did not end even in the aftermath of t great landslide of 1966, which tore aw part of the old town, as well as part of t new development, reminding Italy's natio culture, – and not just that of the urb planners – that there were serious pro lems in the south, and grave problems co cerning the use which was being made of t south's environmental and cultural herita A walking tour of Agrigento (elev. 230 r pop. 55,283; plans on pages 89 and 93) I gins in the Valley of the Temples (Valle c Templi), in which the succession from ea to west of the religious buildings represer the most accurate analysis of them; th were in fact designed to turn their ma front to the east; alongside these there is t regional archeological museum, or Mus Archeologico Regionale, and the Hellenist Roman quarter, which lie along the ro that links the city to the coast, and the cli side sanctuary of Demeter, located near t modern cemetery. Next comes the mode city, which has in the church of S. Maria c Greci and in the cathedral, or Cattedrale, tv major indications of its medieval prospe ty, and in the maritime satellite develo ment of San Leone, which you will need a c to reach, a sadly eloquent example of chac ic urban development.

From the crag, or Rupe Atenea, the spe tacular view of the temples, with the sea the distance, is one of the finest in all of Si ly; in this setting, unrivalled anywhere c earth and enriched by the early blooming the almond trees in the valley, in the first te

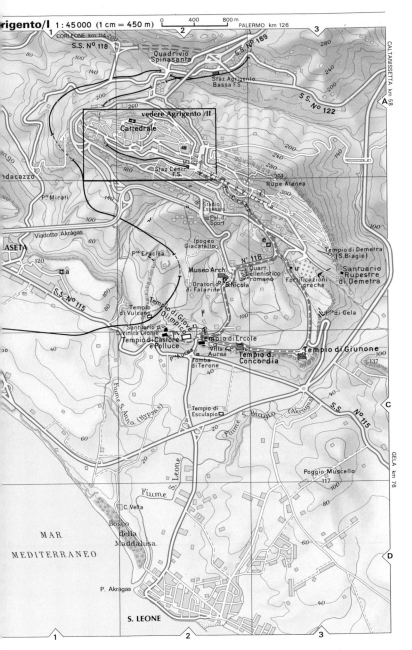

ys of February there is the "Sagra del andorlo in Fiore," or festival of the almond blossoms, a ritual celebrating the arrival of spring.

cheological area*. The ancient city expanded over an area of more than 1,800 ctares: included in it were, to the north-est the hill of Girgenti, just over 300 m. tall ow occupied to the north by the Arabic nter and to the south by the modern ex-

pansion) and the hill of the temples; it featured a Hippodamean layout, with long avenues, running east-west, intersected at right-angles by smaller streets.

The line of the fortifications, partly canceled by the modern expansion, first follows the ridge of the mountain crest, also enclosing the crag, or Rupe Atenea, then runs along the course of the river "Akragas" (now the San Biagio), successively bending off to the west at a right angle (line of the temples)

Springtime in the valley of the temples, with the Temple of Concord in the backgrou

and again to the north, along the river "Hyp-sas" (now the San Leone) and its tributary, until it finally joins up – near the so-called depression, or Avvallamento di Empèdocle – with the walls running out from the crag, or Rupe Atenea; the old city, which the modern state road 118 cuts in two, was thus girt with walls and bastions toward the interior and by temples toward the sea.

The temples of Agrigento all belong to the Doric order and are entirely built of the local limestone with a deep yellow color; traces of white material on the surfaces lead scholars to think that the stone was covered with a plaster made of marble powder.

Before the temple of Juno, or **Tempio di Giunone Lacinia**** (I, C3), set on the summit of the temple hill (Collina dei Templi), stands a large altar for sacrifices; the temple was built in the middle of the 5th c. B.C. – and therefore, just prior to the neighboring temple of Concord (Tempio della Concordia) – with a hexastyle peripteric plan (at the stylobate, 38.15 m. long, and 16.9 m. wide); of the 34 columns (6 on the short sides and 13 on the longer sides) no fewer than 25 are still standing, while the walls of the cella are completely ruined, due to an earthquake in the Middle Ages.

A splendid example of the Doric style (middle of the 5th c. B.C.), the **Tempio della Concordia**** (I, C2), with a hexastyle peripteric plan (at the stylobate, 39.44 m. long, and 16.9 m. wide) and with 34 columns, has been spared much of what happened to the previous temple; it now survives virtually intact, at least in its structural members, as a result of having been transformed (4th c. A.D.) into a basilica with three aisles, which entailed the closure and the reinforcement of the intercolumniation, and the opening, in the walls of the cella, of round arches that can still be

seen; the restoration of 1748 restored i its original form. It was Tommaso Faze who gave the temple its name, and it is s unknown to what deity the temple was c secrated (Castor and Pollux?).

We do know to whom the *Tempio di Erc* (I, C2), or Temple of Hercules, is cor crated; it too is a hexastyle peripteros (at stylobate, 67 x 25.34 m.) but with 38 colur (respectively 6 and 15 on each side); thi probably the oldest of the temples of A gento (end of the 6th c. B.C.).

Before you reach the temple of Olympian J or Tempio di Giove Olimpico, you can dr down, toward the sea, to the *tomb of Teron* C2), which is also visible from the south slope, close to the western edge of the hill of t ples, or Collina dei Templi: set on a high pod is a little temple with a square base, with bl doors obtained by carving into the mass blocks of limestone; at the corners are Do columns, with Ionic capitals and bases, s porting a Doric trabeation, composed of smo metopes and triglyphs. Across the state road a trail leads to the ruins of the temple of Aes lapius, or *Tempio di Esculapio* (I, C2).

The temple of Olympian Jove, or **Tempio Giove Olimpico*** (I, C2), of the hexast pseudo-peripteros type (112.6 X 56.3 n has half columns attached to the outer wa that flank the long inner walls of the cel and six full columns on each short si and was built with the labor of prisone caught on the field of the battle of "Himer it was, however, never completed. It was stroyed by earthquakes, but according the plans of the tyrant Terone it was to l come one of the largest temples of Greek chitecture (it was smaller only than t Artemision of Ephesus and the Didimeon Miletus). The columns, in the fluting which a man could stand, stood some 17 tall, and had a diameter of 4.20 m; coloss nan figures (the so-called telamons), t of stone blocks, supported the weight he interior trabeation like caryatids: in regional archeological museum, or seo Archeologico Regionale, one has n reassembled; a cast of it stands at the ter of the cella of the temple.

four surviving columns of the temple of Dioscuri, or **Tempio dei Dioscuri** (I, C2) e become – for reasons probably bound with the Romantic sense of the pic-esque inspired by the view of the temple as – the symbol of Agrigento. Built toward end of the 5th c. B.C., the temple, a hexa-le peripteros (38.69 X 16.63 m.) with 34 umns, was badly damaged by the sack of Carthaginian conquerors; it was restored he Hellenistic style, and collapsed fol-ing one of the many earthquakes of the t (the present-day configuration was ob-ied during the last century, with the use naterials from other temples).

r the temple there stands a complex of build-s that are believed to belong to the **sanctuary neter and Kore** (I, B2), explored in 1928-32 by 'o Marconi, who reconstructed the develop-it of the complex between the 6th and 5th c. . At the northern extremity are the older ictures, which consist of two y enclosures, with an altar he interior, while in a sec-l phase, probably some-e around the 6th c. B.C., er altars and three small iples were built.

e Museo Archeologico Re-nale** (I, B2), or region-archeological museum, nds in an area of the old vn that was dedicated to olic functions, as is indi-ed by the ruins, quite

conserved up till 1966 in the Museo Dioce-sano (museum of the diocese) and the Museo Civico (civic museum); the material is displayed in accordance with rigorous chronological criteria.

In the first hall (I Sala) you may observe the archeological plan of ancient "Akragas"; this model is very useful in understanding the urbanistic development of the city. The pre-historic material of the first and second milleniums B.C. is visible in the hall II, while the hall III features a rich col-lection of ceramics, both black-figure and red-figure (among the red-figure ceram-ics, we should mention: the *chalice krater*, dating from 490 B.C. – Deposition of a War-rior – originally from the necropolis, or Necropoli Pezzino; a *krater* dating from 430 B.C. – Sacrifice to Apollo – from the necropolis, or Necropoli di Poggio Giache); a splendid *dish with depictions of fish*, from the 4th c. B.C. and, at the far end of the same room, a marble fragment of a *statue of a prostrated warrior* from the temple of Olympian Jove, or Tempio di Giove Olimpi-co (the position of the body, with the legs straight out on the ground, the torso erect, and the body inclined forward, is typical of

Roman sarcophagus featuring the myth of Phaedra

ible, on the esplanade adjoining the irch of S. Nicola, of the "*ekklesiasteri-*', a structure similar to a theater for pop-r assemblies, built in the 3rd c. B.C., h a semicircular cavea, with 28 tiers; ngside it is the so-called oratory, or *Ora-io di Falaride*, a little, 1st-c. B.C. temple, ich was transformed into an oratory in e Middle Ages, by the opening of pointed-h windows. Inaugurated in 1967, the mu-im is located in a building comprising a ently built structure and the old *church* S. *Nicola*, erected in the 13th c. by the Cis-cians (in the 2nd chapel on the right, man *sarcophagus** with the myth of Phae-a, from the 2nd c. A.D.). The museum itains, aside from finds from excavations ne in "Akragas" and the prehistoric sites m the surrounding territory, also works

the sculptures that once adorned the tri-angular composition of the pediment). An original *telamon** (7.75 m. tall) from the temple mentioned above is located in the hall VI, where you can see the heads, set in niches, of three others. The hall VII is ded-icated to artifacts from the Hellenistic-Ro-man quarter: among the works on exhibit, there is a particularly lovely mosaic, de-picting a *gazelle drinking from a spring*, dating from the 1st c. A.D., while the hall IX (open to visitors with special permits) fea tures Greek, Roman, Byzantine, and Nor-man coins, in silver, bronze, and gold. Among the Greco-Roman sculptures in the hall X, we should mention the famous *Ephebus**, dating back to 470 B.C., with re-markable, finely wrought hair. In hall XII and hall XIII, lastly, are finds dating back to prehistoric times (from the Neolithic up to the time of Greek colonization) originally from Sciacca, Palma di Montechiaro, Montallegro, Milena, Favara, and Sant'Angelo Muxaro.

The term *Hellenistic-Roman quarter*, or **Quartiere Ellenistico-Romano*** (I, B2-3), is used to indicate one of the best-preserved sections of ancient city structure in all of Sicily. The area, which covers roughly an hectare, has been the object of archeological explorations ever since the 1950s, which have unearthed buildings and other vertical structures, but also part of the grid of roads, which, in accordance with the prescriptions of Hippodameus of Miletus, consists of regular grids of main streets ("plateiai") intersecting at right angles with secondary streets ("stenopoi"). Over this layout, which developed toward the end of the 4th c. B.C., is juxtaposed the Roman quarter, which in part re-uses – embellishing them with mosaic floors and wall decorations in stucco and fresco – the Hellenistic residential structures; the presence of the peristyle distinguishes those buildings from Roman buildings, which had an atrium and an ambulatory, overlooked by the rooms; also dating from the Roman era are the water pipes and the heating pipes, as well as the sewer facilities for the drainage of rainwater and human waste.

An interesting conclusion of the tour of the old city is the rock-carved sanctuary of Demeter, or **Santuario di Demetra** (I, B3), located in the area around the modern cemetery (you can reach it from the central square, Piazza Marconi, by following the Via Crispi and Via Demetra), a stone building, jutting up against the mount, which marks the presence of the earliest sanctuary of the Agrigento area dedicated to the goddess, built in the 7th c. B.C. (prior, that is, to the foundation of "Akragas"); on the interior, comprising three deep galleries carved into the living rock, the excavations of 1938 unearthed numerous statuettes depicting the goddess and her daughter Kore (Persephone, or Proserpine; the name, in ancient Greek, meant 'maiden').
Not far from the sanctuary stands the little church of *S. Biagio* (I, B3), built in the Norman period on the ruins of the *temple of Demeter and Kore*, an "in antis" building dating back to 480-460 B.C.; of this temple, it is still possible to see, behind the semicircular apse, the structures of the pronaos.

Via Atenea (II, B2-3). This is the main street of Agrigento, as well as the entrance to the historic city; its mouth, off the Piazzale Aldo Moro, is marked by the gate, or *Porta di Ponte*, a 19th-c. reconstruction of the medieval Porta Atenea.

A monastery and a church make up the abbey, **Abbazia di S. Spirito** (II, B3; from the Via Ate you arrive there, taking the Via Porcello and Salita S. Spirito), founded in the 13th c. with tributions from the Contessa di Chiaromo The *church* presents a composite façade, tained by enlarging asymmetrically the old fa and juxtaposing over it, in alignment with the thoroughfare, a wall with single-light window which the bells were to hang: the Gothic po and the 14th-c. rose window are thus off-cen on the plane of the façade; on the interior w and in the presbytery are 18th-c. *stuccoes* tributed to Giacomo Serpotta. The *monas* whose entrance is located on the continuati the façade of the church, has a lovely *cloister* a pointed-arch portal that leads into the chap hall. It contains the *ethnographic and anthro logical section* of the *civic museum*, or Mu Civico, with traditional objects and furnishi

Convento dei Padri Domenicani (II, E This monastery of the Dominican Fathe overlooking the Piazza Pirandello, at end of the Via Atenea, was built in the 1 c. upon the structures of the Palazzo Principi di Lampedusa; it now houses town hall, or Municipio; opening out o the interior courtyard is the 19th-c. to theater, the *Teatro Civico «Luigi Pirandel*

Museo Civico (II, B2), or civic museu This museum is housed in the conv building of the Augustinian Fathers, wh was first built in the 16th c.; it is norma called a "pinacoteca," or art gallery, cause it largely contains paintings, m from the Sicilian school of the 15th to 1 c., as well as the collection, or Collezio Sinatra, of contemporary artists.

S. Maria dei Greci (II, A2). This chu stands on the site of a Doric temple from 5th c. B.C.; of that temple, you can still s remains of columns on the interior and the gallery beneath the left aisle of t church. The façade, surrounded by lo residential structures, presents, in contr with the smooth and simple surface, a lo ly Chiaromonte Gothic portal with lit carved cornices.

Cattedrale* (II, A2), or cathedral. Nam after Gerlando, the first bishop of Agrigen this cathedral was founded around the e of the 11th c. (some scholars say, on t structure of an existing Greek temple) by Normans – who made it the headquarters the bishopric, as was the practice in other cilian cities; the church underwent vario transformations in the 14th, 16th, and 1 c. The *façade*, surmounted by a double-pit pediment and punctuated by pilaster str

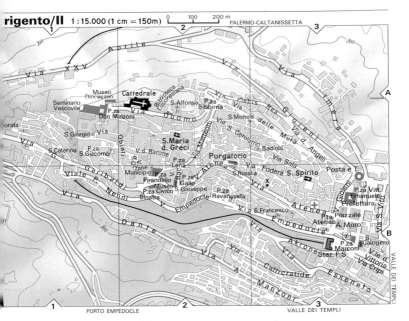

PORTO EMPEDOCLE   VALLE DEI TEMPLI

ing from the surface, is preceded by a
ad and tall staircase. The building is dom-
ted by the *campanile*, with its square
e, begun in the 15th c. and never com-
ted, punctuated on the first two stories by
) orders of blind Moorish-arched win-
ws, and on the third story by a balcony
h rich brackets and a Gothic arcade dec-
ted with zigzag motifs, and on the top sto-
by a number of single-light mullioned win-
ws with simple round arches, with a
ustrade. The church is currently closed
renovation work.

e **interior**, built to a Latin-cross plan, is died into three aisles by high pillars with a
ygonal base, supporting pointed arches;
e ceiling over the side aisles features open
ams, painted with figures of saints and
stocratic heraldic crests dating from the
h c.; the ceiling over the nave, in wooden
unars, was completed in 1682. Note the re-
rkable tomb, or *Arca di S. Gerlando* (in the
apel, or Cappella di S. Gerlando, in the
ht wing of the transept), with a silver reli-
ary dating back to 1639; the Baroque *stuc-
es* in the presbytery – where, due to a re-

markable acoustic phenomenon, it is possible to hear the slightest whisper at the entrance of the church, set 85 m. away – and,
in the right apse, a *Virgin Mary with Christ
Child*, a marble statue dating from 1495.

Museo Diocesano (II, A1), or museum of the
diocese. In a modern building, currently
closed for renovation, this museum has: ancient sculpture; 14th- and 15th-c. frescoes
that were detached in 1951 from the walls of
the cathedral, or Cattedrale, in order to re-
store it to its original Norman Gothic appearance; and fine goldsmithery and sacred
paraments. Adjoining it is a seminary, or
Seminario Vescovile, originally built in the
16th c., but completed in 1611.

San Leone (elev. 2 m.). This beach resort,
some 7 km. from the city, is a favorite with
the people of Agrigento; this is the reason for
the sudden explosion of second-homes that
began in the 1960s, and which transformed,
completely, the old fishing village. In the
nearby area is the *necropolis of Montelusa*,
which dates back to the turn of the 6th c. B.C.

2 The hinterland of Agrigento

e tour runs through territories that are
aracterized by the presence of rural vil-
es founded by the Moors (the area now
ecializes in the cultivation of fine grapes),
d for the permanent echo, in the place
mes and the structure of a number of

towns, of Arabic culture.
This driving route, which leaves Agrigento
in the direction of Caltanissetta, at first
winds along the state road 122 Agrigentina,
reaching Favara, a little town of Islamic origin, from which it is possible to reach Ara-

93

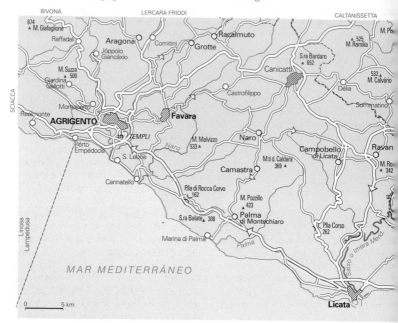

gona (note the little volcanoes, or vulcanelli of Macalube) and Racalmuto, which was also founded by the Moors. A good set of secondary roads then leads on to Naro (interesting for its Baroque appearance), Ravanusa (the immediate surrounding area features the major archeological site of Monte Saraceno), and Licata. The route covers roughly 80 km., to which you should add the 44 m. of the coastal link to Agrigento, along the state road 115 Sud Occidentale Sicula.

Favara

As you observe the city as a whole, extending over a rolling area in the immediate and hilly hinterland of Agrigento (12.5 km. away from the capital), what will strike you is the contrast between the new and massive projects on the outskirts of town, in the foreground, and the structure of the old *church of the Rosario*, in the distance. The city (elev. 338 m., pop. 32,632), a major sulphur-mining town until the turn of the 20th c., clearly shows the signs of the mining crisis, even though lately the new cooperative approach to farming has brought about a slow and difficult recovery.

The name, of Moorish origin ("Fawar") refers to the presence of spring water at the time of the Muslim conquest, when in this territory there was nothing but a hamlet guarding the farmlands. The site was fortified in the 13th c. by the construction of the castle, or Castello dei Chiaramonte, around which clustered the earliest settlement, which was then to grow, over all of the

14th and 15th c., in accordance with the typ[ical] urban layout of the Middle Ages. In the 17th [c.] great process of urban and architectural tra[ns]formation began, starting with the renovation [of] the square that lay before the castle (the pres[ent]day Piazza Cavour), upon which was built in [the] 17th-c. the churches of the Rosario and the P[ur]gatorio, and, between the 18th and the 19th [c.] the Palazzo Fanara and the Palazzo Albergam[...]. The 19th c., finally, witnessed the final form of [the] present-day urban layout, with the creation of [the] Corso Vittorio Emanuele, perpendicular to [the] Corso Umberto I.

The visit can be limited to the *Piaz[za] Cavour*, an elegant piece of 18th-c. urb[an] planning, rare in these towns of south[ern] Sicily, for the compositional harmony [of] the structures and the architectural rigor [of] the façades. Among them all, the façade [–] sadly damaged – of the 14th-c. castle, [the] *Castello dei Chiaramonte*, stands out.

Aragona

This is a small farming town (elev. 400 [m.] pop. 10,416; 9 km. from Favara), founded [in] 1606 by the Conte Baldassarre Naselli, w[ho] named it Aragona in honor of his mothe[r.] Overlooking the little Piazza Umberto I a[re] the *Palazzo Feudale*, built in the 17th [c.] and renovated in the 19th c., now housi[ng] the town hall, or Municipio, and t[he] Baroque *church of the Purgatorio*.
The interior, with a single nave, of t[he] *Chiesa Madre* (17th c.) is decorated wi[th] stuccoes that have been attributed to G[ia]como Serpotta, containing, in a glass cas[e]

andsome wooden *creche* from the 18th c. e attraction of the town, in any case, ghly 3 km. to the south, along a turnoff m the road to Agrigento, is the *Vulcanelli Macalube**; there are signs pointing the y.

e lunar landscape that you will happen on consists of a clayey expanse, shot ough with fissures and openings which pt – alternately – whitish slime and puffs methane gas. It is infact one of the most iking and evocative demonstrations of a e geological phenomenon known as "sedentary vulcanism".

calmuto

is town has become famous as the birthce of the most illustrious contemporary iter focusing on Sicily, Leonardo Sciascia. cated on the summit of a sunny hill, the y (elev. 445 m., pop. 10,752), which until e turn of the century was a major sulur-mining town, now thrives on agriculte and a limited industry based on the ning of rocksalt.

ce Favara (which lies some 16 km. away), e town still preserves its Moorish name d the original medieval urban layout, ich developed in the 14th c. around the stle, or *Castello Chiaramontano*, still preved with its massive corner towers; the *iesa Madre* dates from the 17th c.; the former monastery of S. Chiara*, which now uses the town hall, or *Municipio*, and e foundation, or *Fondazione Sciascia*, was ouilt in 1872; in the atrium note the Roan *sarcophagus*, installed in that same ar, with a depiction of the abduction of oserpine.

aro*

a position overlooking the center of the st region to the east of Agrigento (which about 30 km. away), this little city (elev. 0 m., pop. 10,071) – the origin of its name d the date of its first settlement are unown – occupies one of the highest sites in e district, with a fine view of the valley of e river Naro; among the towns of this ea, this is the one that best preserves its onumental Baroque appearance, one atction that ensures an enjoyable visit. territory, during the Greek era, fell under e sphere of influence of Agrigento, while e early-Christian necropolis of Contrada nale offers evidence of Christianity as rly as the 4th c. In the 14th c., on an exing Norman fortification situated on the ost exposed highland, the castle, or stello Chiaramontano, was built, around ich developed the late-medieval expan-

sion, which incorporated the restructured Norman buildings of the old cathedral, or Duomo Vecchio, and of the church of S. Caterina; between the 15th and 17th c., the urban layout and the directions of the main thoroughfares were sharply conditioned by the religious settlements of the Carmelites, the Dominicans, and the Jesuits, who encouraged the expansion of the city proper outside the enclosure walls. The current image of the historical center is that of the city as it was renovated in the 18th c., with the expansions and the complete late-Baroque renovations of the religious buildings and the construction of the most representative palazzi of the middle class. It is possible to see a good example of this as you walk through the *Via Dante*, which crosses Naro from east to west, drawing a line between the high city and the low city, and along which you may note the Baroque church of the *SS. Salvatore*, the *Chiesa Madre* (1619), and the *Palazzo Destro*, from the same period. A staircase to the left of the church of the SS. Salvatore allows one to climb up to the medieval castle, **Castello**, adorned with a Chiaramonte portal with zigzag motifs, and to the old cathedral, or *Duomo Vecchio*, which dates back to the 12th c. In the stretch of Corso Vittorio Emanuele, beyond the *Piazza Garibaldi*, flanked by elegant, late-19th-c. buildings, you can admire the façades of the *Palazzo Giacchetto*, laid out in the 15th c., and the 18th-c. *Palazzo Morillo*.

Toward the coast, at a distance of 15 km., is **Palma di Montechiaro** (elev. 165 m., pop. 24,077), which can be reached along the state road 410.

A feudal landholding of the princes of Lampedusa until 1812, this is, according to experts on the book "Il Gattopardo," or "The Leopard," the villa of Donnafugata in the novel. Set on *Piazza S. Rosalia* is the superb Baroque façade of the **Chiesa Madre**, built between 1666 and 1703. On the interior, note the *tomb* of the astronomer Giovanni Battista Odierna (1597-1660), who played a role in the urban planning of the little town.

Palma di Montechiaro: the Chiesa Madre

Ravanusa

At a distance of 20 km. from the previous stop, set in the fertile countryside of the Agrigento area, Ravanusa (elev. 320 m., pop. 16,369) blankets, with its buildings, the southern slope of a hill/cliff overlooking the river Salso. This little town, which has grown considerably and which is based on an agricultural economy, was founded in the 17th c. by the duke, or Duca di Montalbano, owner of the fief. The duke also undertook the construction, on the present-day Piazza Umberto I, of the *Chiesa Madre*; the building features, on its main façade, a handsome carved *portal*, attributed to one of the Gagini.

It is interesting to tour the early-Sicilian/Greek archeological site of **Monte Saraceno***, located 1.5 km. to the southeast of the town. The campaigns of digging undertaken so far have uncovered traces of a Greek city, founded by Gela in the 7th c. B.C., and later absorbed into the sphere of influence of Agrigento, arranged at three consecutive elevations: on the highest elevation stood the acropolis, on the middle elevation was the town itself (explorations have uncovered, beneath the level of the Greek city, a layer of buildings that may be attributed to a previous Siculi settlement), while the lowest elevation was occupied by a sacred area.

Licata

Extending over the vast alluvial plain formed by the mouth of the river Salso and at the foot of the Colle Sant'Angelo, which the Greeks called "Eknomos," the city (24 km. from Ravanusa) offers the frantic and fragmentary image of an old town, forced to adapt too quickly to the sudden developments of the contemporary world; endowed with a broad and safe port, whose construction was made possible by the favorable configuration of the coastline and the good seabed just offshore, this town has based its prosperity on that port, acquiring the distinctive features of a port town (elev. 8 m., pop. 41,269).

Artifacts dating back to the Paleolithic and traces of an archaic Greek settlement (6th c. B.C.) on the eastern slopes of the hill, or Colle "Eknomos," demonstrate that this site was frequented from the earliest periods, even though the actual foundation of the city dates back only to the Hellenistic period, under Fintia, tyrant of Agrigento, who gave it the name of "Fintias"; in the 2nd c. B.C. the Romans improved the port structures, laying the foundations for a solid economic structure based on maritime trade.
The intensive agricultural exploitation of the fertile territory, promoted by the Moors, al with its capacity to export products, led town to become one of the most populous dynamic centers of the southern Sicilian co Dating back to that period was the shift of the tlement from the slopes of the "Eknomos" the plain below: this was the first, fortified cleus of the modern city, destined to exp outside its walls, to the present day.
Between the 17th and the 18th c., a massive ject of renovation of the religious and civil bu ings here was undertaken, filling the empty spa in the town and replacing the surviving medie buildings, with a particular expansion along w are now the Corso Vittorio Emanuele and Via S. Andrea. From the first half of the 19th c the early years of the 20th c., the city underw a rapid development, due to the export of sulp and wheat through the port here; the old w were knocked down and replaced with l blocks of buildings, which joined the old and the new one together, through the us type of construction, without taste or quality

In the town of Licata, there coexist arc tectural and environmental motifs of varic styles, all merged together in a generaliz expression of vitality. In the central squa or *Piazza Progresso*, the nexus of the ma thoroughfares, stands the floral-style to hall, or *Palazzo del Municipio*, designed 1935 by Ernesto Basile; in it, aside from fi artworks, are archeological finds from t ancient "Fintias." The civic archeologi museum, or **Museo Civico Archeologico** the Via Dante, comprises two sections: t prehistoric section contains materials th range from the Paleolithic to the Bron Age, while the other section includes a facts from the Greek period (note the teresting funerary funishings from the chaic necropolises), and fine architectu mosaic floors from the Hellenistic era. O of the most noteworthy monumental reli of Licata's past is the **church of t Carmine**, part of the monastery of the sa name, arranged along the Corso Rom which was built in the 13th c. and rebuilt the 18th c.; it features a handsome Baroq façade and contains a lovely little cloist upon which give a number of twin-light m lioned windows and a portal, all adorn with Chiaromonte motifs. Along the Cor Vittorio Emanuele, you will find the *Chie Matrice*, built in the 15th c. with a thre aisled basilican plan, which has the vault the nave decorated by 19th-c. frescoes. It is also worth visiting the *Castel S. Ange* built on the summit of the Colle S. Angelo plans by Camillo Camilliani between 16 and 1640; from the square before it, ye can enjoy a splendid panoramic view of t city and the coast, as far as Gela.

3 The Agrigento coast, from Porto Empèdocle to Sciacca

e route covers the coastal strip stretch-
g between Agrigento and Sciacca, from
ich this route (a total of 63 km.) some-
es wanders, to run through a landscape
ounded hill, covered with orderly fields;
depressions between hills often offer a
mpse of the sea. Near sites that are of his-
ic and artistic interest (suffice it to men-
n the lovely Eraclea Minoa alone), there
towns that appear uniformly dull to the
veler: rows of modern grey houses, ap-
rently unfinished, which conceal behind
ow of buildings their often-very-hand-
me urban cores, of much older origin.
ce you have reached Porto Empèdocle,
other seaside appendix of Agrigento and
point of departure for the islands of
lagie, follow the state road 115 Sud Oc-
dentale Sicula to Siculiana, Eraclea Mi-
a, and Ribera (the two latter towns can be
ched by taking short detours along sec-
dary roads); from Sciacca, the last stop
d an important hot-springs spa which
eserves major ruins from antiquity, you
y want to take a detour to the medieval
vn of Caltabellotta.

me of Luigi Pirandello

ou head down from Agrigento toward
rto Empèdocle, just before Villaseta, you

will reach the Contrada *Caos*, with the home
in which Luigi Pirandello was born in 1867;
the building, a typical example of a prosperous home of the Agrigento countryside,
has been declared a national monument;
several of its rooms have been converted into a *museum* of souvenirs and memorabilia
of Pirandello. In the garden, at the foot of an
age-old cluster pine, beheaded by a violent
storm, cemented into a limestone boulder,
there is an urn with the playwright's ashes.

Porto Empèdocle

Constituting the natural maritime comple-
ment to Agrigento, this town is the city's
trading and shipping center, as well as the
harbor for boats to the islands of Pelagie;
the town (elev. 2 m., pop. 16,755) presents
features that are quite typical of seaside settlements of this zone – a single main thoroughfare lined by private homes of no real
interest – and bases its economy almost
exclusively on sea trade and on a modest
fishing industry.
With the name of Marina di Girgenti, this
town was endowed in the 15th c. with one
of the most important wheat-loading facilities in Sicily, a port structure that was in-
dispensable to the export of Agrigento's
main resource (on the wharf, you can still

97

The marvellous coast of Capo Bianco

see the 16th-c. watch *tower*, built at the behest of Charles V). The first artificial jetty, which was built in part with stones from the Agrigento temple of Olympian Jove, or Tempio di Giove Olimpico, dates back to 1749, while a further improvement of the port facilities took place in the 19th c., to accommodate the export of sulphur, mined along the coast and in the inland regions, as far up as Caltanissetta. With the crisis that followed the closing of the sulphur mines, there began an economic decline, for the port and for the city itself, that still persists. There is an interesting archeological site in the area around the town; the *Villa di Durrueli*, a Roman building dating back to the 1st c. B.C.: overlooking the sea, it features the ruins of a peristyle, around which there are rooms with fine mosaic floors.

Siculiana

If you are coming from Agrigento (19 km. away), this little town (elev. 129 m., pop. 5,070) appears to lie behind the eastern slope of a hill, just above the roadway. The apparent stacking skyward of the buildings, the intertwining welter of lanes and courtyards, the rapid growth of the city's construction, which culminates in the two-tone cupola of the Baroque *Chiesa Matrice*, reveal the Moorish origins of the town, although historical documentation reveals its existence only from the 15th c. on, when it sprang up around the medieval castle, or *Castello*.

The hill settlement corresponds to the coastal settlement, of *Siculiana Marina* (elev. 12 m.), which developed in recent years at the usual feverish pace.

Eraclea Minoa*

At a distance of 15 km. from Siculiana the is a turnoff that will take you (in another km.) to the ruins of the very ancient colo possibly founded by the Myceneans. W its enchanting geographic location, in a tually unspoiled natural setting, this is c of the loveliest and most interesting arc ological sites in Sicily; the cape, or Ca Bianco, on the summit (m 75) of wh stretches out all that remains of the c slopes westward toward the luxuriant v ley of the river Plàtani; to the east, it tu a sheer wall of white rock over a splen arena-shaped beach, surrounded by dense blanket of vegetation, while, to south, it directly overlooks the open se A number of fragments found in the lay beneath the archaic necropolis, dating ba to the 6th c. B.C. might lead us to date origins of this settlement to the Neolith while the oldest coins testify to the presen on this site of a Phoenician colony. In d uments, the city is cited by three differe names: Macara, or city of "Makar," t Phoenician Hercules; Minoa, founded, cording to legend, by the king of Crete, nos, who had chased Daedalus to here; a finally, Eraclea, a Spartan colony named place after the great demigod. After t Phoenicians and the Spartans, it becam subcolony of Selinunte in the 5th c. B.C., a after reinforcing its fortifications, reach the apex of its urban development in H lenistic times. Located at the border tween Greek and Carthaginian spheres of fluence, it passed repeatedly from one to other, until, in 210 B.C., it was conquered the Romans. In the 1st c. A.D., it was defi tively abandoned, possibly due to a lan slide that swept the southern part of t town and its enclosure walls into the sea Archeological exploration here began 1907, unearthing a part of the *residen quarter*, in which it is possible to dist guish, in two successive stratification traces of both the Hellenistic and the Rom city, the northern section of the enclosu walls, and a beautiful *theater*, with proscaenium opening out toward the s from this theater come a number of sar stone blocks, used as seating, and now exhibit in the antiquarium.

Ribera

Another short detour from the state ro runs up (4.7 km.) to Ribera (elev. 223 pop. 21,004), which occupies a verdant hi bluff, not far from the coast. Its traditio agrarian economy has, in recent years, be bolstered by considerable tourist traff

racted by the excavations of Eraclea Mi-
a and by the beaches.

is town owes its foundation and its name
the de Ribera family, which founded it in
2 17th c., and managed to absorb, in the
h c., the feudal landholdings between the
ers Plàtani and Bèlice. Ribera nowadays
esents the typical checkerboard urban
out of founded cities that relied upon
riculture and refeudalization, with a main
roughfare (the present-day *Corso Um-
rto*) from which the entire grid of the old-
section of town extends.

acca*

ing on a natural terrace formation sloping
wn toward the sea, Sciacca (elev. 60,
p. 38,256; plan below), terminus of the
astal route, overlooks the Mar d'Africa,
d is protected to the north by the lime-
one highlands of the Monte San Calogero
d to the west by the cape, or Capo San
irco. The present-day name – concerning
2 meaning of which discussion still rages
vas given it by the Moors in the 9th c., but
ancient times it was called, by the Greeks
hermai Selinuntinai," and by the Romans,
hermae Selinuntinae." The city was founded in the sixth to fifth c. B.C. as a hot-springs
spa, a subject of the nearby and powerful
Selinunte, whose fate it shared in the continual wars with Carthage; it was finally destroyed entirely by Carthage in 409 B.C.
Beginning in the 2nd c. B.C., the Romans –
aside from encouraging the use of the sulphureous hot springs of Monte Cronio –
introduced a system of intensive cultivation,
which led to a sizable increase in population, making this city a major actor in the
fields of culture and the economy along
the axis linking Syracuse-Agrigento-Lilibeo.
The remarkable urban configuration that
still survives here is the product of the successive efforts of the Moors, who interwove their quarters, bounding them with
walls, above and below the main street,
and of the Normans, who enlarged the enclosure walls, making it possible for the
Greeks, Moors, and Franks to coexist within them; and these were the three chief
ethnic groups to shape and characterize the
urban spaces of the future city.
The 15th and 16th c. witnessed the replacement of the undistinguished civil architecture of the medieval period with the
more sumptuous style of the palazzi of the

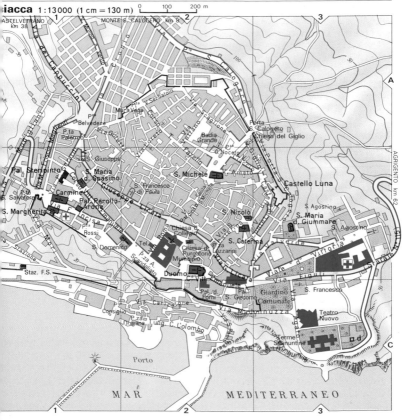

landed aristocracy (Palazzo Steripinto), as well as the construction of the enclosure walls, with bastions, built at the behest of Charles V, while in the 17th c. there were radical restorations of churches and monasteries in the Baroque forms that we still see today. In the 1950s, the construction of the Grand Hotel delle Terme and the spa on the Monte Cronio brought a new flow of tourists and spa-goers to the local economy. The town, which you should tour on foot, has preserved its ancient division into quarters, each lying spread out on one of the three plans of rock, sloping down to the sea. The first of these, the largest, lies to the north of the Via Licata, and is occupied by the medieval quarter known as "Terravecchia": it is a welter of lanes and alleys, many of them with steps, bounded – also to the north – by an enclosure wall with bastions, whose structure still survives in considerable stretches. The second quarter, a narrow strip of elegant religious and civil buildings, extends between the edge of the "Terravecchia" and the main road, the present-day Corso Vittorio Emanuele. The third quarter lies immediately below the buildings along the "corso" and runs steeply down to the jetty; this is the quarter of sailors and ceramist/potters, and it still has its original urban function. On the promontory to the east, a splendid promenade lined with palm trees separates the Grand Hotel delle Terme from the precipice overlooking the sea, while to the west the coastline is adorned with a vast array of recent residential developments.

Even though much of the population earns its living from farming and fishing, much of the fortune of Sciacca is a result of the hot springs, excellent for the treatment of respiratory and rheumatic diseases; the craftsmanship here is quite impressive, especially the pottery, which is found in the older section of the town (art shops, murals).

Piazza Scandaliato (B2). This square is a splendid terrace overlooking the sea, and it is a meeting place for the whole town; embellishing it is the *church of S. Domenico*, an 18th-c. reconstruction of the church built here in 1534 by Tommaso Fazello, and the *Collegio dei Gesuiti*, now the site of town hall, or the Municipio, which, with the adjoining *church of the Collegio*, was begun in 1613.

Duomo (B2) or cathedral. Built the first time in 1108 and rebuilt in 1656; of the original Norman structure, all that survives are the three apses, while the dark yellow col-

or of the unfinished Baroque façade is enlivened by the handsome Gagini marble *statues*, set in niches. The interior, built to a Latin-cross plan, was enlarged to three aisles during the Baroque period, and late adorned with frescoes and polychrom marble work.

S. Margherita (B1). The earliest construction of this church dates back to the 14th but all that survives from that period is th exquisite Gothic *portal** on the side of th church itself. The *statues* and the *bas-r liefs* that adorn it are attributed t Francesco Laurana and Pietro di Bonitad

Palazzo Steripinto (B1). Easily recognize by the diamond-point rustication, the twi light mullioned windows, and the parapet this is a remarkable building in the Ca alonian Sicilian style dating back to 1501 The "Castello Incantato," or enchanted ca tle (B3, off map) is a singular gallery in a olive grove, with hundreds of faces carve into the rock and on the trees by the pea ant/artist Filippo Bentivegna.

Caltabellotta

A tortuous panoramic route of 20 km. ru up to the high Dolomitic mount atop whic stands the town (elev. 949 m., pop. 5,176 The primarily military function that it ha served from its foundation appears to th visitor in the image of compact strengt that contrasts with the gentle slopes of th southern coast. And part of its reputatio was won through its importance in war; peace treaty was signed here, on 31 A gust 1302, between Charles of Valois an Frederick II of Aragon, putting an end to th bloody war of the Sicilian Vespers (Guer dei Vespri Siciliani).

Before acquiring the Arabic name of "Kal'. Ballut" (mountain of oaks), it was calle "Triocala," which means 'three nice thing these three things, according to Diodor Siculus, were its abundance of springwate its fertile soil cultivated with vines an olive trees, and the natural protection of th impregnable crag.

It still enjoys these features, along with i exquisite medieval urban fabric, so t speak, typical of a mountain town of th Mediterranean region.

Among the monuments, we would mentio the *Chiesa Madre*, founded by the Norman and the so-called hermitage, or **Eremo di Pellegrino**, whose architectural mass, s on the western edge of the mount, loom over the city. The sanctuary consists of monastery and a chapel, which stand not f

...om the grotto where, according to an an-...ent legend, there lived a dragon that fed ...n the children of Caltabellotta, suppos-...dly slain by the saint.

...he *grotto necropolises* cut into the rocky wall (you can see them along the road leading out of the town) and ruins of *fortifications*, not yet explored by archeologists, offer indications of an ancient human presence, about which much remains to be learned.

...art of the Lampedusa coastline: the island's natural environment has remained unspoilt

.4 The islands of Pelagie

...attered in the southernmost territorial ...aters of Italy (they are closer to Africa ...an to Sicily), Lampedusa and Lampione to ...e south and Linosa to the north form the ...ttle island group with the somewhat tau-...logical name of the Pelagie (from the ...reek "pelagos," meaning 'sea'). The three ...lets present differing geological charac-...ristics: Lampedusa and Lampione are ...mestone in structure, while Linosa is vol-...anic in origin; moreover, while the first ...vo belong to the African continental shelf, ...e third is considered part of the Sicilian ...ontinental shelf.

...he islands (pop. 5,624) maintain their orig-...al wild appearance, and constitute an un-...valled attraction, especially the wealth of ...nd and sea fauna: on the beaches of ...ampedusa, the sea turtle burrows into the ...nd and lays her eggs; on the rocks, the ...onk seal splashes and suns itself; and on ...e crags high above, the Eleonora's fal-...n perches and observes.

...here are regular flights from Palermo and ...ips running from Porto Empèdocle, so it ... relatively easy to reach the little archi-...lago.

...mpedusa

...nce known for its sponges, this island ...oks like a great inclined rock table, rising

out of the crystal-clear sea, with sheer walls; the coastline is dotted with grottoes and shoals and little sandy inlets, and the waters abound in fish.

Although there are traces of the passage of Phoenicians, Greeks, Romans, and Arabs, the true colonization dates back to 1843, when Ferdinand II of the house of Bourbon established a colony there; until 1940 it was a place of political exile. The town is clustered to the southern extremity, in the Frazione *Lampedusa* (elev. 16 m.). The recent establishment of regular flights from Palermo has encouraged the development of a limited tourist trade.

Lampione
Set to the northwest of Lampedusa, this uninhabited stack formation has only an automatic lighthouse or warning beacon.

Linosa
Constituting the summit of a volcanic cone that has been extinct for nearly 2,000 years, this island's slopes plunge down into the sea to a depth of roughly 100 m. The island has an almost perfectly circular form; the rocky seabeds are popular with scuba divers, attracted by the abundance of fish; it is very nice to stop in the little village of Linoa (elev. 12 m.), with its brightly colored houses.

5 Ragusa and the Ragusa region

The geographic context through which this visit runs largely coincides with the Val di No to, one of the three sections of Sicily as it was divided by the Moors. This is a territory tha is varied and diverse, ranging from the plain, or Piana di Catania to the highlands of th Iblei, from the coastline bathed by the Mar d'Africa, or African Sea, to the Piana di Gel from the inland highlands to the territory of the Calatino, and it represents a complete m

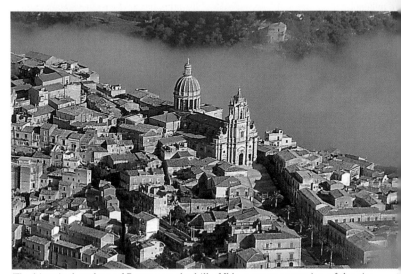

The historical nucleus of Ragusa on the hill of Ibla, eastern extension of the city

crocosm of the finer characteristics of the island as well as its greater contradictions. Th landscape is marked by the imbalances that have emerged in economic development. Once it became clear that there was no real possibility of industrializing the outlying a eas, the farmers of the area around Gela relearned the finest old techniques of irrigatin fields. That was not all: the dairy products of the Iblei – specifically, the cheeses – becam much sought-after in markets everywhere, proving much more lucrative than the phanto wealth from oil wells; indeed, the great landholdings – or "latifondi," from the Latin "lat fundium" – of the Piana di Catania were broken up and cultivated, undermining the collecti policies of the past. The only thing that seems to expand without signs of flagging is th multiplication of greenhouses – the product of a culture better known for pesticides an chemical fertilizers – which are now fetching up against the Mediterranean dunes, whic remain pristine, as of this writing. And it is this astonishing proliferation of greenhouse farr ing which characterizes the coastal landascape – so blighting a landscape that was onc a harmonious patchwork of fields girded by dry-stone masonry walls; however, this for of greenhouse agriculture involves so much money that any objections from enviror mentalists tend to fall on deaf ears.

5.1 Ragusa

Any proper analysis of Ragusa's chief features (elev. 502, pop. 67,535; plan on page 104) must focus on two important factors: the earthquake of 1693 and the city's relationship with the surrounding territory (and vice versa). The earthquake, because it triggered a two-part reconstruction of the city: "Ragusa supra," i.e., the city up on the highland, the one that developed into city proper during the post-earthquak building, and "Ragusa iusu," i.e. Ibla, a most wholly rebuilt along the old mediev. layout. The relationship between city an surrounding territory, on the other hand, a lows one to glimpse the particular lives the inhabitants, who are closely bound t

ıe philosophy of the environment by peas-
ıt traditions which were particularly re-
ıforced and emphasized from the 15th c.
ınward with the institution of the emphy-
:usis, or perpetual lease.

ɾom earliest settlements to the earth-
ᴜake of 1693

ɾaces of settlement in the area around
ıe hill of Ibla have been dated back to the
ɾd millennium B.C., and settlement seems
ɔ have been much more continuous from
ıe 9th to the 7th c. B.C. This favorable ge-
graphic location allowed the early Sicilians
:he Siculi) to found a fortress here, de-
:nding the course of the river Irminio. The
Hibla Heraia" discussed in the early
ɔurces linked its development to the Greek
ɔlony of Kamarina, establishing econom-
: and commercial ties that allowed them to
ɾeserve their independence from the
ɾeek oppressors. Occupied first by the
ɔmans and later by the Byzantines (4th c.),
ɔla was fortified with a strong enclosure
ʌall by the latter. Beginning in A.D. 848,
ınder Moorish domination, the structure of
ıe territory underwent a considerable
ɑnsformation: the countryside was re-
ɔpulated and new crops were planted, us-
ıg new systems of cultivation. Under the
ᵘle of, at first Normans and later the fam-
ᵢes of the Chiaramonte and the Cabrera,
ıe medieval city took shape. To the west,
ᵼ the higher sections, stood the castle, the
ıcient Moorish "Kasr," and to the east the
ɔundary was constituted by what is now
ıe Giardino Ibleo. The principal thor-
ᴜghfare, running east-west, was the "pian-
ɑta," which once crossed the Piazza d'Ar-
ᵢi, now the Piazza del Duomo (cathedral
ᵖuare). The city itself was occupied by
ᴜmerous religious orders. The conces-
ᵢon of enphyteusis, beginning in 1452, at
ᵼe behest of the Conte Cabrera, consti-
ᵼtes a major step forward in the transfor-
ᵃation of the territory and the city. It is in
ᵼct through this economic revolution that
ᵼere was established a direct bond be-
ᵗeen the peasant and the land to be culti-
ᵃted, subordinated only to a lease-rent, to
ᵉ paid to the count. In ensuring years, the
ᵉrritory was broken up and fenced in by the
ᵢstinctive dry-stone walls. From 1693 on, in
ᵼe wake of the earthquake that devastated
ᵃstern Sicily, Ragusa and Ibla became the
ᵗo historic centers of the same city, forced
ᵧ geography and by politics to cohabit.
ᵼe two cities grew necessarily the one
ᵃongside the other, among much bickering,
ıtil 1926, when they were "rejoined" with
ıe single name of Ragusa.

The boundary between the two townships is
constituted by the church of S. Maria delle
Scale; the territory of Ibla includes the working-class quarters that lie on the slopes of the
upland. With the reconstruction of Ibla over
the course of the 18th and 19th c., there was
consolidated a richer array of churches and
aristocratic residences, an array that above
all featured a more harmonious sort of lesser architecture. The new town center, on
the other hand, which has fewer monumental features, extends over the highland. The
growth of the past few decades, however, has
resulted in the marginalization of Ibla, which
is isolated from the economic processes of
the rest of the city.

The itinerary of the visit
The route suggested here allows you to
trace back the expansion of the city in accordance with successive phases of growth.
If you begin from Piazza Libertà, you will
then cross the bridge, or Ponte Nuovo
(1937), which, along with the Ponte dei Cappuccini (1835) and the Ponte Papa Giovanni XXIII (1964) spans the Cava di S. Domeni-
ca. You can then continue along the Via
Roma and then the Corso Italia, heading
down toward the historic centers of the
old city. After you cross the Piazza S. Giovanni, with the cathedral, or Cattedrale,
you can venture into the 18th-c. section of
town, which cuts across a series of streets
at right angles, until you reach the stairs
that run down toward Ibla. At the end of Via
XXIV Maggio, a continuation of the Corso
Italia, you will see a handsome panoramic
view of Ibla. From here, if you walk down the
333 steps of the staircase, or if you follow
the Corso Mazzini, a linking road that was
produced by the demolition done during the
Fascist era, you will find the Piazza della Repubblica, the former Piazza degli Archi,
which constitutes a nexus connecting the
various quarters that climb sharply up toward the highland, and with the entrance to
the medieval section of the city. From the
square, you will continue along, concen-
trating on the route that is richest in historic
and artistic terms, following the old main
thoroughfare – the "piancata" – of the city
as it was before the earthquake: Via del
Mercato, Via XI Febbraio, Via S. Agnese,
Via Tenente Di Stefano, and Via Capitano
Bocchieri as far as the Piazza del Duomo (it
is worth rounding off the tour by pushing into the ancient medieval routes, climbing
and descending stairways in a labyrinth
that makes it possible to discover little
tucked-away jewels and urban settings with
considerable charm). From the spectacular

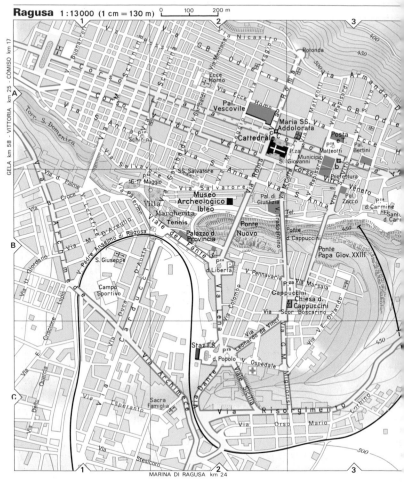

Piazza del Duomo, over which rises the church of S. Giorgio (the Duomo, or cathedral), you will descend to the Piazza Pola, along the Corso XXV Aprile, and along the main thoroughfare, the backbone, as it were of a 17th-c. "forma piscis" (fish shape). From Piazza Pola, which in part coincides with the Piazza Maggiore of the medieval city, take a detour from the Corso XXV Aprile (which runs down toward the Giardini Iblei), and continue along the Via Orfanotrofio; after the church of S. Maria la Nova you will cross the ancient Jewish ghetto, until you reach the Largo Camarina; then take Via Chiaramonte to reach the Baroque church of S. Francesco all'Immacolata. From the church, along the Via Tenente La Rocca and then the Via Monte Ereo, you will return to the Corso XXV Aprile, and then you will reach the park, or Giardino Ibleo.

Piazza Libertà (B2). Once known as Piazza Impero (Empire Square), this area was built during the Fascist era in accordance wit the architecture of Marcello Piacentini; stands at the head of the *Ponte Nuovo*, bridge that was built in order to encourag the city to grow past the Cava S. Domenic; in order to consolidate the 19th-c. quarter the Cappuccini. The square constitutes major example of Fascist architecture, an now constitutes a link between the "third, modern city of Ragusa and its older center;

Museo Archeologico Ibleo (B2). This arch ological museum was established in th wake of the first systematic exploration the territory of the Provincia di Ragusa i the years 1955-60, with emphasis on th chronological sequence in a succession topographical source areas. The installatio of the material is characterized by life-size reproductions of sections of the digs. I the first section, there are displays of flir and volcanic stone tools, and ceramic m; terials from necropolises and villages fron

104

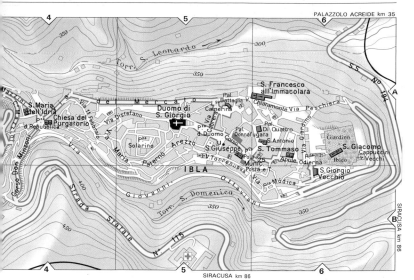

ne Bronze Age. In the section dedicated to amarina, there is documentation concerning the recent excavations in the city, with terracotta figurines from a sanctuary f Demeter, and the archaic and classical ecropolises – of which there are some reconstructions – with Corinthian and Attic eramics. Of particular interest is the material – especially ceramics, local and imported, from the archaic and classical Sicilian towns, while among the Hellenistic owns, special attention is devoted to the aravan center of Scornavacche and its ceamic manufactory (with a reconstruction of kiln). There is also considerable material oncerning Roman and late-Roman centers.

attedrale (A2). This cathedral, the center the urban renewal of 18th-c. Ragusa, was uilt between 1706 and 1760, and was dedicated to St. John the Baptist. It stands on a road terrace supported by a loggia; the çade, which is rendered asymmetrical by e stout bell tower, has a central structure ith two orders, and a monumental portal. ne *interior* is built to a Latin-cross plan and as three aisles, divided by two orders of olumns in a typical Ragusan asphalt stone.

alazzo Zacco (B3). The façade overlooking e Via S. Vito features a harmonious aroque architecture that is characterized y the carvings that decorate the brackets pporting the balconies. The elegant enance portal with the two columns supporting the central balcony, the aristocratcrest held up by putti, the grinning mascaron all point to a school of decorative tists that, in this and in other palazzi of the

historic centers of Ragusa, did sublime work with the carving of white stone.

Palazzo Bertini (A3). This building was erected toward the end of the 18th c., and stands out for the distinctive mascarons set at the keystones of the windows. The most common interpretation is that of the "three potentates," where the first represents the poor man, powerful because he cares for nothing; the second represents the aristocrats, with the firm gaze of one whose power goes beyond the laws; and the third is the wealthy merchant, powerful with the arrogance of money.

Ragusa: the Cathedral

105

S. Maria delle Scale (A-B4). Set at the stop of the staircases that join the two Ragusas, this church for centuries has marked the boundary of the two centers. Built in the 14th c. on the site of an existing Cistercian monastery dating from Norman times, it was rebuilt following the earthquake of

The façade of the S. Giorgio Cathedral

1693. All that survives from the 14th-c. construction is a portal and a Gothic pulpit at the foot of the campanile. The *interior* has three aisles; the left aisle and the nave are rebuilt in a Baroque style, while the right aisle consists of four communicating chapels linked by Catalonian Gothic and Renaissance arches (15th/16th c.). In the third chapel, note the *Death of the Virgin Mary*, a polychrome terracotta relief of the Gagini school (1538).

Salita Commendatore (A4). As you climb along the stairs, narrow lanes, arches, and buttresses of this narrow "salita" (literally, in Italian, 'climb'), you will pass the Palazzo della Cancelleria, the church of the Idria, and the Palazzo Cosentini. These are three noteworthy episodes of Baroque architecture. The *Palazzo Nicastro*, built in 1760, was the site of the *Cancelleria* Comunale (town chancery) of Ibla until the 19th c. On its right, a little further down, is the church and the campanile of *S. Maria dell'Idria*, built in 1626 by the order of the Cavalieri di Malta (Knights of Malta), and rebuilt in 1739. The bell tower is surmounted by a cupola with an octagonal base, sheathed in the bright polychrome tiles of

Caltagirone. Descend even further, and you will find the *Palazzo dei Cosentini*, dating from the early 18th c.

Church of the Purgatorio (A4). This church founded in the 17th c., dominates the Piazza della Repubblica from high atop its staircase. The interior, with three aisles, features among other things a depiction of *Souls in Purgatory*, by Francesco Manno, on the main altar. The campanile, set in the rear and to the left of the church, stands on ancient Byzantine walls, alongside which climbs the *Salita dell'Orologio*.

S. Giorgio* (A5). This cathedral, designed in 1739 by Rosario Gagliardi, was built at the "center of gravity" of the new urban layout. From high atop a very long stairway, which is off-kilter from the axis of the square, it overlooks the surrounding valleys in a handsome setting, emphasized by the sharpness of the slope. The *façade*, articulated in three orders, is convex at the center, and is punctuated by jutting cornices; the cupola is Neoclassical, rises 43 meters high, and dates from 1820; the wrought-iron fencework dates from 1880. The *interior* is built to a Latin-cross plan, and is divided into three aisles. In the nave, 13 polychrome stained glass windows depict the martyrdom of S. George (1926).

S. Giuseppe (A5). The architecture of this church, which overlooks the Piazza Pola (which was called Piazza Maggiore before the earthquake), links it to the Duomo, or cathedral, in a stylistic continuity. The *façade*, attributed to Rosario Gagliardi, or his school, is subdivided into three orders with Corinthian columns and statues. The interior, with an elliptical plan, is decorated with stocco work; the cupola, frescoed in 1793 by Sebastiano Lo Monaco, depicts the *Glory of St. Benedict*.

S. Francesco all'Immacolata (A5-6). The remains of the bell tower and the Gothic portal derive from an early Franciscan church built in the 13th c. The church that now stands here was built in the 17th c., and was rebuilt in the Baroque style after the earthquake. On the *interior*, it is worth noting the wide use of the local pitch-stone both in the flooring and in the holy water font and a tomb slab, set near the presbytery (1577). In Largo Camarina stands the Baroque Palazzo Battaglia (A5), possibly the work of Rosario Gagliardi.

S. Giorgio Vecchio (B6). The Catalonian

Gothic style portal dating from the 14th c. is the sole surviving relic of the large church dedicated to St. George (S. Giorgio), destroyed by the earthquake. In the lunette, you should note a bas-relief of St. George on horseback, slaying a dragon, and, in the rhomboid panels above it, the eagles of Aragon.

Giardino Ibleo (A6). This garden was built in the 19th c. in the area surrounding the churches of S. Giacomo, S. Domenico, and the Cappuccini. Two other churches occupied this location: S. Teodoro, since destroyed, and the first church of S. Giorgio (see above), of which the portal survives. Of the churches that survive, the church of *S. Domenico* (or of the Rosario) is in particularly poor condition due to neglect, though it still has its campanile decorated with colored majolica; *S. Giacomo* (14th c.), originally with three aisles, now features only a central nave dating from the Baroque reconstruction (note the decorated 18th-c. wooden ceiling, and, in the presbytery, a *Crucifix* of the Spanish school of the 17th c.). At the far end of the Giardino Ibleo is the *church of the Cappuccini*, which contains a large altarpiece by Pietro Novelli, known as the Monrealese, with *Our Lady of the Assumption, with Apostles and Angels and Saint Agatha and Saint Agnes*, as well as a *Nativity* of the southern school, dating from 1520, interesting also for its depiction of a medieval village, said by some scholars to be a depiction of Ibla.

5.2 The Ragusa region

This itinerary involves two separate routes that cover the two most homogeneous areas. You should take into account four main locations, two in each area, i.e.: Ragusa and Mòdica for the first excursion; Caltagirone and Gela for the second. For the first route (123 km.), starting out from Ragusa, you should take the old road to Mòdica, the state road 115, which drops down into the valley, or Valle dell'Irminio. To the south, you can see the highest bridge in Europe (168 m.), designed by Riccardo Morandi; the

A "masseria iblea" with pastures bounded by typical drystone walls in the background

bridge crosses the river Irminio, and links the state road 514 to Mòdica. You will leave the state road on a line with Mòdica: you will take it again in the southern stretch, toward Pozzallo. You then follow the coast in the direction of Marina di Ragusa, leaving behind you, immediately on your right, the detour to Scicli, and driving past a number of tourist accommodations. The landscape of the coast road reserves a number of pleasant surprises.

After you reach the last coastal town, Scoglitti, you will follow the local, or provincial road to Vittoria, in a territory that alternates farms and huge dry-wall greenhouses. After you leave Vittoria you will travel east along the state road 115 as far as Còmiso. The road winds among vineyards and watermills, no longer used, that once ran on the flow of the river Ìppari. Before you reach Còmiso, you will note many marble yards, where the traditional working of the local stone, or "pietra di Còmiso," has since been expanded to include imported marble, constituting one of the chief industries of the town. Before you enter the straightaway that runs into Ragusa, on the right a crossroads splits off to the Castello di Donnafugata, a lavish 19th-c. residence. You will leave the city to take the second route (running 111 km.) from the easternmost extremity of Ibla, heading north along the state road 194 to Giarratana. The road runs parallel with the river Irminio through an area with dense vegetation. Once you pass Giarratana, we advise a detour to Chiaramonte Gulfi, where there are magnificent views. Return to the main route, and you will reach Monterosso Almo, the last township in the Provincia di Ragusa, on the boundary with the Provincia di Catania. After a series of twisting switchbacks and

climbs and descents, you will reach Vizzini, birthplace of Giovanni Verga. You leave Vizzini and join the state road 124 heading west toward Grammichele, and from that city with its hexagonal plan you will continue on, crossing the western slopes of the Monti Erei. Once you reach Caltagirone, the third major stopping point on the whole route through the Ragusano, after a brief downhill stretch you will cross the state road Catania-Gela, which runs in a southwesterly direction. Once you have entered the province of Caltanissetta, the vast plain of Gela and, in the distance, the smoke stacks of the petrochemical plant mark an end to the route.

The farms of the Ibla region

Among the green pastures and the dense crosshatch of drystone walls, made with local limestone, in the area around Ragusa and Modica, it is possible to see clusters of buildings. These are the "masserie iblee," great farmhouse complexes organized into small villages, formed around a closed central court of considerable size. In recent periods, some of these "masserie iblee" have become centers for "agriturismo," a sort of agrarian bed and breakfast, or they simply serve unassuming meals. Among the farm complexes that preserve their original structure, we should mention the *Masseria Musso* and the *Masseria Rizza*, privately owned, but possible to view upon request. The former is a small village, with little adjoining church. The courtyard, which is quite large, is bounded by low residential buildings; on the sides there are stables and storehouses. The Masseria Rizza is different in structure and in activities from many others in the area. The regular courtyard is defined by the owner's "palazzotto r mansion, with a little church facing, and wo lower structures, set along either side.

Mòdica

he many descriptions that travellers of he past offered of Mòdica (elev. 296 m., op. 50,529; plan below), tended to describe it as a city torn from the rock, because of its grottoes, which were inhabited ntil a few decades ago, for its stairways, nd for its geographic location. As curious s the city's structure may be, it is also enowned for the remarkable sweets that re made here.

here are traces on the edge of the city nd within the urban perimeter of the pres-ence of humans during the period of the Civilization of Castelluccio (20th to 15th c. B.C.). During Roman times, there is documentation of the existence of Motyka, a "civitas decumana." With the Moorish conquest in A.D. 844-45, Mòdica – with its surrounding territory – underwent a profound shift in the way that agricultural resources were used. Under the Normans, the city, with its powerful strategic location, reached its greatest glory. It was the capital of the county ("contea"), with Peter I of Aragon, and was later ruled by the Chiaramonte, the Cabrera, and the Henriquez-Cabrera, all families of enormous political influence in Sicily. The concession of emphyteusis, or

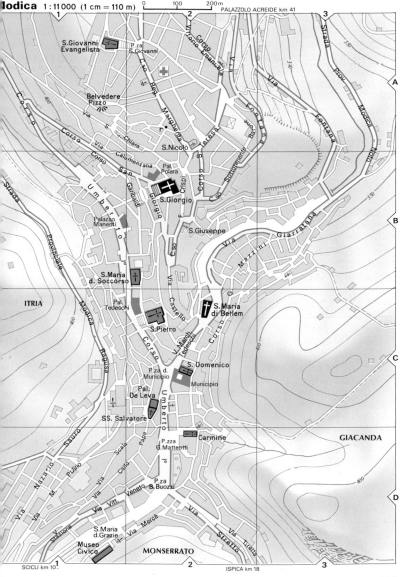

perpetual lease, from the 15th c. on, introduced a number of privileges that allowed
a greater distribution of the wealth that
proceeded from agriculture,with the consequential growth of a strong middle class.
The medieval city, with its two mountain
streams as natural defences, created the fortification of the castle, or Castello on the
ridge of the upland, where the enclosure
wall terminates to the north; not far from
the "cave" outside of the walls rise small villages. The earthquake of 1693 caught the
city in a period of consolidation around
the new settlements founded by the numerous religious orders. The reconstruction, on the same original site, focused in
particular along the axis of the Viale Regina
Margherita and on either side of what is
now the Corso Umberto, with the powerful
contribution of the new agrarian nobility.
The new territorial layout pushed the city
downhill, creating a considerable shift in the
urban structure during the 19th c.
The tour suggested here touches only the
most salient features of a city of easily-
overlooked corners full of charm and atmosphere. If you set out from Piazza Buozzi,
in the southern area of the city, follow the
Corso Umberto I and you will reach the Piazza Matteotti, characterized by the exquisite façade of the church of the Carmine,
later Piazza del Municipio, a nerve center in
this city, set at the confluence of the two
mountain streams, covered over between
the 19th c. and the beginning of this century. You may then continue along the Corso
Umberto I, over the corresponding
streambed of the Torrente Janni Mauro,
skirting the quarter known as Cartellone-San
Francesco, which was home to a Jewish
community until 1474. To the right and to
the left of the "corso" there are rows of
buildings dating back to the 18th and 19th
c., until you reach the Palazzo Manenti; to
the right of that building, if you turn into the
Via Mortillo, you will climb up the spectacular flight of steps that leads up to the
cathedral of S. Giorgio, in the higher part of
town. As you enter the quarter of S. Lucia,
one of the town's oldest quarters, along
the Via S. Chiara, you will reach the
Belvedere Pizzo, a terrace with a panoramic view, at an elevation of 449 m., from
which you can survey most of Modica and
the hills that surround it. From the Via Pizzo, you will reach the church of S. Giovanni Evangelista, and from there you can head
back down to the center of town along the
Corso Regina Margherita, chief thoroughfare of the "città alta," or upper city, marked
by the elevations of 18th- and 19th-c.

palazzi. Once you come even with the
church of S. Nicolò, you can take the Corso
Francesco Crispi, and after it the Via de
Castello, which runs around the enclosur
of the medieval fortress, which was lev
elled by the earthquake of 1693 and neve
rebuilt. Follow the Via Posterla (on th
right, a short detour through the Via Sba
zo makes it possible to view the grottoe
that are now used as stables and ware
houses, but which until a few centurie
ago, were used as homes by peasants) an
the Via S. Maria to head back down to th
"città bassa," or lower section of the tow
once you pass the church of S. Maria o
Betlem you will return, along the Via March
sa Tedeschi, to the Piazza del Municipio.

Convento dei Padri Mercedari (D1). Thi
monastery was built in the 18th c., and no
serves as a town library, an auditorium
and a civic museum, or **Museo Civico**. Th
ethnographic section was founded in 197
as the **Museo Ibleo delle Arti e Tradizior
Popolari**, and occupies the second floor;
offers perfect reproductions of the objec
and tools of a peasant farmhouse or of th
workshop of a master artisan of times gor
by, including: the "scarparu" (cobbler), th
"firraru e firraschecchi" (blacksmith an
farrier), the "mastru ri carretta
(cartwright). Adjoining the monastery, bu
dating back to an earlier period, is th
church of S. Maria delle Grazie, which wa

Mòdica: the S. Giorgio Cathedral

unded to commemoration the "miraculus" discovery, in 1615, amidst mysteriusly burning thorn-bushes, of an image the Virgin Mary with Christ Child, paint-d on a little slab of slate. The image is oused in the main altar of the church.

hurch of the Carmine (D2). This church as rebuilt after 1693, and of the older ructure, all that survives is the pointed-ch portal and a rose-window that surounts it. On the interior, at the second al-r on the left, note the *Annunciation*, a arble group believed to be by Antonello agini (1528-30).

iazza del Municipio (C2), or town square. iis full-fledged hinge of the city's layout and e, the Piazza del Municipio, set at the in-rsection of the Corso Umberto and the ia Marchesa Tedeschi, which are respec-vely the covered-over stream beds of the irrents known as the Janni Mauro and the ozzo dei Pruni, is surmounted by the crag the castle (Rupe del Castello), upon which ands an 18th-c. tower with a clock. To the ght of the square are the former monastery, Convento dei Domenicani, now the town all, or *Municipio*, and the adjoining church S. Domenico (14th c.): destroyed by the irthquake of 1613, it was rebuilt in 1678.

orso Umberto I (B1-C2). On either side of iis street, a series of pieces of architecture store some idea of the enormous impor-nce that this thoroughfare has had over ie centuries: on the left, the *former onastery of the Benedettine*, site of the tri-unal since 1866; further along, the 19th-c. ieater, the *Teatro Garibaldi*; on the right, ie spectacular stairway of the Baroque iurch of S. Pietro; as you continue, you will ote, again on the right, the *Palazzo edeschi* (18th c.), adorned with balconies ipported by typical carved brackets, and ie 17th-c. *church of S. Maria del Soccorso* djoining the former Collegio dei Gesuiti; stly, there is *Palazzo Manenti* with the rackets of its balconies depicting various ersonages of the era (18th c.).

Pietro (C2). This church existed as early the 14th c., and was rebuilt after 1693. You in enter it along a broad staircase embell-hed with statues of the twelve Apostles. he interior has three aisles: in the second iapel on the right aisle, note the *Madonna ell'Ausilio*, a *statue* of the Gagini school; in ie same aisle, at the second-to-last altar, ote the *St. Peter and the Paralytic*, a poly-irome group by Benedetto Civiletti (1893).

S. Giorgio* (B2). Rebuilt on the same site in which it was destroyed and rebuilt repeatedly, the cathedral, or Duomo di S. Giorgio rises atop a stairway of 250 steps, in a spectacular combination of architecture, stage design, and urban design, the work of Rosario Gagliardi. Inaugurated in 1738, it was completed in a number of stages, and as late as 1818 the stairway was finished. The *interior*, with five aisles, transept, and cupola, abounds in numerous works of art; on the main altar is a polyptych attributed to Bernardino Niger (1573); in the chapel to the left of the main altar, note the statue of the *Madonna della Neve* by Giuliano Mancino and Bartolomeo Berrettaro (circa 1510); in the far right side aisle, on the second altar, *Our Lady of the Assumption*, by Filippo Paladino, signed and dated (1610). You should also note the sundial traced in the floor of the transept (1895).

Alongside the church is the 18th-c. **Palazzo Polara**, an interesting example of an aristocratic residence that still preserves its original structure and part of its furnishings. It houses the *Pinacoteca Comunale*, or civic art gallery, with 18th- and 19th-c. paintings of the Sicilian school.

S. Giovanni Evangelista (A1). Destroyed by the earthquakes of the 17th c., this church was rebuilt in 1839. The campanile is the highest point in all Mòdica (elev. 449 m.); from the top of the stairway a road leads off to the left, to the *Belvedere Pizzo**, a spectacular panoramic overlook with a view of the whole city. A detour on the right of the square leads to the *church of S. Maria del Gesù*, built in the 15th c.: with the adjoining monastery, or Convento dei Minori Osservanti, it features a Catalonian Gothic portal, as well as a cloister with double orders of arches. The building, in a poor state of conservation, is now being used as a prison.

S. Maria di Betlem (C2). This church, built in the 15th c. on a site in which there stood the structures of four smaller churches, was damaged by the earthquakes of the 17th c., and was rebuilt in the 18th c. The *interior* has three aisles, with a truss roof and marble flooring. At the end of the right side-aisle, a magnificent 15th-c. portal leads into the chapel, or *Cappella del Sacramento**, a rare example of late-Gothic/Renaissance architetecture; at the altar, a 16th-c. *Virgin Mary with Christ Child* in painted stone.

Pozzallo

This is the only maritime township in the province, or Provincia di Ragusa; the history of Pozzallo (elev. 20 m., pop. 17,176) began with the construction (14th c.) of loading facilities for the exportation of wheat, which gave this town considerable importance in the economy of the county, or Contea di Modica. Traffic was directed by the "maestro portolano," the sole official responsible for the proper operation of the loading facilities. The tower, or Torre Cabrera, which still stands, was built to protect the storehouses from the frequent raids of pirates; later, it was one of the few private towers to form part of the overall systems of defenses along the Sicilian coasts, undertaken at the end of the 16th c. Pozzallo developed with a regular grid network, with straight roads. Behind the *Torre Cabrera* is the Piazza Rimembranza, overlooked by the *Palazzo Musso* (1926), which is characterized by ornamental features in the Liberty, or Art-Nouveau, style. From the square, if you continue along the Corso Vittorio Veneto, the city's main thoroughfare, you will reach the seafront promenade, or Lungomare, surrounding the large port. Pozzallo is linked to the nearby island of Malta through a regular hydrofoil service.

Scicli

This little Baroque jewel is off the beaten tourist track; Scicli (elev. 106 m., pop. 25,225) can be reached along a series of roads arranged radially. Conquered by the Moors in A.D. 864, it became a royal city under the Normans, who are said to have fought a fierce battle with the Moors who had landed along the coast, perhaps in an attempt to win back lost territory. The battle went in favor of the troops of Roger the Norman, and it is commemorated, in accordance with local tradition, by the presence of the sanctuary, or *Santuario della Madonna dei Milici* (a hermitage founded in 1093, in a scenic location, 1.5 km. from Scicli. In further commemoration of the event, each year, on the last Sunday in June, there is a festival known as the Sagra dei Milici). The tour begins from the Piazza Italia, where you can admire the *church of S. Ignazio*, which became the Chiesa Matrice in 1874, replacing the church of S. Matteo; the church dates back prior to the earthquake, and it was rebuilt in 1751. On the interior is the *Madonna dei Milici*, a papier-maché depiction of the Virgin Mary on a white horse, with a drawn sword in hand, in the act of fighting the Saracens, two of which lie under the hooves of her horse. From the square, you can climb up to the *church of S. Bartolomeo* (15th c.), among the few buildings that have been spared by the

great earthquake: inside there is a handsome *creche* made of linden wood, dating from 1573, and renovated by the Neapolitan craftsman Pietro Padula (1773-76). Of the 65 original statues, there survive only 29. You will return to the Piazza Italia along the Via Nazionale, a 19th-c. thoroughfare; branching off from this street are, successively, the Via Duca d'Aosta, with the *Palazzo Beneventano*, noteworthy for its unusual Baroque decorations, and the Via Mormino Penna, marked by a succession of Baroque aristocratic palazzi and monumental churches, culminating in the *church of S. Teresa*, no longer used as a place of worship but now serving as a concert and lecture hall. In Piazza Busacca note the Carmelite monastery, or *Monastero dei Carmelitani*, founded in 1386, destroyed in 1693, and rebuilt between 1775 and 1778; the church was built in 1769. From the square, you can walk to the *church of S. Maria la Nova*, at the foot of the two hills of the Rosario and of the S. Cassa, in one of the oldest quarters in the city; the imposing façade of this church, in Neoclassical style, is a reconstruction, and enlargement of the earlier, 15th-/17th-c. structures, done in 1816. The interior, decorated with stuccoes, features: on the 3rd altar in the right aisle, *Christ Risen*, a wooden statue attributed to Benedetto Civiletti; on the main altar, *Nativity of the Virgin Mary*, by Sebastiano Conca; on the 3rd altar in the left aisle, *Madonna della Neve*, a marble statue of the Gagini school (1496); on the 2nd altar, *Madonna della Pietà*, a statue made of cypress wood, probably of Byzantine origin.

Marina di Ragusa

This is a village that is linked to the capital, some 20 km. away; Marina di Ragusa (elev. 6 m.) grew around the maritime roadstead, protected by the tower built at the behest of the Conte Cabrera in the 16th c. to defend the coast. All that survives of the ancient tower is the square base. The town developed between the end of the 19th c. and the first few decades of the 20th c., a product of the intense activity of the port. A second powerful impulse to development came over the last few decades, in conjunction with the burgeoning phenomenon of vacation homes. Not far from the town, there has recently been established a nature preserve, the *Oasi della Foce dell'Irminio*, a coastal area of great interest in naturalistic terms.

Camarina

The long beach of the Cava di Randello, protected by a forest belonging to the forest rangers, lies near the archeological park

Parco Archeologico di Camarina, an ncient Syracusan colony, located at the outh of the river Ìppari, just a few kilometers outside of the town of Scoglitti. The earliest explorations in 1896, and the systematic survey, which began in 1958 and is still underway, have brought to light the urban layout of this ancient town. Historical sources (Thucydides, Herodotus, Diodorus Siculus) tell of the most important phases in the history of this city founded by the Corinthians of Syracuse in 598 B.C., the third colony after Acre (664 B.C.) and Casmene (644 B.C.). Camarina possessed a vast territory, some 200 hectares, and became a major maritime trading station, with strong links with the hinterland. Devastated and rebuilt repeatedly until 258 B.C., the year in which it was razed to the ground once and for all by Roman soldiers, this town was a major player in controlling this coastline for the three-and-a-half centuries which it existed. The park contains the building housing the archeological museum, *Museo Archeologico*, a typical rural 19th-armhouse, not far from the ruins of the *Temple of Athena*, and the ruins of the ancient town center. It is possible to see parts of the enclosure walls, in some sections 5 meters tall, as well as numerous ancient Roman "insulae" with tenements, and a few public, religious, and civil areas. Of enormous importance, for an understanding of the site and value of the material uncovered there, is the exploration of the many rich necropolises that surround the settlement. Between Punta Secca and Casuzze is an archeological site, the *Parco Archeologico di Caucana*, set amidst greenery: it contains the ruins of some twenty houses and a church with apse and mosaic floors.

Vittoria

Founded in 1607 by the Contessa Vittoria Colonna, Vittoria (elev. 168 m., pop. 55,280) enjoyed a series of privileges: concessions of land, exemption from tariffs, and a ten-year tax amnesty, immunity for criminals and indemnity for debtors. As a result, of course, the original town grew constantly, with an interruption due to the earthquake of 1693. The layout of the city follows a regular checkerboard pattern, oriented around certain piazzas. The most important meeting place is the Piazza del Popolo, with the *Teatro Comunale* (1877) and the church of *S. Maria delle Grazie* (1612, rebuilt in 1754).

Còmiso

There is documentation of the settlement of the territory of Còmiso (elev. 209 m., pop.

Còmiso: the Chiesa Madre

28,906) as early as the Roman period, provided by the unearthing of a mosaic floor (2nd c. B.C.) not far from the Fonte Diana; but the development of the village of Comicio (or Comicini) coincides with the Byzantine period (4th c. A.D.). The earliest documents per se date back to 1125 and 1168 (with a bull from Pope Alexander III), in Norman times, and speak of the growth of the hamlet around the two monastic complexes of S. Nicola (later SS. Annunziata) and Abrazia (S. Biagio). When the town became part of the county, or Contea di Mòdica, on 20 June 1393, the city was enclosed in a set of walls with five gates. In 1453 it passed under the rule of the dynasty of the Naselli, and in 1571 it became a county ("contea") in its own right. The development of the new quarters to the east and south (S. Crispino, S. Cristoforo, S. Leonardo, and S. Francesco) between the 16th and 17th c. marked the city in terms of a specific type of residence: one- and two-story row houses with exterior staircases, to deal with the steep slope of the streets. The reconstruction that followed the earthquake of 1693 give this town its present Baroque appearance. The history of Còmiso in the 1980s was enriched with a controversial chapter linked to the installation of an American nuclear missile base, which was strongly opposed by the pacifist movement. The dismantling of the base in the early 1990s left open the question of the use to which the buildings could be put.

The tour begins with the *Piazza del Municipio*, with a noteworthy fountain, the Fonte Diana, and bounded, in particular, by two buildings of outstanding construction: the *Palazzo Comunale* (or city hall, 1887) and the 17th-c. *Palazzo Iacono-Ciarcià*, rebuilt with its loggia following the earthquake. Not far away extends the Piazza S. Biagio: the adoration of this particular saint (Saint Blaise), the patron saint watching over Còmiso, who is venerated in the *church of S. Biagio*, dates back to Byzantine times. The church, which was rebuilt in the 18th c., still boasts the buttresses of the original structure. Facing it is the castle of the Aragonese counts, or the *Castello* dei Conti Naselli d'Aragona; it has been modified over the course of the centuries, and comprises an octagonal keep, probably Byzantine in origin, and by a square donjon: of particular interest are the two round-arch portals with iron doors; over one of the portals is a 16th-c. serlian window. In 1841, it was converted into a Neoclassical city theater. The church courtyard of the *Chiesa Madre* (S. Maria delle Stelle) dominates the Piazza delle Erbe: founded in the 15th c. on the site of an earlier Gothic church, it was reconsecrated in 1699. The wooden ceiling of the nave was frescoed in the 17th c. From Via Papa Giovanni XXIII you can reach: the *church of S. Francesco* (or of the Immacolata, at the end of the Via degli Studi), inside of which is the marble mausoleum of Baldassar III Naselli, attributed to Antonello Gagini; and the *church of theAnnunziata*, high atop a stairway at the intersection with the Corso Vittorio Emanuele; built in the 16th c., by enlarging the Byzantine church dedicated to St. Nicholas, later rebuilt to plans by G.B. Cascione-Vaccarini in 1772, and completed with a Neoclassical cupola and a campanile dating from the end of the 19th c. The interior, decorated with stuccoes, contains, at the first altar on the right aisle, a wooden polychrome statue of St. Nicholas (S. Nicola; 15th c.); on the altar of the right transept is a *Crucifix*, believed to be the work of Fra Umile da Petralìa.

Castello di Donnafugata

The castle was built at the wishes of the Barone Corrado Arezzo in the second half of the 19th c., on structures dating back to the 17th c., including the square tower at the center; it has been restored many times. The main façade – remarkably theatrical, with the long avenue running up it, lined with the houses of the peasants on either side – was enriched in the early years of the 20th c. with a small loggia in the Venetian Gothic style. The **interior** includes 122 rooms, not all of which can be visited. The rooms that are open to the public, set on the second floor, have period furnishings, a preserve intact the charm of an aristocr ic home. The **park** extends over more th eight hectares, with boulevards emb ished with a Neoclassical coffee-house maze, and a number of 'scherzi,' surpri powered by hidden mechanisms.

Giarratana

The second section of the route beg from Ragusa, heading toward ancient "C retanum," destroyed completely by t earthquake of 1693 and rebuilt at a less evated location, a few kilometers to t south. All that is visible in the old site remnants of the fortified walls, the ruins the castle and of a few churches. Giarrata (elev. 520 m., pop. 3,411), the new town, a regular gridwork layout, with a few m umental structures: the Baroque *church* S. Bartolomeo (18th c.); the *church of S.* *tonio Abate* (mid-18th c.), in the highe point in the city; the *Chiesa Madre*, with broad façade, contains noteworthy c vases from the 18th c.

If you leave Giarratana in the direction Palazzolo Acrèide, at a distance of 1.5 k from the town, turn to the left along a ro that runs up to the Monte Lauro (elev. 9 m.), and in about 7 km. you will reach t Monte Casale not far from the site of *C mene*, a military colony of Syracuse, four ed in 644 B.C.

Chiaramonte Gulfi

This town can be reached via a 15 km. c tour from the state road. Just before you ter the town itself, you will see, set amic the greenry, the sanctuary, or *Santua della Madonna delle Grazie*. From here y can begin a short hike through the pi forest, equipped by the forest rangers comfortable use. Gulfi, the original sett ment that gave rise to the little city that n stands here (elev. 668 m., pop. 8,424) w founded in the 12th and 13th c., and w short-lived, due to the destruction visit upon it in 1299 by the troops of Anjou. T rebirth of this town took place at the behe of Manfred I Chiaramonte, who rebuilt t new city, enclosed it in strong walls, buil castle, and then dubbed it with the name his family. The earthquake of 1693 was f lowed by a reconstruction in the Baroq style. The historic center is well preserv and maintains an easily recognizable m dieval structure. Once you reach the Pia za Duomo, with the *Chiesa Madre* (S. Ma la Nova), built in the 15th c. and restored 1770, you will enter the medieval quarter following the Via S. Paolo, on the right, a n Via S. Giovanni, on the left. The arch, *rco dell'Annunziata* is the only surviving e. In the distance, the *church of S. Giovanni Battista*, on the higher level, domies the surrounding landscape. One of the st noteworthy monuments of the area is sanctuary, or **Santuario di Gulfi**, loed at the edge of town to the north, at a tance of about 3 km.

nterosso Almo

s town (elev. 691 m., pop. 3,503), which sted in Norman times, when it was wn as "Monte Johalmo," owes most of development to Enrico Rosso, count of one, who in the 14th c. built a castle, of ace of which remains. Monterosso Almo s destroyed by the earthquake of 1693 l was rebuilt in the higher section of the . The center of the town is the Piazza S. vanni, higher up, where, atop a broad rcase, stands the *church of S. Giovanni*, ributed to Vincenzo Sinatra, from the ool of Rosario Gagliardi. Lower down, in Piazza S. Antonio, stand the other two in churches: the *Chiesa Madre*, rebuilt in Neo-Gothic style after the earthquake, ntaining two beautiful holy-water fonts m the 12th c. and a wooden Crucifix m the 15th c., and the *church of S. Anto-*, dating from the 18th c.

zzini

st there were prehistoric settlements, l then later, perhaps, the Roman city of lis, mentioned by Pliny and Cicero, and tly there are traces in the city layout of loorish period – these are features of the orly documented origins of Vizzini (elev. m., pop. 8,698). Concerning the devel-

opment and history of the medieval city, there is a fair amount of information from the 13th c. on. The castle, the city walls, and the extension to the east of the present town were all destroyed by the earthquake of 1693. The disaster left very few traces of the main architectural structures, some of which can be recognized in the structures of the *Chiesa Madre*, which is dedicated to the patron saint, St. Gregory; there is a Catalonian Gothic portal that provides evidence of an earlier building, perhaps the ancient Palazzo di Città. The center of the city is the square Piazza Umberto I, overlooked by the city hall, or *Palazzo Municipale* (19th c.) and an 18th-c. aristocratic palazzo, which once belonged to the family of the author Giovanni Verga who, born in Vizzini, set some of his novellas here. From Piazza Umberto I you can easily reach a number of interesting churches. Via S. Giovanni leads to the *church of S. Giovanni Battista*, which was enlarged in the 16th c. and rebuilt in the 18th c.; it has three aisles and stucco decorations. From the Via Vittorio Emanuele you can reach the *church of the Minori Osservanti*; of particular note here, on the main altar, is a *Virgin Mary with Christ Child*, by Antonello Gagini (1527).

Grammichele

Grammichele (elev. 520 m., pop. 13,609) is a 'designed city.' It was founded immediately following the violent earthquake of the Val di Noto, in order to prevent the scattering of the survivors of Occhiolà, a rural village that was completely destroyed. Carlo Maria Carafa Branciforte, assisted by the monk and architect Michele da Ferla, ordered the complex design. The idea of this

e hexagonal central square of Grammichele with the Chiesa Madre and the city hall

learned prince was inspired by the model of of the fortress-city of Palmanova in Friuli, built in 1593; this basic inspiration was enriched by the prince's love for sundials. The result was a design that is still preserved in the city hall, or Palazzo Comunale, where there is a depiction of "Magnus Michael" (which is a version of "Grammichele") carved into a panel of slate. The structure of the city is organized in accordance with a system of concentric hexagons, spreading out from the large square, a sort of center of gravity. The urban development abandoned – as early as the late 19th c. – the original design, with a progressive collapse of the lines of force. In the hexagonal central square stand the city hall, or *Palazzo Comunale*, designed by the

architect Carlo Sada in 1896 (housing Archeological Museum with its interes funeral collections from the Terravecc necropolis 6th c. B.C.), and the *Chi Madre*, dedicated to St. Michael, and b between 1723 and 1765. Take Via Rom. reach *Piazza Alessandro Manzoni*, one of six outlying square plazas, and from th you can continue in a clockwise directi in accordance with the idea of a giant cle by following the former Via Settima, now Cavour, which runs through all of squares of the outlying quarters.

Caltagirone

When you say the name of Caltagirone (e 608 m., pop. 36,898; plan below) to a Sicil he or she will immediately think of a s

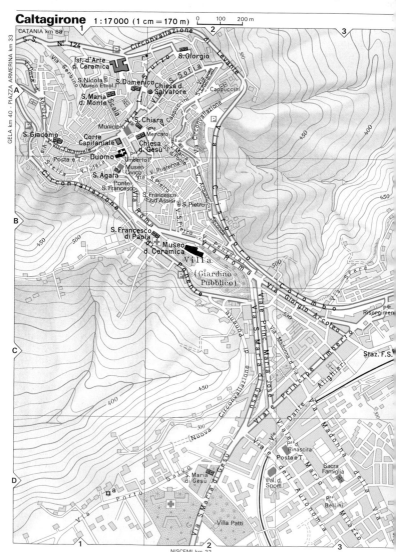

Caltagirone 1:17 000 (1 cm = 170 m)

ing array of colors taking form in objects
le of terracotta. In Caltagirone, in fact,
tradition of ceramics has exceedingly
ent roots. The city has continued this
lition up to the present day, developing
twists to the older ways: among the
t recent and most evident new contri-
ons is the facing of the steps of the
-c. stairway, the Scala del Monte; the
ng was done in 1953. Nowadays, this
s in excellent health, and is thriving on
demand of a steady flow of sightseers,
vell as the crowds attracted by various
ural events and activities: a ceramics
ool and museum, or Scuola della Ce-
ica and Museo della Ceramica, to name
; furthermore there is an exhibition of
ger scenes (at Christmas) and little ter-
otta whistles (at Easter).

merous archeological finds indicate a
tinuous human presence here from the
nze Age to Roman times; one com-
moration of the Moors can be seen in the
tle, to the north of the church of S. Maria
Monte. Roger the Norman conquered it
090, with the assistance of a colony of
urians who had settled there in 1038-
Once it had become a state-owned city,
tected by walls, Caltagirone began to
w, between the 12th and 17th c., in the
n of spread-winged eagle, which is in fact
image that appears in the city coat-of-
as. The crossroads, or "croce di strade,"
ich is constituted by the Via Principe
edeo and the stairway, or Scala del
nte (north-south) and the Corso Vittorio
anuele and the Via S. Sofia (east-west),
established in the 17th c., and it serves
ink the main sections of the city's his-
ic growth, and they are: the castle, or
stello, to the north, along with the
rch of S. Maria del Monte and the
nastery, or Convento degli Agostiniani;
church of S. Giorgio to the east; the
e, or Porta S. Pietro, demolished in the
h c., and the monastery, or Convento dei
ncescani, to the south; and the church
. Giacomo, to the west. In the 17th c., the
y's nerve center was the Piano di S. Giu-
o. Here, an originally Norman church,
church of S. Giuliano, stands alongside
Casa Senatoria, now the art gallery, or
leria Luigi Sturzo, and the Corte Capi-
iale. Ravaged by the earthquake of 1693,
tagirone was rebuilt on the ruins of its
self, with the contribution of the most
ed architects of Sicily.

is route, which follows the main thor-
ghfares of the urban layout, offers a ho-
geneous analysis of the development of
city over the course of the centuries.

The entrance to the old city can be said to
lie at the intersection between the Viale
Principessa Maria Josè and the Via Roma. If
you continue along the Via Roma, you will
pass the public park on the left, with your
first glimpse of polychrome majolica, and
then you will reach the Teatrino, whose
steps lead to the ceramics museum, or

*The tradition of ceramics is visible
everywhere in the city*

Museo della Ceramica. A little further along,
on the right, there is a splendid 18th-c. balcony by the ceramist Benedetto Ventimiglia.
After you pass the 'Tondo Vecchio,' on the
right lies the Piazza S. Francesco d'Assisi,
with a convent. This square, which was integrated into the walled city in the 16th c.,
was linked to the Piano di S. Giuliano with
a bridge (1626-66), later decorated with
majolicas. At the first wide square, you will
find the Bourbon prison, now a civic museum (Museo Civico), and the little church
of S. Agata, site of the confraternity of ceramists. A little further along you will find
Piazza Umberto I, with the ancient pawn-
shop, or 'Monte delle Prestanze,' linked by
two streets with the Piazza del Municipio,
with which it forms the core of the city:
the Via Duomo, overlooked by the Duomo
and the Corte Capitaniale, and the Via
Principe Amedeo, an extension of the staircase of S. Maria del Monte, the thoroughfare
of the ancient city. Once you have passed
the city hall, or Municipio, you will see the
spectacular stairway of S. Maria del Monte:
this route includes the climb up that stairway, tiring, but enjoyable due to the decorations of the 142 steps, as well as a descent

at the end of the visit to the medieval city. The ancient quarters at the summit of the stairway are marked by the presence of numerous churches: S. Maria del Monte, S. Domenico, SS. Salvatore, S. Giorgio (this was the church, in the 11th c., of the Ligurian community). If you take the Via Luigi Sturzo, the second axis in the crossroads (in an east-west direction), you will return to the Piazza del Municipio and you will con-

Thanks to tourism, the production of ceramics has become an important source of local income

tinue along the Corso Vittorio Emanuele, with numerous aristocratic palazzi; at the end of the "corso" you will see the church of S. Giacomo. It is worth making a special trip to the monumental cemetery, or Cimitero Monumentale, designed by the architect Giambattista Nicastro in 1866.

Giardino Pubblico (B2). The first projects for clearing the hill, which was uncultivated, date back to 1846, and in 1850 the Bourbon governor commissioned the architect Giovanni Battista Filippo Basile to plan how to revamp the hill. His design took its inspiration from the model of the English garden, and was completed in the Liberty style (Art-Nouveau) in the early 20th c.

Museo Regionale della Ceramica* (B2), or regional museum of ceramics. You enter the museum from the so-called *Teatrino*, a scenic overlook of the city, designed in 1792 by the architect Natale Bonaiuto, comprising a network of ramps, alternating with steps and benches, adorned with panels and reliefs in polychrome majolica. The Museo, established in 1965, contains many examples of the production of ceramics in Sicily from prehistory to the present day.

S. Francesco d'Assisi (B1-2). This convent was founded by the Blessed Richard (Beato Riccardo), a companion of St. Francis himself: the adjoining church was built in 1226

in the Gothic style, and the Gagini famil[y] so worked on it, beginning in 1592. Reb[uilt] following the earthquake in the Baro[que] style, it was completed with a campani[le] 1852. It preserves, in a chapel adjoinin[g] presbytery, remains of the original Go[thic] structure. The nearby bridge, or *Ponte [S.] Francesco* links the hill of this convent [with] the plain, or Piano di S. Giuliano: bui[lt] 1666, it spans some 50 m. with a differe[nce] in elevation of more tha[n ...] m. From the bridge, o[n a] clear day, you can se[e as] far as the African Sea [and] the Ionian Sea.

Museo Civico (B1), or c[ity] museum. The building t[hat] houses it, erected in 1[...] and completed in 17[...] served as a prison u[ntil] 1890. It later becam[e the] Monte di Pietà (charita[ble] institution) and served [oth]er public functions, and [was] heavily renovated o[ver] time, with the destructio[n of] the main chapel and the torture chambe[r. In] the 1960s, the Museo Civico was mo[ved] here, with three sections – history, arc[hae]ology, and the art gallery.

Duomo (A1). When the Senato decide[d in] 1582 to enlarge the Duomo, or cathedral, [add]ing it three aisles, it was the reversal of [the] orientation of this building – founded [by] the Normans, and dedicated to St. Ju[lian] (S. Giuliano) – that constituted the larg[est] change; till then it had been facing w[est]. Destroyed by the earthquake of 1693 and [re]built in the early 18th c., because of the [se]rious damage it had suffered, the Duomo [had] its elevation demolished in 1838; the ele[va]tion was replaced in 1909 by the present-[day] façade, in a floral style (the campanile da[tes] from 1954). *Inside* are many paintings [by] local artists of the 19th c.; in the left trans[ept] is a marble statue of the Gagini school. [To] the right of the Duomo is the *Corte Cap[i]niale*, a long single-story building dat[ing] from the 16th/17th c.

Scala di S. Maria del Monte (A1). With 1[...] steps, the stairway, or Scala del Monte c[ov]ers a vertical distance of roughly 50 [m], and since 1606 it has joined the higher s[ec]tion of the city with the Piano di S. G[iu]liano. In 1953 the stairway was rebuilt in v[ol]canic stone, and embellished in the ris[ers] with majolica decorations, with patter[ns] that recapitulate the history of local

ics. For the feast of St. James (24/25 Ju-
the stairway is lit with more than four
usand oil lamps, containing a total of
e than five quintals (over a thousand
nds) of oil. Along the stairway there
numerous workshops of ceramists,
re it is possible to watch various phas-
f the production and decoration of ce-
ic products.

Iaria del Monte (A1). Once the Chiesa
rice, this church is thought to date back
'orman times. It is believed that it was
t in the main square of the old medieval
ige. Rebuilt immediately following the
hquake, it still preserves on its main al-
he *Madonna di Conadomini*, a panel of
Lucchese school from the 13th c. The
sure includes exquisite gold work and
ver 15th-c. ostensory.

**omenico or church of the Rosario and
rch of the SS. Salvatore** (A1-2). These
churches face each other in the Largo
omenico: the first dates from 1801, and
arrently used as an auditorium; the oth-
lates from the 19th c. and has an interi-
nriched with fine stucco work, as well as
atue of the Virgin Mary believed to be by
onello Gagini, 1532. Since 1963, more-
r, it has contained the tomb of Don Lui-
turzo, the illustrious sociologist, who
s the mayor of the town in the first
ade of the 20th c., and who was the
nder of the Partito Popolare Italiano.

iiorgio (A2). Local tradition attributes
e foundation of this church to the
10ans who were present in the city as

early as 1030. Of the original church all
that remains are traces of a pointed-arch
portal and sharply splayed narrow loop-
holes. Rebuilt more than once following
the earthquake, it remains incomplete in the
façade (designed in 1830). On the interior,
in the second altar on the left, a very fine
Trinity of the Flemish school (attributed to
Rogier van der Weyden).

S. Chiara (A1). This little church was built
by Rosario Gagliardi between 1743 and
1748, with a polygonal plan and a curvilin-
ear façade. It possess a rich majolica floor,
recently redone. Adjoining it, on the site of
the Clarissan convent, is the old plant of the
Officine Elettriche, built by Ernesto Basile in
1908 in an Art-Nouveau style.

Basilica di S. Giacomo (A1). This church,
dedicated to the patron saint of the town, St.
James, was built, according to tradition, at
the behest of the Conte Ruggero (Roger I).
Destroyed almost entirely by the earthquake, it was rebuilt immediately and completed in 1700. On the inside were placed a
number of works by the Gagini that had
been in the church that was destroyed.
Above the central portal is the great marble
coat-of-arms of the city, carved by Gian
Domenico Gagini; the portal of the relics in
the left transept is by Antonuzzo Gagini. The
statue of *St. James* (S. Giacomo) is by Vincenzo Archifel (1518).

Gela*

In a context in which archeological relics
hearken back to a rich past, the chaotic
urban expansion of Gela (elev. 46 m., pop.

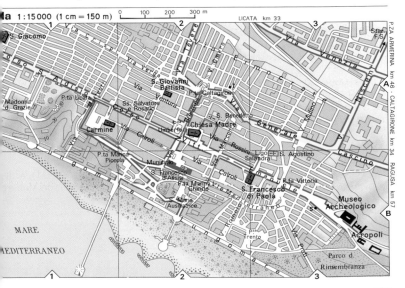

72,535; plan on page 119) over the last few decades flies in the face of common sense. In 668 B.C., colonists from Rhodes and Crete founded the city on the eastern slope of the hill, and they soon dominated coast and plain. The town was destroyed by Carthage in 405 B.C. and was refounded in 338 B.C., only to be razed to the ground in 282 B.C. by the Mamertines and by Finzia, the tyrant of Agrigento, who moved the inhabitants of the city into the town of Phintias, present-day Licata. Scattered to the four winds for more than 1,500 years, it was refounded by Frederick II of Swabia in 1230, with the name of Terranova, on the site of archaic Gela, between the present-day Piazza Umberto I and Largo Calvario, which are crossed by the perpendicular lines of the Corso Vittorio Emanuele and the Via G. Marconi. Becoming a feudal holding at the turn of the 15th c., the city was enclosed with walls in 1582. The urban perimeter was thus contained until the 19th c., and the city began to take on a structure with a gridwork of streets at right angles. In 1927, Terranova assumed its ancient name of Gela. The development of the city has its negative aspects; one is the huge petro-chemical plant run by ANIC, which was built in 1961: this self-contained complex has greatly contributed to the chaotic and jumbled growth of the city, as well as doing overt damage in the form of pollution.

The tour can be broken down into three parts. The first part, dedicated to the me-dieval layout of the city, begins in the Piaz-za E. Mattei. Once you pass the site of the gate, or Porta Caltagirone (A2), which no longer stands, you will follow the Via G. Navarra Bresmes until you reach the Piaz-za Umberto I (A2), where the town's main thoroughfares intersect. Overlooking this square is the main church, or *Chiesa Madre*, rebuilt in 1766, with a Neoclassical façade that was completed in 1844. You will turn to the right along the Corso Vittorio Emanuele (A-B2-3), the main street of the city, where the townspeople take their evening prom-enades: around midway, on the right, note

the 18th-c. *church of the SS. Salvatore* Rosario (A2, 1796). A little further al the Via Trieste, on the left, leads to *church of the Carmine* (A1, 1514). At th tersection, with the Via G. Matteotti (th tersection corresponds to the site of gate, or Porta Licata, demolished in 1 turn to the left and continue along th Miramare, skirting the southern walls w still contain two towers built by Freder (known as "torri federiciane"). Take th F. Morello and the Via Fratelli Cairo reach the *church of S. Francesco d'A* (B2, sec. xvii) in the Piazza S. Franc d'Assisi; nearby is the city hall, or Mu pio. You can then return to the Corso torio Emanuele and, turning onto the str that runs east, toward the Porta Vittoria, will see on the right the *church c* Francesco di Paola (B2-3, 17th c.); on left, in the Largo Salandra, note the faça of the 15th-c. *church of the Agostiniani* gustinians) and the former monastery Convento degli Agostiniani (B3).

The second section of the visit is dedica to the archeological museum, or **Mu** **Archeologico***, and to the *Acropolis* (I which can be reached from Corso Vitt Emanuele, beyond the Porta Vittoria. tablished in 1958, the museum, in its nev stallation comprises two sections: on ground floor are finds from the ancient tlement, while the upper floor is devote the sanctuaries outside of town, the Gr necropolises, and the territory over wh the city had influence. Not far from the seum lies the *acropolis*, with the remain a Doric temple (5th c. B.C.) and of an arc temple dedicated to Athena (6th c. B.C The last part of the tour is of the **arch logical area of Capo Soprano*** (A1 map). From Corso S. Aldisio, after you cr the new urban expansion, you will reach Piazza S. Biagio; from there, you can turr to the left along the Via A. Manzoni, rea ing Capo Soprano. The high sand du have preserved the walls that enclosed town to the west, and which were unc ered between 1948 and 1954.

Syracuse and the Syracuse region

special geological structure of eastern Sicily, and its position in the complex interaction
e continental masses and plates in the Mediterranean, has made it a perennial theater
evastating earthquakes as long as it has been an island. The earthquake of 1693, known
e earthquake of the Val di Noto, after the area that was particularly hard-hit, was – both
use of the historic moment during which it occurred, and because of the consequences
it triggered – an event that can supply us with a way of understanding the nature of
and buildings in the aftermath of that great earthquake; and this is true of the entire
heastern strip of Sicily, to the south of the Piana di Catania. This is equally true for cities

w of the Ortigia promenade at dusk

were wholly destroyed and cities that were only damaged; the ensuing reconstruction
red an excellent opportunity to endow new cities and new buildings with that unique
e of Baroque that in Sicily acquired a radically new and diverse character, unlike the
e elsewhere, clearly influenced by what had gone before and by outside influences.

Siracusa**

ated in one of the loveliest maritime
dsteads of the Mediterranean Sea, Sira-
a (Syracuse; elev. 17 m., pop. 125,941;
n on page 128) is now a modern and dy-
nic city, which proudly boasts its great
noble past in its appearance. The ide-
oute for a spectacular arrival in Sira-
a is by sea, given the beauty of its nat-
port, into which juts the island of Or-
a. The countryside surrounding the port
road and green with trees, and crossed
he streams of the Ànapo and the Ciane;
ind all this is the ledge of the limestone
hland of the Epìpoli; in the distance
nds Mount Etna. Siracusa is a central
yer in the history of the Mediterranean,
art due to the names that it gave to cul-
e and the arts: Epicharmus, a Greek po-

et who invented the "comedia"; Theocritus,
a bucolic poet; Archimedes, physicist and
mathematician; and to name a few illustrious contemporaries, Salvatore Quasimo-
do and Elio Vittorini.
The most important cultural event, recurring every two years, is the performance of
ancient tragedies in the Greek theater. In
July or in September, we should mention
the Palio, or horse race, and the Festival of
the Sea, while on 13 December there is a
celebration of the feast day of the patron
saint, St. Lucy; on the first Sunday in May,
in the context of the adoration of this same
saint, a number of quails are freed, and
flock through the sky over the town. The local crafsmen make paper and papyrus
parchment, as well as reproductions, in

precious and ordinary metals, of ancient Syracusan coins.

The historical background

A reliable historical chronology indicates 734 B.C. as the year of the foundation of Greek Syracuse by a group of Corinthians under the leadership of Archia, though archeological digs have confirmed traces of earlier human settlements. The two core settlements of the first Greek colony were located on the islet of Ortigia and the adjoining mainland (Akradina), in the area of the Foro Siracusano, and were probably at first linked by an earth causeway, and later by a bridge, probably located in the area behind the main post office, or Palazzo delle Poste. In the area around Akradina ran a torrential stream of water, the Syrakò, hence the probable derivation of the name Siracusa. The fact that it had an abundant supply of water from the spring, or Fonte Aretusa and that it was well-defended on every side were the notable advantages of Ortigia. The political and economic growth of the city, as early as the seventh and sixth c. B.C., and above all the transfer en masse of the population of other Sicilian colonies, ordered by Gelon (the tyrant of Gela, who siezed power in Syracuse in 485 B.C.), triggered – over the course of the 5th c. B.C. – a sharp increase in population and a consequential expansion of the city out beyond the original walls, with the creation of two other quarters: "Tyche," situated in the area to the east, and so-called because it is close to a temple of the goddess Tyche (Fortuna), and "Neapolis," which means the new city, where the archeological park, or Parco Archeologico now extends. Three other temples were built in the city, to commemorate victorious military exploits, and they can be easily found: the temple of Olympian Zeus (Zeus Olimpico), set on a hill overlooking the river Ànapo, near the port; the temple of Apollo, which can be toured in the Piazza Pancali; the temple of Artemis (Artemide). Gelon was responsible for the construction of the temple of Athena, which can still be identified in the structures of the cathedral, or Catte-

drale; he was also responsible for muc the city's growth; Syracuse soon bec one of the most important Greek metrɩ lises of the period, and its burgeo growth awoke the concerns of its ne bors. The war against Carthage caused city to come under the rule of the ty Dionysius I, who found himself forced t dertake major fortifications: he also mc away the population of the island of Ort which he then transformed into a fortr putting it exclusively to military use; he larged the little port and built an enorm circuit of walls that extends some 22 meters, which enclosed the quarters the terrace of Epìpoli (Epipolis, or " that stands above"), to the west of the tlement; the strongpoint of this loca was the castle, or Castello Eurialo. death of Dionysius, which took pl around the middle of the 4th c., trigger long period of transition. Thus, even the presence of such major figures as oleon and Agathocles and with a policy liances, aimed at preserving the city's in the Mediterranean basin, there was way to stave off defeat, which came in B.C., with plunder and sack under the mans led by the Consul Marcellus; s Marcellus was long stymied by the brill techniques of defense developed by Ar medes, and only succeeded in conqueɩ Syracuse after two years of siege.

Syracuse in those days must h been spectacular, with its ag temples, buildings, and wa Marcellus himself remained tivated by the town, and in plunder that followed the man victory, he spared all the ligious buildings; Syracu though it remained the capita Sicily and the residence of Roman praetors, and des some modest increase in stock of monuments, entere phase of decline, with the idential section dwindling size.

As early as the first few c turies of the Roman emp Christianity had begur spread, through the t that the city maintai with the major Syrian Palestinian towns. In 3rd c. the first commur

Statue of Venus emerging fr the sea (Museo "Paolo Or

eteries were established, such as the
:ombs, or Catacombe di S. Lucia, Vigna
ia, and S. Giovanni; early-christian re-
us architecture is well exemplified by
churches of S. Pietro and of S. Giovan-
vangelista, beneath the crypt of the
ch of S. Marziano. After a long siege, the
was sacked and devastated by the
rs in A.D. 878; the Moors however left
ep urbanistic sign of their presence:
s and courtyards, enlivened by mar-
and small shops, are especially typical
e island quarters of the Graziella and
iperduta. The most significant factor in
is of the city structure, in any case,
the shrinkage of Siracusa, beginning
isely during the last twenty years of the
c. and extending up to the end of the
c. – for an entire millennium, in other
ds – to only the island of Ortigia, which
long been separated from the main-
by a channel. In the definitive expulsion
e Moors from the island, the Normans
pleted the project that had been begun
he Byzantines under George Maniace,
were responsible for the rebuilding of
ancient fortifications and the con-
ction, at the southernmost tip of Ortigia,
castle (Castello Maniace).
r a brief period of Angevin rule, Siracusa
ived enormous economic benefits from
successive rule of the house of Aragon,
ecially in its trade with the rest of Eu-
e, trade that left is mark in the great ar-
ectural development of the city: the
struction of the bastions that guard the
ld and the construction of a great many
izzi date from this period. The Black
th of 1348 and the feudal conflicts
ught Siracusa under Spanish rule for a
g period; during that period great forti-
tions were built and very fine architec-
l projects were completed. The famines
he 15th c., the earthquake of 1542, the
shing taxes imposed on the citizenry to
for the construction of the fortifica-
s, together with the gradual decline in
le, led to the flight of the great families
own, to the degree that by the end of the
c., the population of Siracusa was no
e than 14,000. One crucial event in the
's history was the terrible earthquake of
anuary 1693. It did not, generally speak-
cause irreparable damage to the build-
of Siracusa, nor did it leave marks in the
ic of the city, but it did offer an occasion
the renovations of style typical of that
iod. Restorations were undertaken of
naged buildings, in some cases through
tial demolition, and often the interiors
the elevations were modified, giving the

city an 18th-c. appearance, concealing its
ancient aspect.
In 1865 Siracusa was made provincial capital again, and this date was an important
one for its future growth. The establishment here of government offices and the
considerable growth in population caught
the city unprepared, enclosed as it still was
within the walls of Ortigia. There was a
rush to build upwards, filling in every empty lot, and reaching the height of feverish
construction madness following the law
suppressing the convents and monasteries
(1866) and with the demolition, beginning in
1886, of the complex of Spanish fortifications. In urbanistic terms, the most significant projects were the great demolition
projects done during the Fascist era, and in
particular the construction of the Via del Littorio, now the Corso Matteotti; while with
the great boom of the 1950s and the 1960s
began the period of living alongside major
industrial plants – however uncomfortable
and at times even unprofitable that proved
to be. All the same, the city's allure has
survived sack, plunder, sieges, earthquakes,
rampant development and speculation, industrialization: indeed, it has been this succession of often traumatic events that has
triggered an interesting process of stratification and juxtaposition, which can be seen
at all and any scale.
The tour of this city can be broken down into two routes, starting from the area of the
archeological area, heading one toward
the mainland and the other toward the island of Ortigia.

The mainland

This mainland route runs through the quarters of the pentapolis of Syracuse, which developed with the growth of the Greek city;
several of the quarters were abandoned in
certain historical periods, because of the
concentration of population on Ortigia.
The tour, logically enough, begins with the
Castello Eurialo, almost a preview of these
imposing Greek fortifications on the highland of the Epìpoli.

Castello Eurialo** (plan on page 124 and on
128: A2, off map). This castle stands at a distance of roughly 8 km. from the center of the
city, but it was linked to the city as part of
the overall defenses of Greek Syracuse,
constituting the most spectacular and at
once historically correct approach to the
city; to go up to the highland, or Altopiano
di Epìpoli means admiring not only Siracusa in its Greek extension, but also admiring one of the finest panoramic views of

123

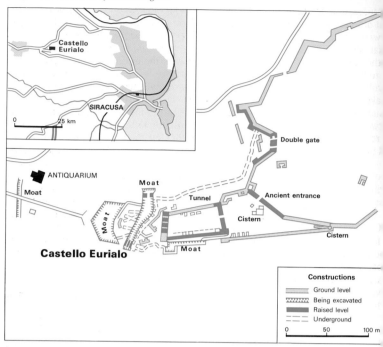

Castello Eurialo

Constructions
Ground level
Being excavated
Raised level
Underground
0   50   100 m

Sicily, from a very evocative location. Built at the turn of the 4th c. B.C. by Dionysius, it did its job very well, thanks to the military genius of Archimedes, until the fall of Syracuse to Roman might. Its strategic location and its structure – interior and exterior, built in accordance with new ideas that were innovative at the time – make this a jewel of military engineering; it is however wise to carry a map to find one's way in the vast expanse of ruins, extending over one-and-a-half hectares. The complex is made up an outlying fortified outworks, preceded by two deep moats, excavated with sheer walls in the living rock, and followed by another moat, 9 m. deep, with a drawbridge, from which there branched out a complex network of tunnels linking the various parts of the castle. Over this outpost extended the great defensive enclosure that contained the entire terrace of the Epìpoli, girt with five defensive towers and split into two separate circuits of walls, with barracks, cisterns, bastions, underground galleries, hidden passages, movable stairways, and crossed-tongs doors.

Teatro Greco** (A-B1), or Greek theater. The monument that stands here today is the most important structure in the archeological park, as well as the greatest expression of theatrical architecture and scenic technology from Greek times to survive to the present day; it is the result of an

expansion made at the behest of Hiero the 3rd c. B.C. of an existing theater that ed back to the 5th c.: tradition reco with considerable pride, that there were jor performances here of tragedies Aeschylus, but the theater was also used popular assemblies. Completely carved of living rock, it is divided into three se rate areas: the cavea, the orchestra, and scaena. The *cavea*, the area reserved spectators, has a diameter of 138 m subdivided into nine sectors, and is di ed roughly midway up by a corridor, the azoma. The northern section of this co dor, or diazoma, is adorned with mouldi and has inscriptions of the names of a n ber of deities, and important personalit after whom various sectors were nam The areas of the *orchestra* and the *scaena* we see them today, are the fruit of tra formation which the Romans undertool adapt the theater for their own uses. abandonment of the monument began v the invasions of the Vandals and the Go in A.D. 440, with the definitive decline classical culture and traditions, and cu nated with the partial destruction of building at the orders of Charles V in 15 who had much marble removed from it a used it in the construction of fortificatio The cavea of the theater is overlooked b terrace carved into the rock; at the cen of the northern wall of this terrace you n note a large manmade grotto, dedicated

Muses, in which there was a bubbling
...t of water from the Roman aqueduct;
...water flowed into a channel cut into
...ar wall, and was then channeled into
...theater's hydraulic system. The rock
...to the west is dotted with little niches
...voltive images linked to the hero cult
...akes). In the southwestern area of the
...ument are the remains of an immense
...way, some 27 meters wide, perhaps
...rchaic theater that predates the clas-
...theater.

...di Ierone II (B2), or altar of Hiero II. This
...ificial altar must have been truly im-
...ssive, to judge from its base, the only
... that survives, which measured 198 x
...0 m. Still visible, on the north side, are
... feet of one of the two telamons that
...d at the entrance. Before the altar there
...bably extended a majestic porticoed
...are, at the center of which was a pool,
...visible, with a base in the middle on top
...hich stood a statue of Zeus.

...iteatro Romano (B2), or Roman am-
...heater. Dating from Roman times is the
...e elliptical amphitheater, visible in the
...carved out of living rock; the upper sec-
... of the cavea, formed of square-hewn
...:ks, has disappeared, destroyed by the
...nents and by plunder. The size of this
...cture is outdone only by the Colosseum
... the Arena of Verona. The cavea is sub-
...ded into quadrants by little staircases,
... is crossed by two corridors. It is still
...sible to make out the inscriptions on the
...e, which served to identify seating. Un-
... the nearby little *church of S. Nicolò* you
... still see the "piscina," or pool, used in
... cleaning of the arena, and which al-
...ed flooding of the arena for the staging
...aval battles.

...mie* (A2), or prisons. These are an-
...t rock quarries from which, as early as
...ek times, large blocks of grey-white lime-
...e were extracted for use in erecting
...dings and walls, giving the city its un-
...takable and distinctive color. What were
...e dark grottoes have been opened up
... to the collapse of the vaults following
...hquakes, and strong sunlight and great
...idity have caused the growth of luxu-
...t vegetation in those former quarries.
...white limestone walls, eroded into
...rd shapes of all sorts, are now dotted
...citrus trees, immense ficus trees, mag-
...as, and delicate maidenhair ferns. On
... interior of the archeological area is the
...st famous group of quarries, ranging in

height from 25 to 47 m.: as a group, at the
foot of the Greek theater (Teatro Greco),
they are known as the prison, or **Latomia
del Paradiso****. There is a renowned cu-
riosity, the ear of Dionysius (*Orecchio di
Dionisio*), which because of its shape and its
remarkable acoustic properties, has engendered the legend that the tyrant had
the place built and used it to listen to the
conversations of the prisoners enclosed
within. It is far more likely that the Orecchio
di Dionisio, originally dug as a rock quarry,
later served as a sounding board for the performances of classical theater that were
held in the adjoining theater. Near the Orecchio di Dionisio is a huge manmade grotto
supported by pillars carved into the rock:
this is the remarkable *Grotta dei Cordari**,
so-called because ropes ("corde") were
manufactured here, making use of the hu-

The Orecchio di Dionisio, an old rock quarry

midity that is so abundant in the grotto, as
moisture is required to make good rope.

For years it has been forbidden to enter the **Latomia dei Cappuccini** (A5), which lies at the foot of
the Convento dei Cappuccini, for safety considerations; you can however see it perfectly from up
on the Via Acradina. The "latomia," or prison, is
quite vast, labyrinthine, and the process of ero-
sion has produced bizarre forms there, enormous caverns, natural bridges, pylons. The odd
relationship between nature and man is here
gently underscored by the little flight of steps created to get over the pits that have been created
by the process of excavation in the "latomia."

Piazza S. Lucia (B4). The *church of S. Lucia*, in accordance with popular tradition, was supposedly built on the same site in which the Syracusan virgin, St. Lucy, met her martyrdom in A.D. 303, not far from the catacomb of St. Lucy (Catacombe di S. Lucia). Originally founded in Byzantine times, it now stands as a three-aisle basilica with semicircular apses: the oldest part (portal, apses, and the first two orders of the campanile) date back to the 12th c., while the rose window dates from the 14th c.; the portico, which extends along the elevation and one of the two sides, was the work of Pompeo Picherali (1727). Alongside the church, and linked to it by an underground passage, is the octagonal chapel, or *Cappella del Sepolcro*, built by Giovanni Vermexio in 1630 to contain the tomb of St. Lucy, whose body however was never moved here (it is still in Venice). The famous painting by Caravaggio depicting the *Burial of Saint Lucy* (1609), formerly in the apse of the church, is a work that is stylistically surprising and daring given the artistic culture of the period, and it is now in the Galleria Regionale, in Palazzo Bellomo.

Museo Archeologico Regionale "Paolo Orsi" * * (A3-4), or regional archeological museum. Located on the interior of the Villa Landolina, a large park abounding in historical relics (prisons, a cemetery, a number of pagan hypogea, or underground ch... bers), this building, with a triangular sh... fits into the setting as if camouflagin... self. With its exhibition area of 9,000 sq... meters, the museum, built to plans by F... co Minissi, has since 1988 housed the... lections that previously were housed in... historic site in the Piazza del Duomo, w... had – with the expansion of the collect... – become insufficient by this point; it... vides a complete presentation of the... lizations that have succeeded one ano... on this territory. At the center of the b... ing a large circular room is not only th... cal and physical point of reference for... museum – in this room one can also fin... necessary information concerning the... tory of the collections and the conten... the three major exhibition areas in wh... those collections are displayed. *Secto*... which begins with a closed geolog... overview of the territory of ibleo, is d... cated to prehistory and early history, f... the Paleolithic to the period of Greek c... nization. *Sector B* is dedicated to the hi... ry of the Greek colonies in Sicily, with ... cial reference to Megara Hyblaea and S... cuse. From Megara Hyblaea we should r... tion the earliest ceramics and a numbe... splendid sculptures*, including a fune... statue of the physician Sambrotidas, f... the middle of the 6th c. B.C. and, from ... same era, a statue depicting a mother n...

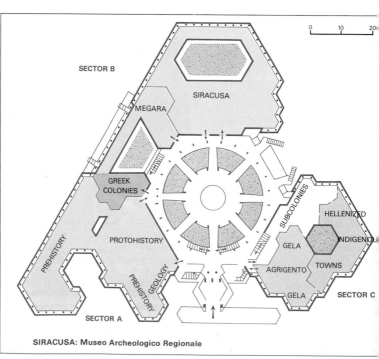

SIRACUSA: Museo Archeologico Regionale

win boys, made of painted limestone. owing these is a series of finds that con te the funerary furnishing found in the opolises of the city. The part concern Syracuse opens with a splendid copy Roman times of the ere Anadiomene**, aning "Venus emerging the sea"; though it is ally Aphrodite), found 804 by Saverio Lan n; it is known as well as Landolina Venus; next e collections of statu and largely ceramic erials from excavations e in the quarter of the adina (Piazza Vittoria) he sanctuary of Deme and Kore, and then the rary furnishings and

gelists; these date back to Norman times. The Byzantine church, of which the apse still stands, was the city's first cathedral ("duo mo"), and was divided into three aisles by columns that still exist. The western façade

A collection of vases at the "P. Orsi" Archeological Museum

itectural terracottas from the Temple pollo. Lastly, in *Sector C* there are finds Eloro, a Syracusan outpost along the st to the south of the city, and from the colonies of Akrai, Kasmenai, and Ka ina, including a terracotta acroterial up (intended for the summit of the roof building that was probably destined to gious use) depicting a horseman. Fur rmore, there is notable material from Hellenized indigenous towns in the Si an hinterland, and the major Doric onies of Gela and Agrigento.

acombe di S. Giovanni* (A3), or cata nbs of St. John. The history of the church racusa has played a major role in the his y of Christianity, a clear indicator of the 's importance even in the face of its pro ssive decline, a result of the Roman con est. The most important catacombs are Catacombe di S. Lucia, di Vigna Cassia, di S. Giovanni. The last-named cata nbs date back to the 4th c., and in their ginal layout, present a regular gridwork ucture that was built by enlarging an old ek aqueduct (traces of which can still be n in the vault of the main corridor). The eries lead to monumental chapels that, to their shape, are known as "rotonde," rotundas: in these were found the hand ne sarchophagus known as the Sarcofa di Adelfia. Adjoining the catacombs are remarkable *crypt of S. Marciano* (St. Mar nus, first bishop of Syracuse; 6th c.) and, ve it, the church of **S. Giovanni Evan ista**, whose altar stands on a line with the nb beneath it. In the *crypt*, Byzantine in out, four pillars were built, with four cap s depicting the features of the four evan

provides clear evidence of the renovation done during the Norman period, but the harshest blow was that struck by the earth quake of 1693, which caused the collapse of the roof, which was not replaced. The city then decided to build a new church, at a right angle to the main aisles of the earlier church, the little church, or *Chiesetta di S. Giovanni Battista*, with a lovely portal with, above it, a rose window. The portico, show ing Catalonian influence, can be dated to the 14th c., and included recycled materials.

Santuario della Madonna delle Lacrime (B3). Built to commemorate the miracu lous appearance of tears on an image of the Virgin Mary, in 1953, this building, begun in 1966, was only completed much later due to the ballooning budgets and to the great outcry over its size and height. De signed as an immense cone some 90 m. tall, the sanctuary today represents an unmis takable feature on the city's skyline.

The island of Ortigia

The approach to Ortigia that is best suited to its island nature is of course by sea: the entrance of the Porto Grande consists of a narrow passage emphasized to the left by point, or Punta del Plemmirio and to the right by the towers of the Castello Maniace. Continuing along, you will see a succession of palazzi with a warm golden hue, cam paniles, and cupolas of churches, until you reach a broad square in which the eye seeks out the mythical spring, or Fonte Aretusa; and then there is the tree-lined boulevard of the Lungomare, and above it the lovely promenade, or Passeggio Adorno. For those who enter this little islet (the 'scoglio,' or

127

'shoal' to the people of Siracusa, not even one square kilometer of surface area) from the mainland, on the other hand, there is a different but no less fascinating impression: you leave behind you the modern quarters, set amongst anonymous blocks of buildings, and as soon as you cross the bridge, or Ponte Umbertino, you are immediately swept up in a world of continuous discoveries, where even the traces of the many eras that have followed one on the heels of the other – Greek, Norman, Aragon, Baroque – give a harmonious and unified character to the setting. Every quarter, historically divided by the main thoroughfares (Via Dione-Via Roma and Via Amalfitania-Via della Maestranza), presents its own characteristics and its own specific qualities, faithfully noted in the place names. Everything tells a story: the temples, the palazzi, the shafts of columns, the courtyards, the façades, the town walls, the portals, the grate work.

Setting out from the square that lies before the archeological area, along the Viale Paolo Orsi, Via Columbia, Via Elorina, with a stop at the *Ginnasio Romano* (a monumental complex dating from the 1st c. A.D., including a theater, a quadriporticus, and a temple), and the roads that skirt the wharf, or Molo S. Antonio, you will find yourself on the bridge, or Ponte Nuovo, the only way for cars to get onto Ortigia. We would suggest that you park in this area, and continue on foot by one of two routes (or one of three, if you choose to take also the most fascinating of routes, the trip around Ortigia by sea; at the Riva della Posta, there are usually plenty of fishing boats that can be hired for this trip). The first route is the trip around the island by land, which emphasizes the relationship between Ortigia and the sea: from Riva Garibaldi and Viale Giuseppe Mazzini you will reach the Largo Porta Marina, and from there you can follow the entire Passeggio Adorno and the Lungomare Alfeo, as far as the Piazza Federico di Svevia. The Lungomare Ortigia marks the furthest section of the island overlooking the open sea, and by following the successive roads – Via Eolo and Via dei Tolomei – you will hook up with the Lungomare di Levante, which ends at the Riva Nazario Sauro, at the Porto Piccolo. The second route penetrates inland into the center of the island: from the Piazza Pancali, to the end of the so-called "straightaway," or Rettifilo (Corso Umberto), you will then reach Piazza Archimede via Corso Matteotti, and then by following the Via Roma, Via Capodieci, and Via Pompeo Picherali, you will reach the Piazza del Duomo.

From that square, you can enter the Saverio Landolina and, after returning the Piazza Archimede via Via Amalfitar you will enter the Via della Maestranza the end of which, via Via Vittorio Vene you can return to the Lungomare di Levar

The Marina (port) and the Passegg Adorno (E4-5). The broad waterfront bou vard, or Lungomare, a tree-shaded pron nade and, above it, and running paral the promenade or Passeggio Adorno, ideal places from which to admire the comparable panoramic view of the Po Grande, this vast body of water that w nessed many great battles, and which terms of size and shape, seems a lake rat than a branch of the sea. The modernizat of the jetty of the port did not result in a tal demolition of the town walls, and inde

km 58

Cittadella d. Sport
Latomia d. Cappuccini
Cappuccini
P.za Cappuccini
Via Foriti

Catacombe di S. Giovanni
S. Giovanni
Museo Regionale
Villa Landolina
Catacombe di Vigna Cassia
S. Maria di Gesù

Viale Teocrito
Viale Teocrito
Sant. Mad. delle Lacrime

Via Bassa Acradina
Via Augusto von Platen
Via Tica

Stadio Comunale

Via Piave
Via Monte Grappa

S. Lucia
Cappella d. Sepolcro
P.za S. Lucia

S. LUCIA

Via Testaferrata
Pza Vittoria
Via Di Natale
Corso Timoleonte
Carabelli
Maniace
Cadorna
Via Gorizia
Via Luigi
Via Ragusa
Via Bignami

Via Mosco
Via Teracati
Via Trapani
Via Statella
Pza d. Repubblica
Pza Euripide

Arsenale Antico

Tel.
ne F.S.
Via Arsenale

Imbarcadero di S. Lucia

MAR IONIO

Sacrario ai Caduti
Agorà
Foro Siracusano
Porto Piccolo

orgo S. Lorenzo
Viale A. Diaz
Via Dante
Via Catania
Via Margherita
Via Umberto
Posta e T.
P.za Posta
Via Trieste

Pza Lepanto
Pza Marconi
Viale Montedoro

Darsena

Crispi
Corso
Via Tripoli
Via Bengasi
Via Rodi
Pza Nuovo
Pza Pancali
Via Resalibera
Tempio di Apollo
S. Pietro

Pontile S. Antonio
Staz. Marittima F.S.
Pza IV Novembre
Mura Greche
Via XX Settembre
Via Savoia
Via Nizzeti
S. Maria d. Miracoli
Via Maniace
Corso Matteotti
Via Mirabella
S. Tommaso
Filippo
Via Maestranza

MAR IONIO

Marina
Traghetto per Malfa, Catania, Napoli, Tripoli
Pza Marina
Porto Trafalco
Ch. del Collegio
Via Cavour
Archimede
Pal. Montalto
Gargallo
S. Francesco
V. Maestranza
Belvedere S. Giacomo

PORTO GRANDE

Pal. Beneventano
Pza Municipio
Munic.
Duomo
Prefettura
ORTIGIA
Via Giudecca
S. Giov. Battista
S. Giuseppe
Pza

Capitaneria di Porto
Acquario Tropicale
Via Capodieci
Pal. Bellomo Gall. Region.

Fonte Aretusa
S. Martino
Via Cavour
Via Castello Maniace
Pal. Blanco
Lungomare Alfeo

MAR IONIO

1° itinerario
2° itinerario
3° itinerario
4° itinerario

Castello Maniace

129

it is atop the high enclosure wall that formed part of the old Spanish bastions that the 19th-c. "hanging" promenade now runs. It is marked by a succession of pink and golden palazzi, culminating in two large buildings that stand side by side, the old hotels *Albergo Miramare* and *Hôtel des Etrangères*; the town still hopes that these hotels will be adequately restored. The two points linking the Marina and the Passeggio Adorno are the *Porta Marina*, one of the entrance gates that formed part of the 16th-c. Spanish system of fortifications of the city, and the little villa overlooking the aquarium, or Acquario, cur-

sions of 51 meters on each side, an[d] formed part of the impressive syste[m] constructions that included earlier work[s] fortification. Its name came from the na[me] of the Byzantine general George Mani[aces] who, on the same site, had built a defens[ive] outpost. The castle stands on the furth[est] point of the island, atop a rocky prom[on]tory, isolated by a manmade channe[l] moat; the imposing square, enclosed [by] massive cylindrical corner towers, sho[ws a] refined construction technique that m[ade] use of three types of stone: limestone [and] volcanic stone for the square-hewn bl[ock]

The Castello Maniace situated on the furthest point of the island of Ortigia

rently being restored, which leads to the area of the spring, or Fonte Aretusa.

Fonte Aretusa* (F5). This thousand-year-old freshwater spring, once enclosed by walls and now populated by ducks, grey mullets, and papyrus plants, is one of the loveliest and most charming places in Siracusa. Legend has it that the nymph Aretusa, a lovely handmaiden of Artemis, was transformed by the goddess into a spring, in the forests of the Elide, in order to preserve the nymph from the unwanted attentions of Alpheus, the river god, who had fallen in love with her: fleeing underground, across the Ionian Sea, Arethusa emerged on Ortigia. But Alpheus, unwilling to resign himself to the loss, followed her, and joined her in the same pool of water.

Castello Maniace* (F5). From the spring, or Fonte Aretusa, if you follow the Lungomare Alfeo, you will reach the Piazza Federico di Svevia; from here, the tour of the rest of the circuit around the island by land is blocked by an iron gate, barring entrance to a military area that is exceedingly difficult to get into; in this area stands the massive structure of the Castello Maniace. This monumental fortress, perfectly square, was built in 1239 by Frederick II with ample dimen-

and sandstone for the fill-rock. Becaus[e] the Spanish modifications – such as [the] gate, or Porta Vermexiana at the dr[aw] bridge, and the modifications cause[d by] the earthquake of 1693 and the great [fire] caused by the explosion of the powder m[ag]azine in 1704, as well as the various use[s to] which it has been put in more recent ye[ars] (first as a prison and later as a barracks), [the] castle has been renovated in many secti[ons] with respect to the original plan; that [plan] can still be understood clearly, howeve[r].

Lungomare di Levante (D-E5). The hist[ory] of Ortigia is essentially the history [of a] fortress-town, whose dominant prob[lem] was always defending itself from the s[ea]. The cartography that has survived, an[d the] scholarly analysis of the traces of the w[alls] that are still visible, as well as the numer[ous] monuments and structures that still [sur]vive, allow us now to describe with s[ome] certainty the city's complex system of [de]fenses. The entire Lungomare di Leva[nte,] even though it was pounded by the open [sea] and by powerful winds, still preserves m[ost] of its military works: the bastion, or [Ba]stione S. Giovannello, the platform, or [Pi]attaforma Cannella (or Piattaforma [di S.] Domenico) and the Piattaforma di S. [Gia]como stand virtually intact.

rder to discover another aspect of Ortigia,
can venture along the *Via Resalibera*, into the
ors quarter, where the twisting narrow streets
tect from the gusts of sea winds and the heat
he sun, creating a cool setting rendered
asant by a complex interplay of light and
dow.

mple of Apollo (D5). The calling card, so
speak, of Ortigia for those who come
m the landward side is presented by the
1s of the temple of Apollo in the Piazza
1cali, one of the first temples built by the
:ient Greeks in Syracuse, and one of the
est temples in Sicily. The fact that it was
licated to Apollo is shown by an in-
iption on the stylobate. The ruins that we
v admire have withstood the powerful
nsformations that have affected this
icture, located as it is in a strategic point
ween the older layout and the more re-
it urban expansion: it was used as a
irch in the Byzantine period, a mosque
he Moorish period, again as a church un-
the Normans, and finally it was incor-
rated into a 16th-c. barracks by the
iniards. It was not until the turn of the
h c. that the temple, freed of all its ac-
tions and superstructures, was finally al-
red to breathe again, as it were.

zza Archimede (E5). At the end of the
g straight thoroughfare of Corso Mat-
tti – once known as the Via del Littorio,
ich shows clear signs, in the stern,
1are-hewn buildings that line its course,
he brutal demolition undertaken through
heart of the city by the Fascist regime –
ens out what is considered the warm
l welcoming drawing room of Ortigia:
zza Archimede. Set at the center of the
1are is a little *fountain*, with burbling jets
vater, depicting Diana the Huntress, sur-
inded by handmaidens, sirens and tri-
s. Overlooking the square is, among oth-
ouildings, the *Palazzo Lanza* with its el-
nt twin-light mullioned windows, along
h the *Palazzo dell'Orologio*, now housing
offices of the *Banca d'Italia*; in the court-
d, there is a 15th-c. staircase in the Cat-
nian Gothic style. From the northeastern
ner, there runs a Via Montalto, which
es its name to the **Palazzo Montalto**: it al-
may be said to possess the most hand-
ne 14th-c. façade of all Siracusa, punc-
ted with exquisite twin- and triple-light
llioned windows, while an elegant
licule with a Latin inscription recalls the
r of its construction, 1397.

lleria Regionale* (E5). This regional art
ery is located in the former monastery,

or Monastero di S. Benedetto, which in turn
comprises the 14th-c. *Palazzo Parisi* and
the 13th-c. *Palazzo Bellomo*, the larger of the
two, characterized on the ground floor by
the distinctive architectural features of the
Swabian period (the portal, the loophole
windows, the masonry structure), while on
the upper floor there are clear signs of the
renovations undertaken to the structure in
the subsequent Catalonian period. Aside
from sizable collections of sculpture and
painting, dating from the high Middle Ages
to modern times (we should mention the
splendid **Annunciation**** by Antonello da
Messina, 1474, and the **Burial of St. Lucy****
by Caravaggio, from the church of S. Lucia,
in Siracusa, 1609, and *statues* by the Gagini
family and by Francesco Laurana) there
are noteworthy collections of the applied
arts: silversmithery and goldsmithery, ivory,
coral work, majolica, religious furnishings,
illuminated codices, furniture, ceramics,
and terracotta.

Duomo** (E5; plan below). The present-day
cathedral of Syracuse, or Duomo di Sira-

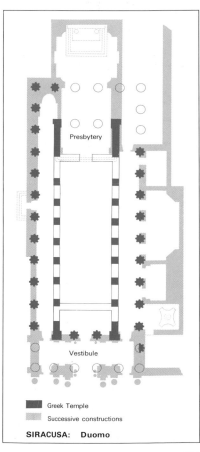

Presbytery

Vestibule

■ Greek Temple

░ Successive constructions

SIRACUSA: Duomo

cusa, stands on the highest point on the island, a location that has always made this a sacred spot. Here is the most astonishing example of the fascinating accretion and layering and coexistence of styles that is so characteristic of Ortigia: inside of this cathedral, there survives the shapes of a Doric temple dedicated to Athena, dating from the earliest decades of the 5th c. B.C., while below it you see clear signs of Sicilian civilization, and what is thought to be an altar ("ara") dating back three centuries previous. The temple is a hexastyle (with a six-columned front) peripteros, which means a building surrounded by a single row of columns; of the 36 original columns, no fewer than 24 are still in their place, cemented in but perfectly visible in the masonry of the cathedral. In the central part, of course, stood the cella, on the walls of which were reproduced scenes of the battles fought on horseback by Agathocles against the Carthaginians, as Cicero noted admiringly. The transformation into a Christian church was done in the Byzantine era, when a wall was raised, enclosing the columns, and when eight arches were cut in either wall of the cella, thus creating a three-aisled basilica. Its appearance must have been that much more splendid in Norman times, when the church was covered with exquisite mosaics, which, sadly, have since been lost. The earthquakes of 1545 and 1693 caused the façade to collapse ruinously; it was rebuilt in accordance with plans by Andrea Palma, in a pure Sicilian Baroque.

Palazzo Municipale (E5). Formerly the senate building, or Palazzo Senatoriale, this palazzo was built in 1629 on a site in which recent excavations have unearthed relics of an Ionic temple from the 6th c. B.C., dedicated to Artemis, but never completed. The work of the Spanish architect Juan Vermexio, nicknamed the lizard, or 'Lucertolone,' bears his unmistakable signature: a small lizard carved into the stone at the left corner of the cornice. Facing the town hall, or Palazzo Municipale, stands the *Palazzo Beneventano del Bosco*, which still preserves part of its original medieval structure, which was embellished, during the Baroque period, by lavish decorative elements in the façade and in the courtyard.

Via della Maestranza and Via Vittorio Veneto (E-D5). In architectural terms, these two streets are the richest in the city; they are a succession of Baroque palazzi, their golden walls adorned with cornices, m carons, splendid wrought-iron balconi supported by equally richly-sculpted bra ets; inside these palazzi sometimes are h den far older structures. If you set out fr the Piazza Archimede, you may note t *Palazzo Impellizzeri*, *Palazzo Bonanno* (n housing the tourist office, or Azienda *A*tonoma di Turismo), and *PalazzoBufard* (with an interesting setting on the inter of the courtyard); past here, a lovely lit square, or piazzetta, is overlooked by t handsome façade of the church of *Francesco* (or church of the Immacolata) you turn sharply to the right, along the *V* della Giudecca, you will enter the quar that housed the large Jewish communi sadly, almost nothing survives of the or inal rooms. Return along the Via della M stranza, and, as you head down toward t water, you may note other palazzi, amo them the *Palazzo Lanza*, the sinuous *Pal zo Rizza*, and a second *Palazzo Impellizz* Also along the Via Vittorio Veneto – whi at the end of Via della Maestranza ru down toward the little marina, or Porto *P*colo, just inland of the open sea – you m note a line of fine large palazzi, or "pal zotti," which still display the graceful st of the Spanish.

Fonte Ciane

The papyrus plant is one of the many tre sures that nature has endowed upon Si cusa, and it has of course been lo

The papyrus plant grows wild along the banks of the river Ciane

renowned for its use in the manufacture paper. From the slender stalk of the pla long strips are obtained, which are first lowed to soak or steep in a special vege solution, and then spread out and arrang in a woven crosshatch, first vertically a then horizontally, and are pressed wit roller and joined with a glue that is o

ned from the stalk of the plant itself. You
n watch all the various phases of manu-
ture, and the current state of the craft of
permaking with papyrus in various work-
ops throughout Siracusa, the most note-
rthy of which are located in the area
und the Museo Archeologico, or arche-
gical museum, and the gate, or Porta
rina a Ortigia. It is also possible to take
a boat from the Marina di Siracusa and
steam along the banks of the *river Ciane* to
the spring, or Fonte Ciane, venerated for the
last few millennia, where it is believed that
Pluto plunged downward into the earth following the abduction of Proserpine. This
area is protected by a special nature preserve, or *Riserva Naturale Orientata*, established in 1984.

2 Noto and the coastline south of Siracusa

e appearance of the southern strip of
e Syracuse region, or Siracusano, is fair-
homogeneous in terms of landscape.
ach of the territory, comprising the south-
stern extensions of the Iblean massif, is
aracterized by the numerous "cave,"
deep cuts in the limestone of the highland,
carved out by the streams and rich in luxuriant vegetation. Differing from this typology is the coastal strip, which is flat and
sandy, and dotted with many marshes.
Even more homogeneous is the cultural na-

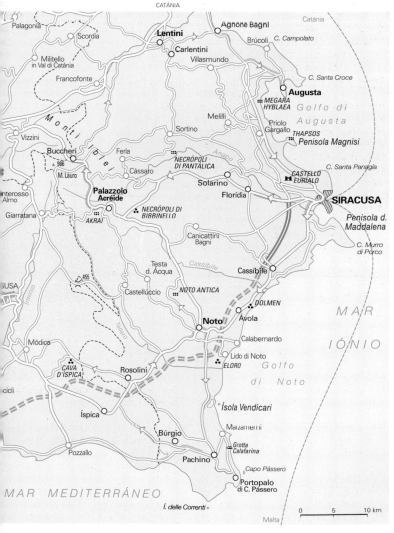

ture of these rural quarters, or "contrade," marked by shared historical heritages. The culture here dates back as far as prehistoric times, with the spread of the culture of Castelluccio, which, from the village of that name not far from Noto, spread from the 18th to the 15th c. B.C. over the entire southeastern area of Sicily. The rise of the mighty city of Syracuse in the 8th c. B.C. and its historical and artistic hegemony over the entire territory, were two further elements of cultural unification. Nowadays in this area there is an alternation of specialized crops – such as almonds in Àvola and Noto and the vineyards of Pachino – with more traditional uses of the land, such as grazing and other sowable crops.

You will leave Siracusa along the Via Elorina, and then you will continue south along the state road 115, crossing the rivers Ànapo and Ciane. Once you are past Cassìbile you will first pass through (24 km.) Àvola, a large farming town, renowned for its production and export of almonds and the distinctive local sweets made from those almonds, and then you will reach (after another 8.5 km.) Noto, which is rightly considered to be the capital of Sicilian Baroque: at the crossroads, or Bivio Testa dell'Acqua, near the town, you will find directions to the ruins of ancient Noto, long silenced witnesses of a once-prosperous past. You may then abandon the main route and get onto a provincial road that runs 22 km. from Noto to Pachino, in a luminous landscape covered with vineyards and almond groves. A detour, not far from the mouth of the river Tellaro, will allow you to reach the ruins of

the city of Eloro, not far from which, in th Contrada Cannedi, it is possible to visit t ruins of a Roman villa (the so-called *Villa the Tellaro*, dating back to the 4th c. A.D The charm of the natural setting in this are is protected by a nature preserve, the Rise va Naturale di Vendìcari, which lies just b fore the township of Pachino. From her you can reach Portopolo, Capo Pàsser and the island, or Isola delle Correnti, the e treme southernmost point of Sicily, which geographic terms lies further south tha Tunisi. From Pachino, it is just 19.5 km. Ìspica and then, again on the state road 1 for another 5.5 km., Rosolini, from which yc must go to see the Cava d'Ìspica. Once yc pass the Contrada Belliscala with its wir cellar, or "Cantina Sociale Elorina," th largest vintner's establishment in easte Sicily, producing excellent table wines, yc will cross the river Tellaro, and in 15 km. (' km. from your starting point, in Siracus you will return to Noto.

Àvola

The busy farming community, surrounde by almond and citrus groves, of Àvola (ele 40 m., pop. 31,322) is the product, in i present refined layout, of the reconstructic that followed the earthquake of 1693, whe the inhabitants of ancient Àvola descende from the hill, or Colle Aquilone (to t northwest) and took up residence in the fe or Feudo Mutubè, overlooking the sea. D signed by the royal architect Frate Ange Italia, the new city presents a hexagon plan with a large square in its center, fro which there extend orthogonal roads c

Noto: the Duomo and the town hall square in a spectacularly uniform Baroque settin

oto 1:13000 (1 cm = 130 m)
0   75   150 m
NOTO ANTICA km 16 - PALAZZOLO ACREIDE km 30

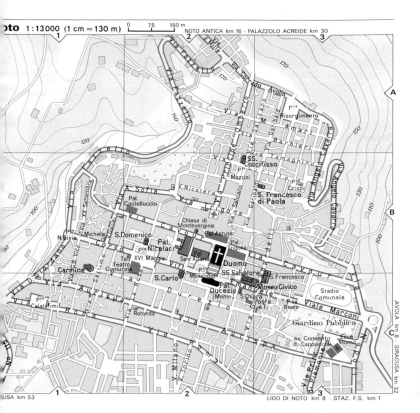

inating in four squares that – along with
e central *Piazza Umberto I* – form a cross,
d mark the entrances to the city. This un-
ual layout is embellished by a number of
th-c. buildings; standing out among them,
r the decorative richness and the Baroque
nse of space, are the *church of the An-
nziata* with its convex front, and the
iesa Madre dedicated to St. Nicholas (S.
cola), with a classic Latin-cross plan, with
ree aisles and a church courtyard surunded by pillars with the characteristic
ures of "saints" designed, again, by An-
lo Italia. There are also many buildings in
e Liberty (Art-Nouveau) style, with splen-
d floral decorations, carved by master
onecutters, to mark the front doors and
e windows of the homes, also embell-
hed with finely wrought railings.

oto *

oto (elev. 152 m., pop. 21,704; plan above)
d its history comprise the remarkable
atures that emerged following the terrible
rthquake of 1693, when a new urban plan
d an entirely different architectural style
placed the memory of an ancient city,
ng since abandoned. The new layout, in
y case, was certainly not created all at
ce; the first, anonymous plan that was

drawn up in fact proved too small, and was
poorly laid out. As time went on, a new
section was added, based upon a road that
divided the city into two parts. This project,
which gave substance to the social structure of the community and its economic
development, was met with approval by
the local aristocracy, which took up residence along the main streets, building their
own fine palazzi. The location, on a slight incline, the equilibrium shown in the dimen-
sions of the squares, the symmetry of the
buildings, the architectural details and the
urban furnishings – all these were the features used in the creation of views, perspective, and what we might describe as
dynamic articulations, all contributing to
the exceptional theatrical and spectacular
qualities of this new Baroque city. The exceedingly characteristic and homogeneous
physiognomy of Noto derives as well from
the adherence over time to the original
techniques of construction and the unbroken use of traditional materials.
The city is laid out in accordance with a
checkerboard pattern, with as its chief thoroughfares the **Corso Vittorio Emanuele***
and its parallel (higher up), the *Via Cavour*,
with the Piazza del Crocifisso as a sort of urban nexus. Preceded by the imposing gate,

or *Porta Reale* (C3), the line of the "corso" is broken by three squares, overlooked by three churches, each of which has a monumental staircase. The first church that you will see as you head west is the church of *S. Francesco* (B-C3) with a monastery, the Convento di S. Francesco, planned and built by Vincenzo Sinatra, one of the most important architects of this period in Sicily, and one of the moving forces behind

Detail of the Palazzo Villadorata in Noto

the architectural rebirth of Noto. As you proceed along the "corso" you will see the monastery, or Monastero delle Benedettine and the adjoining church of *S. Chiara*, by Rosario Gagliardi (another major figure in the history of Sicilian Baroque), on the elliptical interior of which, studded with stuccoes, you can admire a *Virgin Mary with Christ Child*, attributed to Antonello Gagini. The second square represents the central space of the city: this is the town square, or **Piazza del Municipio*** (B-C2), with the broad and impressive stairway of the cathedral, or Scalinata del Duomo. This is an urban space of remarkable charm, a combination of many different presences, each of which is a little masterpiece: the cathedral, or *Duomo* (B2), with its vast façade and its lavish interior (now partially closed, due to the collapse of the cupola and the roof of the nave, which occurred on 13 March 1996), the elegant *Palazzo Ducezio*, now the town hall, the 19th-c. *Palazzo Vescovile* (bishop's palace), and the *Palazzo Landolina*, dating from the 18th c. Between this square and the successive square stands the church of *S. Carlo* (or of the Gesuiti). Concluding the architectural progression of the Corso Vittorio Emanuele is the *Piazza S. Domenico*, bounded on one side by the convent and *church of S. Domenico**; the façade of the church (which, like the church itself, currently closed for renovation, is the work of Rosario Gagliardi) is perhaps the most

noteworthy work of Noto Baroque. On the other side of the square, there is a note of architectural diversity, the 19th-c. *Teatro Comunale*, with the adjoining *Villetta d'Ercole* which contains in its center a 17th-c. fountain originally from ancient Noto. This is just one of the many routes that is possible in Baroque Noto, and it is the simplest, as it follows a direct axis; there could be many other, in a voyage of discovery of monumental and vernacular elements, in which Baroque motifs merge with Islamic reminiscences, rich in details of 'lesser architecture' which contrasts with the architecture of the "noble city."

A dense blanket of vegetation conceals, as if to protect them, the ruins of the buildings of **ancient Noto** (Noto Antica, 16 km. to the northwest). Certainly inhabited in prehistoric times, this city had a moment of particular splendor during Greek times; from that period the gymnasium and places of worship of the heroicized dead have been unearthed. Almost nothing remains, on the other hand, from the Moorish period, though Noto was one of the richest strongholds of that time.

Vendìcari

The three marshes – two to the north and one to the south of the lovely tower, *Torre di Vendìcari*, overlooking the little islet, or Isoletta di Vendìcari, constitute the protected and official nature preserve, *Riserva Naturale di Vendìcari*. It represents an authentic reservoir of nature, with splendid examples of Mediterranean maquis where large populations of birds, such as Audouin's gulls, slender-billed gulls, and black-winged stilts, find their natural habitat. From the entrance to the preserve, "oasi," you can follow a marked trail through the area of the salinas (salt marshes) to the great marsh, or *Pantano Grande*, and you will reach the area of the "tonnara" (tunny-fishing nets) and the Swabian tower, or Torre Sveva. From here, you can enjoy a vast and sweeping view of the entire preserve, set against a lovely marine background, a perfect setting for the little islet mentioned above, and, further off, the cape, or **Capo Pàssero**. From the tower, which marks the center of the preserve, there run two trails: one to the north, ending near Eloro, and another to the south, along the beach toward Marzamemi.

Along the northern route, which skirts the

w rocky shoals, there is a predominance
Mediterranean maquis, with bushes of
ntisk and thyme and dwarf palms: beyond
e small and enchanting bay of Cala-
osche you will reach the mouth of the riv-
Tellaro, which marks the boundary of
e preserve, or Oasi di Vendìcari, beyond
nich you will find the ruins of **Eloro**, iso-
ted and looming over the golden sands of
e beach: of this town, a Syracusan foun-
ation dating from the end of the 8th c.
C., there remain stretches of fortifications,
agments of the road system, a theater and
ligious buildings, and, without the walls,
e sanctuary of Demeter and Kore.

he southern route, on the other hand, is
tirely different: you climb down into the
antano Grande, where you tour an old
andoned salina, or saltworks, with its
d structures in the middle of which was a
rge windmill and then, walking along the
each, you will reach a dune beyond which
the *Pantano Roveto*. In the summer time,
is pond, entirely dry, is covered with a
hite crust of salt, a natural habitat for
ltwort, a curious reddish succulent plant.
he southern most point of Sicily is to the
uth of Vendìcari, namely *Isola delle
rrenti*.

ica

t on a hill, sloping gently down toward the
a, roughly 6 kilometers away, stands the
esent-day town of Ìspica (elev. 170 m.,
p. 14,629), formed by two separate quarrs: one quarter was laidout in the 18th c.,
d constitutes the present-day settlement,
ile the other was laid out in the Middle
es, is now uninhabited, and is part of
e so-called archeological park, or *Parco
cheologico della Forza*, adjoining a rocky
ur upon which is located, along with oth-
ruins, the remains of a fortress that con-
tuted the main core of the city until the
rthquake of 1693. In the area of the pre-
nt-day town, with its regular layout, along
e central thoroughfare of the Via XX Set-
mbre is the church of *S. Maria Maggiore*,
ting from the first half of the 18th c., with
basilican plan, and with three aisles
orned with frescoes; facing it on the ex-
rior is an elliptical portico. From the Via

XX Settembre you can reach the Piazza
Maria José, which marks the location of
the Chiesa Madre and the beginning of the
Corso Umberto I, along which you may note
the *Palazzo Bruno di Belmonte*, now the
site of the town hall, or Municipio: designed
by Ernesto Basile in 1906, the parallelepiped
bulk of the palazzo appears as a latter day
Art-Nouveau (or, in the Italian parlance,
Liberty) castle, with corner towers, den-
telle decorations along the crown of the
building, panels of majolica and elaborate
wrought-iron gratework, a distinctive feature of all of the architecture of this town.

Cava d'Ìspica

The limestone highlands of the Iblei are
characterized by numerous cuttings eroded by streams and watercourses, here
known as "cave," some of them used as far
back as prehistoric times. The most important of these is the Cava d'Ìspica (elev.
338 m.), which you can easily reach from
Rosolini (just a little more than 12 km. away
along the road to Mòdica). Few other environmental settings in Sicily give so powerful an impression, with the human presence mingling with a natural setting that is
perfectly shaped and altered by historical
relics and monuments from every era and
in every style, ranging from the Aeneolith-
ic to the present day. Early Christian catacombs (Larderia, 4th/5th c. A.D.), little
Byzantine cliff churches, now reduced to ruins (S. Pancrati) or built in caverns (S. Nicola), in some cases with a few fragments of
mural paintings, tombs, beehive-style cave
dwellings several stories high, cliff dwellings
from late antiquity and the Middle Ages
(the castle, or Castello), homes in caves,
used until recently and then abandoned,
with everything that they contained, verdant gardens and rough limestone surfaces;
everything seems like a movie, in which
the soundtrack is provided by the numerous farming activities that are being undertaken in the area: a truly stunning array
of stimuli. After much plunder, Cava d'Ìspica is now subject to much closer control,
and it is possible to tour it with the ac-
companiment of local staff and private
guides, who can be hired on the spot.

3 The Ibla highland

e morphology of the northern section of
e Syracuse area, or Siracusano, is not
ry different from that to be found in the
uthern section; we find the same unifying
aracteristics, both physical and histori-
. Here too, the territory, constituted by

the eastern reliefs of the Monti Iblei, is distinguished by the presence of deep hol-
lows ("cave," in Italian) that cut into the
limestone ground, a phenomenon that becomes less marked to the north, as you descend to the Piana di Catania. Here too the

The fascinating and suggestive necropolis of Pantàlica

powerful and unifying presence of Syracuse (Siracusa) and the extensive Baroque reconstruction following the earthquake of 1693 have given the environment a unified appearance. In more recent years, other elements have been added, helping to diversify to some extent the homogeneous cultural and geographic substrate: first of all, the development, beginning in the 1950s, of the industrial zone between Augusta and Siracusa, with the inevitable result of a progressive abandonment of the traditional farming activities in favor of industry. This has led to a considerable modification of the landscape and the types of settlements; it is only inland that there is an array of mountain towns, of feudal origin, that are fairly intact in their typologies.

With this route, which runs a total of 152 km., you will penetrate into the hinterland of Siracusa, by following the course of the river Ànapo and the ridges of the Monti Iblei; through a landscape made particularly vivid by little towns with 18th-c. form and image, and with the ruins of Megara Hyblaea and the oil and petrochemical plants serving as a distant backdrop against the sea, you will travel through a territory in which it is possible to analyze directly a cross-section of Sicilian history, which sinks its roots into prehistoric eras. You will leave Siracusa heading west, along the Viale Paolo Orsi, along the state road 124; amidst olive groves and fields, you will drive along the lower slopes of the Monti Iblei. After Floridia, the views become broader and, amongst handsome olive groves, extend on one side over the valley of the river Ànapo, toward Siracusa, and on the other, toward the highlands dotted with "cave," and toward the distant Mount Etna. You will pass, at 16 km., Solarino, a renowned olive-

growing town, and then, as you contin along the state road, in Contrada Meli on the left you will find two very lovely f tified farmhouses ("masserie fortificate the first and largest of which is open to v itors. After briefly leaving the state road, y will reach Ferla, and from there you w head northeast, following the signs for Pa tàlica, the largest cliffside necropolis Sicily.

After you get back onto the state road 12 you will continue along the course of the r er Ànapo, and you will reach Palazzo Acrèide (26 km. from Solarino); then, aft you pass through Buscemi and Bucche you will turn off toward Francofonte, drivi back down along the northern ridge of t Monti Iblei. From Francofonte, a well-kno center of citrus farming, located 20 k from Buccheri, passing through Lentini a Carlentini, you will proceed directly to t coast, reaching it at Brùcoli, a lovely lit fishing village that stands on a peninsula closed between the inlet of Brùcoli and t mouth of the mountain stream, or Torrer Porcaria. This was the site of the ancie Trotilon, one of the earliest Greek coloni in Sicily; its port has long been used for porting sea salt. Immediately afterwar you will reach Augusta (42 km. from Fra cofonte), a town with a notable histor heritage, increasingly swamped by its a too-modern present. Amidst a succession smokestacks and holding tanks, which ha a weird charm all their own (especially night), you will pass through Megara H blaea, a major Greek colony, and then, at t turnoff for the station of Priolo, you w take the detour to the left to the peninsu of Magnisi, two kilometers long and 7 meters wide, jutting out into the Gulf of A gusta, and linked to the mainland by a ve arrow sandy isthmus. This was the ancient Thapsos, a Bronze-Age and Iron-Age village, a site that still looks much as it was described by Thucydides. The ridge of the ontrada Targia, marked by a docking tructure for oil tankers, is the northern ntrance to Siracusa.

ntàlica*

ne site of a warren of cliff tombs overoking the valley of the river Ànapo, Panlica (elev. 425 m.) possesses a remarkable harm and allure, surrounded as it is by a lendid and uncontaminated nature. There e no houses, there are no trees, and there e no roads; there is only a rocky tableland nclosed by sheer walls carved out over the ourse of the millennia by the waters of he river and its tributary, the Calcinara, isscrossed by exceedingly few paths or ails: all of these characteristics made this safe place in antiquity, nicely suited to beg easily defended. In a territory covering me 80 hectares, enclosed by a perimeter tending roughly 5 km., there is a vast ecropolis comprising more than 5,000 mbs of manmade grottoes, with multiple ccupation (divided into five main clusrs), alongside which stand the few surving ruins of the early-Sicilian city of Hya, which flourished between the 13th and e 8th c. B.C. All that survives of this city,

which Syracuse was meant to survive as a seaport, is the large rectangular square-block base of the *Anaktoron*, the palace of the prince. Tradition has it that the early Sicilians were known as the People of Bees, and by a noteworthy coincidence, the early Sicilian necropolis of Pantàlica is quite reminiscent of a large beehive carved in stone. The site, which was not inhabited throughout the ancient age, was newly occupied in the high Middle Ages, since as a nearly inaccessible place, it offered safe haven from Moorish incursions: from this period there survives a village of cave dwellings and a few small carved-rock churches. Nowadays, to enter the necropolis and wander through it freely – especially during periods during which there are not many tourists, when one can fully enjoy the silence broken only by the cawing of crows – is to take a plunge into the earliest historical times. If you are fond of adventure, you may choose to follow – on foot or by the minibus of the local forest rangers, or Azienda forestale – the dirt road along the route of the old railroad, since abandoned, which once connected Ferla to Sortino, along the banks of the river Ànapo.

Palazzolo Acrèide*

This small city with a 17th-c. style, Palazzolo Acrèide (elev. 670 m., pop. 9,097; plan on

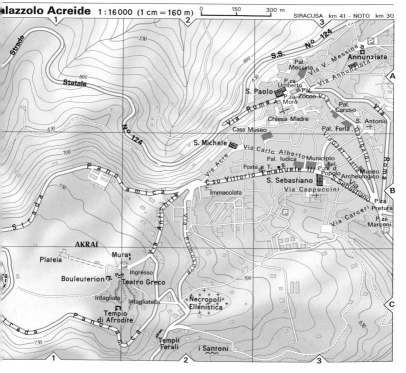

lazzolo Acreide 1:16000 (1 cm = 160 m)

page 139) is the namesake and heir to the Greek town of Akrai, founded by the Syracusans in 664 B.C., as a fortress overlooking the river Ànapo, fundamental to effective control of the hinterland. The current urban configuration of the town, which dates back to the 17th c., is characterized by a network of thoroughfares that links up the chief points of the urban structure. And within this gridwork is a series of architec-

ing the Byzantine-Christian era; above t[...] "latomie," or prisons, are the remains [...] the base of the *temple of Aphrodite* (6th [...] B.C.), which can be reached from the arch[...] ological zone. To the east of the theat[...] are the *Templi Ferali*, a "latomia," or pris[...] cell, whose walls are covered with little v[...] tive tablets (pinakes) dedicated to the c[...] of the heroicized dead; the large relief fro[...] the Hellenistic era is also linked to the sa[...] cult. You can follow a tr[...] to a little valley in whi[...] stands the so-called **Sa[...] toni***, literally, holy me[...] 12 remarkable rock scul[...] tures dating from the 3[...] c. B. C., set into the ro[...] dedicated to the godde[...] Cybele, who is depicted [...] standing or seated: this [...] the largest figurative co[...] plex linked to the cult [...] this Magna Mater, as t[...] ancient Romans called he[...] Once you leave the arche[...] logical area, the tour of t[...] city focuses on the series [...] Baroque buildings that e[...] tend so theatrically alo[...] the two main thoroughfa[...] of the city, the Corso Vitt[...] rio Emanuele and the V[...] Carlo Alberto: these tw[...] roads meet on the Piaz[...] del Popolo where the ma[...] sive bulk of the church of [...] *Sebastiano* stands, reari[...] up its spectacular façad[...] on three orders on a hi[...] stairway. The little city fe[...] tures other interesting re[...] gious structures, such [...] the church of *S. Pao*[...]

The traditional procession of Palazzolo Acreide

tural structures from each of the three phases of urban growth: the period prior to the earthquake of 1693, the period immediately following that earthquake, and the present day. The city still preserves, from the period of its initial formation, in the area around the excavations of Akrai, noteworthy monuments, among them the Greek theater, or **Teatro Greco***, dating back to the 3rd c. B.C. but heavily renovated in Roman times, quite harmonious in its proportions, even though it was designed to contain only 600 spectators. Behind the theater extends the complex of ancient Greek "latomie", or prisons, named the *Intagliata* and the *Intagliatella*, whose walls, carved into reliefs, are clear evidence of their use as homes and burial grounds dur-

which dates from the first half of the 18th [...] with its imposing and spectacular Baroq[...] tower-like façade, and the *church of the A[...] nunziata*, rebuilt in the 18th c. with a ri[...] Baroque portal with tortile columns; on t[...] interior is a handsome altar with marble [...] lays. In Via Machiavelli is the *museum-hom*[...] *of Antonino Uccello*, with an interesting c[...] lection of Sicilian ethnographic material.[...]

Buccheri

This town (elev. 820 m., pop. 2,755), whi[...] already existed during Norman times, [...] the highest township in the province, [...] Provincia di Siracusa, and was made a cou[...] ty, or "contea," during the war of the Sic[...] ian Vespers, or Guerra del Vespro; the or[...] inal site was further uphill, where you c[...]

ill see the ruins of the castle. The section of town that was built after 1693 is dominated by the monumental and very ill church of *S. Antonio Abate*, which is certainly the most impressive piece of architecture here, atop its imposing stairway, and with its three descending orders. The *church of the Maddalena* also has a rich çade; it preserves on the interior a marble atue by Antonello Gagini (1508).

arlentini and Lentini

uilt in 1551 at the behest of the emperor harles V, from whom it took its name, for irposes of defense, **Carlentini** (elev. 200 ., pop. 16,946) is set in a site that dominates the surrounding territory, above the icient city of Lentini; the strong citadel as meant to defend the hinterland from irkish raids. Of the entire defensive sysm, all that remains are a few traces of e walls of the town, which was designed a checkerboard pattern with a large central square, on one side of which now ands the Chiesa Madre. Following the irthquake of 1693, Carlentini was repopated thanks to its healthy location. Just to e north of Carlentini, it is possible to vis-the archeological zone of *Leontinoi*, a mar Greek settlement that existed as early as e 7th c. B.C., as is shown by the perimeter the first enclosure walls; its history was ofoundly and constantly marked by the ri-lry with the powerful and nearby city of racuse, which subjugated it repeatedly. ne research done in the area now enosed by the archeological park, or *Parco rcheologico*, has made it possible to esblish that the city stood on the hill and valy, or Colle San Mauro and the Valle San auro; excavations have brought to light retches of three sets of enclosure walls id a gate, outside of which extends a ecropolis that dates back between the urth and the end of the 3rd c. B.C.

ne city of **Lentini** (elev. 53 m., pop. 27,764), hich is the heir to the Greek colony of eontinoi, dominates a fertile plain, known antiquity by the name of Campi Lestrigo-; partially set below sea level, and im-oved by reclamation projects during the scist era, nowadays the area is devoted to tensive cultivation of citrus fruit. A major ligious center, Lentini was an episcopal e during the early Christian period. Proundly marked by various earthquakes 140, 1169, and 1542), and considering the healthiness of the site, following the great irthquake of 1693, it was decided to ange the city's location; the selection of e new location and the layout of the set-tlement were dictated by Angelo Italia, the architect of Àvola and Noto, but no traces remain of this operation, because the inhabitants did not accept the new project, and chose to rebuild their city exactly where it had originally stood. In the archeological museum, or *Museo Archeologico*, there is a collection of the antiquities of the territory, with special attention to Leontinoi, but also to the other sites in the area.

Augusta

Set on a peninsula that extends over two kilometers in length, separating two ports (Megarese to the west and Xifonio to the east), Augusta (elev. 15 m., pop. 34,189) was built (on a site believed to have been that of the Greek town of Xiphonia) at the behest of Frederick II, who wanted to reinforce a strategically fundamental site at the entrance to the enormous inlet that is closed off to the south by the squat promontory, or Promontorio di Siracusa. Looming over and protecting the city is, in fact, the Swabian castle, or *Castello Svevo*, which underwent considerable renovation to suit it properly to the defensive needs of the port and the hinterland. Recent restoration work on the structures built by the emperor Frederick have uncovered the presence of both military and civil characteristics. The castle has a square plan and four corner towers, which are also square, while the interior rooms are partly covered with splendid vaults; under the Spaniards, the castle was surrounded by a double enclosure wall with bastions. Later heavily renovated and rebuilt, the castle was converted into a prison beginning in 1890, and it continued to be used as a prison until 1978. What surives of Augusta's original military character is an interesting *Museo della Piazzaforte*, or museum of the fortress. Other historical monuments worthy of note include the gate, or Porta di Terra, also known as the Porta Spagnola, and the town hall, or *Palazzo del Municipio* (1699), decorated with a Swabian imperial eagle grasping the town's coat of arms, and with a sundial to commemorate the eclipse of the sun of 1870. The earthquake of 1990 left evident marks upon Augusta, especially on the interior of the quarter of Borgata. The entire town of Augusta and all the surrounding area in any case inevitably provoke a sense of malaise: a predatory and all-powerful development movement and the false sense of prosperity induced by the presence of large-scale heavy industry have irreparably mangled one of the most splendid and noteworthy and historically rich

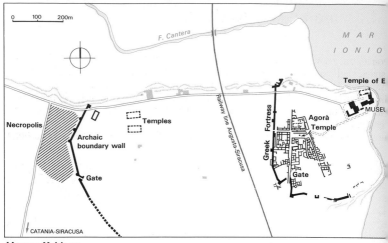

Megara Hyblaea

landscapes in the entire Mediterranean basin.

Megara Hyblaea

From Augusta, skirting the Esso refinery, along the provincial road 193, in the direction of Siracusa, signs will point the way to Megara Hyblaea (plan above). Surrounded by an industrial zone, to the point that at certain times during the day it is difficult to reach it, the area of the ancient city has however been rescued from the looming presences that surround it on every hand, and represents an oasis of greenery and solitude that is certainly worth a stop. Following the first explorations undertaken by Paolo Orsi at the end of the 19th c., since WWII the city has been the subject of regular excavations, making it one of the best-studied western Greek colonies. The visitor is almost led by the hand with a series of charts and explanations (though we would advise at least a short visit to the little museum on the site) through the ruins of the ancient city, which was founded in 728 B.C. by Greeks from Megara, a few years after the foundation of Syracuse, and which

grew thereafter until 483 B.C., when it w razed to the ground by Gelon, the tyrant Gela, who deported its inhabitants. It w refounded by Timoleon in 340 B.C. on t same site; but this second Megara was al completely destroyed, in 213 B.C., by M cellus, in the operations prior to the cc quest of Syracuse and in the context of t Second Punic War. From the 2nd c. B until the 6th c. A.D., there remains all t same evidence of a small settlement. The excavations of the city and the adjoini necropolises have unearthed authentic je els of Greek sculpture, now on display in t archeological museum, or Museo Arche logico di Siracusa.

The tour of Megara Hyblaea takes pla against the backdrop of the gulf, or Golfo Augusta, where there are always oil tanke loading crude oil in the facilities near t port. To walk among the grim industr structures in search of the relics of ancie Megara, in a chaotic environment and tr fic, with a savage vitality, can constitu an experience entirely out of the ordina with respect to the way that we are acc tomed to thinking about the past.

Catania and its territory

ou look at a map of Sicily, your attention will immediately be attracted by a large emp-space, centering around an elevation that is unlikely in this area, characterizing the east-section of the island to the point of breaking up the logic of morphology and settlement: is is the area surrounding Catania which, for better or worse, has always had Mount Et-. as its central point of reference, both in visual and in ideal and cultural terms, as well economic terms.

e volcano does not so much symbolize the distinctive character of this area; rather, it

familiar view to travellers in Sicily: the image of Etna in the background

the area, and with respect to the volcano, the renowned and populous towns, an-ored to its slopes or lying spread out in the plain – in particular, Catania – wind up be-ming little more than parasitic appendages.

impressive is this volcano that not even the Greeks dared to contaminate it with their sto-es of gods and heroes, relegating Vulcan and his forge to the far more accessible depths of e island of Vulcan, certainly in part to the mining of obsidian and pumice that was done there. e favors of Mount Etna are, on the other hand, much less visible, though they certainly en-uraged the endless sequence of human settlements that, at elevations ranging from 500 750 meters, have taken hold here: first of course is the exceedingly fertile earth, the prod-t of the decay of volcanic rock in an eons-long geological process, which, along with the uvial deposits of the river Simeto, constituted the foundation of a very valuable agricul-ral tradition; this tradition, in its turn, with the help of a coastline rich in anchorage and th at least one major seaport, triggered – in part as well thanks to the centuries of hard work d enterprise of the inhabitants – an economic development of great worth and benefit.

.1 Catania**

he remarkable geographic location, with setting that includes Mount Etna and the nian Sea, has played a major role in the ousands of years of history of this city, a story of light and shadows. The growth of atania (elev. 7 m., pop. 333,075; plan on age 148) has clearly been affected, for bet-r or worse, by its relationship with the vol-no: the volcano made the fields remark-ly fertile, as it spewed forth its lava, and

as the lava cooled it served as a quarry for the volcanic stone with which houses were built. Historic settlement here dates back to the earliest Greek colonization in Sicily, when the Chalcideans founded the earli-est core of "Katane," sometime after 729 B.C. according to the documentation pro-vided by Thucydides, in the area that is now occupied by the church of S. Nicolò and the Benedictine monastery of S. Nicolò l'Arena. The traces that still remain of the archaic phase of the settlement find correspondences in the historic sources: they refer to the Catanese origins of the legislator Caronda and the stay in this town of a number of poets, foremost among them Stesicoro, whose tomb gave its name to one of the city gates.

For three centuries, it remained in Greek hands, often at war with Siracusa for hegemony over the territory; in 263 B.C. it was conquered by the Romans, who subjected it to the payment of a tribute; Roman domination left a considerable number of buildings and structures that still stand: the Amphitheater (Anfiteatro) in Piazza Stesicoro, the Theater (Teatro) and the Odeon between the lower section of the Via Vittorio Emanuele and the Via Teatro Greco, the ruins of the Forum (Foro) in the Cortile S. Pantaleone and four thermal complexes (one was transformed during Byzantine rule into the church of S. Maria della Rotonda, the Terme Achilliane lie under the Cathedral, the Terme dell'Indirizzo stand alongside the church of S. Maria dell'Indirizzo, while another structure stands in Piazza Dante).

Early-Christian history is documented in the martyrdom of St. Agatha St. Euplio, prior to the 4th c.; the city was conquered by the Byzantines in A.D. 535, though very few traces now survive of their three centuries of rule. The Saracens conquered Catania in A.D. 875, leaving a strong mark on their relationship with the countryside, establishing new crops and opening new routes of communication (they created the "trazzere", paths for animals across fields, that crisscross Mount Etna).

Under Norman domination, construction began (1071) on the Cathedral, which was linked to the town walls and was endowed with parapets that can still be seen in the apses and transept (this is one of the more interesting examples of an "ecclesia munita"), while an earthquake devastated the city (1169), contributing to the economic crisis that continued until the end of Norman rule. In 1239 Frederick II of Swabia ordered the construction of the Castello Ursino at the edge of town, near the sea, in an area that was later covered by boiling lava in 1669 (a spectacular image of Catania with lava flows lapping at its edges is preserved in a painting that hangs in the sacristy of the Cathedral).

The few years that separated the eruption and the earthquake of 1693, and, to an even greater degree, the years that followed that date, saw a city on its knees, humbled by the destruction of the countryside, overwhelmed by a mass of penniless refugees. In June 1694 Giuseppe Lanza, Duke of Camast right-hand man of the viceroy Uzeda, sembled the surviving members of the Se ate and the clergy, and established a plan a rebirth on the site of the old town. The fo of the city showed greater attention to se mic dangers: straight thoroughfares we built on the older tracks of the Via Uze (now Via Etnea) and the Via S. Frances (first stretch of the Via Vittorio Emanuel which were freed of rubble and rebuilt; t width of the roads was classified into thr different orders of magnitude (eight, s and four "canne") and many large squar were built, offering places of refuge in case new earthquakes (the system of square a roads that now links the old clearing of t Piazza del Duomo to the west with Piaz Mazzini and to the north with Piazza U versità is the concrete result of this plan) In the reconstruction, outstanding amo the clergy was the effort undertaken by the der of the Benedictines who, with their en mous landholdings and new rules concerni purchase and sale of real estate, enlarg old structures (S. Nicolò) and built new on adjoining the walls (Palazzo del Vescov Seminario dei Chierici, church of S. Agata Vetere), violating the rules of the Duke Camastra; among the nobility, only the Prin of Biscari was allowed to build his magnifice palazzo next to the walls, alongside the Pala zo del Vescovo (bishop's palace) and t seaport. Among those who led the recc struction, particular note should be ma of G.B. Vaccarini, who was the city archite from 1730 on, laying the foundations, sho ly before 1750, for an expansion northward far as the existing settlements of Borgo ar Consolazione, founded to house the refuge from the eruption of 1669.

In the early decades of the 19th c., Catar underwent a powerful surge in populatic

The fountain of the elephant, symbol of Catania: detail

Piazza del Duomo, with the Cathedral and the dome of the Abbey Church of S. Agata

which was not met with careful planning in the inevitable urban expansion that ensued, despite the efforts of Sebastiano Ittar; the urban expansion that was done in that century, however, did result in a series of major works: the construction of the railroad, expansion of the port, the monumental cemetery (Cimitero Monumentale) to the south, as well as the public gardens and a theater, both dedicated to Vincenzo Bellini.

The railroad viaduct, whose arches are commonly known as the "l'archi da Marina," forever ended the relationship that this city had long had with its view of the sea, and nowadays there is the quiet but continuous expansion of the residential buildings of the Italian Navy (Marina Militare) to further seal off that view. Sporadic efforts to recover the historic heritage date from the early years of the 20th c., when the Amphitheater (Anfiteatro) was restored, in Piazza Stesicoro, and plans were made for the restoration of the Castello Ursino with the location of the city museum, or Museo Comunale. The chaotic urban development of the past decades witnessed the creation of an immense industrial area between the city and the river Simeto and the ravaging of the quarter of S. Berillo to make way for the creation of a financial center, a project that was however left unfinished.

The development of Catania following the earthquake of 1693 can be seen in the broad panoramic view as you take the highway, or autostrada A18 to Messina: the post-seismic construction, marked by the silhouettes of domes and bell towers; the 19th-c. expansion, which continued until the first few decades of the 20th c., linking Catania with the settlements along the route of the Via Etnea; the current phase, caused by the tumultuous development of the 1950s,

when, once the area of the old farm buildings had been filled, pushed the residential areas along the coast and up the slopes of Mount Etna.

The route, which is a walking tour, runs through the main points of both the older city (the Castello Ursino and the ruins of the Teatro are the most important landmarks) and the post-earthquake section, the most important features of which are the Cathedral (Cattedrale), the Via Crociferi, and the church of S. Nicolò; also interesting are the walks along the Via Etnea and the Viale XX Settembre, with a number of examples of 20th-c. construction.

Catania however is much more than this; it is also the contrast between the Baroque sumptuousness of Piazza del Duomo and the cries of the street vendors in the nearby fish market, or Pescheria, a concert of aromas and descriptions of wares, worthy of the largest and most crowded Moorish souks; Catania is also one of the thousand culinary temptations of its tradition – an almond ice, or "granita," or a cup of coffee with cream, or an orange drink – "arancino," ending in 'o,' because in the rest of Sicily it ends in 'a' – or a thirst-quenching "seltz, limone e sale," meaning seltzer, lemon, and salt, or the cookies in the shapes of bones on the Day of the Dead, and rice "crispelle" (rough translation: crêpes) covered with honey on St. Joseph's Day, almond pastries, the "crispeddi" with anchovies or ricotta, pasta asciutta with eggplants and salted ricotta – known as "Pasta alla Norma," in a tribute to the Catanese composer Vincenzo Bellini – the "sangele" (calf tripe with cooked blood sausage), and "panzerotti," a kind of dumpling filled with chocolate, and the little sweet olives known as the "olivette di S. Agata."

145

Piazza del Duomo* (D3), or cathedral square. The traditional center of Catania was planned immediately following the earthquake of 1693 in the place of the medieval "platea magna," or main square, and was selected as the site of civil and ecclesiastical power, in time becoming the point of convergence of the main thoroughfares. The central fulcrum of the space here is the renowned "fountain of the elephant," or *Fontana dell'Elefante*, designed in 1736 by G.B. Vaccarini; in order to create this emblem of the city, Vaccarini used ancient relics (the volcanic-stone elephant dates from Roman times, and was popularly known as "u liotru" and the Egyptian obelisk, with hieroglyphics linked to the worship of the goddess Isis). The whole, set on a pedestal and surmounted by a sphere and the insignia of St. Agatha, expresses a remarkable mixture of Christianity and paganism. The fountain is soon to be restored.

Cattedrale* (D3), or Cathedral. Dedicated to S. Agata (St. Agatha), patron saint of the city, this cathedral was built by the Count Ruggero in the years 1078-93 on the ruins of the baths, or Terme Achilliane, and rebuilt for the first time in 1169 and again following the earthquake of 1693. The main façade, built by G.B. Vaccarini between 1733 and 1761, has two orders of columns and is adorned on high by a statue of the patron saint, while on the left flank there is a marble *portal* by Giandomenico Mazzola (1577); the rear (visible from the courtyard of the Arcivescovado) preserves the original structure of the fortified religious construction; it is possible to glimpse the massive apses, carved with arches and surmounted by merlons, all in large blocks of volcanic rock. The **interior**, which has three aisles divided by pillars, presents a modern flooring, while the side altars and the carved and gilt wooden frames date back to the 18th c.; among the notables buried here, we should mention the *tomb of Vincenzo Bellini* and that of the cardinal Giuseppe Benedetto Dusmet. In the right transept, in the center, is a marble *portal* (G.B. Mazzolo, 1545), with bas-reliefs depicting scenes from the life of the Virgin Mary; through this portal you can enter the chapel, or *Cappella della Madonna*, on the right wall of which is set the *tomb of Constance of Aragon* (d. 1363), the wife of Frederick III; on the opposite wall is a Roman sarcophagus (3rd c.) which contains the remains of royal members of the house of Aragon who resided in Catania. In the right apse, note the chapel, or *Cappella di S. Agata**; here an exceedingly ornate *portal*

(1495) leads into the sacellum containin the relics and part of the immense **treasure of St. Agatha**, including a silver bu dating from 1373-76 and a *coffer**, a gre reliquary case containing the remains the saint, a fine piece of Gothic work in Sic ly (the Vara, i.e., a sort of litter for tran porting the bust and the coffer in town pr cessions, and the treasure are only acce sible during the St. Agatha festival: 2-5 February). In the left transept, a marb *portal* (Giandomenico Mazzola, 1563) wit Scenes of the Passion marks the entrance the chapel, or *Cappella del Crocifisso*, whic occupies one of the side donjon towers da ing from Norman times. To the left of th transept, the *sacristy*, built in 1675, contai a fresco depicting the *Eruption and La Flow of 1669, Threatening Catania*, and 17t and 18th-c. carved cabinets; the adjoinir Sacrario Capitolare, or chapter sacrariur contains a collection of exquisite parc' ments. The grates in the ground are for th ventilation of the baths, or *Terme Achillia* (entrance on the right side of the façade the cathedral), which run under the churc the seminary, or "seminario," and th square that lies before it.

Porta Uzeda (D-E3). This gate was built 1696, along a direct line with the Via nea, within the fortifications of the cit which in their turn were built between th 14th and the 16th c.; some sections of th enclosure wall can still be seen (outer sic of the Duomo). To the east is the *Seminar dei Chierici*, with a complex plan that e tends along the 16th-c. walls, runs throug the gate and links up with the cathedral.

Pass through the gate and follow the Via Dusm to the left, and you will come to the **Palazzo B cari*** (D-E4), which overlooks this side with more lavish façade – pilaster strips in the for of caryatids and balconies framed by scro and putti – the façade that was built first, for th matter (1707). To enter this building, whic was completed in 1763 to plans by France Battaglia and his son Antonino, and which w the site of the museum assembled in 1758 by t prince Ignazio Paternò Castello, and finally d nated to the township in 1932 (the material now in the city museum, or Museo Comunale you must go around to the Via Museo Bisca The building, made up of structures dating fro various eras, is arranged around a large close courtyard; you can enter the oldest core of t building by climbing a crossed-tongs staircas among the halls on the interior – one of whi contains a collection of canvases depicting t immense landholdings of the prince – one c distinguish the *reception hall*, with a dom vault, where a loft stood for the musicians play during entertainments.

ong the same road, the Via Museo Biscari, u will find in the wall of the rear wall of the Conto di S. Placido a 17th-c. aedicule, with a ref of St. Agatha: the door beneath leads into a mber of subterranean chambers dating from man times, traditionally said to be the birth ace and home of the saint.

a Garibaldi (E1-3). This long thoroughfare

c.; it was enclosed by walls in the middle of the 16th c. and, in the centuries that followed, damaged and restored repeatedly. The building has a square plan, with walls two meters thick, four cylindrical corner towers and two remaining semi-cylindrical towers set midway along the northern

e city center is lined with sumptuous Baroque palazzi

ns from the Piazza del Duomo to the west, d it is lined as far as Piazza Mazzini by th-c. palazzi. To the left of the entrance to e street is a fountain, the *Fontana dell'Ameno* (1867), commonly known as "l'acqua a zolu" (the water sheet), because it gaths up and then pours out the waters of the er Amenano; there are traces of this subrranean river both on the hill of the nedettini and in the Roman theater, or atro Romano, but its exact course has ver been plotted with precision.

Maria dell'Indirizzo (E3). This church, reilt in 1727-35 on the site of the 17th-c. urch destroyed by the earthquake, ands atop the Roman baths, or *Terme ll'Indirizzo* (Piazza Currò), baths that are most wholly preserved (there are still rnaces, air conduits, and drains for the ater).

stello Ursino* (E3). The oldest documentation concerning the commission givby Frederick II of Swabia for the conruction of the castle is a letter of conatulations dating from 1239 for the section of the site – a promontory surunded by the sea – addressed to the dictor of fortifications, Riccardo di Lentini; mpleted in 1250, it was the residence of yalty of the house of Aragon in the 15th

and western sides; on the interior, the halls still preserve a number of original structures, of considerable interest.

In the castle is housed the civic museum, or **Museo Comunale***, formed in 1934 with the assembly of much of the material from the Museo Biscari, the collections of the Benedictines, and the material donated by the Baron Zappalà-Asmundo; restoration work currently underway makes it possible to visit only part of the museum. The collection includes excellent archeological finds (the *torso of an emperor*, said to be a torso of Jupiter or Bacchus, taken from a Catanese basilica; *head of an ephebe**, an Attic sculpture from the 6th c. B.C.; *frescoes* from the catacombs of Domitilla in Rome), medieval and Renaissance sculpture, 18th-c. busts of members of the Paternò Castello family, arms and armor, numerous paintings (*St. Christopher* by Pietro Novelli; *Virgin Mary* by Antonello de Saliba). Also worthy of note are the collections of miscellaneous art, with majolica and porcelain, goldsmithery, ivory, marble inlay, and 18th-c. creches.

Home of Giovanni Verga (E2). On 27 January 1922, Federico De Roberto concluded his obituary of his friend, Giovanni Verga, with the words, "Thus begins immortality." And indeed in the

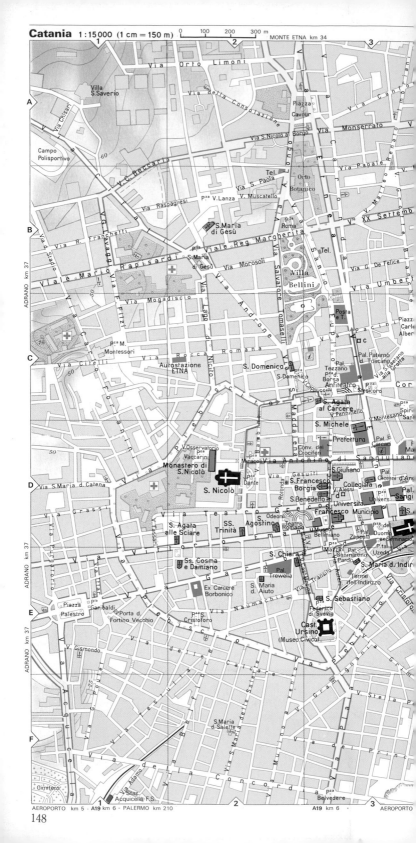

Catania

1:15000 (1 cm = 150 m)

0   100   200   300 m

MONTE ETNA km 34

AEROPORTO km 5 - A19 km 6 - PALERMO km 210   A19 km 6   AEROPORTO

148

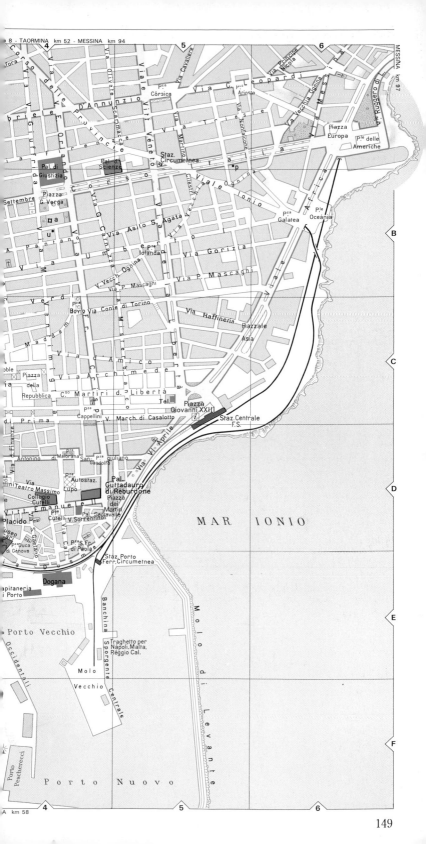

late-17th-c. palazzo where the great author (born in Vizzini in 1840) lived from his early boyhood, a *museum* has been established (entrance in Via S. Anna, n. 8); the house contains objects, furniture, and portraits; the library boasts 2000 volumes by Italian and non-Italian authors, some signed. Nearby, in Piazza S. Francesco, stands the house of another famous citizen, Vincenzo Bellini, with a precious collection of personal effects and sheet music.

Via Vittorio Emanuele (E-D1-3). Running parallel to the Via Garibaldi, the "Strada del Corso," as it was called until the unification of Italy, cuts east and west across the area of the ancient city; framing it on either side are the aristocratic homes and convent buildings that testify whole-heartedly to the Catanese Baroque style.

Teatro Romano (D2-3), or Roman theater. Entirely surrounded by buildings, this theater lies between the Via Vittorio Emanuele (the entrance is in this street, at n. 266) and Piazza S. Francesco. The cavea, which lies athwart the hill upon which the ancient acropolis was built, faced south; it is possible that this structure was Grecian in origin – as tradition would have it – but in any case what is certain is that the surviving structures date solely from Roman times. The theater had a diameter of 87 m., and could accommodate as many as 7,000 spectators; the cavea was built of blocks of limestone, divided into nine wedges and two precincts, and was bounded by three corridors, built in volcanic stone and set at various heights, from which the public could reach the various seating sections through the vomitoria.
The adjoining *Odeon* (D2), which was smaller and was used for rehearsing choruses and for competitions, is semicircular in form and has a cavea capable of seating 1,500.

Via dei Crociferi* (D3). This is one of the most monumental and noteworthy streets of the Baroque section of Catania, partly compromised by archeological excavations underway at the intersection with the Via Antonino di Sangiuliano (ancient Roman roadways and parts of a mosaic have been unearthed). Take this street and you will see, in rapid succession: the *Arco di S. Benedetto* (D2), or arch of St. Benedict, said to have been built in a single night in 1704 by the powerful Benedictine order, determined to overcome the opposition of the secular authorities who opposed the construction on the grounds of seismic dang the majestic church of *S. Benedetto* (17 13), set high on a stairway, with wood doors depicting scenes from the life of Sa Benedict (the interior is embellished with egant stucco work and altars with exquis marble work); the former *Collegio d Gesuiti*, or Jesuit college, now housing t art institute, or Istituto d'Arte, with a pl featuring four courtyards, the first of whi is a handsome cloister believed to be part by G.B. Vaccarini (1742), who certa ly did design the other courtyard, wi strips of white limestone and black co bles, inspired by Borromini; he also c signed the *Palazzo Asmundo Francica No* on the neighboring Piazza Asmundo; t church of *S. Giuliano* (1739-51), also signed by Vaccarini, has a convex façade the center, and a cupola surrounded by small loggia; the *convent of the Padri C ciferi* (by Francesco Battaglia; 1771-80) the crossroads with the Via di Sangiulia which gave its name to the street; the e trance of *Villa Cerami* (from the turn of t 18th c.) at the end of the road, which no houses the law school, or Facoltà Giurisprudenza.

Via Antonino di Sangiuliano (D2-3). Th street constitutes one of the chief the oughfares of the reconstruction order by the Duke of Camastra, and it feature steep rise which is a considerable obstac to the bearers of the giant candles and t litter of St. Agatha, in the procession of 4 and 5th February in the saints honor. the stretch toward the sea, you may n the 18th-c. *Palazzo Manganelli* (D3) ar set off to the side in Piazza Bellini, is

Baroque façades in via dei Crociferi

era house, the *Teatro Bellini* (D4), dedi-
ted to the composer and designed by
rlo Sada on the site of an unfinished
ilding dating from the turn of the 19th c.;
e building, in the Eclectic style, was in-
gurated on 31 May 1890 with a perfor-
nce of the "Norma".

urch of S. Nicolò (D2). Spectacular in size
5x48 m. in the transept; height at the
pola, 62 m.), work on this church began
1687, but was interrupted, first by the
rthquake and later by technical difficul-
s, probably in connection with the size of
e structure, which would have made it the
gest church in Sicily. Because of its state
incompleteness, the façade – which over-
oks the elegant esedra of *Piazza Dante*
tefano Ittar, 1769) – is quite charming
d impressive; note the massive, unfin-
ed columns.

e **interior** features three aisles set on
ssive pylons and a cupola; its vastness is
tounding: the walls, originally pure white,
e interrupted by altars devoid of any fur-
shings, following the anything-but-litur-
al use that has recently been made of the
mplex (it is now a monument to the war
ad, or Sacrario dei Caduti); the pave-
nt of the transept is marked by a marble
eridian with inlaid signs of the zodiac,
ting from 1841.

particular interest – currently being re-
red – is, in the presbytery, the organ,
th a very tall wooden case, carved and
ded, a masterpiece by Donato Del Piano;
e wooden cabinets in the sacristy, in the
coco style, preserve only a faint hint of
eir former splendor.

om a niche in the splay of the largest
rtal, it is possible to climb up to the tam-
ur of the cupola, and from there the eye
n survey everything from Mt. Etna to the
promonte, in Calabria.

joining the church is the **monastery of S.
colò l'Arena**, today the site of the depart-
nt of literature and philosophy (Facoltà di Let-
re e Filosofia) of the University of Catania.
e Benedictines, who had a monastery in Con-
da S. Nicolò l'Arena a Nicolosi, moved into the
y in 1558; the original monastery in Catania,
ich took its name from that section of town,
ich was almost entirely destroyed by the
rthquake of 1693, was replaced, from 1703
, by a new complex, with an even more
andiose structure; among those who worked
it were G.B. Contini and G.B. Vaccarini. In the
urtyard to the east, whose walls are splendid
stimonials to the culture of the expert stone-
tters of the early 18th c., archeological digs
ve unearthed remains of buildings from the ar-
aic Greek period.

This former monastery also houses the *Biblio-
teche Riunite*, or united libraries, assembled
from the original core of the collection of the
Benedictines; another addition came with the collection bequeathed by the Barone Ursino Recu-
pero – particularly valuable in terms of Sicilian
history – and with the library of the poet Mario
Rapisardi. Noteworthy the Naccarini room, famous for its fine majolica floor.

Anfiteatro* (C3), or amphitheater. This immense Roman structure (the entire complex,
which measured respectively 123 and 105 m.
across, at furthest and narrowest, was second
in size only to the Colosseum) probably dates
back to the 2nd c. B.C., and could seat 16,000
spectators; what is visible of the structure
nowadays, from Piazza Stesicoro, represents
only a part of it, with a lava core structure and
marble facing, but its foundations extend
back as far as the Via Penninello.

Via Etnea (A-D3). This street also dates
back to the 18th c., when it was a location
of great prestige among the well-to-do in
Catania; it now largely presents a 19th-c.
style and appearance, a motif that derives
from the fact that at that time the city grew
explosively along this street toward Mt. Etna; much of the urban "boom" in the 20th c.
took place along it as well.

If you follow the northern section of this street,
and occasionally turn off briefly, you will see the
church of *S. Gaetano alla Grotta* (on the Via S.
Gaetano alla Grotta which turns off from the
northeastern corner of Piazza Stesicoro), beneath which is an interesting construction from
Byzantine times; the *Santuario del Carmine*
(1729), a sanctuary overlooking Piazza Carlo
Alberto (where a charming market is held); the
main entrance of the *Villa Bellini*, now a public
park with lavish flowerbeds and old trees; **Viale
XX Settembre**, one of the segments of the
longest thoroughfare in the city, which runs
straight down to the sea; the section running toward the Ionian Sea, on the other hand, features the Piazza Trento and the Piazza Giovanni Verga, and the *Palazzo di Giustizia* (hall of justice), built by Francesco Fichera in 1937-53, and
Villa Manganelli by Ernesto Basile, as well as the
Palazzo delle Scienze (hall of science, 1942),
which houses various geological museums
(*Museo di Mineralogia, Museo di Geologia, and
Museo di Vulcanologia*); the last of the three
museums has interesting collections of material from Mount Etna, the Eolie islands, and other parts of the world.

Collegiata (D3). Also known as the Regia
Cappella, this religious building stands
along a stretch of the Via Etnea that runs toward the center of town; it is one of the masterpieces of the Catanese late-Baroque, and
was built in the early 18th c. to plans by An-

gelo Italia, and completed in the façade by Stefano Ittar (1758); inside, the vaults are frescoed, by Giuseppe Sciuti (late 19th c.).

Piazza Università (D3). This square was built at the behest of the Duke of Camastra, and is hemmed in on the left by the *Palazzo Sangiuliano*, by G.B. Vaccarini (1745), and on the right by the main university building, or *Palazzo dell'Università*, which was completed at the end of the 18th c., with a square courtyard with two orders of loggias, also built by G.B. Vaccarini in 1730. The Università degli Studi di Catania (the "Siculorum Gymnasium" founded by Alphonse of Aragon in 1434) has an exquisite *library* (Biblioteca), one of the richest in all Sicily.

Palazzo Municipale (D3), or city hall. Nowadays also known as the Palazzo degli Elefanti, this building was erected following the earthquake of 1696 on an existing loggia, even though its current form was given it by G.B. Vaccarini who worked on it from 1732 on; fire broke out in 1944 during a popular revolt, and destroyed the furnishings of the interior, as well as the historical archives of the city and the Museo del Risorgimento. The building has a rectangular plan with a central courtyard, porticoed on two sides; at the entrance, a 15th-c. *bust of Saint Agatha*,

the so-called *Carrozze del Senato* (carriag of the Senate), used by the Senate on the casion of the feast day of the patron sai usually open to the public on Sunday.

It was for this same patron saint that G.B. V. carini designed, in 1735-67, on the Via Vitto Emanuele, the **abbey church of S. Agata** (Bad di S. Agata, D3), ending in the massive structu of a large cupola set on an octagonal tambo there is an exceedingly handsome elevati overlooking the Via Raddusa. The interior is signed to a central plan around a regular octago there are four chapels with altars that feature, the right, *statues of St. Euplio and St. Joseph*, a on the left, *Our Lady of the Immaculate Conce tion*, and *St. Benedict*; on the main altar is a s ue *of St. Agatha*. This is only one of the numero churches dedicated to the patron saint of Ca nia; among the other churches dedicated to h we should mention: *S. Agata alle Sciare* (D2), the easternmost extremity of the Via Vitto Emanuele; *S. Agata alla Fornace* (C3) in the Piaz Stesicoro (tradition has it that this was the s of the furnace – "fornace" – where she was m tyred); *S. Agata al Carcere* (C3) in the Piaz Santo Carcere – here, the name "carcere" refe to the belief that the room here dating from F man times was the cell in which the saint w held prisoner before her execution – there are so numerous relics of the saint; *S. Agata la Vete* in the Via S. Maddalena, on the site of an ear Christian basilica; and *S. Agata al Borgo* (A north of the Piazza Cavour.

7.2 Mount Etna and its slopes

Rising 3,323 meters into the air, this volcano dominates the entire Ionian coast of Sicily, and its mass is so vast that it overshadows all other mountains.

A single and complete description of the cone is practically impossible without slipping into generalizations, so great is the variety of landscapes and vegetation that can be found on the volcano: the maquis of prickly pears of Belpasso; the groves of oak, chestnut, hazelnut, and pistachio trees of Bronte; the birch trees (Betula aetnensis), pines, mushrooms, and vineyards, as well as the splendid pine forest of Linguaglossa with its rich underbrush; lastly, as if to join together so many different features, the lava deserts, the sere and lifeless flows that punch through the vegetation, at times creating full-fledged islands of greenery, surrounded by cooled magma. Currently, the prevailing activity takes the form of lateral flows, while the craters on the summit seem to produce most of the explosions of the Stromboli type; full-fledged eruptions are accompanied by diffuse seismic activity throughout the volcanic structure. The oth-

er notable "feature" of the area is the se which laps at the eastern slope along t renowned "Riviera dei Ciclopi" (literal. the Cyclops Coast), embellished by t rock stacks of Aci Trezza and dotted with unending succession of communities.

There is a great variety of possible excu sions, to all sorts of different places: Mount Etna along the trails of the Etr Park (Parco dell'Etna: the administrativ headquarters is at Nicolosi, page 159; t plan is on page 158), to the 150 volcan grottoes (Grotta del Gelo, Grotta dei Lar poni, Grotta delle Palombe, and so on which can be found on the slopes, towar the summit of the volcano; to th renowned "Castagno dei 100 Cavalli" (th 100 Horse Chestnut Tree; its girth is meters) not far from Sant'Alfio; to th snowy ski slopes of the southern slop which offer the excitement of skiing the fiery belly of Mount Etna, while lookir down on Catania and the blue sea glitteri far below; to the Ionian Sea for a refreshi swim in the rainbow-hued waters, and visit the various towns called "Aci."

e automobile tour – which covers a cir-
lar route, 141 km. long – (the tours of
e towns, however, are by foot) runs in
e first section (roughly 42 km. long)
ng the coast, on the state road 114 Ori-
tale Sicula through Aci Castello, Aci
ezza, and the largest of the towns,
reale – its streets are the site of the
est Sicilian carnival – from which sec-
dary roads lead to Zafferana Etnea. At
mefreddo di Sicilia, you leave the state
ad 114 and you skirt the border of the
rco dell'Etna along the state road 120 of
na and the Madonìe, for roughly 80 km.
u will pass through Linguaglossa (an-
er access route to the volcano) and
ndazzo, "marked" architecturally by
e three ethnic groups that lived togeth-
there at some length; then the state
ad 284 Occidentale Etnea leads to
onte – founded in the 16th c. – Adrano,
d Paternò – guarded by an old Norman
stle – and from here you can return to
tania along the state road 121 Catanese
else you can drive up, on secondary
ads, to Nicolosi, the main jump-off point
excursions to the volcano.

Aci Castello and Aci Trezza

The bond linking Aci Castello with Aci Trezza is a long stretch of beachfront, interrupted – as if by a wall – by a bathing establishment, that has been the meeting
place of high-society Catania for decades.
Aci Castello (elev. 15 m., pop. 17,927), which
grew up around a Norman fortress, can no
longer be considered to be a beach resort,
as it has been absorbed into the hinterland
of Catania. Built in 1076 entirely in volcanic
stone, high on a rocky ridge of crystallized
magma, and – after falling under the rule of
Ruggero di Lauria – seized in 1297 by Frederick II of Aragon, the *castle* seems to be an
instrinsic part of the natural product of a
volcanic eruption upon which it stands. It
houses the Civic Museum with specimens of
undersea archeology. From the square before it, bounded by the *Chiesa Madre*, also
made of volcanic stone, it is possible to admire a superb panoramic view of the "Riviera dei Ciclopi," or Cyclops coast, with the
towering silhouettes of the farallons, or
stack formations, in the distance.
Aci Trezza is a village with a maritime tradition, immortalized in the novel "I

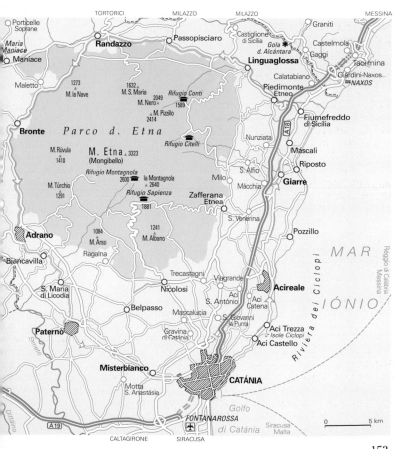

153

Malavoglia" by Giovanni Verga. This is a beach resort but also a town of permanent residents (elev. 5 m.), and it continues to have close ties with the fishing industry: numerous restaurants cluster around the marina, which has now become a mix of tourist pleasure port and fishing port, where large wooden fishing boats dock and where there is a large and active fish market; the selling and buying is done in virtual silence, with only telegraphic gestures and quick nods to mark the bargaining.

Across the water rise up the rock stacks, or **Faraglioni dei Ciclopi*** (now a nature preserve), great shoals of basalt rock, like the rocks hurled in mythology by Polyphemus, the Cyclops, blinded by Odysseus, in a vain

Acireale: the Duomo with the church of Ss. Pietro and Paolo

raging effort to sink the ships of the escaping Greeks, and the *island of Lachea*, now property of the Università di Catania; on the island, there is a biological-research and hydrophysics station.

Acireale*

The name prefix of Aci can be found here too; this name – "reale" means 'royal'– clearly indicated that this was the largest of the seven towns arranged along the eastern slope of Mount Etna. The origin of the prefix has to do with the presence of a stream, cancelled by a series of eruptions, which largely ran underground, and which was linked by tradition to the legend of the loves of the shepherd Aci (in English, Acis) with Galatea, the sea nymph. Polyphemus was in love with the nymph and, in a rage of jealousy, tossed a huge boulder onto Acis, crushing him; the gods, moved by pity, turned the shepherd into a river that, running through subterranean chambers, poured out into the sea to be with his beloved. The tone of this legend is well suited to this little town (elev. 161 m., pop. 46,199; plan on facing page) where the pace

of life is in keeping with the placid nature the people; Piazza del Duomo, the cathed square, with its Baroque magnificence, the fine drawing room of this town – a me ing place where, among the little tables the elegant "gelaterie," or ice cream sho that surround it, people may seem to merely eating ice cream, but in fact they a taking part in an old and noble social ritu The great celebration in Acireale "carnevale," the finest carnival feast in Si ly, with a procession of "carri allegorici," painted carts, and with thousands tourists attracted by the giddy festival, well as by the hot springs, first used baths by the ancient Romans.

The city was built on its current site 1326, after the destructi of the settlement – ori nally Roman and lat Byzantine ("Aquilia") – fi by the earthquake of 11 and later by sea raiders became a feudal holding three centuries, beginni in 1642, by decree of Phi IV of Spain, controlled rectly by the crown, as state-owned town und the name of Aci Reale.

The earliest core of t town stands on what is n the Piazza del Duomo, cathedral square, whi could be said to be complete by the first h of the 17th c. with the completion of bui ings surrounding it (Duomo, 1618; church Ss. Pietro e Paolo, 1642; Palazzo Comuna 1659). Between the 16th and 17th c., t structure of the city branched out from t thoroughfare consisting of the present-d Corso Vittorio Emanuele and Corso U berto I, which respectively led to the roa to Catania and Messina; it was the new s tlements of various religious orders – D minicans to the west, Capuchins to t northeast, Carmelites to the southeast that created new poles of urban develo ment, linked in the center and one to t other: Via Cavour joined the monastery the Dominicans with the Duomo; V Galatea linked the two convents, of the C puchins and the Carmelites, encouragi the eastward growth of the city.

The earthquake of 1693 caused conside able destruction, though it did not da age the urban structure irreparably. R construction was directed by the Duke Camastra, and among those responsib we should mention the Aci-born paint Pietro Paolo Vasta. The nobility and t

althy bourgeois took up residence along
e chief thoroughfare; the clergy repaired
e damage to the existing churches and
lt new ones, thus giving a structure to the
ginal center that persists to the present
y. Expansion in the 19th c. extended the
urse of what is now Corso Savoia, which
ates a triangle with the Viale Principe
nedeo and the Corso Umberto I.
the south entrance to the city stand the
ths, or *Terme di S. Vénera* (D2), at the
ry heart of an immense park that was
ated in 1873; these hot baths take their
ter from a hot spring (the sulfurous wa-
is 22 degrees Celsius, is used in treating
rtain forms of deafness and is excellent
the skin) which is located in the quarter,
Contrada S. Vénera al Pozzo; here stood
e Terme Xiphionie, possibly Greek in ori-
, which the Romans enlarged, with a
nstruction whose ruins still stand there.

The main thoroughfare of this little city is
the *Corso Vittorio Emanuele* (C-D2), which intersects with the Via Ruggero Settimo on a
line with the Piazza Vigo. Overlooking this
square is the church of **S. Sebastiano** (C2),
before which extends a balustrade adorned
with ten 18th-c. *statues* with characters
from the Old Testament. The 17th-c. architectural structure, restored following the
earthquake of 1693, is decorated on the interior by numerous frescoes and canvases
by Pietro Paolo Vasta; also note the 18th-c.
litter used in the procession of the saint.
Walking past 18th- and 19th-c. palazzi, we
will come to the **Piazza del Duomo*** (B2),
enlarged in the 17th c., a setting of rare
beauty. The *Duomo* (B2), or cathedral, dedicated to Our Lady of the Annunciation (Annunziata), and to St. Vénera, was first built
in the years 1597-1618 and was renovated in
the early 18th c.; the two bell towers, with

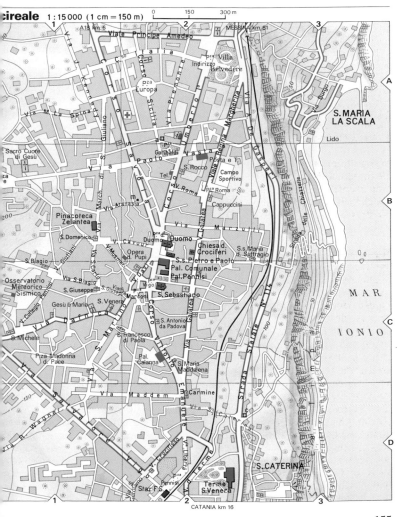

conical cusps sheathed in polychrome ceramics, flank a façade in a pseudo-Gothic style, built at the turn of the 20th c. by G.B. Basile, who incorporated a massive marble portal with 17th-c. *statues of the Annunciation and of Saints Vénera and Tecla*; inside, you can admire numerous works by the Aci-born painter Pietro Paolo Vasta and a sundial dating from 1843, set at the intersection of nave and transept.

Completing the setting of this square is the church of the *Ss. Pietro e Paolo*, with an 18th-c. elevation and a façade with two orders, and only one bell tower, on the right, with cusp and pinnacles (perhaps a second bell tower would have blocked the sunlight to the sundial of the Duomo, or cathedral), and the *Palazzo Comunale* (city hall; B-C2), built in 1659 in the typical flamboyant Baroque of Catania, with balconies supported by carved brackets, depicting bizarre figures and surmounted by ornate railings in wrought iron.

The *Biblioteca Zelantea* and the *Pinacoteca Zelantea* (respectively, library and art gallery; B1) have been located since 1915 in the Via Marchese di S. Giuliano (you can reach it from Piazza del Duomo by following the Via Cavour); the library, which dates back to 1671, has one of the largest and richest collections in all of Sicily; in the art gallery, there are canvases by Pietro Paolo Vasta and a particularly noteworthy *bust of Julius Caesar**, better known as the Busto di Acireale, a Roman sculpture uncovered in 1676.

Beyond the Piazza del Duomo, the main thoroughfare of Acireale is called *Corso Umberto I* (A-B2), and is lined with boutiques and ice cream shops, and the latter truly constitute a distinctive feature of the little town; at the end of the "corso" is the *Villa Belvedere*, a public park and garden with a magnificent view of the Ionian Sea and Mount Etna.

If you go from Acireale to **Zafferana Etnea** (elev. 574 m., pop. 7,381), on the main square of which stands the Baroque *Chiesa Madre*, you can "climb" Mount Etna along the eastern slope; the road is distinguished by the remarkable views and the possibility of looking down over the far edge of the Valle del Bove (turn right at the turnoff for the Monte Zoccolaro).

From Acireale to Riposto

The secondary road, which runs parallel to the state road, juts like a broad terrace high over the Timpa and the coast far below, offering a panoramic view that reaches all the way to the coasts of Calabria, and running through orange groves and rebuilt rural farmhouses.

The little hamlet of *Santa Maria la Sc* (elev. 15 m.), where you can even w down a long stairway with spectacu views, is both a fishing village and a bea resort; the little village is clustered arou the 17th-c. church and the little marina, a setting that is still miraculously intact Rocky beaches of volcanic stone, and ple ant trattorias overlooking the sea char terize the next town *Santa Tecla* (elev. 3 m.), followed by *Pozzillo* (elev. 10 m.), s among countless orange groves and a re tively undeveloped coastal area, and *posto* (elev. 8 m., pop. 14,048), which un 1841 was part of the adjoining town of G rre. Its name comes from the original rol played as a storehouse for goods from land, and it is still possible to see many e amples of industrial architecture from t 19th c., linked to the production and sale wine; nearby there were once famous sh yards, no longer in operation.

Linguaglossa

The name of this town (elev. 550 m., po 5,393) probably comes from a large s ("lingua grossa") of lava from an eruption ter 1634, commemorated by a plaque the city hall. It is easy to reach the pine f est, or *Pineta di Linguaglossa*, and the Pia Provenzana, a ski resort on the northeaste slope, a base camp for expeditions to t summit of the volcano, or to walk the tr that leads around Mount Etna.

Randazzo

Located on the northern slopes of Mount na, this town (elev. 765 m., pop. 11,55 plan on facing page) hearkens back to t Middle Ages, both in terms of the config ration of the center and for the very fact its existence. The presence of the volca is a very vivid and keenly felt thing, not o ly because it bulks so large in the lan scape, but also because its products a used in manufactured artifacts of all sor volcanic stone is used not only to bui drystone walls in the fields but also to co struct buildings in the city and as the r material for sculpted and monumental e ifices, as well as for the paving of the roac Always spared by the magma – even thou it was the town located closest to the v cano's main crater – this little city grew importance during the age of Swabian ru and it soon became the trading center f the entire range of the Monti Nèbrodi. 1154, the Arabic geographer Idrisi describe it as overflowing with merchants: its stru ture stabilized into three main areas, o cupied by the different ethnic commu

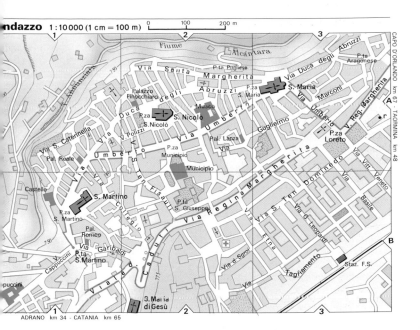

s (the Latins around the church of S. ..ria, the Greeks around the church of S. ..colò, and the Lombards around the ..rch of S. Martino); the equilibrium of the ..mmunity was preserved by giving each of ..ese churches, and consequently each of ..ese ethnic groups, the role of Cathedral .. a year (it was not until after 1916 that S. ..ria was finally named Chiesa Matrice).

..der the rule of Peter of Aragon, the town ..s fortified and enclosed with walls, some ..etches of which still stand in an area ad-..ning the gate, or Porta Aragonese. In the ..th c., the population was estimated to be ..00/6,000; subsequent growth dwindled ..ly at the end of the 16th c. due to an array ..contributing factors: the foundation of ..e nearby town of Bronte (1535); the ..mming of the river Piccolo by a lava flow ..at caused considerable damage to the ..lds; the plague, which broke out between ..75 and 1580, raging so fiercely that it ..ced the abandonment and destruction of ..tire quarters of the city. The recon-..ruction of a number of buildings and the ..ing up of the room within the walls were ..e most notable occurrences of the 17th c. ..e most significant monuments are the ..urches of the ethnic communities. Over-..oking the Piazza Basilica is the church of **Maria*** (A3), which was founded by the ..abians (1217-39), and shows very little of .. original structure; the façade has a ..sped campanile, rebuilt in 1852-63; the ..ses, shaped like battlemented donjon ..wers, date from the 13th c.; on the right

side, note the splendid Catalonian Gothic *portal* (15th c.) complete with an array of triple-, twin-, and single-light mullioned windows. The *interior* has three aisles, divided by columns made of volcanic stone; the addition of a cupola in the early 19th c. partly undercut the harmony that had been attained with the various modifications done during the 16th and 17th c.; the interior boasts numerous frescoes, canvases, and inlaid marble work from various eras: among all of these, we would single out, as a precious piece of iconographic documentation, a painting on panel (*Salvation of Randazzo*), with a view of the 16th-c. town, hanging on the right side door, and attrib-

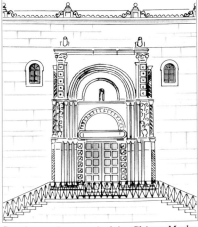

Randazzo: the portal of the Chiesa Madre

157

Parco dell'Etna   1:300000 (1 cm = 3 km)

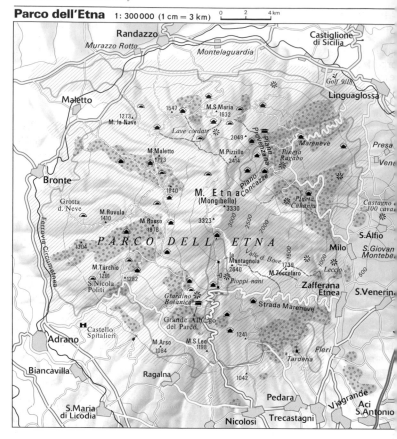

uted to Girolamo Alibrandi.

The original structure of the church of **S. Nicolò** (A2), the second basilican church and the largest one in Randazzo (which is why Peter of Aragon accorded it the privilege of holding general civic assemblies), dates back to the 14th c., but was rebuilt in 1583. In the *interior*, with its Latin-cross plan, there are numerous works by the Gagini, including a notable *statue of St. Nicholas*, set on the altar of the left arm of the transept, and signed by Antonello (1523).

The church of **S. Martino** (B1) was also founded by the Swabians (13th c.), but the bell tower on the right dates from the 14th c.; the 15th-c. *interior* contains canvases from the Gagini school and a polyptych (*Virgin Mary, St. Lucy, and St. Martha*) attributed to Antonello de Saliba. Facing the church are the ruins of the medieval citadel, housing the civic archeological museum, or *Museo Archeologico*, with finds ranging from the Neolithic to early Sicilian and Greek times and a collection of Sicilian puppets.

It is interesting to note in the mediev structure that there are still intact sectio of lesser structures: among the architectu complexes, of particular environment note is the pointed-arch gate, or *Po Aragonese*, in the southern walls, whi dates from 1282.

Not far from Randazzo, a short detour toward (sarò is certainly worth taking, to see the Be dictine **abbey of Maniace***, known as Caste and located not far from the place where t Byzantine condottiere George Maniace defeat the Saracens with the assistance of the N mans (1040). It was founded in 1174 by M garet, the mother of William II, and in 1799 w donated to Admiral Horatio Nelson with t Ducea di Bronte; Nelson's descendants liv there almost uninterruptedly until 1981, tra forming it into a lavish aristocratic residen with a wonderful garden of exotic plants.

Bronte

Under Spanish rule in the 16th c., the po er of the barons had grown out of all pr portion, along with the extensive corrupti of public officials and outright favoritism

e part of the nobility. The decision of
arles V to reorganize the hamlets of the
lages of the Randazzo countryside into a
gle center was a result of the decision to
organize all settlements in administra-
e and fiscal terms; that decision resulted
the foundation in 1535 of Bronte, which
on rivalled its neighbor Randazzo, drain-
g it of population and manpower.

vastated by the eruptions of 1651, 1832,
d 1843, whose lava flows, especially those
the eruption of 1832, still lie nearby, this
wn (elev. 760 m., pop. 18,689) is now a no-
le farming center, known in particular for
biennial pistachio harvest. Among the
urches, the most significant is the church
the Annunziata (1535), on the façade of
ich you may observe a yellow sandstone
rtal; inside are 17th-c. canvases and a
lychrome marble group attributed to An-
ello Gagini.

rano

t on a volcanic highland which juts out to-
rd the Valle del Simeto, this farming
wn (elev. 560 m., pop. 32,717) is particu-
ly devoted to the production and sale of
rus fruit.

cheological relics of the Greek town of
dranon" (5th c. B.C.) have been found in
Contrada Mendolito, not far from which
a bridge, or Ponte dei Saraceni, which
ans the river in question; it declined un-
r Roman rule and revived under the Nor-
ans with the name of Adernò, a name that
kept until 1929.

rticularly impressive is the **Castello Nor-
anno***, or Norman castle, with a square
an, built in the 11th c. by Count Roger; reilt in the 14th c. and recently restored, it
ntains an archeological museum, or
seo Archeologico, with finds dating from
e Neolithic to the early-Sicilian/Greek era,
und in recent excavations, and a museum
crafts, or Museo dell'Artigianato. The

nearby *Chiesa Madre*, dedicated to Our Lady of the Assumption (Assunta), and Norman in origin, was enlarged in 1640-56 and
restored in 1811; tradition has it that the 16
columns supporting the three aisles on the
interior come from the ancient temple of
"Adranon."

Paternò

The little town (elev. 225 m., pop. 44,266),
with an economy based on growing, harvesting, and exporting oranges, was founded by the Normans and has a historical
center downhill from the basalt crag, atop
which looms the inevitable castle, or *Castello*, built by Roger the Norman (1073), but rebuilt after the 14th c., and subjected twice
to restorations in the 20th c. (new work is
now underway, to turn it into a museum);
the massive cubic structure, built of volcanic stone, is interrupted along the sides
by twin-light mullioned windows which
light the armory on the second floor and a
gallery on the third.

From the square opposite, overlooked also
by the *Chiesa Madre* (or S. Maria dell'Alto),
which was rebuilt in 1342 on an existing Norman structure, it is possible to recognize the
way the city developed in the prevailing
colors (the burnt sienna lava black of the
historical center; polychrome hues in the
regular urban development to the north;
concrete grey and brick red in the settlement – largely in violation of the building
codes – to the east and southeast); you
can also admire the broad Piana di Catania,
the mouth of the valley of the river Simeto,
and the spectacular volcano.

Another route providing access to Mt. Etna runs
from **Nicolosi** (elev. 700 m., pop. 5,365), a town
that has been destroyed repeatedly by lava, and
which has now become a choice summer resort for Catania, given the excellent weather,
fine tourist facilities, and considerable hotel capacity. Located here are the offices of the **Parco
dell'Etna***, where it is possible
to get directions concerning
the nature trails running
around the volcano.
Of particular note is the route
to the hut, or *Rifugio Sapienza*;
this trail, like many of the trails
that wind up to the cone, alternates vast expanses of oak,
chestnut, and pine groves with
desert-like volcanic lava flows.
During the summer, it is possible to continue in off-road
vehicles nearly all the way up
to the summit of the crater,
which however is off limits to
visitors.

e incredible vulcanic landscape

8 The region of the Monti Peloritani and the Aeolian islands

Across the Strait of Messina, the continental ridge of the Apennines re-emerges just pa[st] the sandy spit of cape, or Capo Peloro. The orographic alignment, or mountain range, th[at] takes its name from this remarkable feature of the Sicilian coast – to be specific, the Mo[n-]ti Peloritani, with more than one summit rising above an altitude of 1,000 meters – exten[ds] first to the southwest, and is then blocked by the volcanic mass of Etna, which pushes [it] sharply west; from this point on the ridge takes the name of the Monti Nèbrodi until it reac[h-]es the westernmost fringe of the Madonìe. To the east, along the Ionian slope, the coa[st]

is steep and rocky, with [a] littoral strip that leaves l[it-]tle room for farming, ma[nu-]facturing, and residenti[al] communities.The urba[n] settlements from Messi[na] to Taormina are all rough[ly] the same size and equal [in] importance; they basica[lly] revolve around the capit[al.] To the north, on the Ty[r-]rhenian slope, there is [a] much more gradual grad[e] leading from sea level [to] the upper ridges, and t[he] slopes of the Monti Pelo[ri-]tani lend themselves pe[r-]fectly to terrace farmin[g.] The sere and arid appea[r-]ance of the eastern coast [is] a result of the hot siroc[co] winds out of Africa, whi[ch] scalds the flora before [it] can bloom; the norther[n] coast, which receives a "tr[a-] montana" wind and is ri[ch] in mountain streams, on th[e]

Home to fire and winds, the Aeolian islands are set in the midst of a deep blue sea

other hand, is covered wit[h] high-branched forest tree[s] on the middle and upp[er] hills, and by fruit orchards and vineyards at the lower elevations. Milazzo, with its vast ha[r-]bor, in the sheltering lee of the Promontorio di Milazzo, a promontory jutting six km. o[ut] into the Tyrrhenian, and with the fertile rolling hills extending inland, is the second ran[k-]ing city of the Tyrrhenian area, as far as Sant'Àgata di Militello. Across from Milazzo an[d] across from the entire arch of the coastline of Messina, the volcanic archipelago of the A[e-]olian islands constitute one of the greatest tourist attractions of the area.

8.1 Messina, the city on the strait

Any visit to Messina (elev. 3 m., pop. 231,693; plan on page 162) should begin from the sea. From the upper decks of the ferryboats that run across the strait, in fact, you can see a new city; it is fairly evident at a glance just how the urban structure was laid out, punctuated as it is by the transverse axes of the broad river beds, or "fiumare" – which have been converted into roads – and organize[d] into long straight avenues running perpe[n-]dicular to the "fiumare." Old Messina [is] gone: there is the occasional sculpture [or] here and there a little architecture in ston[e,] isolated from the original urban conte[xt,] which only vaguely speaks of the past; the[se] are scattered throughout a landscape of r[e-] rced concrete.

ssina has always played a critical role as
oint of passage of the chief maritime traf-
between east and west and between
th and south. This has been true since the
y's foundation, which dates back to be-
e the Greek colonization – which is to
, before the 8th c. B.C. – by early Sicil-
s, who called it "Zancle," or 'sickle'; fol-
ving its conquest by Dionysius in the 5th
B.C. its name was changed to "Messana."
tween the 3rd c. B.C. and the 5th c. A.D.
 city grew in economic power, in part
e to the construction of the two Roman
sular roads running along the coast:
 Via Valeria toward Catania and the Via
npea toward Palermo. Under the Byzan-
es, the government was entrusted to the
ratigoti" (strategists), interesting politi-
figures of Greek influence; it was in this
iod that the Christianization of the island
ready underway in its Latin form – was
ted in the direction of the Greek rite. Fol-
ing the Arabs came the Normans (1061),
o planted the feudal system on the is-
d.

der the house of Hauteville (11th and
h c.) and under the dynasty of the Ho-
staufen (12th c.), Messina was girded
h a power set of walls – not a trace of
ich is left standing – and numerous
nasteries and churches were built as
l (SS. Annunziata dei Catalani), not to
ntion the foundation of the Duomo, or
hedral, and, at the extremity of what is
v known as the peninsula of S. Raineri,
 titular church of the Greek-rite archi-
ndrite (S. Salvatore dei Greci). The con-
ction of manufacturing infrastructure
 improved communications encouraged
 ring the occupation by both Swabians
 by the house of Anjou – trade in silk,
ol, and leather. The Messina that, in the
1 c., came under the rule of the Spanish
eroys was a wealthy and populous city in-
d. Following an initial period of structural
ovation, a decisive project was under-
en for the expansion of the city bound-
s, with the shift of the enclosure walls;
ong the many building projects that were
ipleted – many of them long since de-
oyed – there still stand the two fortress-
f Forte S. Salvatore, at the sickle-hook of
 harbor, and the Forte Gonzaga, set high
 mount behind the city center.

reat many of the public and private
dings constructed in this period were
troyed by the brutal earthquake of 1783.
he 19th c., communications with the
ital cities of Catania, Siracusa, and Paler-
were improved; a regular ferry boat

service was established across the strait,
and shortly after the unification of Italy,
the first regulatory plan was drawn up,
which further extended the boundary of
the city, this time toward the south.

The catastrophic earthquake of 1908 once
again put a sudden halt to all development,
sapping the will of the people of Messina, a
determination that had already been sore-
ly tried by centuries of traumatic events.
The plan for reconstruction (1911) designed
a city in which there is no room left for historic memory, a city with broad boulevards
and strong, earthquake-proof buildings, organized into blocks on a rigid, checkerboard pattern. Although it has been widely
discussed and criticized, the "Piano Borzì"
– a regulatory plan that was named after its
framer – was nonetheless prompted by the
harsh necessities of the moment, and it did
provide at least a reassuring solidity to the
terrorized city that had survived the earthquake. There was also massive damage
caused by bombing in 1943, another factor
that contributed to the almost totally modern appearance that Messina presents to a
visitor: the few pre-earthquake structures
that still stand are easily noted in the mass
of residential buildings, of late-19th-c. appearance. If you have a car, then you can drive around the eastern branch of the Punta
della Sicilia, or you can venture up into the
nearby Peloritani.

Forte S. Salvatore (B-C3). At the farthest tip
of the peninsula of S. Raineri, which closes
off to the east the natural harbor of Messina, a great fortress was built in the 1540s, at
the behest of the viceroy Ferrante Gonzaga,
to plans by Antonio Ferramolino da Ber-
gamo. The Forte San Salvatore was part of
the plan for the fortification of the city
made necessary by the incessant raids of
the Turks; it constitutes the outlying works
of the city defensive apparatus, construction of which began in 1533, and continued until 1686, with the construction of the
citadel, or Cittadella; the only section of
this immense fortification that remains in
good condition nowadays is the Forte Gonzaga (see page 166).

Cittadella (C-D3, off map), or citadel. On the
central area of the peninsula, now occupied by shipyards and railyards, there still
stand, shrouded by many years of neglect,
the ruins of the fortress built between 1682
and 1686 (it was one of the most important coastal fortifications of the time) following the bloody revolt against Spanish
domination in 1678. Justified both for the de-

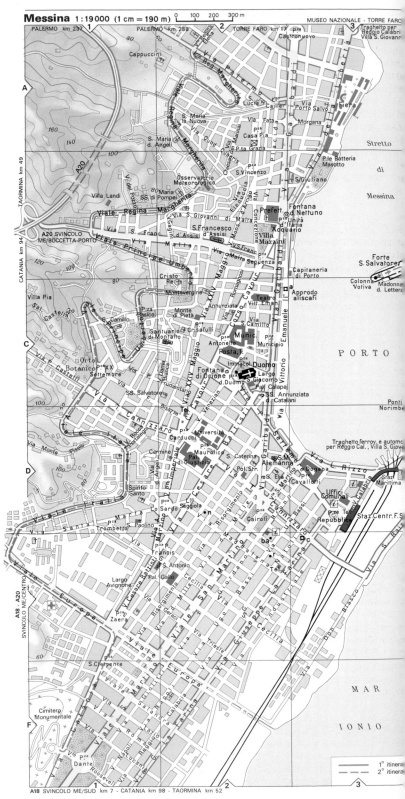

Messina 1:19000 (1 cm = 190 m)   0 100 200 300 m

MUSEO NAZIONALE - TORRE FARO

PALERMO km 237   PALERMO km 258   TORRE FARO km 17   Traghetto per Reggio Calabri Villa S. Giovanni

Castronuovo

Cappuccini

Via Rea Palermo

S. Lucia
Cailler
Via Porto Salvo
Fiera

S. Maria la Nuova

Via Fata
Morgana

S. Maria d. Angeli

Via Oued
Casa Pia

Stretto

Osservatorio Meteorologico

S.P.ta Grazia

P.le Batteria Masotto

Villa Landi

SS. di Pompei

S.Vincenzo

S.Giuliana

di

Viale Regina Margherita

Prefett
Fontana d. Nettuno

Via S. Giovanni di Malta

Messina

Via S. Franc

S.Francesco d'Assisi

Concezione
P.za d'Italia
Acquario

d'Assisi

Villa Mazzini

Via Malta

V.S.Franc

Via Maria Sequenza

Forte S. Salvatore

Cristo Re

Capitaneria di Porto

Colonna Votiva
Madonna d. Lettera

Villa Pia

Montevergine

Teatro Vitt. Eman.

Approdo aliscafi

Castello

P.za Basico

Monte di Pietà

Annunziata

Via S. Camillo

PORTO

S. Camillo

Santuario di Montalto

Crisafulli

Munic.

Orto Botanico
P.za XX Settembre

Antonello
Posta, F.

Municipio

Immacol.
Duomo

Ponti Norimbe

SS. SALVATORE

Fontana di Orione
Largo d.Duomo

Largo Giacomo
Pal.Calapaj

SS. Annunziata d. Catalani

Cannizzaro
Tel.

Carducci

Università

Traghetto ferrov. e automac. per Reggio Cal., Villa S. Giov

Via Monte Piselli

Carmine

Maurolico
Pal. di Giustizia

S. Caterina
Pol.Str.

S.M.
Alemanna

Via L. Rizzo

Spirito Santo

S. Elia
P.za Dogana
(Cavallotti)

Staz Maritima

P.za Seggiola

Lo Sardo

S. Paolino

P.za Cairoli

Uffici Comunali

Via Santa
P.za Maria Trombetta

P.za Francis

P.za Repubblic
Staz.Centr. F.S

ba

Via Santa

S. Antonio

Largo Avignone
Pal. Gallo

Via Cecilia

Tel.

S.Clemente

P.za Zaera

MAR

Cimitero Monumentale

P.za Dante

P.za Roosevelt

IONIO

1° itinera
2° itinera

A18 SVINCOLO ME/SUD km 7 - CATANIA km 98 - TAORMINA km 52

162

se of Messina from attacks by outsiders the time that Ferramolino was building ese fortifications, the peninsula of S. ineri was unguarded to the south, toard the seafront overlooking the strait), d to keep the city itself under control, in fear of possible new outbreaks of unrest; e fortress presented a pentagonal plan, d was endowed with five projecting basns, from which to set up a crossfire, giv it the form of a star that was later adopt in other forts under Spanish, French, d Dutch domination, and which still rks the shape of some towns to the pret day.

e **curtain of buildings facing the port** -C2). These structures were built in the t half of the 20th c., replacing the 19th-c. alazzata," which was destroyed in the thquake of 1908. The architectural and anistic invention of the "Palazzata" of the t dates back to the period of the Spanish eroys (the structures built at that time re first damaged by the insurrection inst the Spanish, and finally destroyed the earthquake of 1783) and was also led the "teatro" or front of the city; ined, the prestigious series of buildings unbroken, like a ribbon, along the part the port's perimeter facing the sickleped area.

I Settembre (D2-3, C2). The present route of this street dates back to 1911, retraces the much older Via Austria, t in the 16th c. to link the Palazzo Reale, ich stood in the area now occupied by Dogana, or customs office, with the omo, or cathedral; the date indicated in name commemorates the outbreak of Sicilian uprising of the Risorgimento.

Maria degli Alemanni (D2). A rare exple of Sicilian Gothic architecture (the inor features three aisles and three apses), church was built in the first half of the h c., possibly by craftsmen and builders n north of the Alps, at the behest of the alieri Teutonici, or Teutonic knights, abandoned it at the end of the 15th c., sing a steady decline and decay; capitals all sorts of depictions are the sole decions surviving.

Annunziata dei Catalani* (C2). This ll church, with a basilican plan and e aisles, with cross vaults over the sides and the transept, was built in the ond half of the 12th c., in the context of Norman campaign of foundations. The

decoration of both the main façade and the side elevations show clear Moorish influence; the presence, surrounding the apse and the tambour, of smooth slender columns supporting the little arches that mark the structure, in place of the traditional brick pilaster strips, differentiates this church from the other churches in the Messina area dating from this same period. The floor level is at a much lower level than the level of the modern city, which has been raised considerably due to the accumulation of rubble produced by various earthquakes.

Duomo* (C2), or cathedral. Built at the behest of the Normans, it was consecrated under the rule of the Swabians (1197) and was partly destroyed a first time by the earthquake of 1783; its current appearance is the result of the reconstruction that was done following the last earthquake and the bombing of 1943: of the ancient structural elements, the only parts that survive are the northwestern corner and the room that now contains the crypt. On the *façade*, it is possible to observe, progressing upward, marble bas-relief bands (15th c.) depicting scenes of the fields and of everyday home life. In the main portal, which was rebuilt with elements that were rebuilt to replace the original elements, since lost, one should pay particular note to the two pillar-bearing

The Duomo (rebuilt after the earthquake)

lions, which date from the 14th c. On the right side is a *portal* by Polidoro da Caravaggio and Domenico Vanello (16th c.; the twin portal, set on the opposite side, is now used as an entrance to the modern baptistery, though this distorts the original composition); in the structure adjoining the side there are Gothic-style twin-light mullioned windows, though only the first of them is original, made of stone and dating from the 15th c. The **interior**, with a Latin-cross basilican plan, is also largely redone: it is divided into three aisles by columns surmounted by pointed arches, and covered by a roof with painted trusses. On the first altar in the right aisle, note the *statue of St. John the Baptist*, attributed to Antonello Gagini (16th c.; it is the sole example to survive the fire of 1943, from a series known as the Apostolate); further along, a stone *portal* from the same period adorns the entrance to the vestibule which leads into the *Tesoro* (Treasury; not open to visitors), while its twin is located in the left aisle as an entrance to a symmetrical vestibule. On the main altar, in the presbytery, there is an interesting bronze panel depicting the Virgin Mary handing a letter to the ambassadors of Messina. In the left apse, note the chapel, or *Cappella del Sacramento*, designed in the last few years of the 16th c. by Jacopo del Duca, a student of Michelangelo; this was the part least badly damaged by the earthquake; it contains the panels depicting the *Supper at Emmaus* and the *Last Supper* and, in the vault of the apse, a 14th-c. mosaic with the *Virgin Mary enthroned*, and surrounded by archangels, female saints, and queens.

Campanile (C2), or bell tower. This tower stands 60 m. tall, and it too was rebuilt after 1908; in 1933 the tower was given a large clock with four dials, one on each face of the tower; on the southern face, moreover, there are two other dials, one showing the calendar and the other the system of planets; lastly, there is a globe showing the phases of the moon. On the west side there are niches that contain a number of mechanical figures, which start working every twelve hours of the day or night: if we look from the bottom up, we see: in the first niche, allegories of the days of the week; in the second niche, allegories of the ages of man; in the third niche the Santuario di Montalto rises from and then disappears into a small mount; in the fourth niche, there are characters from four Gospel scenes; in the fifth niche, the delivery of the letter of the Virgin Mary to the ambassadors of Messina. The first of the two top twin-light mullioned windows, on the same side of the tower, contains two antique bells, and – on the external platform, there is a group of mechanical figures including a rooster and Dina and Clarenza, two popular heroins from the Vespri Siciliani, or the revolt of the Sicilian Vespers.

Fontana di Orione * (C2). Set in the square facing the cathedral, or Duomo, this fountain is one of the few sculptural works that survived the succession of disasters that

struck the town; it was built in 1547 by Giovanni Angelo Montorsoli and Domeni? Vanello in commemoration of the cc struction of the city's first aqueduct, whi captured water from the mountain strea of Camaro and Portalegni: the human figu that adorn it, in fact, represent the rive Tiber, Nile, Ebro, and Camaro, while a nu ber of verses written by the Messine mathematician and philosopher Frances Maurolico, carved into the side of the bas allude to river-related themes.
The square to the left of the Duomo, cathedral, features a marble *statue of Our dy of the Immaculate Conception* (Imma lata), dating back to 1758.

From the Piazza del Duomo, beyond the Cavour, you can reach, along the Via XXIV M gio, the *Monte di Pietà* (C2), which, of its origi structures, preserves the façade by Natale I succio (17th c.); the three-arched portico p serves a 16th-c. fountain; from the atrium, a d ble-ramp staircase (on the first landing, n the 18th-c. fountain with *a statue of Abundar* leads up to the church of *S. Maria della Pietà* which only the façade now survives.

Via Garibaldi (A-D2). This is the main th oughfare of the city, extending from the azza Cairoli (those interesting in shopp should explore the Viale S. Martino, wh runs southward from here) and the Pia Castronuovo. There are few pieces of chitecture dating back to before the rec struction of 1911 (the massive classic-st bulk of the city hall, or *Municipio*, da back to 1934; C2): the 19th-c. *Teatro Vitto Emanuele* and, beyond the Piazza Ur d'Italia, where there is a copy of the Neptu by Montorsoli, now in the Museo, note houses, or *Case Cicala*, built between 1 and 1864.

S. Giovanni di Malta (B2). Incorporatec to the *Palazzo della Prefettura* (1920), this tle church, with its elegant Manner façade, was designed in the 16th c. by copo del Duca, and is one of the few pie of religious architecture from that per still to stand in decent condition; on the terior, note the *funerary monumen Francesco Maurolico* as well as 18th- 19th-c. silverwork, on display in little ha and the sacellum with the tombs of martyred saints, and large silver reliqu busts.

Museo Regionale * (A3, off map). This gional museum was set up in 1914 on premises of a spinning mill not far from Viale Annunziata, and comprises works

from the Civico Museo Peloritano, an
institution that was located in the former
monastery, or Monastero di S. Gregorio,
since destroyed by the earthquake. The interior halls, the vast area surrounding the
old structure and the new museum, under
construction, are cluttered with architectural and decorative elements taken from
the ruins of buildings destroyed by earthquakes and war; for this reason it is still not
possible to admire, among other things,
the original of the lovely statue of Neptune
by Montorsoli, which stood until recently on
the esplanade.

On the left wall of the atrium, 12 18th-c.
panels in gilt bronze recount the *legend of
the Sacred Letter*: since the people of Messina had long been suffering a great famine,
the Virgin Mary, moved to compassion by
the faith the people had shown, offered her

Christ Child, surrounded by a wreath of fruit
and vines (15th c.) and, attributed to
Domenico Gagini, a marble bas-relief of *St.
George, princess, and dragon* (15th c.).

In the list of works influenced by Antonello
da Messina (hall IV), we should note the
marble *Virgin Mary with Christ Child*, interesting for the treatment of surfaces with
polychrome and gilding, attributed to
Francesco Laurana. Antonello da Messina
painted a panel oil painting for the chapel of
the monastery of S. Gregorio in 1473, a
polyptych** depicting the Virgin Mary Enthroned between Saint Gregory and Saint
Benedict; of the five panels, which are now
in relatively poor condition, the two upper
panels depict the archangel making the Annunciation, and Our Lady of the Annunciation (Annunziata). Another panel oil painting (*Pietà and Symbols of the Passion*), by an

...essina and the strait which separates Sicily from Calabria

...sistance by sending to the port of Messina a ship without a crew, but loaded with
wheat and foods of all sorts, along with a letter containing a lock of Her hair and a mes-
sage blessing the city and the people (the
words of the letter can be seen on the interior of the Forte S. Salvatore).

Among the objects dating from the Nor-
man-Byzantine period (12th/13th c.), note
the three *fragments of trusses* that supported the roof of the cathedral, or Duomo,
painted by local master craftsmen with
themes taken from the Old and the New
Testament (hall I); these motifs were probably the inspiration for the recent decoration of the present roof of the church.

Dating from the early Renaissance in Messina is, in hall III, the splendid two-tone glazed
majolica tondo, from the workshop of the
della Robbia, depicting a *Virgin Mary with*

anonymous Flemish painter, also of the
15th c., is a clear indicator of the cultural activity that was in the air in this city during
the Antonello da Messina period; a painter
of the Neapolitan school, Antonello de Saliba, did the 16th-c. panel of the *Virgin Mary
with Christ Child*.

From the fountain, or Fontana del Nettuno,
rebuilt in the Piazza Unità d'Italia comes the
marble *Scylla* done by Giovanni Angelo
Montorsoli in 1557 (hall IV).

There are two large canvases that Caravaggio painted between 1608 and 1609,
during his brief stay in Messina, of the *Adoration of the Shepherds** (hall X) and the
Resurrection of Lazarus* (hall X), paintings
which were done in his last few years of
work (they fit between the Seven Works of
Mercy, for the Pio Monte di Pietà in Naples
and, slightly later, the Beheading of St. John,

in Malta). The two paintings exerted enormous influence upon the local artistic culture, stimulating works of considerable merit: among these, let us cite the *Supper at Emmaus* (hall X) and the *Disbelief of St. Thomas* (hall X) by the Messinese artist Alonso Rodriguez, in which it is easy to see similarities in composition and style to the work of the master.

In the interior courtyard, note the archeological finds from Greek and Roman times.

Circonvallazione a Monte (A2, B-F1-2) or uphill ring road. Long series of boulevards, which you will need a car to explore, which mark the urban perimeter of the 1960s, and from which it is possible to enjoy lovely views of Messina and the strait. The segment that is known as the Viale Principe Umberto is characterized by the votive church of *Cristo Re* (Christ the King; C2), designed by G.B. Milani in 1937 in a Neo-Baroque style (from the square across from it, the Piazza Montorsoli, there is a fine view of the port and the center of town, with the Duomo and the Via I Settembre in the foreground). Not far away is the sanctuary, or *Santuario di Montalto* (C2; you can reach it by following to the left the Via Dina e Clarenza), whose façade was rebuilt (1930), replacing the original apses. On the Viale Italia, which comes next, there is an intersection with the Via Montepiselli, which leads up to the 16th-c. fortress, the *Forte Gonzaga* (D1, off map), which can only be viewed from outside.

Continue along Viale Europa until you reach Piazza Zaera and then turn to the right in the Via

Catania to visit the monumental cemetery, *Cimitero Monumentale* (1872; F1); inside there a fine works of 19th-c. sculpture and architectur including successful works from the Art-Nouveau period (Liberty) inaugurated in Sicily b Ernesto Basile.

The easternmost point of Sicily. Handsom views of the Sicilian and Calabrian coastlin can be enjoyed by driving along the scen route along the strait, as far as the *lakes Ganzirri*, little brackish ponds, linked t the open sea by feeder channels, and tr ditionally used for the breeding and ha vesting of mussels. And precisely on the e tremity of the point stands the village *Torre Faro* (elev. 3 m.), while *Lido di Morte* (elev. 3 m.), one of the favorite beach r sorts of the Messinese, is already part of th Tyrrhenian littoral strip.

The hills, or Colli San Rizzo. The nearb Monti Peloritani, over which runs the sta road 113 Settentrionale Sicula toward Pale mo, are covered with dense mantles of eve greens. Once you have driven up to th crossroads of the Portella di S. Rizzo, the are three possible routes to follow: turn the right to reach *Castanèa delle Furie* (ele 382 m.), a hamlet that lies on one of th ridges of the range; turn to the left, to clim up to the *Monte Antennamare* (elev. 1,1 m.), from the summit of which you can s both the Tyrrhenian and the Ionian se (during migration season, you can see floc of birds riding the updrafts over the mou tains); or turn down toward the sea, reach Gesso (elev. 285 m.), a village e tending along a hilly crest.

8.2 From the Ionian coast to the Tyrrhenian coast

The route, which runs from Messina to Taormina along the Ionian coast and, after crossing the Monti Peloritani and reaching the Tyrrhenian Sea not far from Tìndari, ends after 155 km. at Milazzo, is a succession of remarkably varied landscapes, both in terms of natural environment and in terms of urban and manmade features.

The eastern slope of the Monti Peloritani gives way only to an exceedingly narrow coastal strip, and here winds the road to Catania, which runs through the 'marinas' of towns that developed high on the slopes during the Middle Ages and then moved down to the coast in the late 18th c.; these settlements still preserve their original layout and part of their historic array of religious and public buildings.

Itàla: the Basilian church of S. Pietro

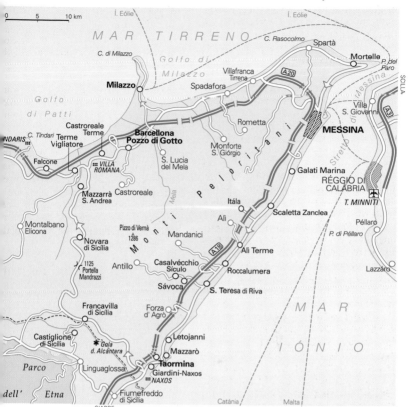

e harsh and almost entirely barren land-ape of the southern slopes of the Monti :loritani is suddenly replaced by another ndscape, on the other side of the moun-in ridge, a landscape in which at first nse conifer forests predominate, favored the northwestern exposure of the slopes, d then farmland.

ong the Tyrrhenian Sea, lastly, there is a rident contrast between the endless suc-ssion of little beach towns, devastated er the past few decades by the creeping ight of illegal construction and second mes, and the hilly hinterland, which pre-rves acceptable conditions of environ-ntal quality.

is route follows, in the stretch between essina and Taormina (53 km.) the state ad 114 Orientale Sicula (two brief de-urs lead to the towns of Itàla and salvecchio Siculo, where the Basilian urches are major documents of the civil d architectural history of the province, or ovincia di Messina). As you shift inland, u will follow the length of the state road 5 di Sella Mandrazzi (69 km), which, after nning through the astonishing canyon, or la dell'Alcàntara, crosses the Monti

Peloritani at an elevation of 1,125 m.; having left Castiglione di Sicilia behind you on the left, you will drop down toward the sea and intersect, near Terme Vigliatore, with the state road 113 Settentrionale Sicula. Between Tindari and Milazzo, the termi-nus of the route, there is a distance of 33 km.; this is also the point of departure for the trip to the Aeolian islands.

Basilian churches

The monasteries founded by the Normans were located in strategic positions (on the banks of mountain streams or on high val-ley platforms) and were built with a wide va-riety of techniques and materials; one ex-ample, among many, can be seen in the church of *S. Pietro* near Itàla, established in 1093 on the site where, according to tradi-tion, the Normans beat the Moors in battle, and the church of the *Ss. Pietro e Paolo**, not far from Casalvecchio Siculo, founded pri-or to the arrival of the Normans and re-stored by them.

The history of the Basilian churches is closely bound up with the effort to con-vert Sicily to Islam; Greek monks, who had escaped the iconoclastic persecution, had emigrated to Sicily in the 8th c., and up until the middle of the 9th c., they had remained under the authority of the Byzantine patriarch, organizing themselves in the territory with sites scattered outside of urban centers, constituting a compact community, apparently no threat whatever to either Catholic or Muslim jurisdictions. The monasteries often provided haven to refugees following the arrival of the Moors, preserving a Christian presence on the island. In the 11th c., Roger (Ruggero I), hearkening back to a clause in the treaty of Melfi, signed in 1059 by his brother Robert Guiscard, succeeded in bringing under Latin jurisdiction the Byzantine dioceses of the reconquered territories. By restoring, founding, and endowing bishoprics, but allowing the abbots of the monasteries of Greek rite to administrate their holdings until death, and then by replacing them with Latin bishops, the Count of Sicily won their loyalty, transforming the monasteries into tools of territorial control, at his service.

Taormina**

This authentic pearl of Sicily is unique in location and in its urban form: two wings of a butterfly extending over the terrace of a crag jutting over the sea, and interwove with exquisite architecture and thread-li streets. From its high and luminous va tage point, protected by the last highland of the Monti Peloritani, Taormina (elev. 2 m., pop. 10,120; plan below) looks nort ward along the coast as far as Messina, a to the south, as far as Mount Etna. Perhap it is its intense luminosity, reflected in th sea and echoed by Mount Etna, that mak its settings and scenery so attractive. A obligatory passage on the route betwee Messina and Siracusa, in the past the ci played an important role in the region economy of eastern Sicily, until the 18th when, with the coastal route linking th two cities, Taormina was left to specialize tourist accommodations, so well suited the remarkable loveliness of the site.

This site, already populated in archaic tim by the early Sicilians and by the inhal tants of "Zancle" (Messina), received ne immigrants from the nearby "Naxos" in 4 B.C., when the tyrant of Syracuse, Dionysi destroyed the town, allowing the survivo to occupy the ledge of the Monte Tau that entered the stage of history, with t name of "Tauromenion." Near the church S. Pancrazio, it is still possible to see rui

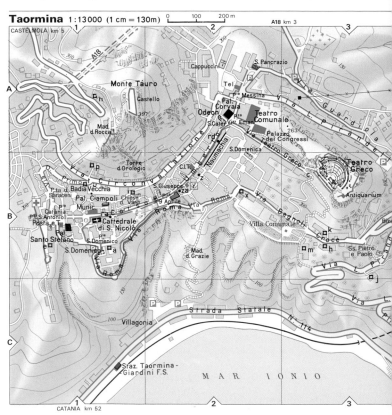

Taormina 1:13000 (1 cm = 130m)

houses that date back to the 3rd c. B.C.: is believed, therefore, that the residential one of the Hellenistic city must have been cated here, since the acropolis stood on the summit of the mount, where the meeval castle now stands; to the south lay the area of the "polis," with the market quare and the agora, surrounded by public and religious buildings (the "bouleurion," the theater, the temples). Monuents that, during the Roman Empire, were renovated and modified, in form and in d use. During the Byzantine era, when Taormina was elevated to the status of episcopal see, it expanded its perimeters, d at the southernmost extremity of the wnship, the first cathedral of S. Maria Assunta was built (now the hospital morgue). he Moors, who ruled here from 962 to 79, enlarged and improved the town's ater supply system, leading to the improved cultivation of the surrounding land d shifting the urban center toward the rlier Byzantine expansion: around the thedral, or Cattedrale, there are resiential quarters (Cuseni), clustering around e gate, or Porta Saracena – a gate that was t into existing walls that were consolited at the time – while in the area of the

Taormina: the Cathedral of S. Nicolò

old Roman Forum, there is a watch tower built to monitor the entrance to the city at the consular road, or Consolare Valeria. Taormina became the great trading and caravan station mentioned by the geographer Idrisi in the 12th c., and consolidates its urban layout with the construction of the village, or "borgo," beyond the Porta di Mezzo, which marked the perimeter of the city's growth in the late Middle Ages. It is from this period that the transfer of the cathedral to its present site dates, while during the centuries that followed there was a great proliferation of palazzi built by the nascent landed aristocracy. Outside of the fortified enclosure, the Franciscan monastery grew up, now a rest home for the aged, and the convent of S. Maria di Valverde; a 10th-c. watchtower, or "torre saracena," which was integrated in the 12th c. with the addition of a separate structure, attained its final version at the end of the 14th c. in the present-day Palazzo Corvaja, home to the new *Museum of Sicilian Popular Figurative Art*, with handcarts, puppets, folklore costumes, pottery, nativity scenes and other specimens of island art.

Between the 16th and 17th c., a new expansion affected the city, this time pushing northward; while in the 18th c., the site of the present-day belvedere was completed with the construction of the church of S. Giuseppe, and foreign travelers blazed the path of tourism to this little city, which had monasteries to recycle as tourist accommodations following the suppression of religious orders in 1866. In the 20th c., the construction of new routes linking up with the ancient Mola (now Castelmola) and the

coast encouraged easy travel to this place by mass tourism, accelerating the growth of the town.

This walking tour runs along the Corso Umberto I, the good 'drawing room' of the city (a short detour leads to the magnificent Greek theater, or Teatro Greco); a stroll along the Via Roma, past the Piazzetta S. Domenico, will allow you to enjoy the many spectacular views that are offered by the coast and Mount Etna; a walk through the dense network of lanes and stairways, here and there interrupted by small squares, winding among the walls of ancient houses and "palazzetti" that are adorned by geraniums and bougainvilles, helps to get into the enchanting atmosphere of this little town.

Corso Umberto I (A-B1-2). This road, whose route follows the ancient consular road, the Consolare Valeria, was the central thoroughfare and, as it were, backbone of the earliest Greco-Roman settlement, filled in where there were empty spaces, or more simply, recycled into the buildings of later periods. It starts out from the gate, or *Porta Messina* (A2), rebuilt in 1808 (immediately outside that gate is the 17th-c. church of *S. Pancrazio*, built on the remains of a temple dedicated to Jove Serapis), and ends at the gate, or *Porta Catania* or *Porta del Tocco* (B1; dating from 1440), the western boundary of the "borgo."

Church of S. Caterina d'Alessandria (A2). Set to the left of the *Palazzo Corvaja*, and comprising three structures (11th/15th c.), with a façade dating back to the 15th-c. renovations, this church was built in the 17th c. atop the ruins of the Roman *Odeon**, which was in turn built during the Empire through the transformation of an existing building (some think that it was a Hellenistic "bouleuterion," others that it was a Doric temple), uncovered during the excavations of 1893. What can still be seen of the earlier structure, behind the church, are the five wedges, with brick steps, constituting the cavea and a stretch of the original stonework on the "frons scaenae".

Teatro Greco** (B3), or Greek theater. This construction, which probably dates back to the Hellenistic era, is built to exploit the natural slope of the hill; the cavea, split up into nine wedges, with 28 steps each, was crowned, at its summit, by two porticoes, one on the interior (there are still some traces of it) and another, larger one, on the exterior; the Romans transformed it from a theater for dramatic performances into an amphitheater for gladiatorial spectacles, replacing the semicircular orchestra with a circular arena, set below the level of the foundation of the steps. The far wall of the scaena, in brick, presents in the center a large gap which allows a view**, as if it were a perfect theatrical backdrop, of the bay of Schisò and Mount Etna.

Naumachiae (A-B2). The Roman not only "modernized" the city, they also endowed it with the service infrastructures needed for its economic development; among those infrastructures was the construction of a system for gathering spring water in large cisterns. The so-called "naumachie" constitute the relics of that effort: this massive wall of masonry, exposed for a distance of 122 m., served to consolidate the embankment uphill for the construction of an enormous cistern, from which ran further hydraulic conduits for the irrigation of farmlands downhill.

Among the buildings that stand atop Roman structures is the church of *S. Maria d Piliere*, now converted into a shop.

Continue along the Corso Umberto I, and you will see on the left the former *church of S. Agostino* (1486), and then on the right, atop a staircase, the *Palazzo Ciampoli* (1412; now a hotel), in a Catalonian Gothic style, with one floor of lovely small twin-light mullioned windows.

Cathedral of S. Nicolò (B1). Built in the 13th c., this church has a façade with two 15th-c. single-light mullioned windows and a 17th-c. portal; the portal on the right side dates from the 16th c., while the portal on the left side, adorned with a floral vine motif, dates from the 15th c. On the interior, which still preserves the Romanesque basilican layout, with evident traces of later renovations, there is a noteworthy *polyptych* panel by Antonello de Saliba (1504) on the second altar.

Palazzo dei Duchi di S. Stefano (B1). This building, dating back to Norman times, features on its façade splendid twin-light mullioned windows with trilobate arches and a crowning frieze with geometric motifs, of clearly Muslim inspiration (the Normans used Moorish craftsmen in construction). The interior is broken up into three stories, the central floor being covered by four cross-vaults with a column in the center; there is a permanent exhibition of the work of the sculptor Giuseppe Mazzullo.

Castelmola* (A1, off map). A scenic route uphill from the city takes you to what

ought to have been the site of the acrop-
is of "Tauromenion," now occupied by
e medieval castle, still in good condition.
he village of Castelmola (elev. 529 m., pop.
123) clearly shows its medieval layout; as
u stroll through the little lanes, you may
ote that the minor adaptations of the build-
gs have done nothing to altar the original
vironmental layout; this is because until
cent decades the city had attracted little
terest from tourism. A number of short
airways lead to the Piazzetta del Duomo;
e church of *S. Giorgio*, whose nave has
en rotated, now overlooks a narrow ter-
ce from which you can enjoy a fine view
the northern slopes of Mount Etna.

axos

n the promontory of the cape, or Capo
hisò, which closes off to the south the bay
the beach resort of *Giardini Naxos* (elev.
m., pop. 8,640), excavations begun in the

Phoenicians had spread about the island
throughout the Mediterranean, with the
goal of preserving their monopoly over the
western markets), even though this colony
did not have a long existence, as it was at-
tacked and razed to the earth in 403 B.C. by
the tyrant of Syracuse Dionysius, who intended to extend his rule over the entire island, and who was hindered in his ambi-
tions by the alliance of Naxos and Athens.
Explorations have shown the existence of
two different phases of growth of the city,
as well as indicating the existence of human
settlements from the Bronze Age on the
promontory. As of this writing, it is possible
to see the walls dating from the 6th c. B.C.,
which enclosed the settlement in its second
configuration, and the urbanistic layout of
the most recent settlement: characterized
by a regular orthogonal grid layout, with a
clear reference to Ippodamo town-plan-
ning, the city had broad roads running

e theater of Taormina with Etna and the bay of Schisò forming a marvellous backdrop

60s have unearthed the ancient Chalcid-
n colony. Tradition has it that the Greeks
ayed far from the Sicilian coasts, because
ey believed them to inhabited by mon-
ers and pirates of unheard-of savagery, un-
the Athenian Theocles was shipwrecked
one of the eastern beaches; he found the
cilian earth to be fertile, and returned
th a contingent of Chalcidians and found-
the first colony. According to the writ-
gs of Thucydides, the construction of
xos began in 735 B.C., the second year of
e eleventh Olympiad, and marked the
art of the Greek colonization of Sicily (the
pression "dicerie fenicie," or "Phoeni-
n rumors" indicates the lies that the

lengthwise (plateas) intersecting with other perpendicular roads, smaller, bounding
the blocks of buildings; the sacred area,
enclosed in a further masonry wall, was located at the southernmost extremity of the
Promontorio di capo Schisò.
As you enter the boundaries of the excavation area, there is a stretch roughly 300 m.
long of the massive western *fortification*,
in very rough-hewn polygonal blocks of
volcanic stone; this wall marks the level of
the city of the 5th c. B.C.; as you walk along
it, you will find the entrance gates and the
enclosure wall of the sacred area in which,
aside from the sacrificial altars, archeologists found the ruins of a *temple*, dating

back to the 6th c. B.C., a temple that measured at each front 14.25x38.40 m. Near the castle, or Castello Paladino, to the north, are the ruins of an archaic settlement, with an *"a pastas" house*, dating back to the 7th c. B.C. Dating back to the earliest settlement (8th c. B.C.), at the intersection between the Platea A and the Transverse 11, is thought to be a house with a square plan and techniques of construction similar to those found in the houses of "Megara Hyblaea," Syracuse, and Eloro.

The furnishings, objects of everyday use, re-

A view of the enchanting Gola dell'Alcàntara

ligious paraments and fragments of architectural decorations found in the area of the excavations are preserved in the two stories of this little museum, installed in a building dating from the 17th/18th c. at the easternmost point of the cape.

Gola dell'Alcàntara*

The river Alcàntara, which received its names from the Moors because there was a stone bridge over that river near Calatabiano ("al cantara" in fact means 'the bridge'), originates on the Monti Nèbrodi and is fed by a spring on the slopes of Mount Etna, just over Randazzo, and by the rivers, or "fiumare," of Castiglione and Francavilla; for much of its length it marks the boundary between the provinces of Messina and Catania, and links the great volcanic cone of Mount Etna with the early limestone formations of the Monti Peloritani. In times prior to the Greek colonization, the eruption of the crater, or Cratere Moio, situated on the northern slope of Mount Etna, formed cape, or Capo Schisò, where Naxos was later founded; in time, the river, which the Greeks called the "Onobala," dug into the basalt flow a deep and lovely canyon. This canyon, or "gola," can be reached on foot or by elevator, and it is possible to walk along the river bed, wearing rubber boots that can be

rented on the site, for a distance of roughly 150 m.

Castiglione di Sicilia

Perched high on a hilltop in the valley of the Alcàntara and accessible from Francavilla di Sicilia with a 5.2-km. detour, this little town (elev. 621 m., pop. 4,551) still preserves the charm of the medieval urban setting, extending around the castle, or *Castel Leone* (hence the name), founded by the Normans and Swabians; the fortification, daringly wedged in amongst the crevices of the rocky ridge at the highest place in the town (from here it is possible to get a good idea of the strategic layout of the settlement, as well as to admire the incredible assortment of shapes and colors of the bell towers of the churches, like so many minarets in a casbah), presents on its façades classic pointed arch mullioned windows in volcanic rock and brick; these windows were taken as models for the religious and civil architecture of the surrounding area.

From Piazza Ruggero di Lauria, after you follow a short uphill lane and cross the Piano S. Antonio (the 18th-c. church of S. Antonio contains fine marble inlays on the interior), you can observe the Neoclassical *church of the Benedettine* and the Norman/Moorish apse (1105) of the Chiesa Matrice di S. Pietro. Embellishing the narrow and charming lanes are balconies and portals made of volcanic stone, which wind and cold have eroded, revealing the porous structure of the material.

Terme Vigliatore

A stop at San Biagio (elev. 24 m.), an outlying section of Terme Vigliatore (pop. 5,941) offers an opportunity to tour a **Roman villa** unearthed in 1953, opened to visitors only recently; it dates back to the 1st c. A.D., which makes it older than the villa of Patti. There survives a part of the *peristyle* with off to the right a small *bath complex* with typical room with floors on hypocaust and surrounded by terracotta tubing for the circulation of steam, and at the center an apsed *tablinum* with a single large exedra, and next to it a slightly smaller room; also in good condition are the black-and white mosaics in a number of rooms and the hexagonal-tile marble floors of the *tablinum*.

ndari*

owadays a destination for religious pil-
ims as well, with its imposing *sanctuary of
e Madonna del Tindari* (1956-79; plan be-
w, A-B2), this town owes its historical im-
ortance to the role it played in the an-
ent history of the island. Founded toward
e end of the 4th c. B.C. with the name of
"yndaris," it was – much like "Taurome-
on," "Mylai," and "Zancle" – a strongpoint
the possessions of the Syracusan tyrant
onysius in eastern Sicily; not unlike "Tau-
menion," it occupied a crag, high over the
a, and protected by the sea, from which
e could easily survey the coast from
pe, or Capo Calavà to the west, to Capo di
lazzo to the east. Like the other Greek
ties that were 'recycled,' it was subjected
considerable renovations by the Romans
its urban layout and in the architectural
onfiguration of its main public buildings; af-
r it partly collapsed into the sea in the 1st
A.D. following a landslide, it was finally
d completely destroyed by the Moors in
e 9th/10th c.

e archeological digs have unearthed the
gular layout of Tindari, with a right-angled
id of decumani and cardines, bounding
e blocks of buildings. Of the fortress *walls*
at surrounded the hilltop occupied by
e city, built in the 3rd c. B.C. and modified
the Romans in correspondence with the
eater in the late-Empire, you can see the
uthernmost stretch, with its towers and
ain gate, beginning from the point where
e road crosses it.

The *basilica** (A1-2), or meeting hall, on
the other hand, is a construction from the
late Roman Empire, with a barrel-vault roof;
it originally extended over three stories,
with two staircases set diametrically opposite each other.

Between the upper decumanus and the
middle one is an "insula*," or block, structured with terraces on at least four levels,
running down toward the sea: on the first
level from the bottom, on the middle decumanus, there are shops and storehouses; on the second level is a little house; on
the third level, there extends a large residential building, probably dating from the
2nd c. B.C. and successively enriched with
mosaic floors (it has an entrance on the
western cardo which led to the peristyle,
onto which in turn opened the rooms and
the tablinum or reception hall); on the
fourth level, the hot baths have floors decorated with mosaics in nearly every room
(in the dressing rooms on either side of the
entrance, *Bull and pilei of the Dioscuri* and
Trinacria; in the frigidarium to the west,
*Struggle between the two athletes Verna and
Afer*, signed by "Agathon slave of Dionysius," and, in another panel, a *Marine Cen-
taur*; in the tepidarium, a tondo with *Dionysius and panther*).

The *Museo* (A1), or museum, features material from excavations and lavish furnishings found in the Hellenistic and Roman
necropolises. A large model reconstructs
the "frons scenae" of the theater.

The *theater** (A1), with an originally Greek

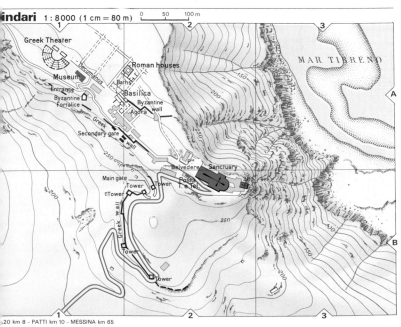

indari 1 : 8000 (1 cm = 80 m)

Greek Theater

Museum

Decumanus

Roman houses

Baths

Entrance

Basilica

Byzantine

Byzantine wall

Fortalice

Agorà

Greek

Secondary gate

wall

MAR TIRRENO

Belvedere Sanctuary

Main gate

Posta

Tower Tower

Te. Tel.

Tower

Greek wall

Tower

Tower

Tindari: Roman ruins

plan dating from the 3rd c. B.C., has a cavea split into 11 wedge segments, with 28 steps; total diameter is 63 m.; the circular arena that now exists is the result of a transformation of the orchestra, done in Roman times.

Milazzo

The port, surrounded to the east by smokestacks and to the west by a wall of modern buildings, offers an image of an entirely new city: the recent, chaotic expansion inland, and the overriding interests of industry, are at the root of this appearance. In reality, although the town has certainly undergone considerable environmental decay, it is still possible to admire the urbanistic history of Milazzo (elev. 1 m., pop. 31,541, plan on facing page), so important to the economy of the entire northeastern area of the island: the 18th-c. city, arranged on the plain and overlooking the waterfront at one extremity; the "borgo," with its 16th- and 17th-c. monuments, arranged around the castle hill, or Collina del Castello, built on the site of the Greek acropolis. Founded by the inhabitants of "Zancle" in 716 B.C. with the name of "Mylai" and conquered by Dionysius in 392 B.C., Milazzo closes off – with the contemporary foundation of the two bridgeheads of Taormina on the Ionian Sea and of Tìndari on the Tyrrhenian Sea – the easternmost territorial triangle of the landholdings of Syracuse. After Hiero II, it became Roman and, in the 7th c., under the Byzantine government, it was made a bishopric.

Between the 9th and 10th c., under the Moors, the city took on new vitality in terms of maritime trade; in 1061, it was returned to the Christian faith by the Normans, and it was fortified at the behest of Frederick (construction of the earliest core of the Castello), while Alphonse of Aragon built the enclosure walls with circular towers, then completed the fortifications in the 15th c. The 16th and 17th c. were a time in which the present-day layout of this section of the city came into being: during the reign of Charles V, Ferramolino, the same architect who designed the system of fortifications of Messina, and Camillo Camilliani were commissioned to oversee the enlargement of the enclosure walls built during the rule of the house of Aragon, an undertaking that was to make Milazzo one of the six most important strongholds in Sicily. The Spanish enclosure walls, originating from the north and south corners of the Aragonese complex, run with two massive arms in both directions to form a giant pincer that encloses the later urban expansion: linking up a little lower down from the eastern front of the castle, or Castello, the line of bastions of the military quarters marks the perimeter of the walled city; on the exterior, in the area of the Spanish quarters, work began on the restructuring of the leading religious and public buildings. In the meanwhile, the development of commercial activities gave renewed importance to the areas surrounding the port; much of the population moved there, originating the distinction between the lower town, or 'città bassa,' as opposed to the upper town, or 'città alta.'

As a confirmation of the new importance of this area in the 18th c., the urban grid was homogenized with the construction of two roads, one running through the center and one running around, the Via Reale (now the Via Umberto I) and the Via alla Marina (now the lungomare Garibaldi). The year 1893 marked the advent of the first urban plan, which, in the wake of the radical restructurings that were so popular at the time, cut with the road now called the Via Cumbo Borgia, the mass of late-medieval buildings, leading to their demolition and replacement.

In your exploration of the historical center you will pay close attention especially to the spectacular Baroque architecture, which emerges between crafts workshops and modest homes; the walking tour begins from the old walled city and then descends through the village, to the more recent lower town, or 'città bassa,' while by car you may drive out along the cape, or Capo di Milazzo.

e walled city. At the highest point, en-
)sed within the Aragon walls with round
wers, from the 15th c., the castle, or
stello di Federico II (1237-40; A2) still
eserves, in its center, the Norman keep
d, inside, the hall, the Sala del Parla-
ento. On the lower esplanade, used in
cent years for the temporary structure of
open-air theater during the summer, is
e façade of the old cathedral, or *Duomo*
2), dedicated to Our Lady of the As-
mption, or Vergine Assunta, and which
nstitutes one of the very few examples of
th-c. Sicilian Baroque; in the vicinity
ere are the ruins of the 15th-c. *Palazzo dei*
urati, the site in the 18th and 19th c. of the
blic council.

e borgo, or village. From the walled town,
taircase lead directly to the *church of the*
idonna del Rosario (A2-3), founded by
e Dominican order in 1538 (this was the

headquarters of the Holy Office and the tri-
bunal of the Inquisition), which still has a
handsome cloister. A monumental double-
ramp stairway runs, a little further along, up
to the 18th-c. façade of the *church of S.*
Francesco di Paola (B2), whose adjoining
convent, now used as a barracks and to
house the art institute, or Istituto d'Arte,
was founded by St. Francis of Paula, in 1464.

The lower city. On the Lungomare Garibaldi is the church of *S. Giacomo Apostolo* (C2),
built in 1432 and over the ensuing centuries
renovated heavily; on the interior is the
main altar of the old cathedral, or Duomo, a
fine piece of 17th-c. marble intarsia. Also
originally founded in the 16th c. were the
church and the *convent of the Carmine* (C2),
whose 17th-c. elevations overlook the Piazza Caio Duilio; in one wing of the convent
was built, at the end of the 19th c., the town
hall, or *Palazzo Municipale* (C2).

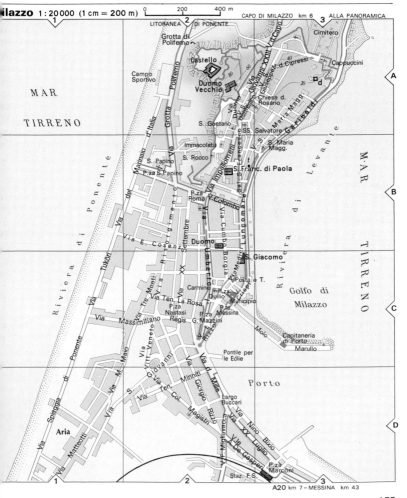

The cape of Milazzo. Two roads, which you should plan on driving, skirt the promontory: the western one, at sea level, leads to the bay of Tono, where there is an old tuna-fishing station ("*tonnara*"), now converted into a residence; the east-

ern one, high over the rocks, leads the end of the peninsula on which th lighthouse stands, amidst bushes prickly pear; a little before it, a stairca: leads down to the cliff sanctuary of *Antonio di Padova*.

8.3 The Aeolian islands

The seven islands are all of volcanic origin, though each one is different from the other six, in terms of the colors that make up the natural and manmade landscape: Vulcano is greenish-yellow, because of the sulphureous incrustations on its summit, and black because of its beaches of volcanic sand; Lìpari is blindingly bright due to the sharp contrast between the shiny black of the obsidian and the white of the pumice; Strómboli is black by day and incandescent red by night due to the continuous eruptions of lava on the "sciara del fuoco"; Salina is a spectacular green, due to its forests high atop the craters that are long

extinct; Filicudi, like Alicudi, is dark gree because of the beautiful caper bush which burst out of the basaltic rocks; P narèa has an amber color, dotted with th bright green of vines and the plaster of th local houses, the "dammusi," buildings wi broad terraces covered with canes, typic in these islands. Set in waters with roc seabeds, waters of a stunning intense da blue, all the islands are wrapped in glitte ing reflections.

The islands, in fact, were not inhabited co tinuously as was the mainland, and the soils, which are largely untouched, off up fragments of civilizations without hi

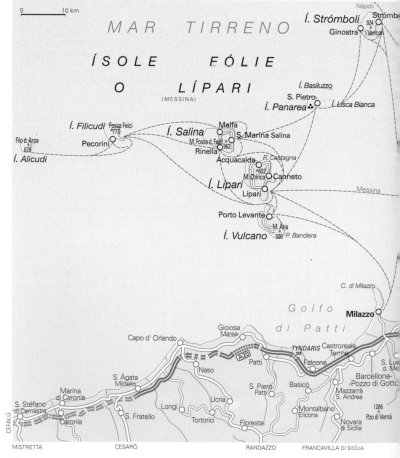

rical overlapping, dating back to the 5th millennium B.C.

Connections with Milazzo are assured by a service of ferry boats and hydrofoils.

Lipari*

This is the largest of the seven islands (37.6 sq. km.; maximum elevation, 602 m.), and the township that includes it and is headquartered here (pop. 10,382) also includes Alicudi, Filicudi, Panarèa, Strómboli, and

demographic increase of the lower city, or "città bassa," and the formation of the villages of Canneto, Acquacalda, Quattropani, and Pianoconte; along the Via Santo Petro (now the Corso Vittorio Emanuele) the urban expansion of the 19th c. was concentrated; and in 1930, lastly, a stairway was built, leading directly to the main portal of the cathedral, or Cattedrale, cutting the 16th-c. enclosure wall.

Much of the Castello has been transformed

Lipari: beyond the ramparts of the boundary wall stands the Cathedral

Vulcano, as well as other smaller islands. Like the others, this island is volcanic in origin; its history is entirely concentrated around the narrow platform of the so-called Castello, a fine natural fortress formed by a riolytic socle, on the flat summit of which, there has accumulated a further earth socle, carried by the wind.

This island was the site of an early settlement in the 4th millennium B.C., and was selected in 580 B.C. by the Greeks of Rhodes and Cnidus for the foundation of one of the last western colonies. "Lipara," so named, after the name of its mythical first king, underwent with Greek rule three phases of expansion, with two resulting shifts of the defensive enclosure walls; beginning in 252 B.C., the acropolis became the first nucleus of the Roman city; it was on the same site that the Normans much later founded the cathedral of S. Bartolomeo (Benedictine order). After a particularly prosperous period, the result of extensive exploration of the sulphur and alum mines, as well as the excavation of pumice, with the exportation of these resources to the larger island of Sicily, Lìpari fell victim, in 1544, to a raid by the pirate Ariadeno Barbarossa (Khair-ed-din Barbarossa, known as Redbeard), who destroyed the town, killing many of its inhabitants. In a few years, the Spaniards rebuilt an effective system of defensive bastions to protect the port of Marina Corta, the "borgo," and the "civita." In the 18th c., the walled city lost population in favor of a

into a museum complex; there are prehistoric, classical, epigraphic, and vulcanological sections, along with a section dedicated to the lesser islands; there is also a small archeological park; the tour of the little town (elev. 44 m., plan on page 178) is obviously a walking tour, and it passes by the Norman cathedral.

Museo Eoliano* (C2). This institution, which uses existing buildings, has one of the finest exhibits in Sicily in terms of scholarship and careful exposition through documents and souvenirs of the development of Aeolian culture.

The 18th-c. ex-*Palazzo Vescovile* (former bishop's palace) now houses the first prehistoric section, dedicated to materials found in excavations done on the acropolis of Lìpari. The second prehistoric section (halls XII-XV) is housed in the little pavilion facing the Palazzo Vescovile (bishop's palace) and features materials found in excavations done on the sites of Panarèa, Filicudi, Alicudi, Salina, and Strómboli. In the pavilion to the north of the cathedral, or Cattedrale, are displayed materials found in excavations done in the necropolises of Milazzo (halls XVI- XVII) and Lìpari (halls XVIII-XXV), along with materials found in underwater archeological campaigns.

The period of settlements prior to the Greeks can be broken down into ten periods, six of which are prior to the Bronze Age. The *Neolithic* covers the first few cen-

Lipari 1 : 8 000 (1 cm = 80 m)

turies of the 4th millennium B.C., the period when people first began to work and export obsidian, a glassy eruptive material that, when reduced to flakes, can be used in manufacturing weapons and cutting or carving tools; these periods are documented by traces of settlements and ceramics decorated in the style of Stentinello, found in Castellaro Vecchio on Lìpari.

Following this, until the middle of the 4th millennium, was the *middle Neolithic*, the time of the first settlement on the site of the Castello di Lìpari, with ceramics decorated in the three colors and characterized by spiral and meanders carved into the surfaces; beginning in the second half of the 4th millennium, it evolved into the refined ceramics of the style of Serra d'Alto (Matera), painted with more complex motifs.

In the 4th period, which includes the end of the 4th and all of the first half of the 3rd millennia, you can find traces of a settlement in

Contrada Diana at Lìpari, which has yielded up shiny red ceramics without designs tubular or spool-shaped.

Following this, after the middle of the 3rd millennium, is the period of the *culture of Piano Conte di Lìpari*, during the course of which the beginning of metallurgy caused crisis in the trade in obsidian, triggering an economic decline.

During the *culture of Piano Quartara di Panarèa* (last centuries of the 3rd and beginning of the 2nd millennia) the archipelago began to form part of the cultural area of Sicily.

The *Bronze Age* is represented, until the 15th c. B.C., by the *culture of Capo Graziano* on Filicudi: the imported ceramics found there testify to ties with the Aegean Sea; we find the earliest settlements with stone huts at first located in areas that are poorly protected (Contrada Diana, Piano del Porto and Contrada Fucile on Filicudi, Punta Peppe aria on Panarèa) and later moved to safer cations (Castello di Lìpari, Serro dei Cian- on Salina, Montagnola di Capo Graziano on lcudi); this marked the beginning of trade alum, useful in tanning hides, and in tin, a omponent in bronze alloys.

etween 1400 and 1270 B.C., Panarèa was e site of the *culture of the Milazzese*: the ce- mics took on forms and decorations sim- r to the contemporary culture of "Thap- s," huts were built on huts from the earlier eriod, and above all there was a first great estruction, which resulted in the depopu- tion of the lesser islands for some time.

the 9th *period*, known as the *Ausonio I* 270-1125 B.C.), the objects of everday e that have been uncovered indicate con- ct with the culture of the late Bronze Age the Italian peninsula, while in the tenth riod (*Ausonio II*; end of the 12th/beginning the 9th c. B.C.) the huts were built with uss roofs and the ceramics were general- thrown on a wheel.

ne final destruction put an end to this lture as well, and the islands were left actically uninhabited until the arrival of e Greeks. The earliest tombs, linked to the *eek period*, were used strictly for burials conjunction with cremation, and date ck to the 8th c. B.C.; they feature cineraria d vases of Aegean importation; by the 6th d 5th c. B.C., simple burial prevailed – at st in stone or brick sarcophagi, and later sarcophagi made of terracotta – marked ove ground by markers of every sort. Of nsiderable value are the tomb furnish- gs, which include finds from the 6th c. B.C. te-Corinthian ceramics and Attic black-fig- e ceramics, but also black and striped ce- mics of local production) running up rough the 5th c. (the subjects consist

largely of depictions of the cult of Dionysius, the god of drunkenness and the theater, who offered happiness in the afterlife to his devotees), and the 4th c. (four kraters are considered to be youthful works of the artist Asteas, of Paestum), during the course of which there was a considerable produc- tion of tragic, satirical, and comic masks, linked to the works of Sophocles, Euripides, and Aristophanes: the examples found on Lìpari – circa 400 – document all the char- acters of their plays. Dating from the 3rd c. B.C. are masks worn in the New Comedy, as well as the innovative work of the Painter of Lìpari, by whom there are some 100 sur- viving vases.

During the *Roman period*, the tombs with large and curved tiles became the only method of burial until 252-251 B.C., while be- tween the 1st c. B.C. and the 1st c. A.D. there is documentation of rough masonry tombs with recycled materials, a trend that in imperial times went so far as to include the re-use of Greek sarcophagi.

The **section of marine archeology** con- tains the relics of about 15 wrecks, found in the seabeds of the Eolie in points that are particularly treacherous to navigation: from the bay of Lìpari comes a prehistoric ship; almost 70 vases belong to the cargo of a ship that dates back to roughly 2000 B.C.

The **vulcanological section** illustrates the formation and geological history of the Ae- olian archipelago, as well as the changes that have been introduced by man.

Cattedrale (C2), or cathedral. Dedicated to St. Bartholomew (S. Bartolomeo) and founded by the Normans, this church was destroyed in 1544 by the pirate Barbarossa; the subsequent reconstruction (1654) re-

ypical homes along the coast of the Aeolian islands

sulted in the present-day Baroque style (the façade dates from 1761).

Parco Archeologico (C2), or archeological park. Various digs, since covered up, have been done on the summit of the Castello, in a vast area, divided by the modern road. The area that has been thoroughly investigated has yielded – from a depth ranging around 4 m. – structures that date from the Bronze Age to Roman times; the lower layers – as much as 9 m. deep – date back to the Neolithic and the earliest metal ages, and have

Fumaroles on the island of Vulcano

yielded abundant materials; special signs, with color-coded indications of the various chronological phases, assist in an understanding of the individual structures.

Salina
This island was called "Dydime" by the Greeks, meaning 'double,' due to the fact that it was composed of two volcanic cones (Monte Fossa delle Felci, elev. 962 m.; Monte dei Porri, elev. 860 m.), separated by a saddle; it takes its present name from the salina, or salt works, of Lingua. It is the second largest in terms of surface area (26.8 square kilometers; pop. 2,581, broken up into three townships) and the most lush of all the Aeolian islands; this latter feature, along with the pleasant environment, still relatively unspoilt thanks to the efforts of a number of groups of dedicated ecologists, make this island one of the favorite resting places of migratory birds.

Vulcano
This island (21 sq. km; 0/500 m.) has fallen

victim in the 20th c. to a tourist frenz which has so damaged the environme that it has hard to imagine how it can r cover; all the same, it still preserves tl charm of its untamed nature, which c be enjoyed by taking a hike to the craters by sailing around the island in a boat.

Panarèa
This is the smallest island (3.4 sq. km.; ele 0/421 m.); it is also the earliest in terms geological formation, although there a still secondary volcanic phenomena, c the beach of the Calcara; with the isle that surround it (Basiluzzo, Spinazzola, L ca Bianca, Dattilo, Bottaro, Lisca Nera, tl Panarelli, and the Formiche), and whic like Panarèa are the tips of a single su merged magmatic basin, it forms a litt archipelago in the sea between Lìpari ar Strómboli, perfect for exploration by boa For the past few decades, the three villag of San Pietro, Ditella, and Drauto have bee invaded, along with the surrounding ter tory, by intensive development for holid; homes and second homes.

Strómboli
Set at the northeastern extremity of tl archipelago, this island has the only pe manently active volcano in thc entire arc ipelago; the island (12.6 sq. km.) is visite especially by tourists interested in the spe tacular eruptive phenomena, which can l admired both from the sea and from tl summit of the highest cone (elev. 924 m if you go up to the cone, we strongly re ommend that you hire an authorized guic (for information, tel. 090-986315). The islar also offers an interesting *Volcanologic Centre* with plenty of information on tl volcano in the form of maps, guides, videc and a permanent direct link with the crate

Filicudi and Alicudi
These are the westernmost islands in tl archipelago: the first, with a maximum el vation of elev. 774 m., has a total area of 9 sq. km.; the second, which rises to an el vation of 675 m., has a total surface area 5.2 sq. km. These are also the islands tha are least popular with mass tourism, bot because of their out-of-the-way locatic and because they are not equipped with a equal level of accommodations. The i lands, however, are ideal for those wh want to spend their holidays far from tl crowds of tourists, even though they are n furnished with what we are accustomed calling modern comforts.

The Tyrrhenian Coast of Sicily

e extensive territory bounded to the west by the river Imera and to the east by the riv-
Simeto has been known historically by the name of Val Demone. The name, despite what
e might well think, means divine valley: valley in the sense of an expanse of land, and
ine in the classical sense, i.e., so beautiful as to be a worthy abode of the gods.
e may consider the area to be divided up into three broad territorial strips, differing in
vironmental qualities that are however nicely complementary. The coastal strip may fair-
be represented as a long beach periodically punctuated by the mouths of mountain
eams and tall rocky promontories. The area beyond the coast appears as a continuous
lt of steep and forbidding mountains, rich in spring water and covered with dense forests,
e home of the "nebros," meaning 'fawn, young of the deer' in Greek. Indeed, it is from this
at the Nèbrodi take their name. The territory inland is a vast upland, which connects –
an elevation of roughly 800/900 meters – directly into the southern slope of the massif
the Madonìe and the range of the Nèbrodi, characterized hills and soft rolling lands that
e ideal for raising grains and sheep farming. The coastal towns – though historically they
share the crucial phase of refoundation, and while their hinterlands all share the his-
ry of Norman feudalism – still present a wide variety of urban layouts.
e differences between towns become far less marked on the upland. This territory, in
ct, was the feudal holding of the family of the Ventimiglia who, from Càccamo to Naso,
sseminated towers throughout the towns, rendering possible their development, and in
me cases, actually presiding at their foundation, and reconsolidating the course of the
cient and vital network of communications linking the eastern coast of Sicily and the cap-
l. The natural heritage of the Monti Nèbrodi and the Madonìe, happily, remains virtually
tact. Largely overlooked, these are areas of dense forests and silent clearings that offer
spectacular contradiction of the stereotype of Sicily as a land of sun and sea. Both the
ountain range of the Nèbrodi and the massif of the Madonìe reach nearly to elevations
2,000 m., and resemble each other in terms of flora and fauna; as low as 1,000 m. of el-
ation, they are covered with oak forests, and above an elevation of 1,400 m. there is a
nse mantle of beech trees, the southernmost in Europe. The fauna is the same as that
the Apennines: foxes, weasels, and wildcats. Among the birds that nest on the rocky ridges
e Bonelli's eagle, the golden eagle, the peregrine falcon, the kite, and the sparrowhawk.

.1 Cefalù*

n state road 113, from Tusa toward Paler-
o or from Tèrmini toward Messina, the
unning beauty of a giant rock in the shape
a head, standing out against a blue-green

sea, unmistakably marks the site. Protected
by the northern winds, Cefalù (elev. 16 m.,
pop. 13,882, plan page 183) is cut into the
western part of the promontory. Corso Rug-

suggestive view of the beach in Cefalù

181

gero, the chief thoroughfare, divides the town into two sections: one with twisting stepped lanes, ending at the rock wall, another with straight roads running down to the beach, or rather down to the unbroken curtain of small buildings that constitutes the seafront of the walled town. This town was founded in the 5th c. B.C., in a site that was certainly inhabited in prehistoric times, as is indicated by the traces found in the grottoes on the eastern slope of the crag, or Rupe Kefaloidon, or "Kephaloidon," as the Greeks called it. The remains of megalithic walls, on the shore near the Porta Giudecca and at the foot of the crag, as well as the so-called Tempio di Diana (Temple of Diana) on the summit, transmit the fragmentary image of the settlement's origins. Historians tell us of the important political role that this town played in the Roman Mediterranean between the 3rd c. B.C. and the 2nd c. A.D., of the role that it played in the Byzantine west up to the 9th c., and the even more important role that it played as a stronghold of Islam in Sicily; still, there are no substantial traces of this history in the urban structure. The Normans took it from the Moors in 1064, and destroyed all vestiges of the eastern style – just as they did in Palermo – rebuilding it completely. With Frederick II of Swabia, nephew of Roger II of Altavilla (Hauteville) and of Frederick I of Hohenstaufen, known as the Barbarossa, the privileges that had been handed down by his predecessors were confirmed, but there began a process of division between the Byzantines and the kingdom of Sicily. In the 13th and 14th c., Cefalù was governed by the Ventimiglia, who had their city residence built here, the so-called Osterio Magno.

Between the 16th and 17th c., the design of the city center was completed: the monasteries, or Convento dei Domenicani, Convento degli Osservanti, and Convento dei Carmelitani either filled in vacant spaces or were built over existing structures; t[...] perimeter of the Piazza del Duomo was [...] tablished by the façades of the Palazzo [...] raino and the Palazzo Martino-Atanas[...] the old enclosure walls with the entry gat[...] to the city were reinforced and the ba[...] tion, or Bastione di Capo Marchiafava w[...] built. In the 18th c., while the local nobili[...] built its own "palazzetti" (Agnello, Bo[...] donaro, Mandralisca), the bishop's pala[...] ("palazzo vescovile") was rebuilt in its pr[...] sent-day form. With the end of the feud[...] regime, in the 19th c., a profound econo[...] ic crisis began for Cefalù, as for the rest [...] southern Italy. The urbanistic consequn[...] was the abandonment, by declining familie[...] of the buildings that they inhabited or p[...] tronized. Cefalù fell victim to the buildi[...] speculation of the last two decades of th[...] 20th c., and now appears with an ugly e[...] tension of buildings reaching out into th[...] plain to the west of the old center.

It is inevitable to begin a tour of Cefalù pr[...] cisely from the Piazza del Duomo.

Cattedrale** (A2), or cathedral. Built [...] the behest of Roger II, according to legen[...] as fulfillment of a vow made when he su[...] vived a tempest and landed at Céfalù, co[...] struction of this basilica began in 1131. Th[...] two towers give the church at once a fasc[...] nating and worrisome appearance. An o[...] tical illusion makes them seem to converg[...] on high, one toward the other, in som[...] sense undercutting the square-hewn an[...] compact shape of the main façade. Th[...] façade was embellished in 1472 with th[...] portico that protects the splendid entranc[...] portal, as at Monreale. If you examine th[...] exterior of the monument from the rigt[...] side (the only side that is unencumbere[...] you will note the battlements (dates u[...] known) and the side apses, which prese[...] decorative motifs featuring entwined arc[...] es, common in the Sicilian architecture [...] the period, while the central apse has Got[...] ic-style pilaster strips with basket arches[...] The **interior** is large and solemn; it ha[...] three aisles, divided by tall columns with fi[...] ured capitals supporting pointed, doubl[...] lintel arches; in the right aisle, note a R[...] manesque baptismal font. From the end o[...] the central apse look down the great dar[...] eyes of Christ Pantokrator, the All-Powerfu[...] gazing at an indefinite point in the unre[...] mosaic universe. "Glittering old Byzantin[...] gold," to cite an expression of Vincenz[...] Consolo: from behind his head, the brillar[...] mosaics** capture the light of the Sicilia[...] sun. And this figure that portrays the Deit[...] even has Sicilian features: blonde hair lik[...]

Cefalù: the Cathedral

e Normans, but dark thick beard and eye-
rows, like the Moors; a straight nose and
in lips, like the Greeks. These mosaics in
e apse can be dated back to the 12th c.,
d they have never been altered over their
ght centuries of existence. The arches
d the walls of the three aisles which,
ith the transept, compose the Latin cross
f the church's plan, have been modified
ore than once, on the other hand. What
e see in the present day is the result of a
ng series of restorations that have not
et been completed. Adjoining the Duomo
a *cloister*, likewise built in the 12th c.; it
as partly destroyed by a fire in the 16th c.
verlooking the Piazza del Duomo are a
umber of small palazzi from the Baroque
ra, such as the *Seminario* (seminary) and
e *Palazzo Vescovile* (bishop's palace),
e *Palazzo Maria*, probably a royal resi-
ence, and the *Palazzo Piraino* at the south-
rn corner of Corso Ruggero II.

Corso Ruggero (A-B2). Along the "corso,"
the original architecture alternates with reconstructions: one thing that should be noted is the curious common denominator of
the brackets supporting the balconies, all in
iron or cast-iron, whether they are applied
to medieval or contemporary buildings. The
Via Caracciolo, one of the stairways/lanes
leading up to the rocky wall, takes one to the
church of the SS. Trinità, with the adjoining
convent of the Dominicans (1521). At the
corner of the Via Amendola, one of the perpendicular roads running down toward the
sea, you will find the remains of the 14th-c.
Osterio Magno, heavily renovated over the
centuries. The "corso" ends at the Piazza
Garibaldi, which links the historic center
with the new settlement, on the site of the
old land gate, or Porta di Terra, through
which people entered the city when arriving
along the old consular road, or Via Consolare Pompea, and from the interior.

Museo Mandralisca (A1). This museum is now a public institution, but it was born of the love for art and science of Enrico Piraino (not at all the same Piraino as in the Palazzo Piraino), Barone di Mandralisca, who lived in his old age in Cefalù, in the years before and after the unification of Italy. A man of varied interests, Mandralisca collected – for his own intellectual pleasure – ancient marble works, coins, paintings, as well as the seashells which formed the chief focus of his studies – malacological studies, to use the scientific term. Among the works of art collected in this building, once the home of Mandralisca himself, the most famous is certainly the **Ritratto d'Ignoto**** (portrait of an unknown man) by Antonello da Messina. The little "pezzo di legno," or 'piece of wood,' with the oil painting dated 1465 was the central character in a wonderful novel by Vincenzo Consolo. An interesting item, among the Greek ceramics, is a renowned *krater with a depiction of a man selling tuna*, and the minter.

Bastione di Marchiafava (A2). If you leave the Piazza del Duomo behind you on your right, the Corso Ruggero will lead down to the Via Carlo Ortolano di Bordonaro, named after a 17th-c. aristocrat of Cefalù. The roa[d] lined with low buildings, follows the coa[st] line. If you climb down the stairway linki[ng] the *church of S. Giovanni* and the *church* [of] *Itria*, at Piazzetta Crispi you will reach t[he] platform of the Bastione di Marchiafa[va;] from here, you have fine views of the coa[st] and you can observe a number of ruins of *[ar]chaic fortifications* in megalithic structur[e]. On the Via Vittorio Emanuele you s[ee] the Norman *church of S. Giorgio* and t[he] medieval *washhouse*, a structure with [a] strong Moorish influence.

Rocca (B2-3), or mountain. As tiring as [it] may be, especially in the month of Augu[st,] a climb up to the Rocca di Cefalù is a mu[st.] Like a relief extracted from the rock throu[gh] cutting and drilling, Cefalù reveals its urb[an] layout from up here: the red of the roofs a[nd] the yellow of the rock of the Duomo, [the] cathedral, with the deep blue of the roc[k and] sea make memorable contrasts. At the ed[ge] of the brink there are are ruins, heavi[ly] renovated, of a fortification that probab[ly] dates from Byzantine times; further back [is] the **temple of Diana** (B2), a massive co[n]struction in megalithic stone blocks, dati[ng] from the archaic Greek period.

9.2 The Madonìe: from Cefalù to Nicosìa

The Tyrrhenian coast, which can be observed from state road 113, is spectacular; in some sections it is rocky, with a series of stunning views westward from Capo Zafferano and Capo Gallo, two capes that mark the extremities of the Gulf of Palermo. After Campofelice di Roccella and the detour to Collesano, in the area of Buonfornello, roughly 18 km. of distance from Cefalù, yo[u] will see on the right the sign for the Temp[le] della Vittoria (temple of victory; 5th c. B.C[.),] the monumental ruins of ancient Himer[a.] Just a few meters further along on the left, [if] you look very carefully, you will see a sig[n]

inting to the excavations ("scavi") and the
tiquarium. The smokestacks of Tèrmini
erese appear directly after Buonfornello.
nning close around the massif of the
adonìe, green with forests, the road winds
er the bare hills of the highland and reach-
the Madonìe towns of Polizzi, Petralìa, and
ngi, still immersed in an agrarian and
storal world of times gone by. Before you
me to Nicosìa, you can admire the vertical
rust of Sperlinga high on its point of rock
the middle of the upland. At Nicosìa you
ll leave the state road 120 and you will turn
to the 117, skirting the eastern slope of
e Monte Sambughetti (elev. 1,558 m.) and
ving to the east the wooded slopes of
e Nèbrodi. At roughly 30 km. from Nicosìa
u will see Mistretta, on the bluff that looks
wn on the riverbed. You will return to the
3 at Santo Stefano di Camastra, heading to-
rd Cefalù; one can hardly help but notice,
the beach of Villa Margi, the enormous
ulpture in the form of a blue window that
arks the area of the Fiumara d'Arte: this is
'land art" circuit that links the towns of
sa, Pettineo, Motta d'Affermo, and Castel
Lucio. Not far from Tusa lie the ruins of an-
ent Halaesa (with a detour through Castel-
ono; from Nicosìa, if you prefer, you can
ntinue along the 120, take the provincial,
local road, to Capizzi and, passing
rough the handsome forest of Caronìa,
ach the sea). In all, 236 km.

imera

is town was founded in 648 B.C. by the
eeks from Zancle, on a plain midway up
e hillside, to the left of the northern
anch of the river Imera. The site of com-
t between Greeks and Carthaginians, it
as definitively destroyed by the latter in
9 B.C. The coins minted here bore a roost-
, which may hint at the root of the name,
"hemera," meaning 'day.' The *antiquarium*
mporarily closed) is contained in a rela-
vely new building. The excavations to
te have unearthed a few remains of the
ty, among them being a *sacred precinct*
th three small archaic sanctuaries, which
ve yielded important material; the most
teworthy surviving relic is the base of a
ric temple.

rmini Imerese

t on a hill on the coastline between Capo
fferano and Cefalù, Tèrmini Imerese (elev.
' m., pop. 26,571; plan on page 186) has
own in economic importance in Sicily
ce WWII, due to the establishment of a
nsiderable industrial complex, including
e Chimica del Mediterraneo, the power

plant that once belonged to TIFEO, and the
Sicilfiat. Now, like much of Southern Italy, it
is plagued with the shutdown fever. Atop
the hill, the ancient Tèrmini still stands,
protected perhaps by the steep roads leading up to it. Occupied in prehistoric times,
it later fell under the influence of Himera; after the destruction of Himera, it took in the
refugees from the town. Conquered in 252
B.C. by the Romans, who renamed it Ther-
mae Himerensis, the town became a thermal
spa for the treatment of urological disturbances. Traces of the old baths remain on
the interior of the former Stabilimento Vecchio and the Grande Albergo delle Terme.
All that remains of the other Roman public
works are a few ruined aqueducts along
the road to Càccamo and the memory of the
shape of the amphitheater in the direction
of the block of buildings overlooking the Via
Anfiteatro, in the town center, near Villa
Palmeri. Fortified twice, in the Middle Ages
and in the 16th c., Tèrmini has been inhabited by religious orders since the 17th c.,
and until the 19th c. it remained enclosed
within its 16th-c. walls.

In the present-day urban layout, you can
make out the tracks of the old city walls,
which have become ring roads, and the locations of the gates, or the Porta Messina
and the Porta Palermo. From these gates the
main thoroughfares ran toward the center
of town: from Porta Messina the Corso Umberto and the stepped Via Roma; from Porta Palermo the Via Garibaldi. The civic and
religious center is the *Piazza Vittorio
Emanuele*, which is overlooked by the 15th-
c. cathedral, or *Duomo*, rebuilt in the 17th c.,
and the city hall, or *Palazzo municipale*
(1610). Nearby, at the mouth of the Via Roma, you can tour the *Museo Civico*. This
civic museum was established in 1873, and
is housed in the halls of the former hospital,
or Ospedale Fatebenefratelli; it contains
three different sections: archeological, with
materials dating back to prehistoric times,
and as recent as the Late Roman Empire; art
history, with fine artworks from the Moor-
ish/Norman period to as late as the 19th c.;
and natural history, still in progress.

The visit ends with a stroll to the *Belvedere
Principe Umberto* (magnificent view of the
city and the coast) and the *Villa Palmieri*,
passing through the Piazza S. Caterina,
where the 15th-c. *church of S. Caterina
d'Alessandria* stands.

Càccamo (elev. 521 m., pop. 8,636) was a
Carthaginian stronghold in the 5th c. B.C. and
caused considerable problems for nearby
Himera, as well as for other Greek colonies in the
area. Documentary sources seem to date the of-

Termini Imerese 1:12000 (1 cm = 120 m)

MAR TIRRENO

Porto

ficial foundation of the little town to 1093; the town appears to remain solidly attached to its past, and a tour is quite interesting. You should certainly see the *Duomo*, or cathedral, founded long ago by the Normans but rebuilt in 1614; the medieval **church of the SS. Annunziata**, which was also entirely rebuilt in the 17th c.; it houses a lovely *altarpiece of the Annunciation*, by Guglielmo Borremans (1725); the *church of S. Benedetto* dates from 1615, with its splendid pavement in decorated Sicilian majolica. But the monument of which the people of Càccamo are proudest, and rightly so, is their medieval castle, the **Castello***, built into the rocky face that juts over the valley (partially being restored).

Collesano

Particularly well preserved is the ancient center of Collesano (elev. 468 m., pop. 4,589), which still maintains the medieval layout from its earliest development around the Norman castle, with narrow lanes linked by alleys and stairways, all converging upon the Piazza Garibaldi. In this area are the r ins of the castle and the earliest churches: *Giacomo*, 1451; *S. Sebastiano*, 1371; and *Maria la Vecchia*, founded in the 12th c. an rebuilt in the 15th c., with a marble statue the interior by Antonello Gagini (1516). C the Corso Vittorio Emanuele, which begin from the Piazza Garibaldi, note the *Chie Madre di S. Maria la Nuova*, built at the en of the 15th c., the period of the Catalonia Gothic portal on the right side (the façac dates from the 20th c.): the interior aboun in artworks, including, in the presbyter 17th-c. *frescoes and wooden choir*.

Polizzi Generosa

Polizzi Generosa (elev. 920 m., pop. 4,74 has the yellow color of the land in June, an it blends in perfectly with the surroundi landscape, a well cultivated territory. twisting lanes, its lack of space, and the ti

lares all contrast with the immense scope
the view of the valley that separates it from
e massif of the Madonie. The *Chiesa Madre*,
dicated to Our Lady of the Assumption
ssunta), possesses, among many fine art
rks, a handsome *triptych** of the 16th-c.
mish school. On the 1st Sunday of Sep-
nber, the famous Festa dello Sfoglio, a
ical cake with cheese and cinnamon.

Petralìe

along an ancient roadway that runs
st/west across Sicily, Petralìa Soprana
ev. 1,147 m., pop. 3,903) and Petralìa Sot-
ia (elev. 1.000 m., pop. 3,770) date back to
earliest times. Ancient Petra, now So-
ina, is mentioned as early as the 3rd c.
C., but it took on an important adminis-
tive and strategic role with the arrival of
e Moors. The Normans, beginning in the
th c., fortified it and endowed it with reli-
us foundations. The halt of urban devel-
ment, due to emigration, around the 17th
makes it possible to enjoy the urban struc-
e of these two small towns virtually intact.
tralìa Sottana, today a town in its own
ht, originally developed as a small de-
ndency of the Norman castle complex
p the hill. The distinction between the two
tlements appears in documents with the
ms "inferior" and "superior" only in the
h c. That both of the settlements were
ed by aristocratic families and were the
urce of much wealth can be seen in the
gnificence of the private and public build-
s as well as religious buildings, and in
e ostentatious richness of the decorations.
is is true of the *Chiesa Madre* of **Petralìa
prana**, founded long ago, rebuilt by the
ntimiglia family in the 14th c. and subse-
ently enlarged and adorned with stucco
rk, gold, and art work of all kinds, includ-
a wooden *Crucifix* by Frate Umile da Pe-
lìa and a statue of the *Madonna della Cate-*
from the 15th c. Also worthy of note is the
urch of *S. Maria di Loreto*, on the site of the
l Norman fortress, with the polychrome
racotta cusps of the bell towers on ei-
er side of the façade. In **Petralìa Sottana**,
the other hand, we would recomment
e interesting 17th-c. *Chiesa Madre*, which
ludes an earlier building (there remains a
e-Gothic portal on the right side), and the
urch of the *SS. Trinità*, which preserves a
rble altarpiece with bas-reliefs by Gian-
menico Gagini depicting the life of Jesus.

ngi

ery year, on the 2nd Sunday of August,
ere is the celebration year of the Sagra
la Spiga, a sort of propitiatory rite of the
goddess of crops, Ceres. Even though nowadays the festival has more of the feeling of a
tourist attraction than of an authentic folk
tradition, it still reveals the rural character of
the town. Gangi (elev. 1,011 m., pop. 8,176)
preserves unchanged its original medieval
layout. The buildings cover the sides of the
hill like a blanket, and they form around the
Castello dei Ventimiglia, the first core of the
settlement, a compact and minutely articulated urban fabric, crossed by the chief thoroughfare of the Corso Umberto and the Via
G. Fedele Vitale, crisscrossed by the steep
and twisting lanes running downhill. Ancient, like the castle, the massive tower, or
Torre dei Ventimiglia was the first residence
of the lords of the place, and was later adapted for use as a bell tower for the *Chiesa
Madre*. The Chiesa Madre, or cathedral, was
built in the 18th c. by enlarging a 14th-c. oratory; inside, among other fine art works, is
a handsome Gagini statue of the *Virgin Mary
with Christ Child*; in contrast, you may note,
in the presbytery, a canvas depicting the
Last Judgement, clearly emulating the fresco
by Michelangelo in the Sistine Chapel. Further down, on the steps of the Via Matrice,
the *church of the SS. Salvatore* (1612) contains
another of the numerous wooden *Crucifixes*
by Fra' Umile da Petralìa. And if you descend
still further, you will find the *church of S.
Maria degli Angeli*, with, adjoining it, the
Convento dei Cappuccini, in the rooms of
which is a *museum* with paintings from the
16th and 17th c., and fine decorated 17th-c.
terracottas.

Sperlinga

Set on a spur of mossy rock, the battlements
and stepped volumes of the *Castello** di
Sperlinga (elev. 750 m., pop. 1,065) seem to
provide a perfect setting for a period piece
set in the Middle Ages. This too was a castle
of Roger's: reinforced by Frederick II in the
12th c., it returned to the Ventimiglia family
until the 16th c., when it became the residence of Giovanni Forti Natoli, founder of the
town. A sort of cliffside fortress cut into the
rock, it comprises a large, unknown number
of chambers (many of them now open to
the sky), passageways, courtyards, and corridors distributed over a great many levels,
in a mazelike complex of great allure. This
was the center of the last, desperate French
resistance during the War of the Sicilian Vespers, as the motto reminds us: "What Sicily
accepted, only Sperlinga rejected."

Nicosìa

Nicosìa (elev. 724 m., pop. 15,029) is the central hinge of the system of fortified cities

Nicosìa: the Cathedral

along the mountain route running from Messina to Palermo. Set on the site of an existing Byzantine settlement dating from the 7th/8th c. was built, in the 9th c., the Islamic city, destroyed by the Normans. The Normans, with an enormous influx of Franco-Germanic ethnic groups, formed a colony that clustered around the first Norman church of S. Maria. In the 14th c. there was already a considerable class of bourgeois large landowners who, until the 18th c., built their own sumptuous homes along the still medieval lanes of the town. Between the 16th and 17th c., the monastic congregations determined, with the buildings they erected, the present-day layout of the historic city. The **Cattedrale**, or cathedral, a 19th-c. reconstruction of a small 14th-c. church of which only the main portal and the campanile survive, preserves a *pulpit*, an *altar frontal*, and a marble Gagini *baptismal font* dating from the 16th c.; in the presbytery it is possible to admire handsome carved wooden stalls dating from the 17th c. and an exquisite *altar frontal* made of repoussé and gilt silver. Among the 18th-c. stuccoes of the *church of S. Biagio*, one should note the interesting and unusual composition of the marble *triptych* by Antonello Gagini (1510) with a Christ surrounded by a host of little angels and free-standing statues of the Virgin Mary and St. John the Baptist. A handsome carved *portal*, carved with non-religious naturalistic and mythological depictions adorns the main entrance of the **Basilica di S. Maria Maggiore**, built near the end of the 18th c. to re-

place the old church of the same nar swallowed up by a landslide in 1757. L the portal, the works contained inside church come from religious and civil bu ings destroyed by the landslide: amo them is the majestic marble *polyptych* in presbytery and the *Virgin Mary with Ch Child* on the altar in the left transept, bc by Antonello Gagini; note the exceedin rare 15th-c. *altar frontal* made of paint wood in lively colors, done for a clea popular audience; lastly, one should nc in the right transept, the wooden 16th throne with an effigy of the Emperor Char V, who stayed in Nicosia in 1535.

Mistretta

Mistretta (elev. 900, pop. 6,195) was alwa a stronghold for the control of the s rounding territory, right up to the end Spanish rule. The town's churches, nea all of which were rebuilt during the 17th preserve traces of the styles of the earl versions. The *Chiesa Madre* dating fr 1630, for instance, has a marble *altar pic* by Antonello Gagini, and presents in t transept a 14th-c. pointed-arch portal a on the right side another portal dating fr 1494. The *Museo Civico* contains canvas from the churches of the town and lo archeological finds.

Santo Stefano di Camastra

The state road 113 to Santo Stefano di C mastra (elev. 70 m., pop. 5,194) is tra formed into an exhibition space of color ceramics. The birth and development of tl crafts activity are linked to the presence numerous quarries for excellent clay, and present survival is perhaps the result of t uncompleted highway from Messina Palermo. The city, which until 1812 w known as Santo Stefano di Mistretta, w centered in the hills, not far from the town the same name (Mistretta). Destroyed by landslide in 1682, it was rebuilt beginning 1693, in its present site: on a rocky platfoi high over the sea. It is interesting to obser the layout of the town which, on a mu smaller scale, is reminiscent of the layout the gardens of Versailles: a ray of stree with a central square, set over a diver comb-like gridwork, with an east-west ax Behind the state road, on the other hand, a the urban developments of the 19th a 20th c., with roads running parallel. Locat in the 18th-c. section of the city is the *Chie Madre* (with a Renaissance portal and, on t inside, a marble Gagini statue), and the c ramics museum, or *Museo della Ceramic* featuring local crafts products.

amara d'Arte is a territorial art museum built
the exposed gravelly river bed and along the
nks of the Tusa, with works by major con-
mporary artists.

ugurated in 1986 with an installation by Pietro
nsagra in the bed of the river Tusa, this project
d not fail to kindle debates and even furious dis-
tes. Next came a project by Tano Festa on the
ach of Villa Margi, not far from Santo Stefano
Camastra; one by Antonio Di Palma on the
ht bank of the river, on a little hill near Motta
Affermo; another by Hidetoschi Nagasawa in a
unmade cave on the road from Motta to Mis-
tta; one by Paolo Schiavocampo on the road to
stel di Lucio and another by Pietro Dorazio and
aziano Marini in town, in the barracks of the
rabinieri; and lastly a project by Italo Lanfredini
a valley at the foot of Castel di Lucio.

Halaesa

This was an ancient Greek colony, founded
in 403 B.C.: transformed and enriched in Roman and Byzantine times, it was destroyed
by the Moors in the 9th c. Dating back to the
fourth or third c. B.C. are the walls and towers, whose ruins can be seen just before the
turnoff that leads to the excavations, while
the columbarium made of "opus reticula-
tum" dates back to Roman times. In the
archeological area, note the interesting ruins
of the acropolis and the agora, with massive
retaining walls in rustication dating from
Hellenistic times, and the regular urban layout from the Byzantine period, linked to the
final building phase of the city.

3 The Monti Nèbrodi

ter a short stretch on the state road 113
ward Palermo, from Sant'Agata Militello
u will turn off to the left onto the state
ad 289. The road, from which you can en-
y splendid panoramic views of the coast
far as Capo d'Orlando, runs through the
untryside around San Fratello, and with
eep switchbacks reaches Portella Fem-
ina Morta (1,524 m.). The pullouts, in the
ints free of forest and rocky outcrop-
ngs, offer a view of three different Sicilian
olcanoes at once: Etna, Vulcano, and
rómboli. The road drops back down toard the highlands and then, in Cesarò,
ins state road 120 which runs west, reach-
g Troina (from here, the state road 575
ads directly to Catania). After Cesarò, the
ate road 120 crosses the river Simeto. On
e left you may note the turnoff to the
ucea dei Nelson, with the abbey, or Ab-
azia di Maniace, directly overlooking the
ver Saracena (the road, which follows the
urse of the Alcàntara, skirts the northern
opes of Mount Etna, and then pours into
e Ionian Sea, just past Randazzo, not far
om Taormina. In this connection, see
apter 7). From Randazzo, if instead you
ke the state road 116, you will come, after
out 21 km., to Floresta, perched high
op the Monti Nèbrodi (at an elevation of
275 m.: this is the highest township in
cily). With fine views of the Monti Pelori-
ni and the Tyrrhenian Sea, with the Aeo-
an islands in the distance, you can then
op back down toward Naso and Capo
Orlando: 175 km. total.

nt'Agata Militello

ecently founded, Sant'Agata Militello (elev.
m., pop. 12,796) owes its development to
s excellent location on the commercial

thoroughfare of the state road 113, as well
as the abundant farming of its hinterland,
and its proximity to Milazzo. Among its few
monumental buildings, we should mention
the *church of the Carmelo*, with an 18th-c.
bell gable, and from the same period, a castle, the *Castello* dei Principi di Trabia e Lanza di Scalea (now the site of a pizzeria),
overlooking the fine broad sandy beach.

San Fratello

This town (elev. 675 m., pop. 5,055), with a
regular grid of streets and houses made of
smooth and square-hewn stone, was founded in the 18th c. following the transfer of the
old city from a location further uphill; it was
founded by Adelasia, the wife of Roger I, in
the 11th c., and it was destroyed by a landslide in 1754. The Norman queen established
a colony of Lombards there, and founded the
first church, which was named after the Santi Fratelli, or sainted brothers (hence the
name of the town) Alfio (Alphius), Filadelfo
(Philadelphus), and Cirino (Cyrinus). Set on
a panoramic point of the Monte Vecchio,
just before the town, accessible by foot from

Cheese making in the Nébrodi

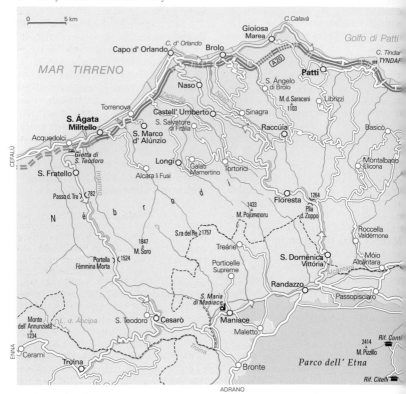

ADRANO

the turnoff to the cemetery, or *Cimitero*, is the sanctuary, or *Santuario dei Tre Fratelli* which still preserves, from Norman times, the plan with a single nave and transept, three apses, and a cylindrical cupola base set on a four-sided tambour.

Outside of town, gentle green hills, covered with pasturage and open Mediterranean maquis prepare the traveller for the highlands of the Monti Nèbrodi, covered with dense forests year round. In these areas, it is not uncommon to see pairs or herds of horses, grazing or galloping across the landscape. The horses are bred in this way, in the wild, and have been for centuries; they are a cross between an Arabian breed and a Norman breed that was imported to the island in the 11th c., at the same time that the town was founded.

Cesarò

Situated on the slope of the Monti Nèbrodi that overlooks the northwestern slope of Mount Etna, this town (elev. 1,150 m., pop. 3,280) has a primarily agrarian economy, with much grazing of sheep. Mentioned in documents dating back to the Swabian era, it was a feudal holding from 1334 on of the Romano Colonna family, which built the castle, whose ruins still stand not far from the town itself. The

Chiesa Madre dates from 1623 and feature a *Crucifix* painted on panel.

Before you enter the town, the state road 289 ru over the crest of the Monti Nèbrodi, near th village of Portella Femmina Morta, at an elevatio of 1,524 m. From there, there are two kilomete of dirt road, to be travelled on foot or with an o road vehicle, which lead to the *Monte Soro* (ele 1,847 m.), the highest peak in the Monti Nèbroc and to the lake, or *Lago Biviere*. This lake, situate at an elevation of 1,274 m., extends over rough 170 hectares, in an area of private property; it necessary, therefore, in order to get to the ban of the lake, to ask permission of the residents the nearby farm. Near the lake there live mar species of animals, including freshwater turtle coots, mallards, and moorhens. The landscape verdant, humid, and wild – features a natural e vironment that, strangely enough, is well pr served, and constitutes a green oasis of gre beauty in the heart of Sicily.

Troìna

Set between Nicosìa and Cesarò, well int the Provincia di Enna, Troìna (elev. 1,121 m pop. 15,029) extends over a narrow terrac in the middle of the highland that ove looks Etna from the west. Here, the view are once again the clean, spare panorama of agrarian Sicily: shallow valleys set amids smooth hills without trees, lying agains

e sharp and vast backdrop of the im-
ense volcanic cone that dominates every-
ing here from its distant abode. The ter-
ory has been inhabited from prehistoric
nes, as is indicated by the discovery of un-
rground tombs carved into the rock of
e nearby Monte San Pantheon and Monte
uganò. And precisely on the site of pre-
nt-day Troìna (the Greek Enghion) there
e stratifications of the various historic
as. On the southeast slopes, you can still
e remains of the Hellenistic fortification in
egalithic blocks and part of the structure
a Roman bathhouse. During Byzantine
nes, Troìna attracted Basilian monks,
o built churches and convents around
e city. Among these, we should mention
e ruins of the monastery, or Monastero di
Michele il Vecchio, set on a nearby high-
nd; the earliest core of it, dating back
evious to the Moorish conquest, was en-
rged during Norman times. In that same
riod, the city Troìna was made a bish-
ric, the first episcopal see in all of post-
amic Sicily. Of the Cattedrale, or cathe-
al, founded by Roger (the *Chiesa Madre*)
ere still survive the apses, the bell tower,
d a cross-vault that covers the passage
rough the tower itself. Among the art-
rks to be found on the interior, we should
ake special mention of a number of late-
zantine panels, such as the *Virgin Mary
th Christ Child* (15th c.) and the *St. Michael*
512). The local Archeoclub was recently
nverted by the young people of Troìna in-
a museum for the preservation and dis-
ay of finds from the excavations done in
e surrounding territory.

Ducea Nelson

is landholding covers an area of 6,556
ctares, which largely belong to the
tanese township of Bronte. It is now pub-
property; its name came about from the
nation in 1799 to the English admiral Ho-
tio Nelson by Ferdinand III of Bourbon, as
reward for having helped to put down
e revolt of Naples. Inside this estate, aside
m the 18th-c. family mansion, there is an
bey, the **Abbazia di Maniace**. This abbey
ands on the site in which the Greek gen-
al George Maniace, leading Byzantine and
rman troops, defeated the Saracens in
40, well before the landing in Sicily of
ger, which took place in 1061. The
urch, according to documents, was
unded in 1174 by Margaret of Blois, the
fe of William I, and was later ceded, along
th its territory, to the Benedictine
onastery of S. Filippo di Fragalà. This in-
resting example of late-Norman archi-

tecture features a handsome stone portal
with figured capitals and a pointed arch, and
it preserves, in the single-nave interior, the
original wooden ceiling, a *polyptych* of the Sicilian school of the 13th c., depicting the Virgin Mary and Saints George, Anthony the
Abbot, and Lucy, as well as a Byzantine
panel, the *Virgin Mary with Christ Child*,
which is said to have been brought by
George Maniace directly from Greece. The
palace, transformed into a sumptuous aristocratic residence by the heirs of Nelson –
now it is a *museum* – features English Vic-
torian furniture, as well as prints and memorabilia of the famous admiral.

Once you pass *Randazzo* (see page 154), you can
take the state road 116 through settings of great
beauty. On the right, after roughly 35 km., there
are markers for the turnoff to *Raccuja* (elev. 640
m., pop. 1,692), whose *Chiesa Madre* has handsome 16th-c. marble statues; along with the
neighboring towns of San Piero Patti, Patti, Montalbano Elcona, and Tortorici, this town forms
a complete system of settlements that live by
growing and harvesting hazelnuts.

Naso

Like other farming towns near the coast, Naso (elev. 490 m., pop. 4,741) shows all the
signs of the decline in the urban environment
that began in the 20th c., including the fringes
of residential development behind the center. All the same, there is a lovely view of the
broad valley, or Valle del Sinagra from the
belvedere next to the main square. Hills,
which were once cultivated in an orderly
manner, and which are now abandoned to
wild thorn bushes, run gently down to the river bed; in the distance, there are nothing
but mountains closing off the view.
This city already existed at the time of the
Norman conquest: a number of documents
state that in 1094 Roger gave half of the
lands of Naso to the monastery, or Monastero di S. Bartolomeo di Lipari. From the
16th c. on, it was feudal possession of the
Ventimiglia family, who were responsible
for its present urban layout and the construction of the main churches and monasteries. These churches and monasteries are
known for their remarkable late-Baroque
sculptures, with decorations in the style of
mischio, tramischio, and rabisco, quite fashionable in Sicily at the turn of the 18th c. The
Chiesa Madre, dedicated to Saint Philip and
Saint James (Ss. Filippo e Giacomo), features – among the Baroque marble curlicues
and the minute colorful inlays of the chapel,
or Cappella del Rosario – a very serious
Gagini statue of the *Virgin Mary with Christ
Child*. Of greater interest is the *funerary mon-*

ument to Artale Cardona, located in the 15th-c. *church of S. Maria di Gesù*, a Renaissance work with four statues of the Virtues, supporting the body of the deceased.

Patti

This is the original core of the relatively new settlement down at the marina (elev. 157 m., pop. 12,959); it declined in population as early as the 19th c., due to the shift in economic interest from farming the countryside to the role of trading station linking Messina and Palermo. It developed in Hellenistic times, an outgrowth of Tìndari, and grew considerably following the influx of refugees from Tìndari when it was destroyed. The Normans founded an abbey there and elevated it to the rank of bishopric. Because of its loyalty to the house of Anjou, during the War of the Sicilian Vespers, it was burned by Frederick II of Aragon and then in 1554 it was plundered and once again burned by the pirate Khair-ed-din Barbarossa (or Redbeard). On the summit of the hill over which the city extends is the complex of religious buildings adjoining the cathedral, or *Cattedrale* (dating from the 18th c.), which stands on the site of the Norman church built by Roger to contain the remains of his mother Adelasia, who died in Patti in 1118: the queen's fine Renaissance *sarcophagus** is located on the left wall of the right transept. On the left wall of the single nave, you may also note a panel by Antonello de Saliba, depicting a *Virgin Mary with Christ Child* (15th/16th c.).

Facing the mouth of the road that runs from Tìndari into the state road 113, you will find the directions for the **Roman villa of Patti***: built during the Roman empire and destroyed in the 5th c. A.D. by an earthquake, the villa of Patti was not unearthed until 1976. It presents similarities in terms of the types of buildings with the less well known villa of Terme Vigliatore: like that one, it has a broad *peristyle*, facing the long sides of which are the private rooms, while on the short side, opposite the vestibule, is the *tablinum*, with the usual three terminal exedrae. A small *thermal complex* is located to the northeast of the peristyle. Unlike in the villa of Terme Vigliatore and the large residence of Tìndari, the floor mosaics are polychrome, and feature geometric and naturalistic motifs, rather than mythological themes: as in the tablinum, where we see geometric and animal motifs enclosed in concave-sided octagons, and in the portico, with panels bounded by festoons of laurel.

Capo d'Orlando

A major farming and trading town, Capo d'Orlando (elev. 8 m., pop. 11,948), along with Sant'Agata Militello and Milazzo, pla▪ a leading role in the economy of t▪ Tyrrhenian coast in the province, or Provi▪ cia di Messina. Its historical origins a▪ ancient and indeed legendary. It is said, ▪ fact, that the promontory upon which t▪ city stands was named Capo Orlando aft▪ an officer, called Orlando, serving und▪ Charlemagne, and that this Orlando foun▪ ed the fortified castle. The ruins of th▪ medieval *castle* preserve traces of ribbi▪ and masonry from the 14th c. Adjoinir▪ the castles is the sanctuary, or *Santuario ▪ Maria SS. di Capo d'Orlando*, which date▪ from 1598.

Between Capo d'Orlando and Sant'Agata,th▪ first turnoff is an interesting halt among the r▪ ins of the **Convento di Fragalà**, near Frazzan▪ Set in a charming location on the highland th▪ overlooks the valley of the river Fitalia, wi▪ the Aeolian islands in the distance, this m▪ be considered one of the prototypes of Sicili▪ religious architecture in the Norman period. ▪ the northern corner stand the ruins of the ori▪ inal Basilian church, dating from the 8th c▪ around which later developed the monast▪ complex built beginning in 1090 with dire▪ funding from Roger I.

Set on a hill, just a few kilometers from the coa▪ in fact, *San Marco d'Alunzio* (elev. 540 m., po▪ 2,396) preserves in its many churches and in i▪ urban layout its original Baroque appearanc▪ The territory of San Marco, comprised betwee▪ the Torrente Favara, a mountain stream, ar▪ the valley of the Rosmarino, was inhabited as e▪ ly as prehistoric times; on the site of the moder▪ day settlement stood the Hellenistic city, ▪ which only the Temple of Hercules (Tempio ▪ Ercole) survives; it was transformed into ▪ church in the 7th c. Destroyed by Moors, th▪ town was fortified and refounded by the No▪ mans in the 11th c., with the name of San Marc▪ Still standing, on the summit of the hill ("rocca" are the ruins of the Norman castle (1061), bu▪ to dominate the coast from Capo d'Orlando t▪ San Fratello. This was a fief of the Filangie▪ princes of Mirto, from the 15th c. until the ab▪ lition of feudalism, in 1812. The *church of the S▪ Salvatore* was built in the 17th c. on the founda▪ tions of a Roman temple; recently sever▪ columns of this temple with their capitals hav▪ been found. The Byzantine *church of S. Teodor▪* known as the Badia Piccola, is of note because ▪ its Greek-cross plan, unusual in this area; it h▪ small calotte cupolas set at the intersection ▪ the arms of the cross. The *Chiesa Madre*, datin▪ from the 17th c., has elegant Baroque portals i▪ its façade, as well as an interior with a single nav▪ and stone walls with Renaissance chapels. Th▪ 17th-c. *church of the Aracoeli* stands out for th▪ imaginative composition of its portals and its i▪ terior with monolithic columns in Rosso Alun▪ no, a precious marble that is similar in color an▪ grain to Rosso Veronese.

0 Inland Sicily

unded lengthwise by the Monti Nèbrodi to the north and by the Monti Erei to the east,
e vast area that slopes down to the Mar d'Africa, with Enna and Caltanissetta in its cen-
, is considered to be an "altopiano," or plateau. The word, which in Italian properly refers
a rolling tableland, considerably elevated above sea level, is a pale attempt at describ-
the immense expanse of rounded hills that intertwine, forming slight depressions and
us restoring the idea of surface not unlike that of a plain.

ere is evidence of human settlement scattered all over the area ever since prehistoric
es, but that evidence becomes more common, of course, in the green and hospitable
leys of the rivers Plàtani and Salso. In these areas are located the two most noteworthy
torical and artistic monuments of the area: the little Hellenistic city of Morgantina and
e Roman villa of Piazza Armerina, a com-
x that is unequalled on earth for the rich-
ss of its mosaic floors, preserved per-
tly in nearly all of the villa's 40 rooms. The
eservation, from the 9th c. to the present
y, of the Arabic place names in many of
e towns and villages, is a clear indication
he enormous role played by the Moors in
onomic and social development, with the
provement of systems of irrigation and in-
ior routes of communications. The Nor-
ns, who were acclaimed as the rescuers
Christianity from barbarous Islam, were
le to return the cities to a Catholic juris-
ction, but they could not change their
mes. What survives from the Moorish pe-
d are the urban grids of the older towns,
ich can be clearly distinguished, howev-
from the new cities, with their orthogonal
d, founded between the 16th and 18th c. in
e context of the policy of the agricultural
lamation of the feudal landholdings, en-
raged by the Spanish. The inland urban

A fresco in the Roman villa of Casale

tem of Sicily comprises the two cities of Enna and Caltanissetta; the first, which is of an-
nt origin, always played a major role in the political and military equilibrium of the island,
en its standing as an impregnable stronghold; the second, devoid of natural defenses, had
le authority in the most important episodes of Sicilian history. Now the situation has been
versed: Enna, with the loss of the need to defend its territory, has stopped growing, and
w has half the population of Caltanissetta.

.1 Enna*

he exact center of Sicily, set amongst fer-
e and gently rolling hills, rises a tall peak,
nilar in shape to a pyramid whose point
d been lopped off with a gigantic hatchet.
the plain that is thus created stands En-
(elev. 931 m., pop. 28,273, plan on page
1), shrouded in fog for much of the year.
t far from the foot of the mountain, a de-
ession of the land, as if to compensate for
e elevation of the peak, led in the distant
st to the creation of a lake, elliptical in
pe. The mount of Enna projects in all di-
tions its own image over the entire landscape of plateaus and valleys of the Sicilian
hinterland, with as a counterpoint only, on
the other side of the ribbon of highway, the
Rocca di Calascibetta. Given its central location, as against the frontal layout of the
maritime cities, and given the multiplicity of
convenient points for the observation of
the surrounding territory, Enna has been
called the "the belly button of Sicily." But
even though it has not been overlooked,
over the centuries, by the interior traffic of
the Sicilian region, becoming one of the
main nexuses in the network of roads, like

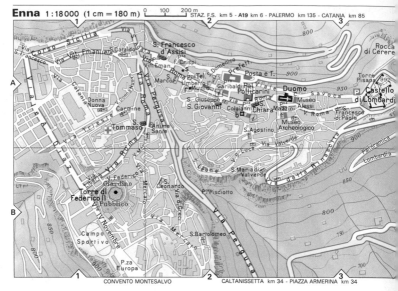

Enna 1:18000 (1 cm = 180 m) 0 100 200 m STAZ. F.S. km 5 - **A19** km 6 - PALERMO km 135 - CATANIA km 85

CONVENTO MONTESALVO   CALTANISSETTA km 34 - PIAZZA ARMERINA km 34

Nicosìa, Enna still preserves its appearance as a historical city. Unlike Nicosìa, however, the city speaks – with its settings and its buildings – a sober medieval language, with little contamination from the flourishes of the Baroque and the 18th c. The preservation of an essentially agrarian economy, which thus hindered the growth of service industries, has probably contributed to the safeguarding of local historical values. These values constitute a substrate of character and a source of lively and productive pride. The clean streets, the carefully maintained buildings, the absence of neon and banner signs, and even the orderly way in which the excellent pastries are displayed in the elegant "pasticcerie" – all these factors tell us that the city of Enna is not only quite different from the chaotic metropolises on the coast, but also from the cities in the depressed areas of Sicily.

The plateau atop the mountain may have been the site of an early Sicilian city when Siracusa (Syracuse), in 664 B.C., 70 years after its own foundation, established the colony of Henna there, for the exploitation of the site's rich agricultural resources; there remain, from the archaic Greek period, the necropolises, and from the Hellenistic period stretches of the enclosure walls, in the area of Santo Spirito. Conquered by the Romans in the 3rd c. B.C., the town saw an improvement in the road network over the surrounding territory, growing grain crops, and the consequential development of the Hellenistic town. Contributing to the consolidation of the city's agricultural production were the technical innovations in irri-

gation introduced by the Moors, who call the town "Qasr Yannah," from the La "Castrum Hennae," which was in time c rupted into Castrogiovanni, a name t stuck until 1927. The Normans, who, in or to besiege the invulnerable fortress camp on the peak of Calascibetta, finally storm it in 1088 and reinforced it with the c struction of a castle to guard the valley low; the Normans also encouraged the tablishment of a Lombard colony in t vicinity. At the end of the 14th c., the city h already acquired its definitive layout. In 17th c., the initiative of the Spanish crown found new villages in the vast feudal la holdings of the interior tableland, in order encourage agricultural production, caus the depopulation of the town, with the suing halt in urban growth.

One characteristic of Enna is the useful c tribution of the ring-roads around the c ter, all streets cut into terraces in the slo or in some cases perched on viaducts. T view that you may enjoy there is unique all of Sicily: it extends, 360 degrees, fr Mount Etna to Èrice, from the Monti Nèb di to the hills of the Caltanissetta provin Once you have reached the castle, or Cas lo di Lombardia, at the easternmost poin Enna, you can begin here the tour that ru entirely along the Via Roma, and all dov hill. You can see, in the near distanc protected behind the entrance gate of Museo Alessi – the massive apses of cathedral, or Duomo and, facing the s portal of that church, the entrance to archeological museum, or Museo Arch logico. Overlooking the successive Pia

lajanni are the façades of the church of S.
iara and the handsome Baroque portal of
lazzo Pollicarini. Running past the love-
façades of the city palazzi of the old land-
aristocracy, the route continues as far as
e Piazza Vittorio Emanuele, where the
urch of S. Francesco stands. A little fur-
er along, the Via Roma intersects with the
a Pergusa and then turns south, crossing
e quarter that was originally built by the
oors, developing, beyond the right side of
e street, in twisting little stepped lanes,
d small secluded courtyards. You will
en reach the more modern section of En-
Alta (upper Enna), and then you may
ke the Viale 4 Novembre, the short dis-
ace to the tower, or Torre di Federico II.

stello di Lombardia* (A3). This castle
unds on the site of an earlier Moorish for-
cation, and was reinforced by the Nor-
uns; Frederick III of Aragona established, in
e 12th c., a powerful curtain wall with tow-
s distributed on every side. The castle
s an irregular plan, since it follows with its
uctures the natural morphology of its
e. Besides the curtain wall, only six of the
original towers still stand, along with the
mplex internal structure of courtyards
ich open in a sequence, one gate after the
her. The closest courtyard to the entrance
used, during the summer, for remarkable
eatrical performances. From the court-

na: the castle of Lombardia

rd, or Cortile di S. Martino, where it is
ssible to see the ruins of the little church,
Chiesetta di S. Martino, you will reach
e entrance to the tower, or *Torre Pisana*,
m the terrace of which you can admire a
endid panoramic view*, when there is
fog. In the immediate vicinity of the cas-
on a rocky crag, you can see the arcaic
ucture of the *temple of Ceres* (Tempio di
ere), which Cicero said was still filled
h statues of the goddess in the 1st c. B.C.

omo* (A3), or cathedral. Originally built
a 14th-c. structure, this cathedral was re-
lt in the 16th c. following a fire. What re-

mains of the ancient structure are the apses and a pointed-arch portal set in the wall
of the right transept. The main façade is
characterized by the 18th-c. campanile that
stands perfectly in the center, directly on
the vaulted roof of the portico. The portico
itself is closed with fencing made of black
iron, with gilded decorations, in the form of
putti and cornucopias. In the side wall,
overlooking the Piazza Mazzini, is a lovely
16th-c. *portal*, which bears a handsome bas-
relief, in the upper aedicule, having to do
with the legend of St. Martin and the poor
man. The Latin-cross basilican **interior** is
broken down into three aisles, with pointed arches on stout columns made of volcanic stone, richly decorated in the bases
and capitals. The coffered ceiling of the
nave was done in the 17th c.; you should
note the odd wooden brackets in the form
of winged and remarkably buxom griffins. In
the chapel, or Cappella della Visitazione,
there are two intarsiaed tortile columns,
framing the 17th-c. canvas depicting the
Visitation of the Virgin Mary, which conceals a Golden Nef (*Nave d'Oro*), a very
valuable litter upon which the 15th-c. statue of the Virgin Mary is carried in procession every year on 2 July.

Museo Alessi (A3). This prestigious institution takes its name from the largest and
most important collection it houses, established by the Enna canon Giuseppe
Alessi, who lived between the late 18th c.
and the early years of the 19th c. Among the
many paintings on exhibit on the ground
floor of the building, there are exquisite
Byzantine icons on panels; on the second
floor, in the great hall, with windows that
look out over a lovely view of Calascibetta,
it is possible to admire sacred paraments,
gold and silver work from the Renaissance,
in the *treasury* of the cathedral, or Duomo;
in the smaller hall, glass display cases contain refined jewels, treasures of the gold-
smith's art: the crown of the Virgin Mary, in
enameled gold, studded with precious
stones, and a gold pin, with an enormous
topaz in its center, depicting a pelican that
has torn its breast to feed its young, a symbol of the sacrifice of Christ.
In the halls on the last floor there is a *numismatic collection*, almost entirely from
the Collezione Alessi; this coin collection is
remarkable, both in terms of the great many
coins displayed, and in that it provides a
broad picture of the economic history of
Sicily of earliest times, and because of the
presence of fine rare examples of Greek, Roman, and Byzantine coinage.

Museo Archeologico Regionale (A3), or regional archeological museum. Established in 1985, this museum occupies the elegant halls of the *Palazzo Varisano*. The ground floor halls are of particular interest, with an exhibition of finds from a number of archeological sites under exploration in the Provincia di Enna. The numerous necropolises that have been discovered have yielded an enormous quantity of funerary furnishings, some of which date back to the 3rd

The Holy Week procession in Enna

or 2nd millennium B.C. But the most interesting material is in the third hall, which is entirely dedicated to the areas around the lake, or Lago di Pergusa; in particular, the explorations have revealed, in the village of Cozzo Matrice, traces of a settlement from the Copper Age, as well as traces of a Greek town from the 5th to 6th c. B.C., with an area sacred to Demeter and Kore within the enclosure walls.

S. Chiara (A2). This church was originally laid out in the 17th c., and was renovated in the 18th c.; it is today a sacrarium which houses the remains of men who fell in the two World Wars. It features a 19th-c. majolica floor, with two panels showing unusual subjects: the advent of steam navigation and the triumph of Christianity over Islam. In a courtyard at n. 467 in the Via Roma stands the *Palazzo Pollicarini*, with architectural details from the Catalonian Gothic period (15th c.).

S. Francesco d'Assisi (A2). This church, first founded in the 14th c., has undergone extensive transformations over the centuries. The entire building stands on a high stone socle with inclined walls, which gives it the appearance of a fortress, more than a church. Contributing to this appearance is the massive 15th-c. *bell tower*, lightened only by the cornices with hanging arches of the upper windows. A staircase, recently reno-

vated, leads to the side entrance of the s gle nave.

Torre di Federico II (B1), or Tower of Fre erick II. This remarkable pure geomet shape with an octagonal base rises 24 atop a little hillock in the center of a pa and can be seen from many places in t town. Built in the 13th c., it clearly shows t stylistic characteristics of Frederick's m tary architecture. The *interior* (curren being restored) which reached by a single por is subdivided into thr stories, the first of whic consisting of a single lar hall, has a handsome vau ed ceiling, with stone arc es. A spiral staircase cut to the thickness of the w (more than 3 m.), leads the rooms on the upp story, much like the firs

Calascibetta
When seen from Enr Calascibetta (elev. 681 pop. 5,014) seems to have been built in t cavea of a natural amphitheater, surrou ed by the steep rock walls that embrace Nothing at all survives from the Roman rlod; of the Moorish period the town p serves its distinctive name, which may ha referred to a hamlet that existed at the tir but the creation of the medieval "borg which still exists in its original urban str ture, dates back to the 11th c., when Rog the Norman was forced to camp here, due the long siege he was laying against En The successive expansion in the 16th a 17th c., taking the form of religious buildir and aristocratic residences, occupied t southwestern area of the slope. The route the present-day Via Conte Ruggero is tha the original thoroughfare that served the quarters of the little town; it bounded the upper section, the area of the medie core, abounding in remarkable settings straitened spaces, overlooked by old wo ing-class houses. The *Chiesa Madre* church dedicated to St. Peter (S. Piet and S. Maria Assunta (Our Lady of the sumption), formerly the Palatine Chap founded back in the 14th c., has undergc a great deal of reconstruction: on the thr aisled interior, it preserves sculptures d ing back to various eras, and a rich coll tion of sacred paraments and liturgical jects. The 18th-c. *church of the Carm* with its classical-style façade, also has an *nunciation* attributed to the Gagini famil

10.2 From Enna to Piazza Armerina

This route runs through some of the loveliest areas in the provinces of Enna and Caltanissetta, characterized by sunny and neatly cultivated hillsides and vast areas of reforestation; there is an abundance of streams and watercourses. From Enna, if you head south and pass the intersection with the state road 117 Bis to Caltanissetta, there is a provincial road that leads, in a few minutes, to the lake, or Lago di Pergusa, and, if you continue south, you will join the state road to Gela: at a distance of about 3 kilometers from the intersection, a turnoff to the left leads to Aidone, where you will find directions for the excavations of the Hellenistic Greek city of Morgantina and the Museo Archeologico that houses the finds. Then return to the state road, and at a distance of about 4 kilometers, you will come to Piazza Armerina, not far from which is the Roman Villa del Casale. From Piazza Armerina it is fairly easy to reach the coast to the south, Caltagirone to the east, or Caltanissetta to the west, while passing through the farm towns of Barrafranca and Pietraperzìa, which form part of this route. In all, you will travel 86 km.

Lake, or Lago di Pergusa

Set in a broad valley, surrounded by a continuous ridge of hills, dense with vegetation, some 9 km. south of Enna, is the innermost natural basin in Sicily. The lake, or Lago di Pergusa, is tectonic in origin, full of shallow brackish water, and has neither inflow nor outflow. We have already referred to the function of this place as the site of a myth (the abduction of Kore); but the charm that must have accrued to this place in the past from this connection is nowadays compromised by the presence of a circular automotive racetrack that entirely surrounds it. The lake, moreover, is seriously threatened by worrisome phenomena of drainage and drying up. In the surrounding area, note the *archeological area of Cozzo Matrice*, one of the hills overlooking the northern shore of the lake; here traces have been found of a fortified settlement dating back to the 8th/6th c. B.C., as well as of its necropolis, with chamber tombs carved into the rock. The finds from the excavations, including numerous tomb furnishings, are now in the archeological museum, or Museo Archeologico di Enna.

Morgantina*

This major archeological station now lies on a road of secondary importance, which links Aidone to Catania over the plain, but at the time of its greatest prosperity, it played a very important role as a commercial city. Built at the center of a gentle valley, surrounded by a ridge of steep hills to the north and the south, Morgantina could be easily defended, and had under its rule enormous and productive territories. When the first settlement of the people of Mor-

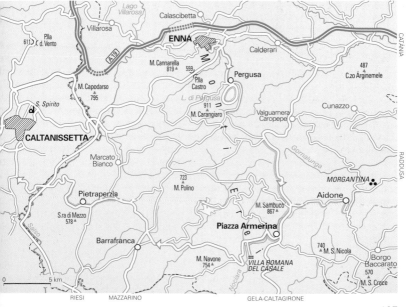

gantina – a tribe from Latium, who migrated here toward the end of the 1st millennium B.C. – was destroyed, the urban center was rebuilt around the 5th c. B.C., and enjoyed its period of greatest growth and prosperity during the Hellenistic era (4th/3rd c. B.C.), under the rule of the tyrant of Syracuse, Agathocles. During that period, the acropolis was built; a few scanty ruins of it survive on the Monte Cittadella, roughly a kilometer-and-a-half from the site of the agora. The city did not live long: in 211 B.C. it was destroyed by hordes of mercenaries at the service of Rome; Rome held the city subject until the 1st c. A.D. The site is particularly charming, because it is far from any towns: the excavations, which were begun in 1955, reveal the interesting layout of the *public square* (agora), arrayed on two different levels, linked by a trapezoidal stairway that also served as seating for the public assemblies. On the upper level, the large open square is occupied, at the center, by the quadrangular structure of the *market*, with clear traces of the walls that divided one shop from the next; and it is bounded respectively on the northern and eastern sides by the Roman "*gymnasium*" and by a *portico* (stoa), on the surface of which it is still possible to recognize the bases of the columns. On the lower level is the *theater*, dating from the 4th c. B.C., preserved in excellent condition with most of the stone benches and the scaena; the long building that faces the scaena of the theater must have been used as a grain silo, with kilns for the production of ceramics at the southeastern end. Behind the northeastern portico, mentioned above, there is a paved road, from which it is possible to climb up to the hill on which stands the ruins of one of the *residential quarters* of the city, comprising a set of terraces sloping down toward the agora. The houses, all of them dating from the Hellenistic era, were probably inhabited by the well-to-do class of the town, judging from the refined wall decorations and by the figures depicted in the mosaic floors, dating from the 3rd c. B.C., found in the interior rooms. Considerable ruins of another wealthy quarter can be toured behind the *theater*, in the western section of the excavated area. Morgantina was, a few years ago, in the news, unfortunately, due to the theft of a marble statue of Aphrodite that had been found during the excavations.

Aidone

This is by and large a farming town; Aidone (elev. 800 m., pop. 7,275) occupies a high plateau in the eastern slopes of the Monti Erei, in a position overlooking the western wedge of the Piana di Catania. The center has a typical medieval layout, which can be traced back to the original development of the settlement in the 12th c., around the castle built by the Normans, whose ruins can still be seen on the rocky spur, at the westernmost extremity of the hill. The town extended, in the centuries following the 17th c. to the south of the center, in accordance with a regular urbanistic scheme. In the 18th c., work had to be done on the reconstruction of the civil and religious buildings that were damaged in the earthquake of 1693, which ravaged all of the Val di Noto. Recently established, the regional archeological museum, or *Museo Archeologico Regionale*, is located in the former monastery or Convento dei Cappuccini and in the 17th c. church of S. Francesco, closed to worship and restored, overlooking the Largo Torres Trupia. The excellent museum installation makes it possible for the visitor, by analyzing the historic phases previous to the Hellenistic settlment of Morgantina, to form a complete idea of the development of the territory from prehistory to the Greek period. The hall known as the Sala di Cittadella contains materials from excavations in the Contrada Cittadella, of a settlement dating back to the end of the 1st millennium B.C. the tomb furnishings of the indigenous necropolises of the 8th to 7th c. B.C. and those from the Greek necropolises from the same period. The hall, or Sala di Serra Orlando contains finds from the area of Morgantina, having to do with the period of its reconstruction. In the former refectory of the monastery, a model of the archeological area prepares a visitor for a tour of the various educational halls.

Piazza Armerina

Extending over three adjoining hills, Piazza Armerina (elev. 697 m., pop. 22,355) – called Piazza until the 18th c. – takes its name from one of the three hills, the Colle Armerino. The settlement is surrounded by land that abound in water and forests with all sorts of trees, making the landscape one of the most fertile in the interior of Sicily. The entrance into the city from the state road is marked by recently built quarters, with fairly shoddy architecture, extending over the plains around the Colle Armerino. On the slopes of this hill, you can still see the old town of Piazza, worth touring for its pleasant streets and most interesting monuments. This site was certainly inhabited from the 8th/7th c. B.C., and must have attracted settlement even in prehistoric times

e Romans settled here, as we can see
the presence of the Villa del Casale, as
d the Byzantines and, in the high Middle
es, the Moors. In the 11th c., the time of
e Norman conquest, we learn of conflicts
tween the Moors and the new con-
erors, who, however, built a fortified
adel to the west of Piazza. Dating from the
me period is the formation of the earliest
nabited nucleus on the Colle Mira, now
own as the Quartiere del Monte. In the
th and 15th c. a first expansion to the
rtheast was followed by a second ex-
nsion to the east and southeast, and was
nsolidated, in the course of the 17th c., by
definitive urban layout, the result of the
nstruction and renovation of the monas-
complexes of various religious orders.
e visit may be limited to the historical cen-
r alone, structured around the Piazza
ribaldi; here is a convergence of the main
oroughfares of the town, onto which give
e narrow lanes of the medieval quarters of
stelina and Monte. On the north side of
e square, separated by the Via Cavour,
nich leads to the cathedral, or Duomo,
ands the 18th-c. *Palazzo di Città*, with its el-
ant wrought-iron balconies, and the 17th-
church of S. Rocco, with a lavish Baroque
ortal in carved tufa stone and a large win-
ow, standing out against the smooth
çade, underscored by heavy corner pi-
ster strips. The **Duomo**, built in 1604, on

the site of an existing church, at the behest
of a munificent local notable, incorporates
– of the various existing structures – only the
campanile, with basket-arch windows in the
first two orders. The interior, built to a Latin-
cross plan, is richly decorated with gilt stucco work; in the chapel to the left of the presbytery, there is a handsome wooden Cross
dating from the 15th c., painted on both
faces. To the right of the cathedral, or Duomo, you can see the long Baroque façade of
Palazzo Trigonia (18th c.).

The 13 and 14 of August every year, there
is a festival of local folklore, the Palio dei
Normanni, which takes its origin from the
historic entrance of the Count Roger (Conte Ruggero) into the city of Piazza after lib-
erating Sicily from the Muslims. A procession of characters in period costumes sets
out from the Piazza Duomo and then
moves, on the second day, to the playing
fields, where there is an equestrian tour-
nament among the representatives of the
quarters of Piazza.

Roman Villa of Casale**

Set in the green environment of the area
around Piazza Armerina, this villa (plan
below) – given the magnificence of its polychrome mosaics and their excellent condition – represents the most important surviving documentation of Roman civilization in Sicily. The excavations, which were

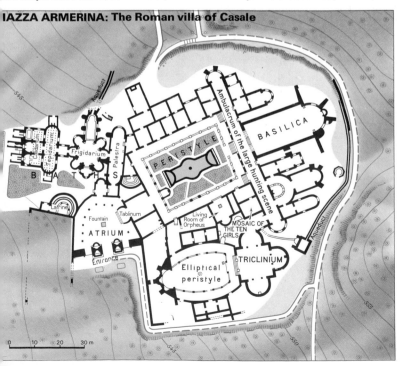

IAZZA ARMERINA: The Roman villa of Casale

undertaken in a systematic manner in 1929, have unearthed a luxurious patrician villa, built sometime between the end of the third and the beginning of the 4th c. A.D., extending over three levels, with a total surface area of some 3,500 square meters. It comprises more than 40 rooms, almost all them artistically paved with mosaic floors. Moreover, the villa is organized into areas with different functions: the area closest to the entrance contains the baths, the successive area clusters around a large peristyle, with bedrooms and guest quarters;

The landscape of inland Sicily

the area across from the entrance vestibule includes the basilica and the private suites of the owners of the villa; the area to the right of the main entrance comprises a large dining hall with a triclinium. The tour follows an obligatory route, over little catwalks suspended above the level of the mosaics.

Just past the entrance, there is a polygonal *atrium* surrounded by a portico, with surviving columns topped by Ionic capitals; on the left, you may note the large exedra of a collective latrine; from the courtyard, you can enter, passing through two small rooms, the large *apsed hall* called the Sala (or *Palestra*) della Gara di Quadrighe del Circo Massimo (after the mosaic floor, depicting a chariot race in the Circus Maximus); adjoining it is an octagonal *frigidarium* with exedrae/dressing rooms and two pools, one facing the other. Next comes the *tepidarium*, and the *calidarium*, which is a sort of sauna, in which you can clearly see the "suspensoria" that support the "hypocaustum," the raised flooring of the baths. In the flooring of the *vestibule* (tablinum) there are depictions of figures welcoming guests, with candelabra and olive branches. Next comes the *rectangular quadriporticus* (peristyle), which features Corinthian marble columns and medallion mosaics with figures of animals. In the

rooms of the western wing, you may admire, in two cubicles, the exquisite pirouettes of a *dancing girl** with a fluttering outfit, and the recurring theme of *cupid fishing,* and, in a "diaeta" (living room), the little hunting scene, or *Piccola Caccia* with scenes of the sacrifice to Diana in the fields. The large corridor with thermal apses, opening onto the quadriporticus, is separated from the quadriporticus by two little stairways, and serves as a connection to the group of rooms to the left of the basilica and the private apartments to the right: this corridor is called the **ambulacrum of the large hunting scene***, o Grande Caccia, because its mosaic floor depicts an African safari, with the killing, capture, and loading of animals onto ships: in the left apse you can admire the allegory of Armenia flanked by wild beasts; in the right apse is a depiction of Africa, with animals fleeing in terror. Among the *mosaics* of the eastern wing, we should point out, for its stylistic elegance, the mosaic of ten girls, each dressed in a sort of very modern looking bikini, doing calisthenics, in one of the cubicles, and, in the large apsed "diaeta" that opens onto the portico, the mosaic based on the myth of Orpheus, who enchanted animals by playing the lyre. In order to tour the private apartments, the basilica, and the northern corner, it is necessary to exit and to follow a beaten-earth trail that winds along the rear of the villa. The decoration of the *apsed hall**, preceded by an atrium giving onto the ambulacrum of the large hunting scene, depicts the legend of Arion, who, threatened with death by his sailors, who are now mutineers, was transported to safety by a dolphin. In the square vestibule of the northern corner there is a *mosaic** depicting Ulysses and Polyphemus, one of the finest mosaics in the villa, with the powerful naturalism of the representation of the scenic setting, the movements of Ulysses and his companions, and the kid goats in the foreground. Return to the interior of the villa and, along the south side of the quadriporticus, you will reach the little passage that leads into the elliptical peristyle. Lining the curving sides of the portico are two groups of rooms with mosaic floors with naturalistic motifs. On the short side of the portico is the *triclinium**, a large dining hall with three apses, where the mosaic floors depict the mythological subject of the Labors of Hercules, in which the depiction takes on a dramatic tone, especially in the scene of the battle against the Titans.

Barrafranca

xtending over the slopes of a hill, at the outhern edge of the interior highlands, arrafranca (elev. 450 m., pop. 13,667) has layed in the past the two-fold role of cen- er of strategic control of the region and readbasket to that same region. Its terri- ory shows traces of settlements dating ack to before the arrival of the Greeks, ut the origins of the present-day city date ack only to the Moorish occuption; the loors in fact first coined the early name of onvicino. Conquered by the Normans, the ity was rebuilt around the Norman castle nd, in the 16th c., passed into the hands of latteo Barresi di Pietraperzìa, who hanged its name to Barrafranca. In that ame period, the *Chiesa Madre* was built, ith its slender campanile with corner pi- ster strips and a small arabesqued cupo- ; and in the same era, the orthogonal grid f the center was developed, to continue for ll of the following century, with the dis- nctive style of the provincial Baroque of e Val di Noto.

Pietraperzìa

et on a highland overlooking the verdant alley of the river Salso, Pietraperzìa (elev. 476 m., pop. 8,015), which was once in the sphere of influence of the town of Caltanis- setta, is predominantly a farming town. Its rich territory has been inhabited every since prehistoric times, and some people say that the site on which present-day Pietraperzìa now stands is the same as that of the ancient Petra. According to docu mentary sources, the city originated from a Norman quarter founded in the 11th c.; dat- ing from the same period is the castle, sit- uated on the steepest part of the hill, in a po- sition that dominates and surveys the val- ley and the city. In the 16th c., it was ruled by Matteo Barresi who, with the aquisition of the feudal landholding of Convicino (Bar- rafranca), made Pietraperzìa an important farming and administrative center. Barresi himself reinforced the castle, and began the expansion of the medieval "borgo," or village, with the usual orthogonal grid. Be- yond the *Chiesa Madre*, a project ordered by Barresi in the 16th c. and rebuilt in the 18th c., it is interesting to note the so-called *Palazzo del Governatore*, with its corner balcony, with its curious brackets, carved in the shape of human heads; all that survives of the *castle* are a few ruins clinging to a rocky crag.

10.3 Caltanissetta

altanissetta (elev. 568 m., pop. 61,319, lan page 203) stands on a site that is easy reach, a hill that is scarcely 500 m. high, ith gently sloping sides. There are various ypotheses concerning the origins of the ame, which is clearly Arabic in form, and the present settlement, which devel- bed, according to the documents, begin- ng in the 11th c. In 1086, in fact, Count oger (Conte Ruggero), in accordance with s vast plan for the territorial and urban- tic reorganization of Sicily, brought the ty back under the jurisdiction of the Latin hurch, conquering the fortress, or Fortez- a di Pietrarossa, of which the ruins still and on a plateau to the southeast of the enter, and founding, on another eminence the northeast, the abbey, or Abbazia di S. pirito, which is still perfectly intact. From ese two opposite poles, set up to defend e city, there run two roads which con- rge in the present-day Via V. Emanuele II, the south of which it is still possible to cognize the earliest core of the city, con- ined within enclosure walls that ran down om the castle. From the 15th c., when this idal landholding became the property the Moncada family, until the 17th c.,

the town, which had already extended be- yond the medieval enclosure walls, ex- panded still further, dividing up into four dif- ferent quarters. The 17th-c. urban struc- ture, based on the axes of the present-day Via Vittorio Emanuele and the Corso Um- berto, can still be seen clearly. It is also very easy to see the differences in the lay- out of the three new quarters, characterized by straight roads and long blocks, and that of the original quarter, behind the cathedral, or Cattedrale, with its narrow twisting lanes. Dating from the 19th c. are the reconstruc- tions and restorations of the buildings over- looking the two main thoroughfares, as well as the current appearance of the Piazza Garibaldi, with the construction of the town hall (Municipio) on the site of the ancient church of S. Maria Annunziata, a church that still stood in the 18th c., and the com- pletion of the two facing façades of the cathedral, or Cattedrale, and the church of S. Sebastiano. Following the construc- tion of the Catania-Palermo highway and the main fast road leading to Agrigento, this city replaced Enna as the major inland city. Cal- tanissetta has been the site of the most im- portant trials for Mafia killings, since this is the headquarters of the Pretura, or magistrate's court, that has jurisdiction for the territory, closest to Palermo. A recent urban expansion created the area that greets the visitor just arriving, while the center of town, clustered around the Piazza Garibaldi, shows clear signs of a complex and even urban history. The 19th-c. Neoclassical style of the main streets, here and there punctuated by a few minor Baroque relics, is set off by the simple and humble image of the quarters immediately outside the well-to-do section of town. Relatively unimportant in strategic terms, after a long past as a rural town, this little city enjoyed phases in the 19th c. of great prosperity, from the exploitation of the mineral resources to be found underground in its territory; today its economy is based on the agricultural sector and the service industries.

During Holy Week, it is possible to watch a remarkable religious festival, with processions and sacred performances, beginning on Palm Sunday and ending on Easter Sunday. On the morning of Holy Wednesday, the procession of the "Real Maestranza," comprising representatives of the various crafts guilds, wends its way through the streets of the city. These guilds are responsible both for maintaining the tradition and preserving the "Vare," papier-maché simulacra made in the last century, each depicting a different moment of the Passion of Christ. On the evenings of Thursday and Friday, respectively, there are the processions of the "Vare" and of the "Cristo Nero," or "Black Christ," while on the Saturday before Easter, there is a performance of the Passion of Christ.

Starting from Piazza Garibaldi, the route includes the most prestigious architectural episodes, dating from different historical era. The fragmentary image of the historical city is, however, made up for by the unified appearance of the urban fabric in each of the quarters, with their unassuming but dignified architecture. After a stop in Piazza Garibaldi for a tour of the cathedral, or Cattedrale, and of the church of S. Seba-stiano, you can climb uphill for a short distance along the Corso Umberto, and you will reach the church of S. Agata; in the surrounding area, behind the town hall, or Municipio, is the unfinished Palazzo Moncada, dating from the 17th c.If you veer to the left of the Cattedrale, and take the Via S. Domenico, you will reach the church of S. Domenico, set in the heart of the medieval quarter; from there the steep Via Angeli leads up to the castle, or Castello di Pietrarossa. It will also be a pleasure, during the course of the tour, to see the lively cultural interests of the people here, which is responsible for there being two interesting museums, one of mineralogy, the other of archeology.

Cattedrale (B2), or cathedral. Commonly known as the church of *S. Maria la Nuova*, this cathedral is also dedicated to S. Michele Arcangelo (St. Michael Archangel), the early patron saint of the city. Built between the end of the 16th c. and the beginning of the 17th c. in a late-Renaissance style, it underwent considerable transformations in the 19th c., with the reconstruction of the transept and the cupola. *Inside*, in the vault of the central aisle, or nave, you may admire 18th-c. frescoes by Gugliemo Borremans depicting the *Immaculate Conception* and the *Coronation of the Virgin Mary*, as well as the excellent altarpiece on the main altar, by the same artist. Facing the cathedral, or Cattedrale, is the *church of S. Sebastiano*, originally laid out in the 16th c., but with a high 19th-c. façade with a classical style.

Sant'Agata (B2). Also known as the *church of S. Ignazio*, it adjoins the Collegio dei Gesuiti accessible from the side ramp, and was built in the early years of the 17th c. The elegant Baroque façade, plastered in a warm orange hue, is the work of Natale Masuccio, and closes off the perspective of the Corso Umberto, with a fine theatrical effect. The interior, with a Greek-cross plan, is richly decorated with stuccoes and polychrome marble work, and preserves masterpieces of religious art, including the interesting marble altarpiece on the altar of the left transept, depicting the saint in glory.

S. Domenico (B3). This church, founded in 1480 at the behest of Antonio Moncada, was enlarged and renovated in the 18th c. Dating from that period is the handsome curving façade and the interior stuccoes. Among the art works housed here, we should point out the canvas by Filippo Paladino on the main altar, depicting the *Madonna del Rosario* (1614).

Castello di Pietrarossa (C3), or castle of Pietrarossa. Even though there now survive only scattered ruins of this ancient fortress, it is interesting to take a stroll up to the rock on which the castle once stood; from here, you can enjoy a view of the city and the surrounding territory, as far as the valley, or Valle del Salso. Probably founded by the Moors, it was reinforced, with the addition of three corner towers, by the Normans, and then later by the Aragonese. In its halls, the barons of Sicily gathered to proclaim Fredrick II of Aragon king. The castle, complete with towers, is depicted in the town coat-of-arms.

Museo Archeologico (C1), or archeological museum. Recently reinstalled with materials from the Museo Civico, this museum features finds from digs dating back to the 1950s, in various areas of the territory of Caltanissetta, Gibil Habil, Sambucina, and Capodarso. On exhibit are objects from prehistoric times (vases and tools from the late Bronze Age), furnishings from indigenous and Greek necropolises, decorated terracottas, Greek and early-Sicilian ceramics.

Museo Mineralogico (B1, off map) or museum of mineralogy. In the halls of the Istituto Tecnico Industriale, an interesting collection of minerals from the territory of the capital of Sicilian sulphur has been on display to the public since 1979. Outstanding colors and shapes can be seen in the crystals of sulphur and celestine, chalks and aragonite, a sulphureous mineral found in abundance in the mines of Aragona. The museum also has minerals found in other parts of the world, and a section devoted entirely to the machinery used in the past in the extraction and processing of sulphur which will soon become an actual *Sulphur Museum*.

Founded by Roger the Norman in the 11th c. and consecrated in the 12th c., the abbey, or **Abbazia di S. Spirito**, presents the typical appearance of Sicilian religious architecture of the Romanesque period. The frescoes on the walls inside date back to the 15th c. To the right of the entrance is a Romanesque *baptismal font*, while in the left apse, you can see an epigraph with the date of consecration.

Caltanissetta 1:13 000 (1 cm = 130 m)

Caltanissetta: corso Umberto I, the city's main thoroughfare, leads to the Cathedral

Gibil Habil means, in Arabic, "mountain of death"; the name was given to this area because of the presence of numerous necropolises carved into the rock cliffs. The fortifications, discovered over the course of the campaigns of excavation, overlook the river Salso and date back to the 6th c. B.C.; they contain an urban layout of the Hippodamean variety, with a regular grid. Finds from the excavations are now in the archeological museum, or Museo Archeologico di Caltanissetta.

Archeological excavations, carried out on the hi known as the **Sabucina**, reveal the interesting r ins of a Sicilian Greek town that, along with th town of Capodarso, controlled the routes lead ing up into the valley of the river Salso. Art facts dating back to the early Bronze Age, foun in tombs and within the circular perimeters c the huts, testify to the existence on this site of a indigenous village dating back to the end of th 1st millennium B.C.

10.4 From Caltanissetta to Mussomeli

This route offers a tour of the mining towns to the west of the river Salso, towns that lived a boomtown illusion of prosperity based on sulphur mining. You will see farming and mining towns that bear the marks of a bitter history, and villages in which, instead, there is a genuine atmosphere of rural life. As you leave Caltanissetta along the state road 122, heading west, you will see San Cataldo and the turnoff for Marianopoli; from the state road and the provincial road, running amidst hills that are here cultivated and there bare and arid, on the way to Milena, which, continuing along, joins the fast road 189 to Palermo, along which you will then find the turnoff to Mussomeli. The total distance traveled is 137 kilometers. In a period of historic transition, the shift – between the end of the 18th c. and the end of the 19th c. – from the rule of the house of Bourbon to the rule of a unified Italian government, we can place the history of sulphur in Sicily. The mining of the mineral was

still a marginal activity at the end of the 18t c., when the nascent French and Englis manufacturers began to demand more an more sulphuric acid. In a short time, th "solfare," or sulphur mines, of central Sic ly multiplied in number; in 1834, of the 19 sulphur mines in Sicily, 88 were in the te ritory of Caltanissetta. The miners, inclu ing many boys under the age of 15 (th "carusi"), were forced to work in inhuma conditions, and many died in the dangerou narrow tunnels, without bracing, suppor ed only by plaster. In the second half c the 19th c., Sicily staked its fortunes on th "windfall" of sulphur, which extended unt the end of the century, when America sulpur hit the market at cheaper price The inevitable crisis hit hard, and little d it avail to found, after WWII, the Ent Minerario Siciliano. After long and pointles struggles, many sulphur miners, or "zo fari" found themselves forced to choos between a life of misery and emigration.

...n Cataldo

...n Cataldo (elev. 625 m., pop. 22,507) owes ...s name to the saint and bishop of Taranto, ...hose relics were once preserved in the *...hiesa Madre*. Founded in the earliest ...cades of the 17th c., in the context of a ...st agrarian reform of the Sicilian lati-...ndium, or large landholding, the town ...llowed a regular grid plan; in the 19th c., ...ter a modest expansion in the 18th c., ...e town grew still more due to the new ...osperity brought by mining. This town ...ew considerably over the last few ...cades, especially as a residential center, ...ven the proximity to the capital. In the sur-...unding area, it is worth touring the *arche-...ogical area of Vassallaggi*, where remains ...ve been found of an early-Sicilian/Greek ...ttlement, on five rocky highlands.

Mussomeli

Mussomeli (elev. 726 m., pop. 11,537) is a major center for the farmers of the area. For centuries, the city lived on an economy based on farming and herding; in the last few years the city has shown a certain vo-cation for the service industry. The city was founded with the name of Manfreda in the 14th c. by Manfredi III Chiaramonte, lord of the great fief of Mussomeli. The ear-liest core of the present-day city can still be glimpsed in the quarter of Terravecchia, in the western section of the historical center. At the same time, Manfredi founded the *Chiesa Matrice*, which was later renovated in the 17th c., and the splendid castle, or *Castello**, restored in the 15th c., which now stands on an isolated peak, 2 km. to the east of the town.

...ilena

...stop at this little farming town may be of ...terest, due to the unspoilt atmosphere of ...e setting, a result of the preservation of ...d peasant traditions. The township of ...ilena (elev. 436 m., pop. 3,644) was es-...blished in the 1920s through the merger ... thirteen villages, the so-called "robbe," ...hich were scattered around the farm, or ...asseria di Milocca, now an urban quarter. ...he adjoining archeological areas, recent-...y explored, of *Monte Campanella*, *Serra del ...lco*, and *Rocca Amorella* have all con-...med the fact that the territory of Milena ...s been inhabited ever since the earliest ...mes, with prehistoric settlements and ...cropolises dating back to the end of the ...t millennium B.C.

Marianòpoli

The little town of Marianòpoli (elev. 720 m., pop. 2,675), founded recently, presents the checkerboard-pattern urban layout that is so typical of new cities in the 18th c. The ter-ritory abounds with traces of settlements from a variety of eras, from the third mil-lennium B.C. to the Hellenistic era; you will find archeological zones on the hills of *Mimi-ani*, *Polizzello*, and *Castelfilici*, but the most important one is in the village of *Castellazzo*, where excavations have revealed the exis-tence of a prehistoric necropolis and a Hel-lenistic settlement,. The ceramic materials and the coins found there are all now in the archeological museum, or *Museo Arche-ologico* di Marianòpoli, in the halls of the town hall, of Palazzo Comunale.

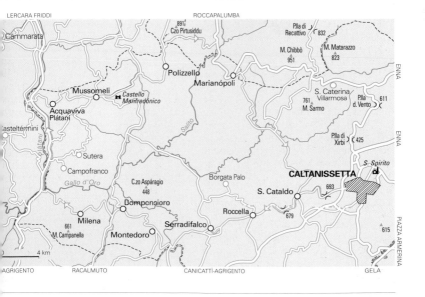

Information for Travellers:
Hotels, Restaurants, Places of interest

Town by town, this list includes hotels, camping grounds, and youth hostels, ranked according to the official classification of the establishment, expressed by number of stars in accordance with the Italian law, Legge Quadro per il Turismo, dated 17 May 1983. The restaurants listed are rated by general price category: ¶ under 45,000 Lire; ¶¶ between 46,000 and 65,000 Lire; ¶¶¶ between 66,000 and 85,000 Lire; ¶¶¶¶ between 86,000 and 105,000 Lire; ¶¶¶¶¶ over 105,000 Lire. As of 18th December 1998, each location's code must also be used for local calls, indicated in the following list next to the symbol ☏. For those calling from abroad, the local code (including the 0) must be dialled after the international code for Italy, followed by the subscriber's number. The following information has been carefully checked before going to print. We would, however, advise readers to confirm certain data which is susceptible to change, before departure. All observations and suggestions are gratefully accepted.

Aci Castello
☒ 95021 ☏ 095

Page 153

ℹ️ *Pro Aci Trezza*, Via Provinciale 218, tel. 276074.

Hotels, restaurants, campsites, and vacation villages

★☆★ President Park. Via Litteri 88, tel. 7116111, fax 277569. Number of rooms: 95. Air conditioning, elevator; parking, garden, swimming pool, private beach.

¶ **Villa delle Rose.** Via XXI Aprile 79, tel. 271024. Closed Monday. Parking, garden. Classic Italian and Sicilian cooking – seafood.

at Aci Trezza, km. 2
☒ 95026

★★★ **Eden Riviera.** Via Litteri 57, tel. 277760, fax 277761. Number of rooms: 33. Air conditioning; parking, parking garage, garden, swimming pool.

★★★ **I Malavoglia.** Via Provinciale 3, tel. 276711, fax 276873. Number of rooms: 83. Air conditioning, elevator; parking, parking garage, garden, swimming pool, tennis.

¶¶ **Cambusa del Capitano.** Via Marina 65, tel. 276298. Closed Wednesday. Air conditioning. Sicilian cooking – seafood.

¶¶ **Holiday's Club.** Via dei Malavoglia 10, tel. 7116811. Closed Monday, part of August and November; open only in the evening. Air conditioning, parking, garden. Classic Italian and Sicilian cooking – seafood.

at Cannizzaro, km. 2
☒ 95020

★☆★ **Baia Verde.** Via A. Musco 8/10, tel. 491522, fax 494464. Number of rooms: 127. Accessible to the handicapped. Air conditioning, elevator; parking, parking garage, garden, swimming pool, tennis, private beach.

★☆★ **Sheraton Catania.** Via Antonello da Messi-

na 45, tel. 271557, fax 271380. Number rooms: 170. Accessible to the handicappe Air conditioning, elevator; special term for parking garage, garden, swimming poo tennis, private beach.

¶¶¶ **Alioto.** Via Mollica 24/26, tel. 494444, fa 492209. Closed Tuesday, August. Air co ditioning, parking. Sicilian cooking seafood.

¶¶ **Oleandro.** Via A. Musco 8/10, tel. 49152 Air conditioning, parking. Classic Italia and Sicilian cooking.

Museums and cultural institutions

Museo Civico. Castello Normanno, tel. 737150 Closed Monday. Open to the public: *winter, 9 and 3-5.*

Acireale
☒ 95024 ☏ 09

Plan, page 154

ℹ️ *Azienda Autonoma*, Corso Umberto 17 tel. 604521 (A2).

Hotels, restaurants, campsites, and vacation villages

★☆★ **Aloha d'Oro.** Via De Gasperi 10, tel. 60434 fax 606984. Number of rooms: 119. Air co ditioning; parking, garden, swimming poo tennis, private beach (D2-3, **c**).

★★★ **Orizzonte Acireale.** Via C. Colombo, te 886006, fax 7651607. Number of room 127. Accessible to the handicapped. El vator; parking, garden, swimming pool (A off map).

¶¶ **La Brocca d'u Cinc'oru.** Corso Savoia 49/ tel. 607196. Closed Sunday evening an Monday, mid-July-August. Air conditio ing. Sicilian cooking (B2, **m**).

Å★★ **Panorama.** Via Santa Caterina 55, te 7634124, fax 608708. Annual.

Capo Mulini, km. 4

* **La Perla Jonica.** Via Unni 10, tel. 877333, fax 877278. Number of rooms: 370. Accessible to the handicapped. Air conditioning, elevator; parking, garden, indoor and outdoor swimming pools, tennis, private beach.

Santa Maria Ammalati, km. 4 ⊠ 95020

Panoramico. Viale Jonio 12, tel. 885291. Closed Monday, for a period in November. Parking, garden. Sicilian cooking – seafood.

Santa Tecla, km. 4   ⊠ 95020

* **Santa Tecla Palace.** Via Balestrate 100, tel. 7634015, fax 607705. Number of rooms: 215. Air conditioning, elevator; parking, garden, swimming pool, tennis, private beach.

griturismo (real Italian country living)

zienda Agricola Il Limoneto. In Scillichenti; Via Amico 41. A farm with 4 hectares of fruit or-ards and olive groves. Guided tours, and tours farm. For information: Gabriella Raciti, tel. 6568, fax 7647788.

Giarre, km. 13.5   ⊠ 95010

zienda Agricola Codavolpe. In Trepunti; Stra-87 N°35. This is a fruit and vegetable farm of-ring accomodation in apartments inside the old rmstead. Guided tours. For information: Angelo uto, tel. 939802.

ot springs/Spas

rme Regionali di Acireale. Via delle Terme, l. 601250-601508. Hot springs, with therapeutic aths, muds, inhalations, and massages.

afes and pastry shops

storina. Corso Umberto I 63, Corso Savoia 9, tel. 601546-601547. Nougat, stuffed dates.

pillon. Corso Umberto I 130, tel. 606755. Home-ade almond pastries and nougat (torroncini).

starelli. Piazza Duomo, tel. 601864. Home-ade ice-cream.

Giarre, km. 13.5   ⊠ 95014

rimi. Via Gallipoli 166, tel. 931564. Specialty veets: torroncini and sweets made of almonds d hazelnuts.

olisano. Via E. Filiberto 27, Macchia di Giarre, l. 931019. Specialty: almond pastries.

useums and cultural institutions

blioteca and Pinacoteca Zelantea. Via March-e di S. Giuliano 15, tel. 604480. Open to the pub-:: *summer, Monday and Wednesday 9-12; winter, onday 9-12, Wednesday 4-7.*

ultural Events

rnevale di Acireale. One of the most beauti-l Sicilian carnivals with floral and allegorical ats. For information: tel. 895111.

Shops, crafts, and curiosities

Maria Chiarenza. Via Vittorio Emanuele 97, tel. 606805-601987. Craftsmen making Sicilian 'pupi,' or puppets.

at Giarre, km. 13.5

Giuseppe Cicala. Via L. Sturzo 59, tel. 930767. Craftsmen making Sicilian 'pupi,' or puppets. Along the same via there are shops of various local craftsmen, working in wood, iron, copper, and terracotta.

Agrigento   ⊠ 92100   ☎ 0922

Plan, pages 89 and 93

[i]   *AAPIT*, Viale della Vittoria 255, tel. 401352 (II, B3).
Azienda Autonoma, Via Empedocle 73, tel. 20391 (II, B3). Information Office, Via Battisti 15, tel. 20454 (II, B3).

Hotels, restaurants, campsites, and vacation villages

★★★ **Foresteria Baglio della Luna.** Contrada Maddalusa, tel. 511061, fax 598802. Number of rooms: 24. Air conditioning, elevator; parking, garden, private beach (J, C1, **b**).

★★★ **Kaos.** Villaggio Pirandello, tel. 598622, fax 598770. Number of rooms: 105. Accessible to the handicapped. Elevator, air conditioning, parking, garden, swimming pool, tennis (I, C1, **a**).

★★★ **Colleverde Park Hotel.** Strada Panoramica dei Templi, tel. 29555, fax 29012. Number of rooms: 48. Accessible to the handicapped. Air conditioning, elevator; parking, garden (I, B3, **e**).

¶ **Black Horse.** Via Celauro 8, tel. 23223. Closed Sunday. Air conditioning. Sicilian cooking – seafood (II, B3, **x**).

¶ **Le Caprice.** Strada Panoramica dei Templi 51, tel. 26469. Closed Friday, for a period in July. Air conditioning, parking. The cooking of Agrigento – seafood (I, B3, **u**).

at Villaggio Mosè, km. 8

★★★ **Jolly dei Templi.** Parco Angeli, tel. 606144, fax 606685. Number of rooms: 146. Accessible to the handicapped. Air conditioning, elevator; parking, garden, swimming pool.

★★★ **Tre Torri.** Contrada Fegotto, tel. 606733, fax 607839. Number of rooms: 118. Air conditioning, elevator; parking, indoor and outdoor swimming pools.

at San Leone, km. 7

¶¶ **Pescatore.** Via Lungomare Borsellino Falcone 20, tel. 414342. Closed Wednesday (except in summer), mid-November/mid-January. Air conditioning. The cooking of Agrigento – seafood.

△★★★ **Internazionale San Leone.** Contrada Dune, tel. and fax 416121. Annual.

Cafes and pastry shops

Pasticceria La Promenade. Via Panoramica dei Templi 8, tel. 23715. Almond specialities.

Bar Sajeva. Viale della Vittoria 61/65, tel. 20671. Dry pastries, plumcake, "panettoni."

Bar Pasticceria La Galleria. Via Atenea 123, tel. 26091. Crepes, ice cream, and tea room.

Museums and cultural institutions

Area Archeologica. Open to the public: *9 pm.*

Museo Civico. Piazza Pirandello 16, tel. 20722. Closed for restoration. Ethno-anthropological section: Monastero di S. Spirito. Closed Sunday. Open to the public: *summer, 9-2, Tuesday and Thursday also 3:30-6:30; winter, 9-1, Tuesday and Thursday also 3:30-6:30.*

Museo Diocesano. c/o Cattedrale, tel. 401352. Closed for restoration.

Museo archeologico regionale. Contrada San Nicola, tel. 401565. Open to the public: *Monday, Tuesday, Sunday, 9-1:30; all other days 9-1:30 and 2:30-5:30.*

Quartiere ellenistico-romano. Open to the public: *9-one hour before sunset.*

at Villaseta, Contrada Caos, km. 5.6

Casa Pirandello. Tel. 511102. Open to the public: *9-one hour before sunset; Saturday and Sunday 9-1.*

Cultural Events

Festa di S. Calogero. An entire week of festivities, from the 1st-2nd Sunday of July. For information: tel. 20391.

Shops, crafts, and curiosities

Zambuto Salvatore. Via Saponara 8, tel. 23924. Creations made of cork.

Convento di Santo Spirito. Via Santo Spirito. The nuns here, in various seasons, prepare an excellent pistachio cous-cous with candied fruit and chocolate, Paschal lambs made of "pasta reale" with a core of pistachio, "buccellati" with sweet dough and figs, and "minni di vergine".

Musicò. Lungomare di San Leone and Viale della Vittoria. "Panni con panelle."

Aidone ✉ 94010 ☎ 0935

Page 198

ℹ️ *Pro Loco,* Via Mazzini 1, tel. 86557.

Hotels, restaurants, campsites, and vacation villages

★★ **Morgantina.** Via Adelasia 42, tel. 88088, fax 87941. Number of rooms: 18. Covered parking.

Museums and cultural institutions

Museo Archeologico Regionale. Largo Torres Trupia, tel. 87307. Open to the public: *9-1; 3-7.*

at Morgantina, km. 3

Archeological digs. Open to the public: *9-1 a 3-1 hour before sunset.*

Àlcamo ✉ 91011 ☎ 09

Plan, page 84

ℹ️ *Pro Loco,* Via Vittorio Veneto 3, tel. 264⸱

Hotels, restaurants, campsites, and vacation villages

at Àlcamo Marina, km. 7

★★ **La Battigia.** Via Lungomare 503, tel. 5972⸱ fax 598432. Number of rooms: 14. Parkir

Hot springs/Spas

in the township of Calatafimi, km. 6

✉ 910

Terme Gorga. Tel. 23842. Hot springs, with the apeutic baths, muds, inhalations, and massage

Cafes and pastry shops

Pasticceria San Gaetano. Via S. Gaetano 16, t⸱ 21942. Home-made pastries, ice-creams and d⸱ icatessen.

Sports

Circolo Tennis Concordia. Contrada Tem Rossi, tel. 26066.

Aragona ✉ 92021 ☎ 09⸱

Plan, page 94

Natural areas, parks and reserves

Riserva naturale integrale Macalube. Unspo nature reserve. Organisor: Lega Ambiente, V Salvatore La Rosà 53, tel. 699210.

Augusta ✉ 96011 ☎ 09⸱

Hotels, restaurants, campsites, and vacation villages

at Faro Santa Croce, km. 6

🍽️ **Donna Ina.** Tel. 983422. Closed Monday, f⸱ a period in January. Air conditioning. ⸱ cilian cooking – seafood.

at Monte Tàuro, km. 6

★★ **Europa Club.** Località Acquasanta, te 983080, fax 978696. Seasonal. Number ⸱ rooms: 35. Parking, garden, tennis.

★★ **Villa dei Cesari.** Tel. 983311, fax 98309 Number of rooms: 24. Air conditionin⸱ parking, garden.

⚓☆ **A' Massaria.** Scogliera Acquasanta, tel. 983078, fax 978696. Seasonal.

at Brùcoli, km. 7   ✉ 96010

⚓☆ **Baia del Silenzio.** Località Campolato, tel. 981881, fax 981881. Annual.

Cafes and pastry shops

Bar Pasticceria Nuovo Alberobello. Via Umberto I 146, tel. 978295; Piazza Castello 1, tel. 522966; Via Libertà Baucoli 28, tel. 981359. "Buccellati," almond pastries, and a great variety of pizzas, arancini," "bombe" with cheese and prosciutto, cipolline," and "scacciate".

Pasticceria Lo Giudice. Via Umberto I 286, tel. 977808. "Pasta reale" in lovely little wooden crates.

Curobar. Via Principe Umberto 256, tel. 975652. In summer, the breakfast of kings: almond "grania," espresso and cream, with a brioche.

at Melilli, km. 15.5   ✉ 96050

Pasticceria Scamporrino. Via Dante Alighieri 7, tel. 951262. You should try the "cucciddrato," a pastry filled with dried figs, walnuts, candied fruit, and almonds.

Museums and cultural institutions

Antiquarium of Megara Hyblaea. Archeological zone, tel. 512364. Closed for restoration.

Archeological digs of Megara Hyblaea. Tel. 512364. Open to the public: *9-one hour before sunset.*

Bagherìa   ✉ 90011 ☎ 091

Page 52

ℹ️ Municipio, Corso Umberto I 1, tel. 943111.

Hotels, restaurants, campsites, and vacation villages

★★ **Zabara Park Hotel.** State road 113 at km. 246, tel. 902333, fax 903104. Number of rooms: 66. Accessible to the handicapped. Air conditioning, elevator; parking, garden, swimming pool, tennis.

Cafes and pastry shops

Gelateria Anni 20. Via Mattarella 13, tel. 902140. Fruit "gelati" in the most exotic flavors. Excellent lemon, orange, nectarine, cantaloupe sherbets, and frozen cakes.

Museums and cultural institutions

Galleria Comunale d'Arte Moderna e Contemporanea. Villa Cattolica, State road 113, tel. 905438. Open to the public: *10-6.*

Shops, crafts, and curiosities

at Casteldaccia, km. 6   ✉ 90014

Casa Vinicola Duca di Salaparuta. State road Nazionale, tel. 945111.

Barcellona Pozzo di Gotto

✉ 98051 ☎ 090

ℹ️ *Ufficio informazioni turistiche,* c/o Municipio, tel. 97901.

Hotels, restaurants, campsites, and vacation villages

⚓☆ **Centro Vacanze Cantoni.** Località Cantoni, tel. 9710165. Seasonal.

at Castroreale Terme, km. 6   ✉ 98050

★★★ **Gabbiano.** Località Marchesana, lungomare marchesana 4, tel. 9782343, fax 9781385. Seasonal. Number of rooms: 39 (36 with bath or shower). Access for disabled. Air conditioning, elevator; parking, garden, private beach.

Hostels

at Castroreale, km. 9   ✉ 98053

🏠 **Ostello delle Aquile.** Youth hostel. Salita Federico II d'Aragona, tel. 9746398. Open: *April-October.*

Hot springs/Spas

at Castroreale Terme, km. 6

Terme Fonte di Venere. Tel. 9781078-9781079. Hot springs, with therapeutic baths, beverages, muds, inhalations, and massages.

Cafes and pastry shops

Bar Pasticceria Munafò. Via Roma 240, tel. 9798114. Beginning in the spring, you can have fruit "granite," ice cream, and frozen cakes here.

Bronte   ✉ 95034 ☎ 095

Page 158

ℹ️ *Pro Loco,* Corso Umberto I 226.

Hotels, restaurants, campsites, and vacation villages

★★ **Parco dell'Etna.** Contrada Borgonovo, tel. 691907, fax 691907. Number of rooms: 14. Accessible to the handicapped. Air conditioning; parking, garden, swimming pool.

Cafes and pastry shops

Conti Gallenti. Corso Umberto I 247, tel. 691165. Specialty: pistachio pastries.

Museums and cultural institutions

Masseria Lombardo. Museo dell'antica civiltà locale. Contrada Cuntarati, tel. 691635. Visits only by appointment: 9-1; closed Sunday and public holidays.

at Maniace, km. 18

Castello Nelson. Tel. 690018. Open to the public:

9-sunset. The duke's apartment is being restored.

at Adrano, km. 14

Museo Archeologico and Museo dell'Artigianato. Castello Normanno, Piazza Umberto I, tel. 7692660. Closed Monday. Open to the public: *9:30-1:30; Sunday 9-12:30.*

Caltagirone   ✉ 95041 ☎ 0933

Plan, page 116

i   *Azienda autonoma*, Via Volta Libertini 3, tel. 53809.

Hotels, restaurants, campsites, and vacation villages

★★★ **Villa San Mauro.** Via Porto Salvo 14, tel. 26500, fax 31661. Number of rooms: 92. Accessible to the handicapped. Air conditioning, elevator; parking, special terms for parking garage, swimming pool (D1, **a**).

⍟ **San Giorgio.** Via Regina Elena 15, tel. 55228. Closed Tuesday, for a period in September. Air conditioning. Sicilian cooking (A1-2, **r**).

Agriturismo (real Italian country living)

Azienda Agricola La Casa degli Angeli. Contrada Angeli. This is a hillside working farm, with citrus grove, olive grove, and vegetable garden; accommodations, some with heating and bath. For information: Crispino and Ines Testa, tel. 25317/095-442025.

Museums and cultural institutions

Museo Civico and Pinacoteca Sturzo. Via Roma 10, tel. 41315. Closed Monday. Open to the public: *9:30-1:30; Tuesday, Friday, Saturday 9:30-1:30 and 4-7.*

Museo Regionale della Ceramica. Via Roma, tel. 21680. Open to the public: *9-6:30.*

Mostra dei Pupi Siciliani. Exhibition of Sicilian, puppets. Ex Teatro Stabile dell'Opera dei Pupi, Via Roma 65, tel. 54085 (Coop. Eliotour). Closed Sunday. Open: *10-1 and 3:30-7.*

Caltanissetta   ✉ 93100 ☎ 0934

Plan, page 203

i   *AAPIT*, Corso Vittorio Emanuele 109, tel. 29532 (B2).

Hotels, restaurants, campsites, and vacation villages

★★★ **San Michele.** Via Fasci Siciliani, tel. 553750, fax 598791. Number of rooms: 136. Accessible to the handicapped. Air conditioning, elevator; parking, garden, swimming pool (A1, *off map*).

★★★ **Plaza.** Via B. Gaetani 5, tel. 583877, fax 583877. Number of rooms: 21. Rooms only.

Accessible to the handicapped. Air conditioning, elevator; parking garage (B2, **a**).

⍟ **Cortese.** Viale Sicilia 166, tel. 591686. Closed Monday, for a period in August. Air conditioning. Sicilian cooking – seafood and mushrooms (B1, *off map*).

Cafes and pastry shops

Bar pasticceria Fiorino. Via E. Vassallo 67, tel. 583109. Excellent bignets with cream filling, coffee, "gianduia," and chocolate, with glaze.

Laboratorio Pasticceria Cordaro e Toscano. Via dei Mille 42, tel. 22615. Open only Sunday. Authentic pastry shop; reasonable prices.

Caffè Pasticceria Rair. Corso Umberto 163, tel. 21402. "Cannoli" and "cannolicchi alla ricotta," dusted with cinnamon, with ground hazelnut and almonds.

Museums and cultural institutions

Museo Archeologico. Via Colajanni 3, tel. 25936. Closed Sunday. Open to the public: *9-1 and 3-7.*

Museo Mineralogico. Viale della Regione 73, tel. 591280. Closed Sunday. Open to the public: *10-1.*

Cultural Events

Settimana Santa. Holy week. From Palm Sunday to Easter Sunday, processions and religious events. For information: 167-019699.

Campofelice di Roccella   ✉ 90010 ☎ 092

Hotels, restaurants, campsites, and vacation villages

★★★ **Plaia d'Himera Park Hotel.** Contrada Pistavecchia, tel. 933815, fax 933843. Seasonal. Number of rooms: 139. Accessible to the disabled. Air conditioning, elevator; parking, garden, swimming pool, tennis, private beach.

★★★ **Le Roi Soleil.** State road 113 at 203.8 km, tel. and fax 933822. Seasonal.

Canicattì   ✉ 92024 ☎ 0922

Hotels, restaurants, campsites, and vacation villages

★★★ **Collina al Faro.** Via Puccini 29, tel. 853062, fax 851160. Number of rooms: 28. Accessible to the handicapped. Parking.

Cafes and pastry shops

Pasticceria Carusotto. Via Garilli 17, tel. 857997. "Babas," "pasticciotti alla conserva," and almond sweets.

Pasticceria Mantione. Via Cavour 154, tel. 851429. "Amaretti," "sospiri," and "torroncini," including orange-flavored ones.

Shops, crafts, and curiosities

Turco Salvatore. Via Vittorio Emanuele 232, tel. 859646. Lamps and objects made of wrought iron.

Capo d'Orlando   ✉ 98071 ☎ 0941

Page 192

ℹ️ *Azienda Autonoma*, Via Piave 67, tel. 912784, 912517.

Hotels, restaurants, campsites, and vacation villages

★★★ **Il Mulino.** Via A. Doria 46, tel. 902431, fax 911614. Number of rooms: 34. Accessible to the handicapped. Air conditioning, elevator; parking.

★★★ **La Meridiana.** Località Piana, tel. 957713. Number of rooms: 45. Access for the disabled. Air conditioning, elevator; parking, garden, swimming pool.

★★★ **La Tartaruga.** Località Lido San Gregorio, tel. 955012, fax 955056. Number of rooms: 38. Air conditioning, elevator; parking, swimming pool.

❝❞ **La Tartaruga.** Località Lido San Gregorio, tel. 955012, fax 955056. Air conditioning, parking. Classic Italian cooking and the cooking of Messina – seafood.

★★★ **Santarosa.** Località Tavola Grande, Via Trazzera Marina, tel. 901723, fax 912384. Seasonal.

at Fiumara di Naso, km. 10   ✉ 98074

❝❞ **Bontempo.** Tel. 961188. Closed Monday. Air conditioning, parking, garden. The cooking of Messina.

Agriturismo (real Italian country living)

at San Gregorio, km. 2

Azienda Agricola Milio. This working farm has 150 hectares of olive trees and fruit orchards, just 500 m. from the sea. It offers horseback riding, with rides in the Parco dei Nebrodi. Bicycling and fishing. For information: Gaetano and Luciano Milio, tel. 955008.

Museums and cultural institutions

at San Salvatore di Fitàlia, km. 24

Museo Siciliano delle Tradizioni Religiose. Via Umberto, tel. 486027. Closed Monday. Open to the public: *10-1*.

Shops, crafts, and curiosities

at San Gregorio, km. 2

The fishermen prepare the fish "vivo vivo," i.e., freshly caught, for connoisseurs; contact them directly on their fishing boats or by knocking on the door of the handsome little houses along the road. For information: Mr. Carlos Vinci, tel. 955157.

Carini   ✉ 90044 ☎ 091

Page 48

ℹ️ Municipio, Corso Umberto I, tel. 8661102.

Hotels, restaurants, campsites, and vacation villages

at Villa Grazia di Carini, km. 6   ✉ 90040

★★★ **Portorais.** Via Piraineto 125, tel. 8693481, fax 8693458. Number of rooms: 44. Air conditioning; parking, garden, tennis, private beach.

★★★ **Residence Hotel Azzolini.** State road 113 at km. 286.600, tel. 8674755, fax 8675747. Number of rooms: 69. Air conditioning, elevator; parking, garden, swimming pool, tennis, private beach.

Agriturismo (real Italian country living)

at Montelepre, km. 11   ✉ 90040

Don Vito - La Fattoria del Sorriso. Località Piano Aranci. Rooms with bath, or else you may camp in a handsome olive grove; there are horses, and riding is available. For information: Salvatore Calafiore, tel. 8784111.

Carlentini   ✉ 96013 ☎ 095

Page 141

ℹ️ *Pro Loco*, Via Marconi 23, tel. 991108.

Agriturismo (real Italian country living)

Azienda Agricola Terias. Contrada Corridore del Pero. Independent rooms in renovated farmhouses, in an estate of 35 hectares, with a citrus grove, a vegetable patch, and other crops, along the river S. Leonardo and the sea. Bocce ball, bicycling, ping-pong. For information: Francesco Cirelli, tel. 381301-997212.

Tenuta di Roccadia. Contrada Roccadia. Accommodations in independent rooms, on a farm growing citrus, olives, and almond trees; swimming pool, horseback riding; guided excursions. For information: Piero Vacirca, tel. 990362.

Castelbuono   ✉ 90013 ☎ 0921

ℹ️ *Pro Loco*, Corso Umberto I 69, tel. 673467.

Hotels, restaurants, campsites, and vacation villages

❝❞ **Vecchio Palmento.** Via Failla 4, tel. 672099. Closed Monday, part of September. Garden. Sicilian cooking.

at San Guglielmo, km. 5

❝❞ **Romitaggio.** Tel. 671323. Closed Wednesday, mid-June/mid-July. Parking. Sicilian cooking.

Castellammare del Golfo

✉ 91014 ☎ 0924

Page 85

ℹ️ *Ufficio Turistico Comunale*, Via De Gasperi 6, tel. 30217.

Hotels, restaurants, campsites, and vacation villages

★★★ **Al Madarig.** Piazza Petrolo 7, tel. 33533, fax 33790. Number of rooms: 33. Accessible to the handicapped. Air conditioning, elevator; parking garage.

▲★★★ **Nausicaa.** Località Forgia, tel. 33030, fax 35173. Seasonal.

at Scopello, km. 10
✉ 91010

🍴 **Torre Bennistra.** Via Natale di Roma 19, tel. 541128. The cooking of Trapani – seafood.

▲★★★ **Baia di Guidaloca.** Contrada Guidaloca, tel. 541262. Seasonal.

▲★★ **Lu Baruni.** Contrada Barone 16, tel. 39133. Seasonal.

Agriturismo (real Italian country living)

Azienda Agricola Camillo Finazzo. Località Baida Molinazzo. Accommodations on a small farm with livestock and olive groves and vineyards. For information: tel. 38051.

Azienda Agricola Marmora. Contrada Marmora. Accommodations on a small farm, with olive groves, cattle, sheep, poultry, and horses, some 800 meters from the sea at Scopello. Horseback riding with an instructor, tours of the farming activities: fishing, and swimming pool. For information: Francesco Paolo Fontana, tel. 39254.

Cultural Events

Festa di Maria SS. del Soccorso. Folkloristic shows and famous nocturnal sea procession. From 19-21st August. For information: 592111.

Hot springs/Spas

at Terme Segestane, km. 8

Terme Segestane. Località Ponte Bagni, tel. 530057. Hot springs, with therapeutic baths, in natural and manmade pools, grottoes, muds, inhalations, and massages.

Sports

Circolo Tennis La Ferula. Contrada Bocca della Carruba, tel. 33913/30941.

Centro Nautico Eolo. Contrada Cerri, tel. 30041.

Catania

✉ 95100 ☎ 095

Plan, page 148

ℹ️ *AAPIT*, Largo Paisiello 5, tel. 7306222 (C3).
Azienda Autonoma, Corso Italia 302 (temporary premises), tel. 373084.

Uffici informazioni: aeroporto, tel. 730626(Stazione centrale, tel. 7306255 (C5).

Hotels, restaurants, campsites, and vacation villages

★★★ **Central Palace.** Via Etnea 218, tel. 32534 fax 7158939. Number of rooms: 107. A conditioning, elevator; parking garage (C c).

★★★ **Excelsior.** Piazza Verga 39, tel. 537071, fa 537015. Number of rooms: 163. Accessible t the handicapped. Air conditioning, elevato special terms for parking garage (B4, **a**).

★★★ **Jolly Trinacria.** Piazza Trento 13, te 316933, fax 316832. Number of rooms: 15 Air conditioning, elevator; parking (B3, **b**

★★★ **Forte Agip.** Via Messina 628, tel. 712230(fax 7121856. Number of rooms: 56. Room only; no dining facilities. Elevator; parkin (A6, *off map*).

★★★ **Nettuno.** Viale Ruggero di Lauria 121, te 7125252, fax 498066. Number of rooms: 8(Accessible to the handicapped. Air condi tioning, elevator; parking, garden, swim ming pool (A6, *off map*).

🍴🍴🍴 **Costa Azzurra.** Via De Cristofaro 2, te 497889, fax 494920. Closed Monday. Park ing. Classic Italian and Sicilian cooking - seafood (A6, *off map*).

🍴🍴🍴 **Siciliana.** Viale Marco Polo 52/A, tel. 37640(fax 7221300. Closed evenings on Sunda and evenings on holidays, part of August Garden. Sicilian cooking (A5, *off map*).

🍴🍴 **Lampara.** Via Pasubio 49, tel. 383237 Closed Wednesday, August. Air condition ing. Classic Italian and Sicilian cooking - seafood (A5, **p**).

🍴🍴 **Pagano.** Via De Roberto 37, tel. 537045 Closed Saturday at midday, August. Ai conditioning. The cooking of Catania (B4, **u**

🍴🍴 **Poggio Ducale-da Nino.** Via Paolo Gaifam 5, tel. 330016. Closed Sunday evening anc Monday at midday, for a period in August Air conditioning, parking. Refined Siciliar cooking – seafood (A4, *off map*).

▲★★ **Jonio.** Località Ognina, Via Villini a Mare 2 tel. 491139, fax 492277. Annual.

Agriturismo (real Italian country living)

Azienda Agricola Molinari. Via San Giuseppe L: Rena, Fondo 23. Accommodations in a farm house amidst the greenery, at a distance of 5 km from the city; you can camp, do archery, play bowls, horse ride, or rent bicycles. For infor mation: Enrico Molinari, tel. 592521.

at Misterbianco, km. 8
✉ 9504 5

Azienda Agricola Alcalà. Località Terrebianche Via Muscatello 11. Accommodations on a farm with a botanical garden, on the slopes of Moun Etna. Mountain streams of natural interest. Fo information: Anna Sapuppo, tel. 7130029.

Cafes and pastry shops

...via. Via Etnea 302, tel. 322335. Home-made almond pastries, cassata and pinoli.

...aprice. Via Etnea 30, tel. 320555. Torroncini ...ugat, cassata, ice-cream; and restaurant.

...antegna. Via Etnea 350, tel. 311918. A century-...d shop sign.

...rivitera. Piazza S. Maria del Gesù 1-2, tel. ...5403. Home-made pastries.

...uovo Caffè Italia. Corso Italia 247, tel. 388807.

. Moritz. Viale R. Sanzio 4-12, tel. 437282; e via ...nea 198, tel. 320936. Home-made pastries and ...e-cream.

...hioschi. Piazza Vittorio Emanuele (known as ...e "Piazza Umberto"). Non-alcoholic bever-...ges, orange, lemon, and nectarine flavored.

Museums and cultural institutions

...arcere romano. Church of S. Agata al carcere. ...pen to the public: *Thursday and Saturday 4-7; ...unday 9:30-12.*

...asa di Giovanni Verga. Via S. Anna 8, tel. ...50598. Closed Sunday. Open to the public: *9-1; ...onday, Tuesday, Thursday and Friday also 3-6:30.*

...useo Belliniano. Piazza S. Francesco 3, tel. ...150535. Open to the public: *weekdays 9-1:30, ...uesday and Thursday also 3-6, holidays 9-12:30.*

...useo Comunale. Castello Ursino, Piazza Fe-...erico di Svevia, tel. 345830. Open to the public: ...-1, Tuesday, Wednesday and Thursday also 3-6.

...usei di Paleontologia, Zoologia, Geologia, ...ineralogia e Vulcanologia. Corso Italia 55, tel. ...195764 and 312355. Open to the public: *9-1 (on-...- weekdays by appointment).*

...rto Botanico. Via A. Longo 19, tel. 430901. ...losed Sunday. Open to the public: *9-1.*

...useo di Zoologia. Via Androne 81, tel. 312355. ...losed Saturday and Sunday. Open to the public: ...y appointment.

...eatro Romano. Via Vittorio Emanuele 266. ...pen to the public: *9-one hour before sunset.*

Excursions and organized tours

...ightseeing tour of Catania. A complete tour of ...he city in one hour. AMT: 167-018696.

...xcursion to Etna. Bus service from the Central Sta-...on to the Sapienza Refuge. AST: 347330/7461096.

Sports

...iscina Poseidon. Via G. Deledda 15, tel. 552883.

...iscina Altair. Via F. Riso 11-19, tel. 437487.

...iscina Paguros. Via Nizeti, tel. 498785.

...ennis Club Il Tavoliere. Via Passo Gravina ...53, tel. 336427.

...ennis Club Gierre. Via Nizeti, tel. 491160.

...ennis Club Umberto. Via Monsignor Orlando 6, ...el. 497191/7126080.

...entro Equitazione La Plaia. Viale Kennedy 52, ...el. 281826.

Società Catanese Equitazione. Via Boschetto Plaia, tel. 395678.

Theater and music

Teatro Lirico Bellini. Via Perrotta 12, tel. 312020. Opera and concert season; in September, Festival of Bellini.

Teatro G. Verga. Via dello Stadio 35, tel 363545. Season of theater, at the Teatro Stabile di Catania.

Metropolitan. Via S. Eupilio, tel. 322323.

Teatro A. Musco. Via Umberto I 312, tel. 535514.

Shops, crafts, and curiosities

Ferraro. Via Monserrato 86, tel. 438039. Furniture, furnishings, and objects in wicker and bamboo.

Il Sigillo. Via Asilo S. Agata 18, tel. 537817. Stringed instruments, guitars, and musical instruments played with a bow – made by a master craftsman.

Terra e Fuoco. Viale Africa 31 (int. 5), tel. 533347. Terracotta and artistic ceramics.

Cefalù   ✉ 90015 ☎ 0921

Plan, page 183

ℹ️ *Azienda Autonoma*, Via Amendola 2, tel. 421050 (B2).

Hotels, restaurants, campsites, and vacation villages

★★★ **Kalura.** A Caldura, Via V. Cavallaro 13, tel. 421354, fax 423122. Number of rooms: 75. Air conditioning, elevator; parking, garden, swimming pool, tennis, private beach (D3, *off map*).

★★★ **Le Calette.** at Caldura, Via V. Cavallaro 12, tel. 24144, fax 423688. Seasonal. Number of rooms: 50. Air conditioning; parking, garden, swimming pool, private beach (D3, *off map*).

🍴 **Gabbiano-Da Saro.** Lungomare Giardina 17, tel. 21495. Closed Wednesday (except in summer), Christmas. Garden. Classic Italian and Sicilian cooking – seafood (B1, r).

🍴 **La Brace.** Via XXV Novembre 10, tel. 423570. Closed Monday, mid-December/mid-January. Air conditioning. Sicilian cooking (B1, **u**).

🍴 **Osteria del Duomo.** Via Seminario 5, tel. 421838. Closed Monday, for a period in December. Sicilian cooking (A-B2, **ab**).

⚠️★★★ **Costa Ponente.** Contrada Ogliastrillo, State road 113 at km. 190.3, tel. 420085, fax 23122. Seasonal.

⚠️★★ **Sanfilippo.** Contrada Ogliastrillo, State road 113 at km. 190.3, tel. 20184. Seasonal.

at Capo Plàia, km. 8

★★★ **Carlton Hotel Riviera.** Tel. 420200, fax 420264. Seasonal. Number of rooms: 144. Air conditioning, elevator; parking, garden, swimming pool, tennis, private beach.

at Mazzaforno, km. 5

★★★ **Baia del Capitano.** Tel. 420005, fax 420163. Number of rooms: 39. Accessible to the handicapped. Air conditioning, elevator; parking, garden, swimming pool, tennis, private beach.

at Sant'Ambrogio, km. 7   ✉ 90010

🏕 **Plaja degli Uccelli.** State road 113 at km.
★★ 180.4, tel. 999068, fax 999068. Seasonal.

Museums and cultural institutions

Museo Mandralisca. Via Mandralisca 13, tel. 421547. Open to the public: *summer, 9-12:30 and 3:30-7; winter, 9:30-12:30 and 3:30-6.*

Cesaro   ✉ 98033 ☎ 095

Page 190

Agriturismo (real Italian country living)
Azienda Agricola Destro Pastizzaro Sergio. Contrada Scalonazzo. Country holiday with organized hikes. For information: tel. 697331.

Chiaramonte Gulfi   ✉ 97012 ☎ 0932

Page 114

Hotels, restaurants, campsites, and vacation villages

🍴 **Majore.** Via Martiri Ungheresi 12, tel. 928019. Closed Monday, July. Air conditioning. Sicilian cooking.

Còmiso   ✉ 97013 ☎ 0932

Page 113

ℹ️ *Pro Loco*, Via Di Vita 6, tel. 961586.

Hotels, restaurants, campsites, and vacation villages

★★★ **Cordial.** State road 115, Contrada Deserto, tel. and fax 967866. Number of rooms: 37. Rooms only; no dining facilities. Accessible to the handicapped. Air conditioning, elevator; parking, tennis.

Corleone   ✉ 90034 ☎ 091

Page 56

ℹ️ Municipio, Piazza Garibaldi, tel. 8461151.

Cafes and pastry shops
Bentivegna. Piazza Vittorio Emanuele 1, tel. 8464633. Specialties: "cannoli" and ricotta-based sweets.

at Bisaquino, km. 21.7

Pasticceria Caronna. Piazza Triona. Specialties: "cannoli" and typical Sicilian sweets and pastries.

Museums and cultural institutions

at Bisaquino, km. 21.7

Museo dell'Artigianato Locale, Antico e M derno. Via Orsini, tel. 8351111. Open to the pu lic: *9-1 every day, only by appointment.*

Theater and music
Teatro Martorana. Via Caduti in Guerra. Perf mances of local theater.

Ègadi (Isole, or islands of)   ☎ 09.

Map, page 69

ℹ️ *Pro Loco* at Favignana, Piazza Matrice 8, t 921647.

Hotels, restaurants, campsites, and vacation villages

at Favignana   ✉ 910.

★★★ **L'Approdo di Ulisse.** Località Calagrand tel. 922525, fax 921511. Seasonal. Number rooms: 126. Parking, garden, swimmir pool, tennis, private beach.

★★ **Egadi.** Via Colombo 17, tel. 921232, f 921232. Seasonal. Number of rooms: 1 Accessible to the handicapped. Air con tioning.

🍴 **Sorelle Guccione.** Via Colombo 17, te 921232. Seasonal, closed at midday. Sicili cooking – seafood.

🏕 **Miramare.** Contrada Costicella, tel. 92133
★★★ fax 922200. Seasonal.

🏕 **Egad.** Contrada Arena, tel. 921555, f
★★★ 539370. Seasonal.

Museums and cultural institutions

Aree Archeologiche. Not always open; always r serve in advance with the professional touris guide, Vitalba Patti, tel. 921411; *Pro Loco* te 921647.

Tonnare. Not always open; for information, co sult the guide Vitalba Patti, tel. 921411; *Pro Loc* tel. 921647.

at Lèvanzo   ✉ 9101

★★ **Pensione dei Fenici.** Via Lungomare, te 924083. Number of rooms: 10. Air cond tioning.

Enna   ✉ 94100 ☎ 093.

Plan, page 194

ℹ️ *AAPIT*, Via Roma 411/413, tel. 528228 (A2)
Azienda Autonoma, Piazza Colajanni 6, te 26119/500875 (A2).

Hotels, restaurants, campsites, and vacation villages

★★★ **G.A. Sicilia.** Piazza Colaianni 7, tel. 50085(

fax 500488. Number of rooms: 76. Rooms only; no dining facilities. Accessible to the handicapped. Elevator; parking garage, garden (A2, **b**).

Ariston. Via Roma 365, tel. 26038. Closed Sunday, for a period in August. Sicilian cooking (A2, **s**).

Centrale. Piazza VI Dicembre 9, tel. 500963. Closed Saturday (except in high season). Classic Italian and Sicilian cooking (A2, **r**).

⚑ Pergusa, km. 10 ✉ 94010

★ **La Giara Park Hotel.** Via Nazionale 125, tel. 541687, fax 541521. Number of rooms: 20. Air conditioning; parking, garden, swimming pool.

★ **Riviera.** Via Autodromo di Pergusa, tel. 541267, fax 541260. Number of rooms: 26. Air conditioning; parking, garden, swimming pool.

afes and pastry shops

asticceria Il Dolce. Piazza Sant'Agostino 40, l. 24018. Excellent "cannoli," "sfogliatine alla cotta," and almond cookies.

ar Pasticceria Caprice. Via Firenze 17, tel. 25281. uit ice creams, cakes, and ricotta "cassatelle."

asticceria Rugolo. Via Roma 425, tel. 25769. es, "cassate," sweet "buccellati," black and hite "taralli," and "cicche" stuffed with dried uit and must.

luseums and cultural institutions

useo Alessi. Via Roma, tel. 503165. Closed onday. Open to the public: *9-1 and 4-7*.

useo Archeologico Regionale. Piazza Mazzini tel. 518200. Open to the public: *9-1 and 3-6:30*.

astello di Lombardia. Tel. 500962. Open to the ublic: *9-1 and 3-5*.

hops, crafts, and curiosities

ornasier Giuseppe. Via Michelangelo, Enna assa, tel. 29425. This craftsman makes stained-ass and also creates embossed painted mo-aics.

---

olie (Isole, or Aeolian islands) ☎ 090

ap, page 176

t Lìpari ✉ 98055

🛈 *Azienda Autonoma*, Corso Vittorio Emanuele 202, tel. 9880095 (A1).

lotels, restaurants, campsites, and acation villages

t Lìpari

★★ **Villa Meligunis.** Via Marte 7, tel. 9812426, fax 9880149. Number of rooms: 37. Acces-

sible to the handicapped. Air conditioning, elevator; garden, private beach (D2, *off map*).

★★★ **Carasco.** Località Porto delle Genti, tel. 9811605, fax 9811828. Seasonal. Number of rooms: 89. Elevator; parking, garden, swimming pool (D2, *off map*).

★★★ **Gattopardo Park Hotel.** Via Diana, tel. 9811035, fax 9880207. Number of rooms: 75. Garden (C1, **d**).

¶¶¶ **Filippino.** Piazza Municipio, tel. 9811002, fax 9812878. Closed Monday in the low season, mid-November/mid-December. Air conditioning, garden. The cooking of the Aeolian islands – seafood (B2, **r**).

¶¶ **E Pulera.** Via Diana, tel. 9811158. Seasonal. Closed at midday. Garden. The cooking of the Aeolian islands – seafood (C1, **c**).

⛺ **Baia Unci.** Località Canneto, Via Marina Garibaldi, tel. 9811909, fax 9811715. Seasonal.

Hostels

🏠 **Lipari.** Ostello per la Gioventù (youth hostel). Via Castello 17, tel. 9811540. Posti letto 120. Open: *March-October*.

at Panarea ✉ 98055

★★★ **Cincotta.** Contrada S. Pietro, tel. 983014, fax 983211. Seasonal. Number of rooms: 29. Accessible to the handicapped. Air conditioning; garden, swimming pool.

★★★ **La Piazza.** Via S. Pietro, tel. 983176, fax 983003. Seasonal. Number of rooms: 25. Rooms only; no dining facilities. Accessible to the handicapped. Garden; swimming pool.

at Malfa, on the island, or Isola Salina ✉ 98050

★★★ **Signum.** Via Scalo 15, tel. 9844222, fax 9844102. Number of rooms: 16. Garden.

★★ **Punta Scario.** Località Scario, tel. 9844139, fax 9844077. Seasonal. Number of rooms: 17.

at Santa Marina Salina ✉ 98050

¶ **Portobello.** Via Bianchi 1, tel. 9843125. Closed Wednesday in winter, November. The cooking of the Aeolian islands – seafood.

at Strómboli ✉ 98050

★★★ **La Sciara Residence.** Località Piscità, Via Barnao 5, tel. 986004, fax 986284. Seasonal. Number of rooms: 62. Accessible to the handicapped. Garden; swimming pool, tennis.

★★★ **La Sirenetta.** Località Ficogrande, Via Marina 33, tel. 986025, fax 986124. Seasonal. Number of rooms: 43. Air conditioning; garden, swimming pool.

¶ **Zurro.** Via Picone 18, tel. 986283. Seasonal. The cooking of the Aeolian islands – seafood.

Excursions and organized tours

Guided visits to the volcano. Guide Alpine; for information: tel. 986263/986211.

at Vulcano ✉ 98050

★★★ **Eolian.** A Porto Ponente, tel. 9852151, fax 9852153. Seasonal. Number of rooms: 88. Accessible to the handicapped. Parking, garden, swimming pool, tennis.

★★ **Conti.** A Porto Ponente, tel. and fax 9852012. Seasonal. Number of rooms: 62. Garden.

❦ **Vincenzino.** Porto di Levante, tel. 9852016. Parking. The cooking of the Aeolian islands – seafood.

Hot springs/Spas

at Lìpari

Terme di San Calogero. Therapeutic baths, muds, grottoes. Being renovated.

at Vulcano

Porto di Levante. Therapeutic baths in natural swimming pool and in the sea, where there is a hot spring, and muds.

Cafes and pastry shops

at Lìpari

Pasticceria del Corso. Corso Vittorio Emanuele 232, tel. 9812536. Always open in the summer. Specialties: almond pastries.

Museums and cultural institutions

at Lìpari

Museo Eoliano. Acropoli, tel. 9880174. Open to the public: *9-2 and 2-7; holidays 9-1 and 4-7*.

Eraclea Minoa ✉ 92011 ☎ 0922

Page 98

Museums and cultural institutions

Antiquarium and Zona Archeologica. Tel. 846005. Open to the public: *9-one hour before sunset*.

Èrice ✉ 91016 ☎ 0923

Plan, page 67

ℹ️ *Azienda Autonoma*, Viale Conte Pepoli 11, tel. 869388 (B1).

Hotels, restaurants, campsites, and vacation villages

★★★ **Elimo.** Via Vittorio Emanuele 73, tel. 869377, fax 869252. Number of rooms: 21. Elevator; parking, parking garage (B2, **c**).

★★★ **Moderno.** Via Vittorio Emanuele 63, tel. 869300, fax 869139. Number of rooms: 40. Accessible to the handicapped. Elevator; parking garage (B2, **a**).

★★ **Edelweiss.** Cortile Padre Vincenzo 3, tel. 869420, fax 869252. Number of rooms: 1 Parking garage (B2, **b**).

❦❦ **Cortile di Venere.** Via Sales 31, tel. 86936 Closed Wednesday, for variable vacatic periods. The cooking of Trapani (B3, **r**).

❦❦ **Monte San Giuliano.** Vicolo S. Rocco tel. 869595. Closed Monday, part of N vember and in January. Garden. Sicilia cooking (B2, **m**).

❦ **Taverna di Re Aceste.** Via De Martino 4, te 869084. Closed Wednesday, Novembe The cooking of Trapani – seafood (C2, **t**)

Agriturismo (real Italian country living

Azienda agricola Pizzolungo. Contrada Sa Cusumano. Accomodation in the master's villa a citrus fruits and vegetable farm. Bicycles ar canoes for rent. For information: Francesc Adragna, tel. 563710.

Hostels

🏠 **G. Amodeo.** Ostello per la Gioventù (yout hostel). Strada Provinciale Trapani-Eric tel. 552964. Posti letto 52. Open: *all year*

Museums and cultural institutions

Museo Civico Cordici. Piazza Umberto I, tel. 86925 Closed Sunday. Open to the public: *8:30-1:30*.

Museo Agro-Forestale. Località S. Matteo, te 869532. Open to the public: *8:30-5 (from Nove ber to March), 8:30-6:30 (from April to October*

Cultural Events

Seven-day Festival of Medieval and Renai sance Music. Every year in August; for inform tion: tel. 869085 (city hall).

Falconara ✉ 93011 ☎ 093

Hotels, restaurants, campsites, and vacation villages

★★★ **Stella del Mediterraneo.** State road 11 at km. 243.4, tel. 349004, fax 349007. Nun ber of rooms: 17. Accessible to the hand capped. Air conditioning; parking, garde private beach.

⛺ **Eurocamping 2 Rocche.** Contrada Faine State road 115 at km. 241.8, tel. and fa 349006. Annual.

Favara ✉ 92026 ☎ 092

Page 94

ℹ️ Municipio, tel. 34233.

Cafes and pastry shops

Antico Caffè Italia. Piazza Cavour. Closed Wedne day. Almond pastries in distinctive gift packs.

Caffè Patti. Via Vittorio Emanuele. Closed Mo day. "Latte di mandorla" and a vast assortmer of "pasticcini."

useums and cultural institutions

useo Civico A. Mendola. Piazza Cavour 56, tel. 233. Closed Sunday. Open to the public: *9-1 and 5; Saturday 9-1.*

ops, crafts, and curiosities

ntina Sociale Chiaramonte (wines). Traversa ana, tel. 32689.

---

orza Agrò Mare   ✉ 98030 ☎ 0942

otels, restaurants, campsites, and acation villages

Forza Agrò Mare. Località Buzzuratti, State road 114 at km. 39.3 tel. 751158. Seasonal.

---

rci Sìculo   ✉ 98023 ☎ 0942

otels, restaurants, campsites, and acation villages

Foti. Via Milano 34, tel. 791815, fax 793203. Number of rooms: 27. Accessible to the handicapped. Air conditioning, elevator.

---

angi   ✉ 90024 ☎ 0921

griturismo (real Italian country living)

nuta Gangivecchia. Contrada Gangivecchia. untry Hospitality, of hotel standard, in rooms uated in the restructured stables. For information: tel. 689191.

---

anzirri   ✉ 98165 ☎ 090

ge 166

otels, restaurants, campsites, and acation villages

Napoletana-da Salvatore. Via Lago Grande 18, tel. 391032. Closed Wednesday. The cooking of Messina – seafood.

---

ela   ✉ 93012 ☎ 0933

an, page 119

📍 *Azienda Autonoma,* Via Navarra Bresmes 104, tel. 913788 (B2).

otels, restaurants, campsites, and acation villages

★ **Motel Agip.** State road 117 bis, località Giar-dinelli, tel. 911144, fax 907236. Number of rooms: 91. Air conditioning, elevator; parking (A2, *off map*).

Aurora. Piazza Vittorio Veneto 1, tel. 917711. Closed Sunday, for variable vacation periods. Sicilian cooking (B2, **s**).

🍴 **Gelone 2.** Via Generale Cascino 39, tel. 913254. Closed Sunday. Air conditioning. Sicilian cooking – seafood (A2, **t**).

Cafes and pastry shops

Bar Pasticceria Bongiorno. Corso Vittorio Emanuele 338, tel. 908846. Marzipan, "piparelli" and almond cookies.

Bar Pasticceria Incardona. Via Navarra 98, tel. 924496. Home-made pastries, especially the ricotta "pasticcini."

Museums and cultural institutions

Museo Archeologico Regionale. Corso Vittorio Emanuele 1, tel. 912626. Closed the last Monday of each month. Open: *9-1 and 3-6; summer 9-1 and 3-8.*

Archeological digs of Capo Soprano. Tel. 930975. Open to the public: *9-one hour before sunset.*

Giardini Naxos   ✉ 98035 ☎ 0942

Page 171

ℹ️ *Azienda Autonoma,* Via Tysandros 54, tel. 51010; information office, motorway exit, tel. 50371.

Hotels, restaurants, campsites, and vacation villages

★★★ **Hellenia Yachting.** Via Jannuzzo 41, tel. 51737, fax 54310. Number of rooms: 112. Air conditioning, elevator; parking, parking garage, garden, swimming pool, private beach.

★★★ **Ramada Hotel.** Via Jannuzzo 47, tel. 51931, fax 56128. Number of rooms: 298. Accessible to the handicapped. Air conditioning, elevator; parking, garden, swimming pools, tennis, private beach.

★★★ **Arathena Rocks.** Via Calcide Eubea 55, tel. 51349, fax 51690. Seasonal. Number of rooms: 37. Accessible to the handicapped. Elevator; parking, garden, swimming pool, tennis.

★★★ **Nike Hotel.** Via Calcide Eubea 27, tel. 51207, fax 56315. Number of rooms: 50. Parking, garden, private beach.

★★ **Palladio.** Via IV Novembre 269, tel. and fax 52267. Number of rooms: 16. Rooms only; no dining facilities. Elevator; special terms for parking garage, private beach.

at Trappitello, km. 3   ✉ 98030

🍴 **A Massaria.** Via Arancio 6, tel. 776009. Closed Tuesday (except in summer) and at mid-day on Monday and Friday. Parking, gar-den. Sicilian cooking – mushrooms and fish.

Cafes and pastry shops

Caffè Cavallaro. Via Umberto 165, tel. 51259. Founded in 1937, this cafe offers excellent ricotta puff-pastries for breakfast, the white buttery "rollò di crema" or its chocolate counterpart, a "fetta moka super," and, an excellent dessert, the glazed lemon "cassatelle," and other fine hand-made pastries.

Bar Pasticceria Salamone. Via Vittorio Emanuele 236, tel. 51398. Excellent lemon, coffee, mulberry, and almond granita, and brioches and fruit ice cream cakes.

Museums and cultural institutions

Museo Archeologico of Naxos. Capo Schisò, tel. 51001. Open to the public: *8-2 and 4-7; Sunday 8-1 and 4-7.*

Archeological digs of Naxos. Capo Schisò, tel. 51001. Open to the public: *9-one hour before sunset.*

Shops, crafts, and curiosities

La Fauci Gaetano. Store in the Via Vittorio Emanuele, 204, tel. 51254. Wrought-iron objects, ranging from clothing valets to magnificent headboards for beds, all rosettes and curlicues with a vaguely Arabian style.

Patané. Via Regina Margherita 111, tel. 51149. Wrought-iron objects.

Qui è Lanfranchi. Via Umberto 367, tel. 52322. Old Sicilian-style ceramics ("siceliote"). The owner loves to tell of the history and the tradition of each object and decoration.

Gioiosa Marèa ⊠ 98063 ☎ 0941

Hotels, restaurants, campsites, and vacation villages

⚶ **Cicero.** Località San Giorgio, Contrada Cicero, tel. 39551, fax 39295. Seasonal.

Isnello ⊠ 90010 ☎ 0921

Hotels, restaurants, campsites, and vacation villages

at Piano Torre, km. 8

⋆⋆⋆ **Piano Torre Park Hotel.** Tel. 662671, fax 662672. Number of rooms: 27. Accessible to the handicapped. Air conditioning; parking, garden, swimming pool, tennis.

Isola delle Femmine ⊠ 90040 ☎ 091

Hotels, restaurants, campsites, and vacation villages

⋆⋆⋆ **Eufemia.** Via Nazionale 28, tel. 8677800, fax 8678002. Number of rooms: 54. Air conditioning, elevator; parking, private beach.

⋔ **Cutino.** Via Palermo 10, tel. 8677062. Closed Tuesday. Air conditioning. Sicilian cooking – seafood.

⚶ **La Playa.** Località Pozzillo, Viale Marino 55, tel. 8677001, fax 8677001. Seasonal.

Lentini ⊠ 96016 ☎ 0

Page 141

ℹ️ Municipio, Piazza Duomo, tel. 941600.

Cafes and pastry shops

Pasticceria Navarria. Via Conte Alaimo 12, t 941045. You should try the ricotta pastries a the excellent fruit ice creams.

Museums and cultural institutions

Museo Archeologico. Via del Museo, t 7832962 and 902383. Closed Sunday. Open the public: *9-6.*

Letojanni ⊠ 98037 ☎ 09

ℹ️ Municipio, tel. 657326.

Hotels, restaurants, campsites, and vacation villages

⋆⋆⋆ **Park Hotel Silemi.** Via Silemi 1, tel. 3622 fax 652094. Seasonal. Number of room 49. Air conditioning, elevator; parkin special terms for parking garage, garde swimming pool, private beach.

⋔ **Paradise Beach Club.** Contrada Silemi, t 36944. Seasonal. Parking, garden. Sicili. cooking – seafood.

⚶ **Eurocamping Marmaruca.** Contrada M maruca, Via Leto, tel. 36676. Annual.

Cafes and pastry shops

Niky Bar. Piazza Durante, tel. 36104. Specia ties: "Meringato al bacio," or peach and m berry granitas, with cream.

Pasticceria Caminiti. Via Vittorio Emanuele 22 tel. 36339. Excellent pastries, especially the " gnolata," during Carnival.

Rosticceria La Rupe. Via Vittorio Emanuele 16 tel. 37344. Excellent vegetable "panzerotti typical fried pizzas of the Messina region, ar the "mozzarella in carrozza."

Licata ⊠ 92027 ☎ 09

Page 96

ℹ️ Municipio, Piazza Progresso 10, tel. 86811

Cafes and pastry shops

Pasticceria Porrello. Via Stazione Vecchia 14, t 774161. "Torroncini" and almond liquors.

Museums and cultural institutions

Museo Civico Archeologico. Via Dante 12, t 772602. Open to the public: *weekdays 9-1 and 7; holidays 9-1.*

do di Mortelle ✉ 98164 ☎ 090

tels, restaurants, campsites, and cation villages

Alberto-Sporting Mortelle. Via Nazionale at km 12.3, tel. 321009. Closed Monday, November. Air conditioning, parking. Sicilian cooking – seafood.

nguaglossa ✉ 95015 ☎ 095

ge 156

] *Pro Loco*, Piazza Annunziata, tel. 643094.

seums

seo delle Genti dell'Etna. Pro Loco, Piazza nunziata, tel. 643094. Open to the public: *9-1 d 4-7:30; Sunday and holidays 10-12:30.*

rina di Ragusa ✉ 97010 ☎ 0932

ge 112

tels, restaurants, campsites, and cation villages

* **Terraqua.** Via delle Sirene 35, tel. 615600, fax 615580. Number of rooms: 77. Elevator; parking, garden, swimming pool, tennis, private beach.

Alberto. Lungomare Doria 48, tel. 239023. Closed Wednesday, for a period in November. Sicilian cooking – seafood.

* **Baia del Sole.** Lungomare Andrea Doria, tel. 239844, fax 230344. Annual.

seums and cultural institutions

Camarina, km. 16.5

seo Archeologico. Tel. 826004. Open to the blic: *9-2 and 3:30-6.*

rco Archeologico di Camarina. Tel. 826004. en to the public: *9-one hour before sunset.*

rco Archeologico di Caucana. Open to the blic: *9-one hour before sunset.*

rsala ✉ 91025 ☎ 0923

n, page 75

] Via XI Maggio 100, tel. 714097.

tels, restaurants, campsites, and cation villages

* **Cap 3000.** Via Trapani 161, tel. 989055, fax 989634. Number of rooms: 61. Accessible to the handicapped. Air conditioning, elevator; parking, swimming pool (A3, *off map*).

* **President.** Via Nino Bixio 1, tel. 999333, fax 999115. Number of rooms: 128. Accessible to the handicapped. Air conditioning, elevator; parking, garden, swimming pool (C3, *off map*).

¶¶ **Delfino.** Lungomare Mediterraneo 672, tel. 998188. Closed Tuesday in the low season. Air conditioning, parking, garden. The cooking of Trapani – seafood (C3, *off map*).

Agriturismo (real Italian country living)

Azienda Agricola Baglio Vajarassa. Località Spagnola. Accommodations in an old restored farmhouse; exhibition of objects from the old peasant culture, archery. For information: Leonardo Agate, tel. 968628.

Cafes and pastry shops

Pasticceria Lilibeo. Via Salemi 5, tel. 982605. Ice creams and hot foods.

Pasticceria Tahiti. Contrada Casazze 22, tel. 964252. Ice creams and hot foods.

Museums and cultural institutions

Enomuseum. Contrada Berbano. State road 115, tel. 969667. Open to the public: *9-1 and 3-7.*

Museo degli Arazzi. Via Garraffa 57, tel. 712903. Closed Monday. Open to the public: *9-1 and 4-6.*

Museo Archeologico. Baglio Anselmi, Lungomare Bolo, tel. 952535. Open to the public: *April September 9-14, Wednesday, Thursday and Saturday also 4-7, Sunday 9-1 and 4-7; October-March 9-14, Wednesday and Saturday also 3-6, Sunday 9-1 and 3-6.*

on the Island of Mozia

Archeological digs of Mozia and Museo. Tel. 712598. Open to the public: *winter 9-1; summer 9-1 and 3-one hour before sunset (afternoon visits only by appointment).*

Sports

Circolo Velico Marsala (sailing). Vicolo Saline 5, tel. 951162.

Shops, crafts, and curiosities

Enoteca Gran Galà. Via Mazara 253/B, tel. 721485. This wine cellar features fine wines of the Marsala region, with tastings. Open to the public: *9-1, by appointment.*

Marzamemi ✉ 96010 ☎ 0931

Hotels, restaurants, campsites, and vacation villages

ᴁ ** **Il Forte.** Contrada Spinazza, tel. 841011, fax 841132. Annual.

Shops, crafts, and curiosities

The wives of the fisherman prepare home-made tuna fish, preserved in oil, as well as tomatoes, eggplants, and peppers in oil, and smoked swordfish. They generally set out the large jars with the preserves on their windowsills or outside the front doors of their homes. You can also enquire in the shop of Salvatore Campisi, tel. 841166.

Màscali
⊠ 95016 ☎ 095

Hotels, restaurants, campsites, and vacation villages

🏠
★★ **Mokambo.** At Fondachello, Via Spiaggia 211, tel. and fax 938731. Seasonal.

Agriturismo (real Italian country living)

Azienda Agricola Russo Rocca. Località Artale Marina. Accommodations in apartments inside a fine late 19th c. building. Surrounded by large garden with citrus fruits and fruit trees. Excursions nearby and around the farm. For information: Giovanni Russo, tel. 931259 or 0347-3672714.

Mazara del Vallo
⊠ 91026 ☎ 0923

Page 77

ℹ️ Municipio, Contrada Affacciata, tel. 942776.

Hotels, restaurants, campsites, and vacation villages

★★★ **Hopps.** Via Hopps 29, tel. 946133, fax 946075. Number of rooms: 240. Accessible to the handicapped. Air conditioning, elevator; parking, garden, swimming pool, private beach (D3, **a**).

🍴 **Papaya.** Via Romano 1, tel. 946221. Closed Wednesday. Air conditioning. The cooking of Trapani – seafood (B3, **v**).

🍴 **Pescatore.** Via Castelvetrano 191, tel. 947580. Closed Monday. Air conditioning, parking. The cooking of Trapani – seafood (D3, *off map*).

🏕️ **Sporting Camping Club.** Contrada Bocca Arena, tel. and fax 947230. Annual.

Museums and cultural institutions

Museo Civico. Piazza del Plebiscito, tel. 941777 and 940266. Closed Sunday and holidays. Open to the public: *8:30-2.*

at Castelvetrano, km. 21.5
⊠ 91022 ☎ 0924

Enoagrimuseum. Baglio Montalto, Contrada Santa Teresa, State road 115, tel. 44060. Open to the public: *9:30-1 and 2:30-6:30.*

Museo Civico. Via Garibaldi, tel. 904932. Open to the public: *9-1 and 3:30-7:30.*

Theater and music

at Castelvetrano, km. 21.5

Teatro Selinus. Via Garibaldi 11, tel. 901732.

Melilli
⊠ 96010 ☎ 0931

Hotels, restaurants, campsites, and vacation villages

🏠
★★ **Happy Holidays.** Contrada Campana, State road 114 at km. 128.3, tel. and fax 914082. Annual.

Messina
⊠ 98100 ☎ 0

Plan, page 162

ℹ️ *AAPIT*, Via Calabria is. 301/bis, tel. 6753 (D3). Information office: Via Calabria corr Via Capra, tel. 674236; motorway Tremestieri, tel. 730713.

Azienda Autonoma, Piazza Cairoli, t 2935292 (D2).

Hotels, restaurants, campsites, and vacation villages

★★★ **Jolly dello Stretto.** Via Garibaldi 126, t 363860, fax 5902526. Number of rooms: 9 Accessible to the handicapped. Air con tioning, elevator (C2, **a**).

★★★ **Royal Palace Hotel.** Via T. Cannizzaro 22 tel. 6503, fax 2921075. Number of room 106. Accessible to the handicapped. *I* conditioning, elevator; parking garage (E3, **c**).

🍴 **Pranpron.** Via Ugo Bassi 157, tel. 293858 Closed Sunday evening and Wednesda September. Air conditioning. The cooki of Messina – seafood (E2, **r**).

🍴 **Savoya.** Via XXVII Luglio 36/38, tel. 29348(Closed Monday, part of August. Air con tioning. Sicilian cooking (D-E2, **ba**).

🍴 **Piero.** Via Ghibellina 121, tel. 71836 Closed Sunday, August. Air conditionir The cooking of Messina – seafood (D2, **r**

at Contemplazione, km. 5

★★★ **Paradis.** Via Consolare Pompea 441, t 310682, fax 312043. Number of rooms: 9 Air conditioning, elevator; parking garag

at Pistunina, km. 6

★★★ **Europa Palace Hotel.** State road 114 km. 5.47, tel. 621601, fax 621768. Number rooms: 115. Air conditioning, elevatc parking, garden, indoor swimming po tennis.

at the San Rizzo gate, km. 10

★★ **Panoramic.** State road 113 at km. 8.5, t 340228, fax 42520. Number of rooms: 14. *I* cess for the disabled. Parking, garden.

Cafes and pastry shops

Bar Pasticceria Pisani. Via Tommaso Cannizza 45, tel. 2938158. The "cannolata" is a speci "pignolata" enclosed in an enormous "cannol that is "sheathed" in chocolate. "Arancini" rice and ragu, butter, and meatless.

Chiosco di Piazza Cairoli. Here they ma "limone al limone," "mandarino al limone "amarena al frutto," and many other tradition Sicilian fruit drinks.

Pasticceria Billé. Piazza Cairoli 7, tel. 67935 First-rate "pignolata," and an artistic "frutta m torana" in the traditional fisherman's baske for splendid gifts.

asticceria Irrera. Via Boccetta 4, tel. 344209.
he black and the white "pignolata," egg-white
d glazed pastries.

asticceria La Spada. Via Natoli 19, tel. 674655.
uit ice creams, granitas, and "cassate" in the
est tradition.

heater and music

atro Vittorio Emanuele. Via Garibaldi, tel.
5233.

useums and cultural institutions

useo Regionale. Via della Libertà 465, tel.
1292. Closed Sunday afternoon. Open to the
blic: *winter, 9-1:30, Tuesday, Thursday and Sat-
day also 3-5:30, Sunday 9-12:30; summer, 9-1:30,
esday, Thursday and Saturday also 4-6:30, Sun-
y 9-12:30.*

ultural Events

rocessione della Vara. Important religious
ent on 15th August. For information: tel.
4236.

asseggiata dei Giganti. Two papier-maché gi-
ts are paraded around the city on 13th and
th August. For information: tel. 674236.

ilazzo   ✉ 98057 ☎ 090

an, page 175

✑   *Azienda Autonoma*, Piazza Duilio 10, tel.
    9222865 (C2).

otels, restaurants, campsites, and acation villages

Eolian Inn. Via Cappuccini 21, tel. 9286133,
fax 9282855. Seasonal. Number of rooms:
250. Air conditioning, elevator; parking,
garden, swimming pool, tennis (A3, **d**).

Silvanetta Palace Hotel. Via Mangiavacca
1, tel. 9281633, fax 9222787. Number of
rooms: 130. Accessible to the handicapped.
Air conditioning, elevator; parking, garden, swimming pool, tennis (D3, *off map*).

Villa Esperanza. Via Baronia 191, tel.
9222916. Closed Monday, November. Air
conditioning, parking, garden. Classic Italian cooking and the cooking of Messina
(A3, *off map*).

Covo del Pirata. Via Marina Garibaldi 2, tel.
9284437. Closed Wednesday. Air conditioning. Classic Italian cooking and the
cooking of Messina (B2, **t**).

Riva Smeralda. Strada Panoramica, tel.
9282980. Annual.

useums and cultural institutions

astello di Milazzo. Via del Castello, tel. 9221291.
losed Monday unless it is a holiday. Guided vis-
s: *on the hour 10-12 and 3:30-6:30 (telephone in
dvance).*

Museo enologico Grasso. (Wines) Via Albero 5,
tel. 9281082. Closed Sunday. Open to the public:
8-1 and 3:30-7:30.

Milo   ✉ 95010 ☎ 095

Hotels, restaurants, campsites, and vacation villages

🏠 **Mareneve.** Contrada Piano Grande, Via
★★★   Bosco 30, tel. 7082163, fax 7083417. Ann-
    ual.

Misilmeri   ✉ 90036 ☎ 091

Page 61

ℹ   Municipio, tel. 8732536 and 8711040.

Cafes and pastry shops

Nocilla. Via Vittorio Emanuele 122.

Misterbianco   ✉ 95045 ☎ 095

Hotels, restaurants, campsites, and vacation villages

★★★ **Gelso Bianco.** At km. 3 from A19, tel.
573834, fax 573757. Number of rooms: 91.
Air conditioning, elevator; parking, garden, swimming pool, tennis.

Agriturismo (real Italian country living)

Azienda Agricola Alcalà. Contrada Terrebianche. A 22 hectare complex situated on the
near hills of the Piana di Catania. Guided nature
walks, fishing. For information: Anna Maria Sapuppo, tel. 7130029.

Mistretta   ✉ 98073 ☎ 0921

Page 188

ℹ   *Pro Loco*, c/o Municipio, Piazza V. Veneto,
    tel. 382053

Cafes and pastry shops

Extra di Lo Jacono. Piazza Marconi 3, tel.
381006. Especially "pasta reale".

Italia di Capicotto Anna. Corso Umberto I 2,
tel. 382184.

Pasticceria Rosticceria Testa. Via Monte 2, tel.
382580. Specialties: "pasta reale" and typical
pastries of Mistretta.

Primavera. Via Primavera 14, tel. 383172. Bar,
pastry shop, restaurant. Specialties: "pasta reale"
and "savoiardi."

Museums and cultural institutions

Museo Civico. Corso Umberto I, tel. 382053.
Closed Sunday and Monday. Open to the public:
8-2; Tuesday and Thursday also 3:30-6:30.

221

Mòdica ✉ 97015 ☎ 0932

Plan, page 109

i *Pro Loco*, Via I Galfo 7, tel. 752820.

Hotels, restaurants, campsites, and vacation villages

★★★ **Motel di Modica.** Corso Umberto I, tel. 941022, fax 941077. Number of rooms: 36. Rooms only; no dining facilities. Parking, parking garage (A1, *off map*).

❢ **Fattoria delle Torri.** Vico Napolitano 14, tel. 751286. Closed Monday, for a period between June and July. Garden. Sicilian cooking (A2, **r**).

Cafes and pastry shops

Antica Dolceria Bonaiuto. Corso Umberto I 159, tel. 941225. Specialties: "i'mpanatigghi," pastries made of meat and chocolate.

Museums and cultural institutions

Museo Civico. Ex Convento dei Padri Mercedari, Via Mercé, tel. 945081. Closed Sunday. Open to the public: *9-1.*

Museo Ibleo delle Arti e Tradizioni Popolari. Ex Convento dei Padri Mercedari, Via Mercé, tel. 752747. Open to the public: *10-1 and 3:30-6:30.*

Pinacoteca Comunale. Corso S. Giorgio (Palazzo Polara). Closed Sunday. Open to the public: *8-2.*

at Ìspica, km. 10.8 ✉ 97014

Cava d'Ìspica. Open to the public: *winter, 8:30-1:30 and 3:30-5:30; summer, 8:30-1:30 and 3:30-7:30.*

Parco Archeologico della Forza. Open to the public: *from 1 October to 31 March, 8:30-12 and 2:30-4:30; from 1 April to 30 September, 9-12 and 3-7.*

Monreale ✉ 90046 ☎ 091

Plan, page 50

i *Azienda Autonoma*, Piazza Vittorio Emanuele (Palazzo Municipale), tel. 6564570 (B3).

Hotels, restaurants, campsites, and vacation villages

★★★ **Carrubella Park Hotel.** Via Umberto I 233, tel. 6402188, fax 6402189. Number of rooms: 30. Elevator; parking, garden (A3, **o**).

❢ **La Botte.** State road 186, Contrada Lenzitti 416, tel. 414051. Seasonal, closed from Monday to Thursday. Parking, garden. Classic Italian and Sicilian cooking (C1, *off map*).

Museums and cultural institutions

Chiostro dei Benedettini. Tel. 6404403. Open to the public: *9-1; Monday, Tuesday and Thursday also from 3-6 (summer 3-7; holidays 9-12).*

Theater and music

Opera dei Pupi Orlando. (Sicilian puppets) Cortile Manin 15, tel. 6404542.

Nicolosi ✉ 95030 ☎ 09

Page 159

i *Azienda Autonoma*, Via Etnea 32, te 911505.

Hotels, restaurants, campsites, and vacation villages

★★★ **Biancaneve.** Via Etnea 163, tel. 914139, fa 911194. Number of rooms: 83. Accessible ❢ the handicapped. Elevator; parking, ga den, swimming pool, tennis.

★★★ **Gemmellaro.** Via Etnea 160, tel. 91106 fax 911071. Number of rooms: 56. Elevato parking.

❢❢ **Grotta del Gallo.** Via Madonna delle Graz 40, tel. 911301. Closed Monday in the lo season. Air conditioning, parking, garde Sicilian cooking.

⚠ **Etna.** Via Goethe, tel. 914309. Annual.
★★

Hostels

🛏 **Etna.** Ostello per la Gioventù (youth ho tel). Via della Quercia 7, tel. 7914686. Pos letto 50. Open: *all year.*

Cultural institutions

Ente parco dell'Etna. Via Etnea 107, tel. 821111

Nicosìa ✉ 94014 ☎ 093

Page 187

i c/o Municipio, Via Roma, tel. 646852.

Hotels, restaurants, campsites, and vacation villages

★★★ **Pineta.** Via S. Paolo 35/A, tel. 647002, fa 646927. Number of rooms: 48. Accessible ❢ the handicapped. Elevator; parking, par ing garage, garden.

Agriturismo (real Italian country living

Masseria Mercadante. Contrada Mercadant Rural construction from the 17th c. Room furnished traditionally. Olive groves and veget bles grown. Fishing, nearby excursions. For i formation: Sigismondo Castrogiovanni, tel. 64077

Noto ✉ 96017 ☎ 093

Plan, page 135

i *Azienda Provinciale Turismo,* Piazza XV Maggio, tel. 836744 (B2).

Hotels, restaurants, campsites, and vacation villages

at Lido di Noto, km. 8

★★★ **Eloro Hotel Club.** Località Pizzuta, te 812244, fax 812200. Seasonal. Number o rooms: 222. Accessible to the handicapped. Air conditioning, elevator; parking, garden, swimming pool, tennis, private beach.

★ **Helios.** Località Pizzuta, tel. 812366, fax 812378. Number of rooms: 141. Air conditioning, elevator; parking, garden, swimming pool, tennis, private beach.

griturismo (real Italian country living)

▮ Vendìcari, km. 10

zienda Agricola Il Roveto. This farmhouse ands in the middle of an estate of 57 hectares, erlooking the sea, with a lovely inlet and a small and. Guided nature walks, birdwatching. For formation: Giuseppe Loreto, tel. 66024.

afes and pastry shops

ar Pasticceria Sicilia. Corso Vittorio Emanuele 5, tel. 835013. Since 1892, supreme producers of e almond granita and the "latte di mandorla," or mond milk. It is also possible to get "crema di andorla," or almond cream, to eat as it is, or to ssolve in hot water, to make "latte di mandorla."

useums and cultural institutions

printendenza alle Antichità per la Sicilia rientale. Tel. 835588.

useo Civico. Corso Vittorio Emanuele II 124, tel. 6462. Closed for restoration.

ultural Events

fiorata or Primavera Barocca. Every Year, a the third Sunday of May, Via Nicolaci is vered with religious images composed at of flower petals. For information: tel. 6744.

nops, crafts, and curiosities

▮ Rosolini, km. 14 ✉ 96019

ooperativa Elorina. Contrada Belliscala. Tel. 7068. Local wine.

---

alazzolo Acrèide ✉ 96010 ☎ 0931

an, page 139

[ ] Ufficio Turistico Comunale (Town Tourist Office), Piazza del Popolo, tel. 882000 (B3).

otels, restaurants, campsites, and acation villages

★ **Senatore.** Largo Senatore Italia, tel. 883443, fax 883444. Number of rooms: 21. Accessible to the handicapped. Air conditioning, elevator; parking, garden (A3, **a**).

Anapo da Nunzio. Corso Vittorio Emanuele 7, tel. 882286. Closed Monday. Sicilian cooking – seafood (B3, **s**).

n the State road 287, km. 7

La Trota. Contrada Pianette, tel. 883433.

Closed Monday. Air conditioning, parking, garden. Sicilian cooking – seafood.

Cafes and pastry shops

Antica Pasticceria Corsino. Via Nazionale 2, tel. 875533-875035. This pastry shop is always open. They prepare ice creams, wonderful "pasticcini alla crema," and almond pastries.

Museums and cultural institutions

Archeological area. Closed Monday. Open to the public: *9-one hour before sunset.*

Home-museum of Antonino Uccello. Via Machiavelli, tel. 881499. Open to the public: *9-1.*

at Pantàlica, km. 31

Necropolis of Pantàlica. Tel. 953695. Open to the public: *9-8.*

Palermo ✉ 90100 ☎ 091

Plans, pages 28-29 and pages 32-33

[i] *AAPIT*, Piazza Castelnuovo 34/35, tel. 6058111/6110977 (II, C3).

Azienda Autonoma, Salita Belmonte 1, tel. 540122 (I, C4).

Hotels, restaurants, campsites, and vacation villages

★★★ **Villa Igiea Grand Hotel.** Salita Belmonte 43, tel. 543744, fax 547654. Number of rooms: 117. Accessible to the handicapped. Air conditioning, elevator; parking, garden, swimming pool, tennis (I, C4, **a**).

★★★ **Astoria Palace.** Via Monte Pellegrino 62, tel. 6371820, fax 6372178. Number of rooms: 326. Accessible to the handicapped. Air conditioning, elevator; parking (I, D4, **h**).

★★★ **Forte Agip.** Viale Regione Siciliana 2620, tel. 552033, fax 408198. Number of rooms: 105. Air conditioning, elevator; parking (I, D3, **aa**).

★★★ **Grande Albergo e delle Palme.** Via Roma 398, tel. 583933, fax 331545. Number of rooms: 187. Accessible to the handicapped. Air conditioning, elevator; special terms for parking garage (II, C4, **b**).

★★★ **Jolly del Foro Italico.** Foro Italico 22, tel. 6165090, fax 6161441. Number of rooms: 235. Air conditioning, elevator; parking, garden, swimming pool (II, E6, **c**).

★★★ **Politeama Palace.** Piazza Ruggero Settimo 15, tel. 322777, fax 6111589. Number of rooms: 102. Air conditioning; special terms for parking garage (II, C3, **g**).

★★★ **Bel 3.** Via Ruffo di Calabria 20, tel. 223560, fax 223560. Number of rooms: 67. Accessible to the handicapped. Air conditioning, elevator; parking, garden (I, E2, **f**).

★★★ **Europa.** Via Agrigento 3, tel. and fax 6256323. Number of rooms: 73. Air conditioning, elevator (II, B3, **q**).

★★★ **Mediterraneo.** Via Rosolino Pilo 43, tel. 581133, fax 586974. Number of rooms: 106. Air conditioning, elevator; parking garage (II, C4, **e**).

★★★ **San Paolo Palace.** Via Messina Marine 91, tel. 6211112, fax 6215300. Number of rooms: 290. Accessible to the handicapped. Air conditioning, elevator; parking, swimming pool, tennis (I, E5, **m**).

★★ **Villa Archirafi.** Via Lincoln 30, tel. 6168827, fax 6168631. Number of rooms: 29. Accessible to the handicapped. Elevator; parking, garden (II, E-F6, **o**).

🍴 **Charleston.** Piazzale Ungheria 30, tel. 321366, fax 321347. Seasonal, closed Sunday. Air conditioning. Classic Italian and Sicilian cooking – seafood (II, C-D3, **s**).

🍴 **L'Approdo Ristorante Renato.** Via Messina Marine 224, tel. 6302881. Closed Sunday, for a period in August. Air conditioning. Refined Sicilian cooking (I, E5, **z**).

🍴 **Il Ristorantino.** Piazzale De Gasperi 19, tel. 512861, fax 6702999. Closed Monday, August. Air conditioning, garden. Sicilian cooking (I, C3, **r**).

🍴 **Scuderia.** Viale del Fante 9, tel. 520323, fax 520467. Closed Sunday evening, for a period in August. Air conditioning, parking, garden. Classic Italian and Sicilian cooking – seafood (I, C3, **ra**).

🍴 **'A Cuccagna.** Via Principe Granatelli 21/A, tel. 587267. Closed Friday, for a period in August. Air conditioning, parking. Classic Italian and Sicilian cooking – seafood (II, C4, **x**).

🍴 **Friend's Bar.** Via Brunelleschi 138, tel. 201401. Closed Monday, for a period in August. Air conditioning. Sicilian cooking – seafood (I, D3, **rs**).

🍴 **Gourmand's.** Via della Libertà 37/E, tel. 323431. Closed Sunday, August. Air conditioning. Classic Italian and Sicilian cooking – seafood (II, B3, **u**).

🍴 **Regine.** Via Trapani 4/A, tel. 586566. Closed Sunday, August. Air conditioning. Sicilian cooking – seafood (II, B3, **ba**).

🍴 **Santandrea.** Piazza S. Andrea 4, tel. 334999. Closed Tuesday and in January. Air conditioning. Sicilian cooking – fish (II, D4-5, **rb**).

at Mondello, km. 10 ✉ 90151

★☆★ **Mondello Palace.** Viale Principe di Scalea 2, tel. 450001, fax 450657. Number of rooms: 83. Accessible to the handicapped. Air conditioning, elevator; parking, garden, swimming pool, private beach (I, A3, **ap**).

★★★ **Splendid Hotel la Torre.** Via Piano Gallo 11, tel. 450222, fax 450033. Number of rooms: 179. Accessible to the handicapped. Air conditioning, elevator; parking, garden, swimming pool, tennis, private beach (I, A3, **aq**).

🍴 **Charleston-Le Terrazze.** Viale Regina Elena, tel. 450171. Seasonal. Classic Italian and Sicilian cooking – seafood (I, A3, **rg**).

🍴 **Al Gabbiano.** Via Piano di Gallo 1, te 450313. Closed Wednesday, for a period November. Parking. Sicilian cooking seafood, shellfish (I, A3, **rh**).

at Sferracavallo, km. 13 ✉ 9014

★ **Degli Ulivi.** Via Pegaso 25, tel. 533021. A nual.

Agriturismo (real Italian country living

Tenuta Gangivecchio. Località Gangi. Pi turesque 14th c. Benedictine monastery su rounded by the Madonie mountain landscap For information: tel. 689191.

Azienda Agrituristica Ogliastro. Località Sa Mauro Castelverde. Once the seat of an ancie feud at the entrance to the Parco delle Madoni

Cafes and pastry shops

I Peccatucci di Mamma Andrea. Via Principe Scordia 67, tel. 334835. This shop offers the pa tries of Sicilian tradition, in refined packages. Sp cial "olivette di mandorla" with cioccolato, an chocolate-covered balls of pistachio. For co noisseurs, the strawberry or herb "rosolio."

Bar Pasticceria Mazzara. Via Generale Maglio co 15, tel. 321443. "Pizze fritte alla siciliana calzones filled with "tuma" cheese and salted a chovies.

Pasticceria Svizzera e Siciliana. Via M. Stabile 15 tel. 588551. Chocolate galore: white, bittersweet milk chocolate, and with hazelnuts, this is the b sis of a wonderful and entirely Sicilian pastry.

Roney Bar. Via Libertà 13, tel. 32427.

Bar Pasticceria Alba. Piazza San Giovanni Bosc 7/C, tel. 309016/6256390. Ricotta "cannoli."

Bar Pasticceria La Cubana. Via G. Pitré 141, te 213410. Pastries and ice-cream, and pizza an delicatessen. Climatised interior.

Bar Stancapiano. Via Notarbartolo 51, te 6817244. Hot foods as well, in one of the more e egant neighborhoods in Palermo.

Pasticceria Costa. Via D'Annunzio 15, tel. 34565 Closed Monday. It produces "cassate," in th finest Palermitan tradition.

at Mondello, km. 10

Caflish. Viale Regina Margherita di Savoia, te 6840444. Ricotta "cannoli" and the tradition "testa di turco," a special kind of "blancmange with thin layers of puff pastry, dusted with fir colorful sugars.

at Sferracavallo, km. 13 ✉ 9014

Pasticceria Gianfranco Graziano. Via dei Ba caioli 42, tel. 530125. Handmade and tradition Sicilian pastries, breads, and breadsticks.

Museums and cultural institutions

Cappella Palatina. Palazzo dei Normanni, te 7054879. Open to the public: *Monday-Friday 9-1 and 3-5; Saturday 9-12; Sunday 9-10 and 12-1.*

Civica Galleria d'Arte Moderna E. Restivo. V

...ati 10, tel. 588951. Closed Monday. Open to public: *9-1 and 3-6; Sunday 9-1.*

...ba. Corso Calatafini 100, tel. 590299. Open to public, enquire at the Caserma Tuköry: *weeks, 1st and 3rd Sunday of the month, hours 9-...; Monday and Thursday also 3-6.*

...ndazione Mormino. Viale della Libertà 52, 6259519. Closed Sunday. Open to the public: *...and 3-5; Saturday 9-1.*

...leria Regionale della Sicilia. Palazzo Abatel-Via Alloro 4, tel. 6164317. Open to the public: *...30; Tuesday, Thursday and Friday also 3-6:30; ...day 9-12:30.*

...seo Regionale Archeologico. Piazza Olivella, 6116805. Open to the public: *9-1:30; from ...nday to Friday also 3-6:30.*

...seo Diocesano. Via Bonello, tel. 6077111. ...sed for a new installation.

...seo Etnografico Siciliano G. Pitrè. Palazzina ...ese, tel. 6711060. Closed Friday. Open to the ...lic: *9-1; 3:30-6:30.*

...seo Internazionale delle Marionette. Via ...era 1, tel. 328060. Closed Sunday. Open to the ...lic: *9-1 and 4-7; Saturday 9-1.*

...seo del Risorgimento di V.E. Orlando. Piaz-...an Domenico, tel. 582774. Open to the pub-...Monday, Wednesday and Friday 9-1.

...o Botanico. Via Lincoln 2B. Tel. 6161493. ...en to the public: *winter, 9-5, Saturday and Sun-...9-1; summer, 9-6, Saturday and Sunday 9-1.*

...soro della Cattedrale. Corso Vittorio ...anuele, tel. 334373. Closed Sunday. Open to public: *9:30-12 and 4-5:45.*

...a. Piazza Guglielmo il Buono, tel. 6520269. ...en to the public: *9-1 and 3-7; Sunday and holi-...s 9-12:30.*

...cursions and organized tours

...ursions of the Palermo hinterland. Guided ...ts after reservation. AAPT, Piazza Castel-...vo 35, tel. 586122/583847.

...e Hundred Churches. Itinerary, some un-...al, of the city's churches. Soc. Coop. Kemo-..., Via E. Tricomi 10, tel. 584228.

...ermo Sightseeing Tour. Seven bus tours ...und the city. AAPT and AMAT; tel. 350415.

...ermo Sotterranea. Guided visits of the city's ...cative underground areas. Visits: *9-1, except ...day and Friday.* For information: tel. 7033320.

...getto carrozze. Five itineraries by horse and ...around the city. Palermo City Council, tel. ...2285.

...lia Excursions. Guided tours all over the is-...l. Via Emerico Amari 124, tel. 582294.

...ggi in Sicilia. Interesting guided tours around ...y to discover villas and private houses not usu-...open to the public. Via delle Croci, tel. 30872.

...eater and music

...ro Biondo. Via Teatro Biondo 11, tel.588755.

...ro Golden. Ente Autonomo Orchestra Sin-...ca Siciliana. Via Terra Santa 60, tel. 305217.

Teatro al Massimo. Piazza Verdi 9, tel. 589070. Music hall.

Teatro Massimo. Piazza Verdi, tel. 6053111.

Teatro Politeama. Piazza Politeama at the corner with the Via Turati, tel. 6053321.

Festino di S. Rosalia. From 10-16th July every year, one week of festivities in honour of the patron saint, tel. 167-234169.

Palermo di Scena. Theatre, dance, music and cinema. Every year in August. For information: tel. 167-234169.

Compagnia Bradamante di Cuticchio. Via Lombardia 25, tel. 6259223.

Sports

Campo Ostacoli della Favorita. Parco della Favorita 1, tel. 6790911.

IRES Ippodromo Alla Favorita. Viale Fante 9, tel. 6703462.

Tennis Club Palermo 2. Via Lorenzo Colli 13/A, tel. 6887926.

Shops, crafts, and curiosities

Ceramiche De Simone. Via Principe Lanza di Scalea 698, tel. 363190. Gift shop.

Centro Storico and Lungomare, or center and beachfront. Especially in the picturesque "Vucciria" there are many vendors who sell the distinctive bread and "panelle," pork "stigghiole," "pane e milza," and chickpea "frittelle."

Il Laboratorio Italiano. Via Privata di Villafranca, tel. 333177. Palermitan ceramics and terracotta.

The crafts tradition of the Sicilian cart, or "carretto," is being lost. In order to see a master craftsman at work, phone the Associazione Artigiani della Provincia di Palermo, tel. 581445.

Pantelleria ✉ 91017 ☎ 0923

Map, page 71

[i] *Associazione per il turismo* a Pantelleria, tel. 912948; *Pro Loco*, Via Roma, tel. 911838.

Hotels, restaurants, campsites, and vacation villages

★★★ **Port Hotel.** Via Borgo Italia 6, tel. 911299, fax 912203. Number of rooms: 43. Accessible to the handicapped. Air conditioning, elevator.

🍴 **I Mulini.** Contrada Tracino, tel. 915398. Closed Tuesday in winter, February. Parking, garden. The cooking of the surrounding territory.

at Mursia, km. 4

★★★ **Cossyra.** Località Cuddie Rosse, tel. 911154, fax 911026. Seasonal. Number of rooms: 80. Parking, garden, swimming pool, tennis.

★★★ **Mursia.** Tel. 911217, fax 911026. Seasonal. Number of rooms: 74. Accessible to the handicapped. Air conditioning; parking, swimming pool, tennis, private beach.

Excursions and organized tours

Boat Excursions. Only on reservation, tel. 918306 and 918170.

Guided Minibus tours. Only on reservation, tel. 911272.

Paternò   ✉ 95047 ☎ 095

Page 159

ℹ️   Municipio, Contrada Ardizzone, tel. 841777.

Cafes and pastry shops

Gran Caffè Italia. Piazza Regina Margherita 12, tel. 854379. Almond pastries and torroncini.

at Belpasso, km. 10   ✉ 95032

Pasticceria Condorelli. Via V. Emanuele 536, tel. 912205. Specialties: "torroncini."

Shops, crafts, and curiosities

at Belpasso, km. 10

Salterio. Località Piano Tavola. IX Strada privata, tel. 391182. Since 1928, production and sale of classical guitars, mandolins, and banjos.

Patti   ✉ 98066 ☎ 0941

Page 192

ℹ️   *Azienda Autonoma*, Piazza Marconi 11, tel. 241136.

Hotels, restaurants, campsites, and vacation villages

at Marina di Patti, km. 2   ✉ 98060

★★★ **Park Philip Hotel.** Via Lungomare 57, tel. 361332, fax 361184. Number of rooms: 43. Accessible to the handicapped. Elevator; swimming pool, private beach.

Cafes and pastry shops

Bar Pasticceria Jolie. Via Trieste 20, tel. 22102. Closed Thursday. Ricotta "cardinali" and "pasticciotti" stuffed with meat.

Laboratorio Pasticceria Praticò. Via Vittorio Emanuele 10, tel. 21818. Closed Sunday. Fruit baskets, with short pastry, chocolate, and pastry cream.

Pasticceria del Bignè. Via XX Settembre, tel. 21959. Exquisite almond pastries and typical Sicilian pastries.

Museums and cultural institutions

Villa Romana. Località Patti Marina, along the State road 113, tel. 361593. Open to the public: 9-one hour before sunset.

at Tindari, km. 10; plan, page 173

Archeological digs of Tindari. Tel. 369023. Open to the public: 9-two hours before sunset.

Shops, crafts, and curiosities

at Marina di Patti, km. 2

Ceramiche Caleca. Via Giovanni XXIII, tel. 36. Full settings of dishes, with hand-painted decorations and other objects.

at Tindari, km. 10; plan, page 173

The fishermen sell freshly caught fish, and the are even willing to cook it for you for a mode fee. Look for them alongside their boats, in the shallows.

Pedara   ✉ 95030 ☎ 0

Hotels, restaurants, campsites, and vacation villages

🍴   **La Bussola.** Piazza Don Bosco, tel. 78002 Closed Monday in winter, for a period November. Sicilian cooking – mushroo

Pelagie (Isole, or islands of)   ☎ 0:

Page 101

at Lampedusa   ✉ 92

ℹ️   *Agenzia Le Pelagie*, Via Roma 155, 970170.

Hotels, restaurants, campsites, and vacation villages

★★★   **Guitgia Tommasino.** Via Lido Azzurro tel. 970879, fax 970316. Number of roo 37. Air conditioning; parking, garden.

🍴   **Gemelli.** Via Cala Pisana 2, tel. 970699. S sonal, closed Monday. Sicilian cooking

⛺   **La Roccia.** Località Cala Greca or C ★★   Stretta, tel. 970964, fax 970055. Annual

Cafes and pastry shops

at Lampedusa

Bar Roma. Via E. Duse. Here you will find classic array of Sicilian pastries.

Shops, crafts, and curiosities

at Lampedusa

Da Famularo. Via F. Riso, tel. 970090. Fish, served in oil.

Petralia Sottana   ✉ 90027 ☎ 0

Page 187

ℹ️   *Pro Loco*, Corso P. Agliata 16, tel. 6416

Agriturismo (real Italian country livi

Azienda Agricola Monaco di Mezzo. Contr Monaco di Mezzo. Accommodations in an ol stored farmhouse, on an estate that grows for and olive groves, with livestock. Swimming p tennis, archery, horse riding. For information 0934-673949.

ana degli Albanesi ✉ 90037 ☎ 091

ge 55

Biblioteca comunale, Via Kastriota, tel. 8571787.

fes and pastry shops

na. Via G. Matteotti 36, tel. 8575602. Special-: Sicilian "cannoli".

sticceria Di Noto. Via Portella della Ginestra tel. 8571195. Specialties: ricotta "cannoli" d "ravioli di ricotta."

useums and cultural institutions

seo antropologico. Corso Kastriota 213. sed Monday. Open to the public: *9:30-12:30 d 3-6:30; Saturday 10-1.*

eater, music and cultural events

ema Teatro Vicari. This theater is now per- nently closed to the public, except for once or ce a year, when old plays are performed, in Al- nian. For information, enquire at the Pastic- ia Di Noto.

ster at Piana degli Albanesi. From the Thurs- y before Easter to Easter Sunday, numerous kloristic events. Sunday's procession of old Al- nese costumes is particularly picturesque. r information: Municipio, tel. 8574144.

ops, crafts, and curiosities

e artists in this town create, in their home stu- s, icons, stone and wooden sculptures, and saics. For information, enquire at the Pastic- ia Di Noto.

San Cipirello, km. 10 ✉ 90040

ntina Sociale dell'Alto Belice (wines). Piazza azione, tel. 8573558.

azza Armerina ✉ 94015 ☎ 0935

ge 198

Azienda Autonoma, Via Cavour 15, tel. 680201.

otels, restaurants, campsites, and cation villages

Park Hotel Paradiso. Contrada Ramaldo, tel. 680841, fax 684908. Number of rooms: 35. Accessible to the handicapped. Air con-ditioning, elevator; parking, garden, swim-ming pool, tennis.

Mosaici-da Battiato. Contrada Paratore Casale 11, tel. 685453, fax 685453. Number of rooms: 13. Parking, parking garage, garden.

Mosaici-da Battiato. Contrada Paratore Casale 11, tel. 685453. Closed mid-Novem-ber-Christmas. Parking, garden. Sicilian cooking – grilled meats.

griturismo (real Italian country living)

ienda Agricola Il Glicine. This farm raises

olives, grains, and fruit, and is located among small durmast and hazelnut trees. Guide to the farming activities; bicycle rides, and use of the swimming pool. No hunters. For information: Santi Francesco Sillitto, tel. 684119.

Azienda Agricola Savoca. Loc. Polleri, 13. Ac-commodations in a restructured nineteenth-century farmhouse, in an estate of 170 hectares, with a stream. Bicycling, fishing, guide to farm-ing activities. For information: Elio Savoca, tel. 683078.

Museums and cultural institutions

Villa Romana del Casale, tel. 680036. Open to the public: *9-sunset.*

Porto Empèdocle ✉ 92014 ☎ 0922

Page 97

Hotels, restaurants, campsites, and vacation villages

⋆⋆⋆ **Dei Pini.** Località Vincenzella, tel. 634844, fax 632895. Number of rooms: 124. Accessible to the handicapped. Elevator; parking, gar-den, swimming pool, tennis, private beach.

Portopalo di Capo Pàssero

✉ 96010 ☎ 0931

ℹ *c/o Municipio*, tel. 842687.

Hotels, restaurants, campsites, and vacation villages

🍴 **Alta Marea.** Via L. Tasca 1, tel. 843081. Closed Wednesday, November. Air condi-tioning. Classic Italian cooking.

⛺⋆⋆ **Capo Passero.** Contrada Vigne Vecchie, tel. 842333, fax 842333. Seasonal.

Cafes and pastry shops

at Pachino, km. 6 ✉ 96018

Caffè Pasticceria Al Ciclope. Piazza Vittorio Emanuele, tel. 846577. Chocolate "cannoli" with pistachio and candied fruit, and an excellent "fetta moka."

Shops, crafts, and curiosities

at Pachino, km. 6

Casa Vinicola Capo Pàssero. Via dello Stadio 38, tel. 801533.

Pozzallo ✉ 97016 ☎ 0932

Page 111

Hotels, restaurants, campsites, and vacation villages

⋆⋆ **Villa Ada.** Corso Vittorio Veneto 3, tel. 954022, fax 954022. Number of rooms: 30. Air conditioning, elevator; parking.

Prizzi
✉ 90038 ☎ 091

Page 59

i *Pro Loco*, Piazza Crispi 5, tel. 8346901.

Cafes and pastry shops

Pasticceria Compagno N., Corso Finocchiaro Aprile 30, tel. 8345457. Specialties: cannoli, cassata, home-made ice-cream.

Ragusa
✉ 97100 ☎ 0932

Plan, page 104

i *AAPIT*, Via Bócchieri 33, tel. 621421.

Hotels, restaurants, campsites, and vacation villages

- *⋆↑⋆* **Mediterraneo Palace.** Via Roma 189, tel. 621944, fax 623799. Number of rooms: 92. Access for the disabled. Air conditioning, elevator; covered parking (B2, **a**).

- *⋆↑⋆* **Rafael.** Corso Italia 40, tel. 654080, fax 653418. Number of rooms: 22. Accessible to the handicapped. Elevator; parking, parking garage (A2, **c**).

- *⋆⋆⋆* **Montreal.** Corso Italia 70, tel. 621133, fax 621133. Number of rooms: 50. Accessible to the handicapped. Air conditioning, elevator; parking garage (A-B3, **b**).

- ¶¶ **Villa Fortugno.** Strada per Marina di Ragusa at km. 4, tel. 667134. Closed Monday, for a period in August. Air conditioning, parking, garden. Classic Italian and Sicilian cooking (C2, *off map*).

- ¶ **U Saracinu.** Via del Convento 9 (Ibla), tel. 246976. Closed Wednesday. Classic Italian and Sicilian cooking (A5, **u**).

at Camarina, km. 33   ✉ 97010

- 🏠 **Club Méditerranée Kamarina.** In the Scoglitti area, tel. 911333, fax 911719. Seasonal.
⋆⋆⋆

at Donnafugata, km. 17   ✉ 97017

- ¶ **Il Gattopardo.** Via B. Brin, tel. 619313. Closed Wednesday (except in summer) and part of November. Sicilian and classic cooking.

Agriturismo (real Italian country living)

Eremo della Giubiliana. Contrada Giubiliana. Impressive structure set in a 15th c. monastery, with antique furnishings. For information: Vincenza Nifosì, tel. 669119.

Cafes and pastry shops

Caffè Pasticceria Ambassador. Via Archimede 6, tel. 624701. Also Enoteca.

Pasticceria Di Pasquale. Corso V. Veneto 104, tel. 624635. Almond biscuits.

Museums and cultural institutions

Museo Archeologico Ibleo. Via Natalelli, tel. 622963. Open to the public: *9-2 and 3-6.*

Sports

Palestre Comunali (gyms). Via S; Roberto B larmino, tel. 643553; Via Sirene, tel. 615574; V Moro, tel. 643342; Via Marsala, tel. 653954.

Piscina Comunale (pool). Contrada Selvagg tel. 621827.

Shops, crafts, and curiosities

Giuseppe Criscione. Ponte Giovanni XXIII. Ar tic creation of objects in terracotta.

Randazzo
✉ 95036 ☎ 0

Plan, page 157

i Municipio, tel. 7991863 and 921028.

Hotels, restaurants, campsites, and vacation villages

- ¶ **Trattoria Veneziano.** Via dei Romano 8, 7991353. Closed Monday and evenings Sunday. Sicilian cooking – mushrooms (A3,

Agriturismo (real Italian country livin

Azienda Agricola L'Antica Vigna. Via Monte guardia. White building, with a little access ro lined with low walls in volcanic stone, on a wo ing farm that raises olives and grapes. For formation: Silvana Zuccarello, tel. 924003, f 923324.

Cafes and pastry shops

Musumeci. Piazza S. Maria 5, tel. 921196. Ric ta-based pastries.

Museums and cultural institutions

Museo Civico Archeologico Paolo Vagliasin Castello Carcere, Piazza S. Martino, tel. 7914 Open to the public: *9-6 (by appointment).*

Museo Civico di Scienze Naturali. Istituto Giovanni Antida, Via C. Beccaria 1, tel. 79912 Open to the public: *9-1 and 4-7.*

Museo dei Pupi Siciliani. Castello Svevo, t 7991214 (temporarily closed due to work on t archeological museum).

Shops, crafts, and curiosities

Local crafts and artisan market. Every Sund morning. Clothing, tools, wooden and me products, typical of the Etna region.

Ribera
✉ 92016 ☎ 09

Page 98

Hotels, restaurants, campsites, and vacation villages

- *⋆⋆⋆* **Miravalle.** Via Circonvallazione 2, t 61383, fax 61863. Number of rooms: 3 Parking, parking garage.

- 🏕 **Kamemi.** At Seccagrande, Contrada Cam
⋆⋆⋆ mi Superiore, tel. 69212, fax 61986. Annu

age 81

otels, restaurants, campsites, and acation villages

* **Florence.** Località Monte delle Rose, tel. 68511. Number of rooms: 22. Parking, parking garage, garden.

luseums and cultural institutions

luseo Civico and Raccolta di Cimeli Risorgimentali. Via F. d'Aguirre, 982248. Open to the ublic: *8-2 and 4-6.*

t Gibellina Nuova, km. 7.5 ✉ 91024

luseo Civico d'Arte Contemporanea. Viale egesta 1, tel. 67428. Closed Monday. Open to the ublic: *weekdays 9-1 and 4-7; holidays 10-1.*

luseo Antropologico-Etnologico. Via Vespri ciliani. Tel. 67877. Ask at the Museo Civico 'Arte Contemporanea for information.

ultural Events

esta di S. Giuseppe. On the 19th March each ear, tables are sumptuosly laid in the village nes and decorated with bread sculptures. For iformation: tel. 991111 (Municipio).

t Calatafimi, km. 14 ✉ 91013

ultural Events

esta della Primavera o del Crocifisso. This estival dates back to 1657 and takes place each rd May. For information: tel. 951988.

an Cataldo ✉ 93017 ☎ 0934

age 205

otels, restaurants, campsites, and acation villages

** **Helios.** Contrada Zubbi S. Leonardo, tel. 573000, fax 588208. Number of rooms: 40 – 36 of them with bath or shower. Air conditioning; parking, garden, swimming pool.

  Al 124. at the turnoff for the station, tel. 569037. Closed Monday, for a period in August. Air conditioning, parking, garden. Sicilian cooking – seafood.

afes and pastry shops

asticceria Gelateria Sollami. Via Garibaldi 93, el. 571486. Specialties, with ricotta: puff pastries, ignets, "cannoli," and "cannolicchi."

anta Flavia ✉ 90017 ☎ 091

lotels, restaurants, campsites, and acation villages

** **Kafara.** Località Sant'Elia, tel. 957377, fax 957021. Number of rooms: 63. Accessible to the handicapped. Air conditioning, elevator; parking, garden, swimming pool, tennis, private beach.

★★★ **Zagarella and Sea Palace.** Località Sòlanto, Via Nazionale 77, tel. 903077, fax 901422. Seasonal. Number of rooms: 360. Accessible to the handicapped. Elevator; parking, garden, swimming pool, tennis, private beach.

🍴 **Muciara-Nello El Greco.** Località Porticello, Via Roma 105, tel. 957868, fax 957271. Closed Monday. Air conditioning. Sicilian cooking – seafood.

Museums and cultural institutions

at Sòlunto, km. 1

Archeological digs and Antiquarium. Open to the public: *9-one hour before sunset; holidays 9-12:30.*

Sant'Àgata Militello ✉ 98076 ☎ 0941

Page 189

Hotels, restaurants, campsites, and vacation villages

★★★ **Roma Palace Hotel.** Via Nazionale, tel. 703516, fax 703519. Number of rooms: 48. Accessible to the handicapped. Air conditioning, elevator; parking, garden.

Museums and cultural institutions

Museo Etno-Antropologico dei Nèbrodi. Tel. 701000. Closed Sunday. Open to the public: *9-12.*

Shops, crafts, and curiosities

at Santo Stefano di Camastra, km. 28.7 ✉ 98077

Fratelli Frantantoni. Via Nazionale 92, tel. 0921/331833. Ceramics manufactory. Always open in the summer. By request, it is possible to tour the workshop, with the stone kiln and the potting wheel, and watch the decorators at work. In particular, note the decorated "bricks" and the plates with St. George (San Giorgio).

Maioliche Val Demone. Contrada Favatà, tel. 0921/339761. Splendid centerpieces, candelabra, and cache-pots with an old-fashioned appearance.

Ceramiche La Giara. Via Nazionale 100, tel. 0921/331524. Majolica crockery and objects.

San Vito Lo Capo ✉ 91010 ☎ 0923

Page 86

ℹ️ *Ufficio Turistico Comunale*, Via Savoia 57, tel. 974300.

Hotels, restaurants, campsites, and vacation villages

★★★ **Capo San Vito.** Via Principe Tommaso 29, tel. 972122, fax 972559. Seasonal. Number of rooms: 35. Air conditioning, elevator, private beach.

★★ **Riva del Sole.** Via G. Arimondi 11, tel. and fax 972629. Number of rooms: 9. Air conditioning.

¶¶ **Alfredo.** Zona Valanga, tel. 972366. Closed Monday in the low season, for a period between October and November. Parking, garden. Classic Italian cooking and the cooking of Trapani.

¶ **Tha'am.** Via Abruzzi 32, tel. 972836. Closed Wednesday from October a June. Air conditioning. Classic Italian cooking and the cooking of Trapani – seafood.

★★★ **El Bahira.** Località Salinella, tel. 972633. Seasonal.

★★★ **Pineta.** Via del Secco 88, tel. 972818, fax 974070. Annual.

Shops, crafts, and curiosities

Sul Lungomare. Production of bags, baskets, and hats made of dried, woven palm leaves.

Sports

Circolo Nautico Costa Gaia. Via Faro 10, tel. 972189.

Sciacca   ✉ 92019 ☎ 0925

Plan, page 99

ℹ *Azienda Autonoma*, Corso Vittorio Emanuele 84, tel. 21182 (B2).

Hotels, restaurants, campsites, and vacation villages

★★★ **G.H. delle Terme.** Lungomare Nuove Terme 1, tel. 23133, fax 21746. Number of rooms: 72. Accessible to the handicapped. Elevator; parking, garden, swimming pool (C3, **d**).

¶ **Hostaria del Vicolo.** Vicolo Sammaritano 10, tel. 23071. Closed Sunday, Monday evening and part of October. Air conditioning. Classic cooking – fish (B2, **m**).

¶ **Le Gourmet.** Verso San Calogero, Via Monte Kronio 7, tel. 26460. Closed Tuesday in winter, November. Air conditioning, parking, garden. Classic Italian and Sicilian cooking – seafood (A2, *off map*).

on the state road, toward Agrigento, km. 8

★★★ **Torre Macauda.** Tel. 997000, fax 997007. Seasonal. Number of rooms: 297. Accessible to the handicapped. Air conditioning, elevator; parking, garden, indoor and outdoor swimming pools, tennis, private beach.

★★ **Baia Makauda.** Contrada Tranchina, tel. 997001. Seasonal.

Agriturismo (real Italian country living

Azienda Agricola Montalbano. Locali Scunchipani. Accommodation in a delightful an modern rural house surrounded by olive and c rus groves. Bicycles available. For informatio Giuseppe Montalbano, tel. 80154.

Hot springs/Spas

Nuove Terme. Via Agatocle, tel. 961111. H springs, with therapeutic baths, muds, inha¹ tions, and massages.

at San Calogero, km. 7

Stufe Vaporose Naturali di S. Calogero. Te 961111. Natural grottoes with steam vents; the apeutic baths, muds.

Cafes and pastry shops

Bar Gelateria La Favola. Corso Vittori Emanuele 234, tel. 82777. Ice creams and froze cakes with fruit.

Pasticceria Pierrot. Via Licata 6, tel. 26466. Sp cialties: almond and ricotta. Exquisite pastrie served with "granita" for breakfast in the summe

Museums and cultural institutions

Museo Scaglione. Piazza Duomo, tel. 8308 Closed Sunday. Open to the public: *Tuesda Thursday and Friday 9-1 and 3-7.*

Shops, crafts, and curiosities

Perconte Ceramiche. Contrada Stancapadror and Via Marco Polo, tel. 994005.

Marchese ceramica. Via Ghezzi 19, tel. 99322?

Cascio ceramiche. Corso Vittorio Emanuele 11: tel. 82829.

Cantina Sociale Enocarboj (wines). via Lion 2/4, tel. 21992.

Segesta   ✉ 91013 ☎ 092

Page 83

Museums and cultural institutions

Tempio. Open to the public: *9-sunset.*

Selinunte   ✉ 91022 ☎ 092

Plan, page 80

Hotels, restaurants, campsites, and vacation villages

at Marinella, km. 1

★★★ **Alceste.** Via Alceste 21, tel. 46184, fax 4614 Number of rooms: 26. Air conditioning, e evator; parking, garden.

★★★ **Paradise Beach Hotel.** Contrada Belice Mare, tel. 46333, fax 46477. Seasonal. Nun ber of rooms: 250. Air conditioning, elev tor; parking, garden, swimming pool, ter nis, private beach (B3, *off map*).

Pierrot. Via Marco Polo 108, tel. 46205. Closed Tuesday in winter, at Christmas and in January. Parking. Traditional cooking of Trapani.

Maggiolino. Contrada Garraffo, tel. 46044, fax 906450. Annual.

griturismo (real Italian country living)

Marinella, km. 1

zienda Agricola Marinella di Selinunte. Via ..tomie. An 8 hectar fruit and olive farm with ooms available for guests. For information: An-..la Bonagiuso De Stefano, tel. 902863.

useums and cultural institutions

rea archeologica and Antiquarium. Tel. 46277.)en to the public: *9-two hours before sunset.*

---

iracusa (Syracuse)   ✉ 96100 ☎ 0931

...n, page 128-129

AAPIT, Via S. Sebastiano 43, tel. 461477 (A3).

Azienda Autonoma, Via Maestranza 33, tel. 464255.

Uffici Informazioni (information offices): Via Maestranza 33, tel. 65201 (E5); Largo Teatro Greco, tel. 60510 (B2).

otels, restaurants, campsites, and acation villages

Forte Agip. Viale Teracati 30, tel. 463232, fax 67115. Number of rooms: 87. Accessible to the handicapped. Air conditioning, elevator; parking (A3, **c**).

Jolly. Corso Gelone 43/45, tel. 461111, fax 461126. Number of rooms: 100. Accessible to the handicapped. Air conditioning, elevator; parking (C3, **b**).

Palace Hotel. Viale Scala Greca 201, tel. 491566, fax 756612. Number of rooms: 136. Accessible to the handicapped. Air conditioning, elevator; parking (A2, *off map*).

Panorama. Via Necropoli Grotticelle 33, tel. 412188, fax 412188. Number of rooms: 55. Rooms only; no dining facilities. Elevator; parking (A2, *off map*).

Jonico-'a Rutta 'e Ciauli. Riviera Dionisio il Grande 194, tel. 65540. Closed Tuesday, Christmas, Easter Monday, Feast of the Assumption (15 August). Garden. Sicilian cooking – seafood (A-B5, **s**).

Arlecchino. Via del Tolomei 5, tel. 66386. Closed Monday, for a period in August. Air conditioning. Classic Italian cooking – seafood (E5, **v**).

Dafne. Via Elorina 97, tel. 21616. Closed Monday, for a period in November. Air conditioning, parking, garden. Sicilian cooking – seafood (D1, *off map*).

Darsena-da Iannuzzo. Riva Garibaldi 6, tel. 66104. Closed Wednesday. Air conditioning. Sicilian cooking – seafood (D4, **r**).

Minosse. Via Mirabella 6, tel. 66366. Closed Monday, for a period in July. Air conditioning. Sicilian cooking – seafood and mushrooms (D5, **x**).

Don Camillo. Via Maestranza 92/100, tel. 67133. Closed Sunday, November and Christmas. Air conditioning. Sicilian cooking – fish (E5, **t**).

Rinaura. Contrada Rinaura, tel. 721224. Annual.

at Fontane Bianche, km. 15   ✉ 96010

★★★ **Fontane Bianche.** Via Mazzarò 1, tel. 790611, fax 790571. Number of rooms: 164. Accessible to the handicapped. Air conditioning, elevator; parking, swimming pool, tennis, private beach.

Spiaggetta. Viale dei Lidi 473, tel. 790334. Closed Tuesday in winter. Air conditioning, parking. Sicilian cooking – seafood.

★★ **Fontane Bianche.** Via dei Lidi 476, tel. 790333, fax 700571. Seasonal.

Agriturismo (real Italian country living)

Azienda Agricola Rinaura. Contrada Rinaura, State road 115 at km. 4. Accommodations in rooms of a citrus farm at a distance of 2 km. from the sea; possible to play bocce ball, mountain bikes for rent. For information: Paolina Menozzi Sindona, tel. 721224.

Strada provinciale 14 Mare-Monti, km. 9

Azienda Agricola Limoneto. A model farm, with farmhouse, set amongst garden, with lemon trees, olive trees, and other fruit trees. Possible to follow the work in the orchards. For information: Adelina Norcia, tel. 717352.

Cafes and pastry shops

Pasticceria Rizzo. Viale Polibio 78, tel. 35771. Closed Monday. Try the ricotta and the confectioner's cream pastries.

Bar Pasticceria Tunisi. Viale Tunisi 74, tel. 37078. Closed Monday. Excellent ricotta "cannoli" but also the chocolate cream "tartufi."

Bar Nuovo Centrale. Piazza Archimede 22, tel. 66466. Specialties: fruit puddings (try the strawberry puddings and the citrus fruit puddings), Sicilian "cannoli" and the almond dough cookies.

Bar Duomo. Piazza Duomo 16, tel. 21544. Some of the finest pastry chefs in the city have formed an association to establish this cafe/pastry shop. Try the "buccellati," the ricotta "cannoli," the "frutta martorana," and the tiramisù.

Museums and cultural institutions

Acquario Tropicale (aquarium). Foro Italico. Closed for restoration.

Castello Euriialo. Open to the public: *9-one hour before sunset.*

Castello Maniace. Temporarily closed for renovation. Guided tours: Mr. Castello, tel. 0360/655648.

Galleria Regionale. Via Capodieci 14, tel. 69617. Open to the public: *9-1*.

Museo Archeologico Regionale Paolo Orsi. Villa Landolina, Viale Teocrito 66, tel. 464022. Closed Monday. Open to the public: *9-1*.

Museo del Papiro. Via Teocrito 66, tel. 61616. Closed Monday. Open to the public: *9-1*.

Parco Archeologico della Neàpoli. (archeological site: Greek theater, altar of Hiero II, Roman amphitheater, Latomie, or prisons). Viale Rizzo. Open to the public: *9-one hour before sunset*.

Excursions and organized tours

Excursions to the Ciane Springs. For information: Mr. Vella, tel. 69076.

Theater and music

Teatro Greco (Greek theater). Information on performances at the Istituto Nazionale del Dramma Antico. Corso Matteotti 29, tel. 67071-67415.

Shops, crafts, and curiosities

Ricami Farina. Via Grotticelle 16/A, tel. 412200.

P.I.C.A. Centro Lavorazione del Papiro (papyrus). Viale Teocrito 70, tel. 461731. Guided tours, by appointment (French, English, German): *from Monday to Friday 8 am-8 pm; Saturday 8-1; 2:30-8*.

Taormina   ✉ 98039 ☎ 0942

Plan, page 168

ℹ️   *Azienda Autonoma*, Piazza S. Caterina, tel. 23243 (A2).

Hotels, restaurants, campsites, and vacation villages

★★★ **San Domenico Palace.** Piazza S. Domenico 5, tel. 23701, fax 625506. Number of rooms: 111. Accessible to the handicapped. Air conditioning, elevator; parking, parking garage, garden, swimming pool, private beach (B1, **a**).

★★★ **Bristol Park.** Via Bagnoli Croce 92, tel. 23006, fax 24519. Seasonal. Number of rooms: 50. Air conditioning, elevator; parking, parking garage, swimming pool, private beach (B3, **k**).

★★★ **Excelsior Palace.** Via Toselli 6, tel. 23975, fax 23978. Number of rooms: 88. Accessible to the handicapped. Air conditioning, elevator; parking, garden, swimming pool (B1, **e**).

★★★ **Méditerranée.** Via Circonvallazione 61, tel. 23901, fax 21231. Seasonal. Number of rooms: 50. Air conditioning, elevator; parking, garden, swimming pool (B1, **p**).

★★★ **Villa Diodoro.** Via Bagnoli Croce 75/E, tel. 23312, fax 23391. Number of rooms: 102. Air conditioning, elevator; parking, special terms for parking garage, garden, swimming pool, private beach (B3, **m**).

★★★ **Villa Paradiso.** Via Roma 2, tel. 23922, fa 625800. Number of rooms: 35. Accessible the handicapped. Air conditioning, elevtor; special terms for parking garage, tenn (B2, **x**).

★★★ **Bel Soggiorno.** Via Pirandello 60, tel. 2334 fax 626298. Number of rooms: 19 – 17 them with bath or shower. Rooms only; n dining facilities. Accessible to the hanc capped. Parking, garden (B-C3, **j**).

★★★ **Continental.** Via Dionisio Primo 2/A, te 23805, fax 23806. Number of rooms: 43. A conditioning, elevator; parking, garde (B1, **t**).

★★★ **Vello d'Oro.** Via Fazzello 2, tel. 23788, fa 626117. Seasonal. Number of rooms: 5 Elevator; parking (B1, **i**).

★★★ **Villa Belvedere.** Via Bagnoli Croce 79, te 23791, fax 625830. Seasonal. Number rooms: 48. Rooms only; no dining facilitie Elevator; parking, garden, swimming poc (B3, **h**).

★★★ **Villa Sirina.** Contrada Sirina, tel. 5177 fax 51671. Number of rooms: 15. Air co ditioning; parking, special terms for par ing garage, garden, swimming pool, pr vate beach (C1, *off map*).

★★ **Villa Ducale.** Via L. da Vinci 60, tel. 28153, fa 28710. Number of rooms: 10. Rooms only; n dining facilities. Access for the disabled. A conditioning; parking, covered parking, pr vate beach (A1, **l**).

★★ **Villa Schuler.** Piazzetta Bastione, tel. 2348 fax 23522. Seasonal. Number of rooms: 26 (? of which with bath or shower). Rooms onl no dining facilities. Elevator, parking, covere parking, garden (B2, **b**).

🍴🍴🍴 **Giara.** Vico Floresta 1, tel. 23360, fax 2323 Closed at midday and Monday from Octo ber to March, for a period between Januar and February. Air conditioning. Refined S cilian cooking – seafood (B2, **za**).

🍴🍴 **Al Duomo.** Via Ebrei 11, tel. 625656. Close Wednesday in low season. Air conditioning Sicilian cooking – fish (B1, **r**).

🍴🍴 **'A Zammàra.** Via F.lli Bandiera 15, te 24408. Closed Wednesday in the low sea son, part of January. Garden. Sicilian cook ing – pastas and soups (B2, **rb**).

🍴🍴 **Griglia.** Corso Umberto 54, tel. 2398(Closed Tuesday. Air conditioning. Th cooking of Messina – seafood (A2, **rd**).

🍴 **Ciclope.** Corso Umberto, tel. 23263. Close Wednesday, for a period between Januar and February. Air conditioning. Cookin of Messina – seafood (B1, **ra**).

🍴 **Delfino-da Angelo.** Via Nazionale, tel 23004. Seasonal. The cooking of Messina seafood (A5, **rg**).

at Capo Taormina, km. 3   ✉ 9803

★★★ **G.A. Capotaormina.** Via Nazionale 105, te 24000, fax 625467. Seasonal. Number o rooms: 203. Accessible to the handicappec

Air conditioning, elevator; parking, parking garage, garden, swimming pool, private beach (C4, **d**).

Mazzarò, km. 4   ⊠ 98030

* **Mazzarò Sea Palace.** Via Nazionale 147, tel. 24004, fax 626237. Seasonal. Number of rooms: 87. Air conditioning, elevator; parking, parking garage, swimming pool, private beach (A5, **aa**).

* **Villa Sant'Andrea.** Via Nazionale 137, tel. 23125, fax 24838. Number of rooms: 67. Air conditioning, elevator; parking, garden, private beach (A5, **ab**).

  Pescatore. Via Nazionale 107, tel. 23460. Seasonal, closed Monday. Parking. The cooking of Messina – seafood (B4, **re**).

Hot springs/Spas

Alì Terme, km. 25

Terme Granata Cassibile. Via Crispi 1/13, tel. 5029-701494.

Terme Marino. Via Roma 25, tel. 715031. Hot springs, with therapeutic baths, muds, inhalations, and massages.

Cafes and pastry shops

Pasticceria Saint Honoré. Corso Umberto I 208, tel. 24877. Jasmine ice-cream, almond paste, and "torrone," a kind of nougat, with aroma of orange.

Pasticceria Vasta. Via Giardinazzo 18/A, tel. 5567. Aside from the confectionery specialties, they offer fine pasta dishes, such as Pasta alla Norma, or Pasta alle sarde, to eat at the counter.

Castelmola, km. 5

Caffè San Giorgio. Piazza San'Antonio 1, tel. 228. A cafe with an old tradition, where you can enjoy sweet almond wine, sitting on distinctive "scanni," or stools.

Museums and cultural institutions

Museo delle Arti figurative popolari della Sicilia. Palazzo Corvaja. Piazza S. Caterina. Open to the public: *9-1 and 4-8.*

Palazzo Duchi di Santo Stefano. Closed Sunday. Open to the public: *summer, 8:30-12:30 and 3-7; winter, 8:30-12:30 and 3-5.*

Teatro Greco (Greek theater). Via Teatro Greco, tel. 23220. Open to the public: *summer, 9-6:30; winter, 9-4.*

Motta Camastra, km. 15   ⊠ 98030

Gola dell'Alcàntara. Tel. 985010. Open to the public: *summer 8-8:30, winter 8-5:30.*

Theater and music

Teatro Greco Romano. Via Teatro Greco 40, tel. 23220. In summer there is a revue of film, theater, dance, and music – "Taormina Arte", tel. 142. Open to the public: *9-4; summer 9-7.*

Villa Comunale e Palazzo Corvaja. Series of musical and theatrical performances organized by the Azienda di Soggiorno e Turismo, tel. 23243.

Tèrmini Imerese   ⊠ 90018   ☎ 091

Plan, page 186

🛈 c/o Municipio, tel. 8128253.

Hotels, restaurants, campsites, and vacation villages

*⭐⭐ **G.H. delle Terme.** Piazza delle Terme 2, tel. 8113557, fax 8113107. Number of rooms: 69. Accessible to the handicapped. Air conditioning, elevator; parking, garden, swimming pool (B-C2, **a**).

*⭐⭐ **Himera Polis Hotel.** State road 113 - area of Buonfornello, tel. 8140566, fax 8140567. Number of rooms: 55. Air conditioning, elevator; parking, private beach (D3, *off map*).

at Buonfornello, km. 13

⛺⛺ **Himera.** Tel. 8140175, fax 8159206. Annual.

Hot springs/Spas

Stabilimento Termale. Piazza delle Terme 2, tel. 8113557. Hot springs, with therapeutic baths, muds, inhalations, grottoes, mists, and massages.

Cafes and pastry shops

Cristal. Via Vittorio Amedeo 58, tel. 8145148. Ice creams, pastries, hot foods.

Pasticceria del Vicolo. Via Mazzarino 100, tel. 8114052.

Museums and cultural institutions

Museo Civico. Via del Museo, tel. 8128279. Closed Monday. Open to the public: *9-1; Wednesday, Thursday, Saturday and Sunday also 4-7.*

Cultural Events

Il Carnevale di Termini. Impressive procession of allegorical floats in February. For information: tel. 8128253.

at Buonfornello, km. 13

Archeological digs of Imera and antiquarium. Open to the public: *9-one hour before sunset.*

Terrasini   ⊠ 90049   ☎ 091

Page 48

Hotels, restaurants, campsites, and vacation villages

*⭐⭐⭐ **Azzolini Palm Beach.** Via Ciucca, tel. 8682033, fax 8682618. Number of rooms: 38. Air conditioning, elevator; parking, garden, private beach.

Androni. Via Cala Rossa, tel. 8681712. Air conditioning, parking, garden. Classic Italian and Sicilian cooking – seafood.

Museums and cultural institutions

Museo Civico-Antiquarium. Via Calarossa, tel. 8682652. Closed Monday. Open to the public: *9-12:30.*

233

Museo Civico-Museo del Carretto Siciliano. Via Della Chiesa 38, tel. 8685636. Open to the public: *9-12:30.*

Museo Civico-Natural History section. Via Calarossa 4, tel. 8682467. Closed Monday. Open to the public: *9-12:30.*

Trapani   ✉ 91100 ☎ 0923

Plan, page 64-65

[i] *AAPIT*, Via San Francesco d'Assisi 27, tel. 545511 (B2).

Ufficio Informazioni (information office), Piazzetta Saturno, tel. 29000 (B2).

Hotels, restaurants, campsites, and vacation villages

⋆⋆⋆ **Crystal.** Via S. Giovanni Bosco 12, tel. 20000, fax 25555. Number of rooms: 70. Air conditioning, elevator; parking garage (A-B3, **g**).

⋆⋆⋆ **Astoria Park Hotel.** A San Cusumano, lungomare Alighieri, tel. 562400, fax 567422. Number of rooms: 93. Accessible to the handicapped. Elevator; parking, garden, swimming pool, tennis, private beach (A4, *off map*).

⋆⋆⋆ **Nuovo Albergo Russo.** Via Tintori 4, tel. 22166, fax 26623. Number of rooms: 36 – 31 of them with bath or shower. Rooms only; no dining facilities. Elevator; parking (B2, **z**).

⋆⋆⋆ **Vittoria.** Via Crispi 4, tel. 873044, fax 29870. Number of rooms: 65. Rooms only; no dining facilities. Air conditioning, elevator (A3, **a**).

¶¶ **P. e G.** Via Spalti 1, tel. 547701. Closed Sunday, August. Air conditioning. The cooking of Trapani (A-B3, **r**).

¶ **Meeting.** Via Fardella 321, tel. 23366. Closed Sunday, August. Air conditioning. Classic Italian cooking and the cooking of Trapani – seafood (A5, **t**).

¶ **Peppe.** Via Spalti 50/52, tel. 28246. Closed Monday. Air conditioning, parking. The cooking of Trapani – seafood (B3, **w**).

¶ **Trattoria del Porto.** Via Ammiraglio Staiti 45, tel. 547822. Closed Monday (except in July and August), Christmas-New Year's Day. Air conditioning. The cooking of Trapani – seafood (B2, **v**).

Cafes and pastry shops

Colicchia. Via delle Arti 6, tel. 547612. Ice-cream and typical pastries.

Cafè Classique. Via G.B. Fardella 112, tel. 26626. Home-made pastries and ice-cream; also some hot dishes.

'900. Via G.B. Fardella 84, tel. 22502. Home-made pastries and ice-cream.

at Paceco, km. 5   ✉ 91027

La Cialda d'Oro. Via Verderame 69, tel. 883166. Home-made pastries.

Museums and cultural institutions

Museo della Preistoria. Torre di Ligny, tel. 2230 Closed Monday morning. Open to the public: *12:30 and 4-7.*

Museo Regionale Pepoli. Via Conte Agostin Pepoli 200, tel. 553269. Open to the public: *9-1:3 Tuesday and Thursday also 3-6; Sunday 9-12:30*

Excursions and organized tours

Turistic itineraries around the city only for grou and reservation. AAPT: tel. 29000.

at Bonagìa, km. 10.5   ✉ 9101

Le Tonnare. One of the oldest tuna-fishing st tions, no longer in operation, is in Bonagìa, nc far from Trapani, along the provincial road t Custonaci. Still operating, on the other hand, the "tonnara" at Favignana, on the island of th same name, known as the Tonnara di ! Cusumano, a couple of kilometers from Trapan toward Custonaci.

at Paceco, km. 5

Museo del Sale (salt museum). Contrada Nùbi tel. 867442. Open to the public: *9-12 and 3-6.*

Theater, music and cultural events

Cine Teatro Ariston. Corso Italia, tel. 21659.

Luglio Musicale Trapanese (concerts in July Villa Margherita, tel. 21454.

I Misteri. The splendid procession of the "Vare antique statues representing the Passions. Goo Friday, every year. For information: tel. 29000.

Sports

Circolo Canottieri. Viale Regina Elena 94, te 28084.

Circolo Tennis Trapani. Contrada Milo, te 532488.

Shops, crafts, and curiosities

Platimiro Fiorenza. Via Osorio 36, tel. 2078! Production of coral objects.

Trecastagni   ✉ 95039 ☎ 09

Hotels, restaurants, campsites, and vacation villages

¶ **Uliveto.** Via Perni 4, tel. 7806988. Close Monday and at midday except Sunday i winter. Parking, garden. Sicilian cooking

Ùstica   ✉ 90010 ☎ 09

Page 54

Hotels, restaurants, campsites, and vacation villages

⋆⋆ **Diana.** Contrada San Paolo, tel. 8449109, fa 8449109. Seasonal. Number of rooms: 34. E evator; parking, garden, private beach.

aldérice   ✉ 91019 ☎ 0923

otels, restaurants, campsites, and acation villages

★★ **Baglio Santacroce.** State road 187 at km. 12.3, tel. 891111, fax 891192. Number of rooms: 25. Accessible to the handicapped. Parking, garden, swimming pool.

★ **Lido Valderice.** At Sant'Andrea Bonagìa, Via del Dentice 15, tel. 573086. Annual.

ittoria   ✉ 97019 ☎ 0932

age 113

otels, restaurants, campsites, and acation villages

★★ **Grand Hotel.** Vico III C. Pisacane 53/B, tel. 863888, fax 863888. Number of rooms: 27 – 26 with shower or bath. Rooms only; no dining facilities. Air conditioning, elevator; parking garage.

at Scoglitti, km. 13   ✉ 97010

★★★ **Agathae.** Via Montale 33, tel. 980730, fax 871500. Number of rooms: 27. Elevator; parking, garage, garden, swimming pool.

Zafferana Etnea   ✉ 95019 ☎ 095

Page 156

ℹ️ *Pro Loco*, Piazza Luigi Sturzo 3, tel. 7082825.

Hotels, restaurants, campsites, and vacation villages

★★★ **Airone.** at Airone, Via Cassone 67, tel. 7081819, fax 7082142. Number of rooms: 50. Accessible to the handicapped. Elevator, parking, parking garage, garden.

★★★ **Primavera dell'Etna.** at Airone, Via Cassone 86, tel. 7082348, fax 7081695. Number of rooms: 57. Elevator; parking, parking garage, garden, tennis.

Index of Places and Monuments

CALTAGIRONE
CITTA' DELLA CERAMICA

REGIONE
SICILIANA
ASSESSORATO
TURISMO

AZIENDA
AUTONOMA
TURISMO
CALTAGIRONE

Informazioni

0933.53809